Grindhouse

Global Exploitation Cinemas

Series Editors
Johnny Walker, Northumbria University, UK
Austin Fisher, Bournemouth University, UK

Editorial Board
Tejaswini Ganti (New York University, USA)
Joan Hawkins (Indiana University, USA)
Kevin Heffernan (Southern Methodist University, USA)
I. Q. Hunter (De Montfort University, UK)
Peter Hutchings (Northumbria University, UK)
Ernest Mathijs (University of British Columbia, Canada)
Constance Penley (University of California, Santa Barbara, USA)
Eric Schaefer (Emerson College, USA)
Dolores Tierney (University of Sussex, UK)
Valerie Wee (National University of Singapore)

Also in the Series:
Disposable Passions: Vintage Pornography and the Material
Legacies of Adult Cinema, by David Church

Grindhouse

Cultural Exchange on 42nd Street, and Beyond

Edited by
Austin Fisher and Johnny Walker

Bloomsbury Academic
An imprint of Bloomsbury Publishing Inc

B L O O M S B U R Y
NEW YORK · LONDON · OXFORD · NEW DELHI · SYDNEY

Bloomsbury Academic
An imprint of Bloomsbury Publishing Inc

1385 Broadway
New York
NY 10018
USA

50 Bedford Square
London
WC1B 3DP
UK

www.bloomsbury.com

BLOOMSBURY and the Diana logo are trademarks of Bloomsbury Publishing Plc

First published 2016

© Austin Fisher & Johnny Walker

All rights reserved. No part of this publication may be reproduced or transmitted in any form or by any means, electronic or mechanical, including photocopying, recording, or any information storage or retrieval system, without prior permission in writing from the publishers.

No responsibility for loss caused to any individual or organization acting on or refraining from action as a result of the material in this publication can be accepted by Bloomsbury or the author.

Library of Congress Cataloging-in-Publication Data
A catalog record for this book is available from the Library of Congress.

ISBN: HB: 978-1-6289-2747-4
PB: 978-1-6289-2749-8
ePub: 978-1-6289-2746-7
ePDF: 978-1-6289-2745-0

Cover design: Seventh Tower Creative Solutions

Typeset by Integra Software Services Pvt. Ltd.

Contents

Acknowledgments — vii
Introduction: 42nd Street, and Beyond — 1
Austin Fisher and Johnny Walker

1. Grinding Out the Grind House: Exploitation, Myth, and Memory — 13
   Glenn Ward

2. "This Is Where We Came In": The Economics of Unruly Audiences, Their Cinemas and Tastes, from Serial Houses to Grind Houses — 31
   Phyll Smith

3. Temporary Fleapits and Scabs' Alley: The Theatrical Dissemination of Italian Cannibal Films in Melbourne, Australia — 53
   Dean Brandum

4. Run, Angel, Run: Serial Production and the Biker Movie, 1966–1972 — 73
   Peter Stanfield

5. "The Smashing, Crashing, Pileup of the Century": The Carsploitation Film — 93
   Robert J. Read

6. Cars and Girls (and Burgers and Weed): Branding, Mainstreaming, and Crown International Pictures' SoCal Drive-in Movies — 107
   Richard Nowell

7. From "Sex Entertainment for the Whole Family" to Mature Pictures: *I Jomfruens Tegn* and Transnational Erotic Cinema — 129
   Kevin Heffernan

8. "Bigger Than a Payphone, Smaller Than a Cadillac": Porn Stardom in *Exhausted: John C Holmes the Real Story* — 145
   Neil Jackson

9. From Opera House to Grindhouse (and Back Again): Ozploitation in and beyond Australia — 163
   Alexandra Heller-Nicholas

10 Go West, Brother: The Politics of Landscape in the
    Blaxploitation Western   181
    Austin Fisher

11 Red Power, White Movies: *Billy Jack, Johnny Firecloud,*
    and the Cultural Politics of the "Indiansploitation" Cycle   197
    David Church

12 Sleazy Strip-Joints and Perverse Porn Circuses: The Remediation
    of Grindhouse in the Porn Productions of Jack the Zipper   217
    Clarissa Smith

Select Bibliography   236
Contributors   247
Index   250

Acknowledgments

We would like to collectively thank our contributors. As they know all too well, *Grindhouse* went through a number of ups and downs during its development, so we thank them for being patient with us as we juggled our other commitments. In this regard, we'd particularly like to recognize Dean Brandum, Kevin Heffernan, Richard Nowell, Peter Stanfield, and Phyll Smith. Thank you to Katie Gallof at Bloomsbury for commissioning this book, and the new Global Exploitation Cinemas series for which it is one of the flagship volumes (the other being David Church's *Disposable Passions: Vintage Pornography and the Material Legacies of Adult Cinema*). Thanks also to Steve Jones, to the anonymous peer reviewers who provided some useful feedback at the proposal stage, and to Mark McKenna, who designed the excellent cover (again). Finally, we'd like to recognize the help and support of those scholars who sit on the editorial board of the Global Exploitation Cinemas series: Tejaswini Ganti, Joan Hawkins, Kevin Heffernan, I. Q. Hunter, Peter Hutchings, Ernest Mathijs, Constance Penley, Eric Schaefer, Dolores Tierney, and Valerie Wee.

Introduction: 42nd Street, and Beyond

Austin Fisher and Johnny Walker

*In the heart of little old New York,
You'll find a thoroughfare.
It's the part of little old New York
That runs into Times Square.*

—Title song, *42nd Street* (1933)

Up until the release of Lloyd Bacon's musical *42nd Street* in 1933, the movie's namesake had, for international audiences which had heard of it at all, been just that: one "part" of New York City. The film's title song, however, told of something much more colorful: an avenue where one could "hear the beat of dancing feet," find "sexy ladies … who are indiscreet," and where "the underworld … meet the elite." It was arguably here, within the confines of a Warner Brothers musical, where the first seeds of 42nd Street's global film mythology were sown.

The pervasive image of 42nd Street as a hub of sensational thrills, vice and excess, is from where the focus of this book—"grindhouse cinema"—stemmed. It is, arguably, an image that has remained unchanged in the mind's eye of many exploitation film fans and academics alike. Whether in the pages of contemporaneous fanzines or in more recent scholarly works, it is often recounted how, should one have walked down this street between the 1960s and the 1980s, one would have undergone a kaleidoscopic encounter with an array of disparate "exploitation" films from all over the world: movies that were being offered cheaply to urbanites by a swathe of vibrant "grind house"[1] theaters. The year 1964 would see the publication of perhaps the most famous grind house chronicle of all, Bill Landis's since-lionized journal *Sleazoid Express*, which was committed to dissecting, theater-by-theater, the auditoria that exposed cinemagoers to sights they had hitherto never experienced: from hardcore roughies at the Globe to splatter films at the Rialto and mondo films at the Times Square.[2]

At its most basic level, this is a book about such films, their exhibition contexts, and the grindhouse mythology that—rightly or wrongly—has underwritten their legacy. It is a book about exploitation movies that, in most other contexts, would be scrutinized on the grounds that they are weird, zany, and transgressive examples of globally celebrated "paracinema,"[3] which have been said to contravene industry movements and types and which have made "it their business to challenge" the "routines" one might typically associate with mainstream film production and distribution.[4] It has been commonplace for exploitation films—which span a broad range of genres, production contexts, and historical periods—to be examined under the rubric of "cult," to the extent that, as Ernest Mathijs and Jamie Sexton note, one "may form the impression that cult cinema is actually synonymous with exploitation cinema."[5] Yet, as the empirical works of Eric Schaefer, Kevin Heffernan, Richard Nowell, Peter Stanfield, and others attest, there is more to exploitation cinema than cult criticism alone can account for.[6] One might argue further that, while a lot of scholarship has sought to look beyond "cult," it has nevertheless been "paracinema"—the ironic, transgressive "reading protocol" that Jeffrey Sconce identified as emerging from trash and cult film fan communities[7]—that has guided much academic study of exploitation cinema. As David Church has argued in his important recent book *Grindhouse Nostalgia: Memory, Home Video and Exploitation Film Fandom*, such an approach invites the erroneous impression that "paracinema" refers not to a mode of consumption but to a group of films.[8]

Of course, the kinds of films our contributors discuss in this volume—which include, among others, US biker movies, Danish hardcore sex films, and blaxploitation westerns—have been either ignored by mainstream discourse or dismissed on account of their unsavory content and "trashy" production values, and, as a result, some are now celebrated in cult film circles for these very reasons. However, while there may be political advantages to championing exploitation cinema's implicit differences to the mainstream, there is also a risk in assuming that *all* exploitation films are somehow imbued with such anti-mainstream, "cult," status. To consider exploitation movies solely on the grounds of their alleged transgressions, or because they are curious cult oddities, in many cases risks undermining the historical and industrial contexts that birthed these films in the first place, or lays claims to cult recognition that, frankly, isn't there. Not all of the exploitation films from the 1960s, 1970s, and 1980s were made "beyond" the mainstream. In fact, many were made *because of* the mainstream, or *as part of* profitable cycles of films that were proving popular with theater-going audiences. By the same token, there are many exploitation films (some of which are examined in this volume) that have yet to receive what could be described as "cult" recognition of any sort.[9] With that said, it is not our intention to disavow the usefulness of any such critical models; indeed, Alexandra Heller-Nicholas ably blends a "paracinematic" framing with a historically grounded study (of Australian exploitation cinema) in these very pages. Rather, our aim is to avoid the trap of uncritically buying into what Church summarizes as a "thoroughly romantic mythology of excess, hedonism and transgression," which can so easily creep into academic work on exploitation films.[10]

The mystique of the American grind house in the wake of the generic interplay of Quentin Tarantino and Robert Rodriguez has unquestionably contributed to this "romantic mythology." Most overtly, their codirected anthology, *Grindhouse* (2007), sought to embellish the romantic pastness of exploitation cinema-going, as Church has also recognized, by using the "digitally simulated appearance of celluloid print damage," to recapture a sense of authenticity that is allegedly lost when old exploitation films are "cleaned up" for "remastered DVDs."[11] Celebrating the scuzzy imperfections of grindhouse cinema's past constitutes one of several ways in which these filmmakers seek to "differentiate themselves ... from the cultural 'mainstream.'"[12] It should come as no surprise that filmmakers whose careers have been largely predicated upon purposeful nostalgia for long-gone exploitation cycles should invest in such exercises. What is telling, and indicative of prevailing trends, is how scholarship has tended to coalesce around these very same parameters when discussing exploitation cinema. Across recent academic work, we find a similar kind of irreverence for the "mainstream": one that is used less to challenge grindhouse mythology, than to prop it up.

For example, in his foreword to John Cline and Robert G. Weiner's academic collection *From the Arthouse to the Grindhouse*, Chris Gore claims that:

> Grindhouse films are never safe. They have the power to alter your perspective by exposing life's brutal truths: the cruel consequences of a life of crime; merciless monstrosities terrorizing innocents in ways that will haunt your dreams and your nightmares; bizarre and strangely erotic fetishes that you'd never heard of and perhaps wish you'd never seen. You'll even be exposed to the documentation of real death in horrific forms.[13]

While Gore is not an academic, but rather the editor of the cult magazine *Film Threat*, his words here serve a clear scholarly purpose. A "foreword," as a framing device, acts as a means of providing weight to (or perhaps "validating") a book's content, by harnessing the words of an authority: in this case, an expert on exploitation films. It is therefore notable that there is in Gore's words a marked lack of specificity and a hyperbolic prose style when discussing "grindhouse films." Far from clarifying the cultural significance of such historical practices of cinematic exhibition and consumption, his words serve further to obfuscate them, perpetuating the kind of idealized mythos that continues to enshroud the study of exploitation cinema. "Grindhouse films," it would appear, do not need to be defined or contextualized, for it is assumed the reader will know what they are.

Consider also this quotation from the opening page of Ian Olney's recent monograph *Euro Horror: Classic European Horror Cinema in Contemporary American Culture*, which explores the cult following of "golden age" European horror films that has been "garnered since the late 1990s," in the United States:

> Between the mid-1950s and the mid-1980s, these Euro horror movies emerged from countries like Italy, Spain, and France in astonishing numbers and were shown in the United States at rural drive-ins and at urban grindhouse theaters of the sort that once filled Times Square in New York City. Gorier, sexier, and just plain stranger than most British and American horror films of the time, they were embraced by hardcore genre fans and denounced by critics as the worst kind of cinematic trash.[14]

While Olney writes with more candor than Gore, he uses similar rhetorical devices to identify exploitation cinema's alleged capacity to transgress and destabilize cinematic norms. Euro horror, thus, is a "stranger" strand of horror. Such films, like the kinds

Gore alludes to, are seen to be more extreme ("gorier, sexier") than other types of horror films, and, despite the fact that they were produced in "astonishing" numbers, were apparently only truly understood and appreciated by a committed "hardcore." Euro horror films, thus, have developed "cult" followings because of their transgressive content, and because they were originally exhibited in theaters of a "sort" that is alternative to the mainstream (i.e. drive-ins and grind houses). These films inhabit the fringes because of their content, but also, and crucially, because of their distribution trajectories, which, it is implied, exposed only a select, discerning few to their exotic thrills.[15]

To rehearse the "paracinematic" mythology of the grind house offers a blinkered view of exploitation film history, and it is our intention that this volume should go some way to redressing the balance. It is, for example, telling that the one chapter in this collection to consider European horror cinema (by Dean Brandum) revolves around the "infamous"[16] Italian cannibal films: a cycle that, according to Olney, "quickly became notorious even among hardcore fans of Euro horror cinema."[17] Yet Brandum demonstrates that this cycle's forerunner, *Man from Deep River* (1972), was not necessarily seen as a marginal oddity, but was instead a mainstream smash when it played for a number of years in Melbourne, Australia. The crucial point here is that, while it has been tempting for academic writing to uncritically champion the allure of the grind house and all the cult pleasures it was said to offer,[18] much work remains to try to distance ourselves from it, so that a fuller picture can be painted of exploitation film history. A more nuanced apperception of these films' varied exhibition contexts is required, more fully to interrogate the cultural implications of "grindhouse" mythology.

Clearly then, "grindhouse" is a term that has traversed all sorts of cultural boundaries and has a number of discernible functions. In one respect, it is used to refer to an original exhibition context for international exploitation films. In other respects, it is used as a lens—not unlike say, "paracinema" or "video nasty"[19]—through which otherwise disparate global exploitation film traditions can be delineated, compartmentalized, and made sense of.[20] Bill Landis's *Sleazoid Express* encapsulated this dual role, being at once a chronicle and myth-generator. While Landis (who was later joined by Michelle Clifford) may attest to the disparate audiences of cinemas such as the Times Square Theater—"Popeyes, inner city denizens, kids playing hooky, and bored Midnight Cowboys"—and even the disparities between the kinds of films that were screened there—"triple bills of westerns," "chop-socky flicks," and various "exploitation double bills on half-week runs"—such experiences and films are seen to have "grindhouse" in common, and are thus frequently homogenized under one universalizing rubric.[21] This may partly explain why, in some quarters, "grindhouse cinema" is thought of as a genre in its own right,[22] which is now capitalized on by a host of international home media distributors. So, the UK distribution company Tartan Films can release the Canadian horror film *Black Christmas* (Bob Clark, 1974) and the very different Spanish "double bills" *Dracula: Prisoner of Frankenstein/The Curse of Frankenstein* (Jess Franco, 1972/1973) and *Devil's Island Lovers/Night of the Assassins* (Jess Franco, both 1974) under the offshoot label "Tartan Grindhouse." Online, the global presence of grindhouse can also be felt, as with the Grindhouse Cinema

Database, which proclaims itself to be "the classic-international exploitation & cult film encyclopedia," and which runs features about films that have emerged from countries as diverse as the United States, the UK, Canada, Mexico, the Philippines, Australia, Italy, France, Germany, and Spain.[23] As Church has argued, the "grindhouse" brand is "a highly sellable commodity" in "a post-theatrical era in which the grind house as historical referent has vanished from the physical landscape."[24] "Grindhouse" is therefore inherently global, transcending the various national contexts from which the term, and the films that grind houses exhibited, first emerged.

This insistence on the phenomenon's transnational aspect notwithstanding, Jamie Sexton and Ernest Mathijs are justified in claiming that "the most recognized non-American exploitation films are those that established themselves in the American marketplace."[25] The specific "marketplace" in question is often that of the New York grind house, since Olney is certainly not alone in prioritizing the American exhibition context as the main inroad into the study of global exploitation cinema. Indeed, the same accusation might be leveled at this book and the geographical referent contained within its title. Our intention is not, however, to position the United States as an inevitable hub of cinematic consumption. Rather, it is to examine the particularities of a cultural moment during which disparate cinematic traditions, emerging from diverse backdrops, found themselves being exhibited and consumed side-by-side. We seek to look beneath the lurid marquees of the popular imagination, to investigate and contextualize both the "grindhouse" concept and grind houses themselves, and thereby to illuminate the complexities at work within the various national, local, and subcultural contexts that surrounded the films and the theaters alike. The word "beyond" in this volume's title has not been merely inserted as a modish scholarly accoutrement pandering to a trend toward transnational cinema studies, but is instead a recognition that "grindhouse" is always already "beyond" 42nd Street.

The contributors to this volume therefore consider "grindhouse cinema" from a variety of cultural and methodological positions. Some seek to deconstruct the etymology of "grindhouse" itself, add flesh to the bones of its cadaverous history, or examine the term's contemporary relevance in the context of both media production and consumerism. Others offer new inroads into hitherto unexamined examples of exploitation film history, including a number of international movie cycles, their production and exhibition contexts, and the audiences for whom they were intended. Ultimately, *Grindhouse: Cultural Exchange on 42nd Street, and Beyond* presents several revisionist histories, snapshots of historical moments that many of us thought we already knew, and the deconstruction of terms that are rife within the lexicon of global exploitation cinema studies.

To begin, Glenn Ward's chapter, "Grinding Out the Grindhouse: Exploitation, Myth, and Memory," investigates the development of the cultish mystique that retrospectively surrounds the term "grindhouse." Ward argues, building on recent developments in scholarship, that this term now mediates a craving for an age of lost exploitation cinema. By placing "grindhouse" within the academic field of "memory studies," Ward asks, which elements of this idealized cinematic past are preserved and curated, by whom, and for whom? The chapter analyzes the means by which "grindhouse" is mediated, approaching the term as an elusive, fluid category, which tends to be framed through inconsistent, occasionally disingenuous "cult" discourses that disavow the cultural and political complexities of this mode of cinematic distribution, exhibition, and consumption.

Phyll Smith moves the discussion on from the mythology of "grindhouse" examined by Ward to the more tangible arena of grind house historiography. Smith's chapter, "'This Is Where We Came In": The Economics of Unruly Audiences, Their Cinemas and Tastes, from Serial Houses to Grind Houses," draws on original trade papers and news stories in what is perhaps the most rigorous assessment to date of the grind house's earliest days. Exploring the original technical uses of "grind," Smith traces the development of "grindhouse" as an industry-standard term, and, through an examination of the continuities and discontinuities that existed between grind house and "serial house" theaters, Smith constructs "a new, more comprehensive and accurate etymology" of "grindhouse" than historians have been offered thus far.

Dean Brandum's chapter, "Temporary Fleapits and Scabs' Alley: The Theatrical Dissemination of Italian Cannibal Films in Melbourne, Australia," is similarly concerned with exhibition contexts, but also considers the pervasiveness of grindhouse mythology as outlined by Ward. Taking Melbourne in the 1970s as his historical context, and the Italian cycle of "cannibal" movies as a case study, Brandum shows how "grindhouse" is a term commonly favored to the detriment of historical accuracy. Indeed, films like *Man from Deep River*, Brandum reveals, proved to be mainstream successes when they played in major Melbourne theaters. While images of US grind houses are more pervasive in Western thought than those of the "temporary fleapits" of Melbourne— dubbed so by Brandum due to their programming of major Hollywood films one week, then exploitation films the next—the chapter stresses how US mythmaking cannot fully account for the original exhibition histories of global exploitation cinema.

Peter Stanfield, in the chapter "Run, Angel, Run: Serial Production and the Biker Movie, 1966–1972," examines how US film producers cultivated "biker movies" for young American audiences in the 1960s and 1970s. Biker-themed exploitation films, Stanfield argues, were broadly responsive to trends in mainstream cinema and were precisely designed as commercial hits. In other words, these films, though clearly "exploitation" movies, were not of the sort since celebrated in cult criticism for eschewing commonplace industry strategies. On the contrary, a marketing strategy focused firmly on the target audience was of utmost importance to the success of the "serial" films that Stanfield (following on from Smith) discusses, which provide insights into how the grind house provided a parallel economic model to "an atrophied Hollywood production system that had long lost the ability to regulate and promulgate itself."

Continuing to focus on how grind houses mediated the United States's love affair with automotive transport (now shifting from motorcycles to automobiles), Robert J. Read, in his chapter "'The Smashing, Crashing, Pileup of the Century': The Carsploitation Film," explores grindhouse films whose *raison d'être* was the "excessive demolition of automobiles as pure destructive sensation." Read's argument positions this "carsploitation" cycle, which responded to contemporaneous big-budget car chases, as a symptom of both a move toward regional film production and a wider "mainstreaming" of low-budget independent film in North America in the 1970s. By focusing (as does Stanfield) on the fiscal pragmatism of exploitation film production as it tried to anticipate audience approval, Read positions these films as documents for sociological shifts in the United States' engagement with automotive transport and associated escapist consumer dreams.

Richard Nowell then provides insight into an alternative model of exploitation film distribution and consumption, which was contemporaneous with the grind house, and therefore provides an important contextual factor for this volume's remit: the US drive-in circuit. His chapter, entitled "Cars and Girls (and Burgers and Weed): Branding, Mainstreaming, and Crown International Pictures' SoCal Drive-in Movies," analyzes the marketing strategies of Crown International Pictures for their purposefully middlebrow exploitation products. Nowell firmly locates the films in their historical moment, identifying how Crown responded to the consumption habits of their young target audiences. This chapter therefore challenges historians of 1970s American exploitation cinema to look beyond "grindhouse" mystique, and to consider the calculatedly anodyne and prosaic output of contemporaneous drive-in circuits. Nowell's chapter, as with Stanfield's and Brandum's contributions to this volume, thus equally challenges prevailing scholarly trends around "cult" cinema, by arguing that much "exploitation" did not seek to subvert the "mainstream," but was in fact entwined within it.

Kevin Heffernan, in his chapter "From 'Sex Entertainment for the Whole Family' to Mature Pictures: *I Jomfruens Tegn* and Transnational Erotic Cinema," locates Scandinavian hardcore pornography within the context of the US grind house and the discourse surrounding "porno chic." Heffernan examines a transnational process by which the Danish adult film *I Jomfruens Tegn* (Finn Karlsson, 1973) found its way into American inner-city neighborhood cinemas, when re-titled *Danish Pastries*. The chapter investigates how *Pastries*—a movie arising from Copenhagen's late-1960s status as a global center of the sex industry—translated into the divergent cultural and legal contexts of the early 1970s US grind house circuit and, in the process, passed from a context in which it was considered "sex entertainment for the entire family" into a system of production, distribution, and exhibition entirely separated from mainstream popular entertainment. The film's American distributors, the chapter argues, were exploiting what Heffernan recognizes as a US fascination with culturally homogenized notions of "Scandinavian" attitudes to sex.

Neil Jackson is also concerned with the contemporaneous discourses surrounding "porno chic," albeit in the context of American hardcore or, rather, one of its biggest male stars. Jackson's chapter, "'Bigger Than a Payphone, Smaller Than a Cadillac': Porn Stardom in *Exhausted: John C Holmes The Real Story*," takes the documentary *Exhausted* (Julia St Vincent, 1981) as an inadvertent document of a cultural moment in which the adult film industry was on the cusp of profound transformation, and in it Jackson examines the discursive construction of porn actor (and, thus, grind house regular) John Holmes's onscreen persona. *Exhausted*, as Jackson has it, is a "document of the relationship between the hardcore film industry and its potential consumers, as well as between filmmakers and their subjects," therefore Holmes's cultural status, analogous to that of a "cult" film star, acts as a synecdoche for the historical trajectory of an industry on the verge of crisis.

Alexandra Heller-Nicholas's chapter, "From Opera House to Grindhouse (and Back Again): Ozploitation in and beyond Australia," returns us once more to Australia. In it, she explores the "Ozploitation" cycle: a series of films that, as with countless other examples of global exploitation cinema, have been reframed as "grindhouse cinema" due to endorsements from "gatekeeper" auteurs such as Quentin Tarantino.[26] Heller-Nicholas identifies a tension in such films between a parochial vernacular and an international outlook, diagnosing white Australia's desire to position itself culturally as a part of the Western world. She thereby maps equivalent tensions in Australia's liminal postcolonial identity, through which oppositional, "paracinematic" taste cultures emerge organically from the national psyche. The Ozploitation film's ambivalent position vis-à-vis this movable national identity (appealing simultaneously to domestic and US export markets) is seen to be a symptom of anxieties surrounding the influence of US popular culture in postwar Australia more broadly.

Austin Fisher reappraises the cultural significance of the blaxploitation westerns that played on urban film circuits in the early to mid-1970s, in his chapter, "Go West, Brother: The Politics of Landscape in the Blaxploitation Western," identifying in such films as *The Legend of Nigger Charley* (1972) and *Boss Nigger* (1974) purposefully anachronistic transpositions onto the tropes of the Hollywood western. This chapter analyzes the blaxploitation western's black outlaw heroes as representatives of a 1970s urban sensibility, facilitating a particular mode of address and exploitation located firmly in the films' immediate distribution contexts, when US film producers were waking up to the lucrative returns on offer from the inner-city black market and tailoring their products accordingly.

David Church, in "Red Power, White Movies: *Billy Jack*, *Johnny Firecloud*, and the Cultural Politics of the 'Indiansploitation' Cycle," takes an alternative approach to exploitation cinema's engagement with the turbulent racial politics of the late 1960s and early 1970s (studies of which most commonly focus on the Black Power movement and, consequently, the blaxploitation film cycle), to investigate the contemporaneous trends of "Indiansploitation," which show a response within grind house circuits to the growing "Red Power" political activism among Native American groups. In these films about retributive violence by modern-day Native Americans, the chapter uncovers a transcultural flow within and between coexistent countercultures: just as the Red Power movement took inspiration from African American advances in self-determination, so the Indiansploitation cycle merged the tropes of blaxploitation with Native American themes to capitalize on the era's tumults. What emerges is a complex snapshot of a cultural moment in US politics, whereby the appropriation of Native concerns for white countercultures, and the tensions between separatist and integrationist strands of the Red Power movement, carried over into exploitation cinema.

In the volume's final chapter, "Sleazy Strip-Joints and Perverse Porn Circuses: The Remediation of Grindhouse in the Porn Productions of Jack the Zipper," Clarissa Smith returns to the contemporary mythology of American "grindhouse" and examines how, in the age of the mainstream "retrosploitation pastiche"—that is, the work of directors such as Tarantino and Rob Zombie—contemporary pornography producers have sought to embellish the cultural mythology of grindhouse cinema and the theaters that originally exhibited them.[27] Through an examination of the director Jack the Zipper, whose films are "excessively stylish re-masterings of the experiences and memories of the grind house," Smith shows how Zipper's work fuses exploitation film aesthetics with "memories" of their original "screening places." Smith demonstrates that, for herself as a researcher of the digital age, where images of sex are ubiquitous (even "mainstream"), the films of Zipper offer retroactive imaginings of a historical moment where hardcore sex imagery remained on the peripheries and was enjoyed, so the legend goes, by "oddballs" and social "deviants."

This introduction began by quoting the title song from *42nd Street*. It should now be clear, however, that this volume is about much more than a "part of little old New York." The ostensibly "local" reference to 42nd Street in its title should not be thought of as a geographical or cultural limitation on its remit: quite the opposite. Tom Conley has described cinema as "the privileged geopolitical medium … at once local and global."[28] For our purposes, this now-legendary strip of downtown New York City acts as a conceptual stage on which to explore the ever-shifting meanings of "grindhouse," as well as a symbol for how the historical exhibition and consumption of exploitation cinema illustrates the veracity of Conley's words.

Notes

1. For the sake of consistency, it is our practice throughout this volume to use the compound word "grindhouse" as an adjective to describe the culturally constituted concept under investigation, but to use the separate words "grind house" as nouns when referring to the physical movie theaters that exhibited such films.
2. Bill Landis and Michelle Clifford, *Sleazoid Express: A Mind-Twisting Tour through the Grindhouse Cinema of Times Square* (New York: Fireside, 2002).
3. Jeffrey Sconce, "'Trashing' the Academy: Taste, Excess, and an Emerging Politics of Cinematic Style," *Screen* 36:4 (1995): 371–393.
4. Ernest Mathijs and Xavier Mendik, "Cult Case Studies: Introduction," in *The Cult Film Reader*, eds Ernest Mathijs and Xavier Mendik (Maidenhead: Open University Press, 2007), 163.
5. Ernest Mathijs and Jamie Sexton, *Cult Cinema* (Oxford: Wiley-Blackwell, 2011), 145.
6. See, e.g., Eric Schaefer, *"Bold! Daring! Shocking! True!": A History of Exploitation Films, 1919–1959* (Durham and London: Duke University Press, 1999) as well as *Sex Scene: Media and the Sexual Revolution*, ed. Eric Schaefer (Durham and London: Duke University Press, 2015); Kevin Heffernan, *Ghouls, Gimmicks, and Gold: Horror Films and the American Movie Business, 1953–1968* (Durham and London: Duke University Press, 2007); Richard Nowell, *Blood Money: A History of the First Teen Slasher Cycle* (New York: Continuum, 2011); and Peter Stanfield, *The Cool and the Crazy: Pop Fifties Cinema* (New Brunswick: Rutgers University Press, 2015).
7. Sconce, "Trashing the Academy."

8. David Church, *Grindhouse Nostalgia: Memory, Home Video and Exploitation Film Fandom* (Edinburgh: Edinburgh University Press, 2015), 14.
9. The blaxploitation westerns discussed here by Austin Fisher are cases in point of films that appear to have been overlooked in cult discourse. As Johannes Ferle argues, Quentin Tarantino's claims of originality for *Django Unchained* (2012), which is clearly indebted to these earlier films, are particularly surprising, given the director's famed penchant for "cult" intertextuality (Johannes Ferle, "'And I would call it "A Southern"': Renewing/Obscuring the Blaxploitation Western," *Safundi: The Journal of South African and American Studies* 16:3 (2015): 295–298).
10. David Church, *Grindhouse Nostalgia*, 14.
11. Ibid., 104.
12. Ibid., 105. Glenn Ward's contribution to this volume explores this issue further.
13. Chris Gore, "Foreword: Grinding Out a New Form of Entertainment," in *From the Arthouse to the Grindhouse: Highbrow and Lowbrow Transgression in Cinema's First Century*, eds John Cline and Robert G. Weiner (Lanham, MD: Scarecrow, 2010), ix.
14. Ian Olney, *Euro Horror: Classic European Horror Cinema in Contemporary American Culture* (Bloomington and Indianapolis: Indiana University Press, 2013), xi.
15. On "Euro horror" discourse, see, e.g., Peter Hutchings, "Resident Evil? The Limits of European Horror: *Resident Evil* versus *Suspiria*," in *European Nightmares: Horror Cinema in Europe since 1945*, eds Patricia Allmer, David Huxley, and Emily Brick (London and New York: Wallflower Press, 2012), 13–24; and, related, but in reference to Italian horror cinema specifically, David Church, "One on Top of the Other: Lucio Fulci, Transnational Film Industries, and the Retrospective Construction of the Italian Horror Canon," *Quarterly Review of Film and Video* 32:1 (2015): 1–20.
16. Olney, *Euro Horror*, 36.
17. Ibid., 191.
18. See Landis and Clifford, *Sleazoid Express*.
19. "Video nasty" is a term given to thirty-nine horror and exploitation films that were banned on video in Britain in the early 1980s. See Kate Egan, *Trash or Treasure? Censorship and the Changing Meanings of the Video Nasties* (Manchester: Manchester University Press, 2007); on the term's longevity in contemporary film cultures, see Johnny Walker, *Contemporary British Horror Cinema: Industry, Genre and Society* (Edinburgh: Edinburgh University Press, 2015), 38–58.
20. Church, *Grindhouse Nostalgia*, 75.
21. Clifford and Landis, *Sleazoid Express*, 154. Church has subsequently identified the importance of such fanzines to cultural history, for their editors "took up the mantle of researching, archiving and assigning value to a wide swathe of cinema history that had been overlooked or deliberately ignored by film historians, high-minded critics and various arbiters of cultural taste" (Church, *Grindhouse Nostalgia*, 13). Subsequently, these zines, and others like them, have been anthologized, widely discussed on the Internet, or used by scholars as academic sources. The collusion of fannish idealism with scholarship has, in some respects, shaped the reception of exploitation films, and film history more broadly, in a very specific, romantic, way, whereby exploitation films constitute "a cinematic corpus tied together by a sense of pastness" (ibid., 3). The New York "grindhouse," thus, is but one of many "spaces that can be imaginatively inhabited," "past spaces of consumption" that "can be nostalgically linked to particular time periods and audiences" including the "grindhouse era" (ibid., 5).

22. Gore, "Foreword," ix; Church explores the "genrification" of "grindhouse" in *Grindhouse Nostalgia*, 75–76.
23. Available at www.grindhousedatabase.com/ (accessed December 29, 2015).
24. David Church, "From Exhibition to Genre: The Case of Grind-House Films," *Cinema Journal* 5:4 (2011): 24.
25. Mathijs and Sexton, *Cult Cinema*, 151.
26. On Tarantino as a "gatekeeper auteur," see the essay where the connection was originally made: Leon Hunt, "Asiaphilia, Asianisation and the Gatekeeper Auteur: Quentin Tarantino and Luc Besson," in *East Asian Cinemas: Exploring Transnational Connections on Film*, eds Leon Hunt and Leung Wing-Fai (London: I. B. Tauris, 2008), 220–236.
27. See Church, *Grindhouse Nostalgia*, 176–242.
28. Tom Conley, "Foreword," in *Frontiers of Screen History: Imagining European Borders in Cinema, 1945–2010*, eds Raita Merivirta, Heta Mulari, Kimmo Ahonen, and Rami Mähkä (Bristol: Intellect, 2013), x.

1

Grinding Out the Grind House: Exploitation, Myth, and Memory

Glenn Ward

Grind houses once existed, but "grindhouse cinema" and "grindhouse films," as they are imagined today, never did. To put it less starkly, the term "grindhouse" has been used in the United States at least since the 1930s, but its transnational cultist aura is of fresher vintage, and for that we may have to thank or blame Quentin Tarantino, the most prominent propagator of grindhouse mystique. The cultification of grindhouse took a while. In the 1980s, the foundational texts of exploitation film fandom in the United States conferred no special value on the label. Michael Weldon's foreword to his *Psychotronic Encyclopedia of Film* noted that the cinemas of New York's 42nd Street specialized in exploitation films,[1] but the term "grindhouse" was practically absent from the book. One of the key early sites for popularizing mainly North American exploitation films as cult treasures was the 1986 volume *Incredibly Strange Films*, a compendium of interviews and subgenre overviews edited by Jim Morton. The term "grindhouse" is a scarce signifier in Morton's book: the filmmaker Frank Henenlotter, for example, reminisces about the drive-in cinemas and "sleaze theaters"[2] of the 1960s and 1970s, but of grind houses he makes no mention. Even as the "paracinema" cult solidified in the 1990s, the grindhouse myth was barely nascent. The 1995 catalogue for Something Weird Video—a key company in the shaping of current definitions of cult American exploitation film—advertised myriad low-budget movies on tape across a variety of genres, but it only labeled striptease and burlesque films specifically as "grindhouse," as part of a series of compilations titled *Grindhouse Follies*. Similarly, in the pages of fanzines such as *Videoscope*, *Cult Movies*, and *Dreadful Pleasures* advertisements for exploitation specialists like Something Weird, Video Vault, and Sinister Cinema were apt to promote "sleaze," "retro," "trash," and "psychotronic" products rather than what we now call "grindhouse." That the term was not as widely adopted by cult communities of the 1980s and 1990s as it has been in the years since Tarantino and Rodriguez' *Grindhouse* project (2007) suggests that the notion of grindhouse cinema as it presently circulates in global consumption circuits is a recent invention.

Grindhouse desire

Even in countries where other terms play a similar role—such as Great Britain, where "fleapit" is (or was) the nearest equivalent—"grindhouse" resonates with fantasies of cinematic mischief and glamorous squalor. To take just one example, a showing of Jess Franco's *Venus in Furs* (1969) at London's Barbican Centre in 2015 was advertised as "a winning combination of soft-core grindhouse and avant-garde techniques." As a Briton (typifying the arguably still hegemonic demographic of the cult film viewer as described by Jeffrey Sconce,[3] Barbara Klinger,[4] and Jacinda Read[5]), gazing across the Atlantic to images of 1970s Times Square and similar locations, I find the grind house a seductive fantasy. Rather than perpetuate it, however, this chapter uses a handful of cultist texts to consider how the mystification of grindhouse mediates a craving for an age of exploitation cinema, and of "cinema" as such, presumed lost. As arenas for film consumption multiply online, the "golden age" of American grindhouse cinema—particularly in the 1970s—is idealized in forms of what David Church calls grindhouse nostalgia.[6] Yet, what this moment of origin comprised, and why its seeming disappearance might matter, is not settled. Historiography and memory alike narrativize partial versions of the past, and the cultist narration of grindhouse history is part of a widespread commodification of "imagined memories."[7] What counts as cult, what constitutes grindhouse, and what is considered memorable are mediated by the production of texts and commodities, and by the maintenance of niche markets: as Barbara Klinger points out, the home cinema "collector's trade" in deluxe reissues encourages fan attachment by promoting mass-produced DVDs and Blu-rays through ideas of scarcity and connoisseurship;[8] though committed to an ostensibly non-elitist film culture, grindhouse fan websites and blogs likewise deal in a specialized discourse of auteurism and arcane knowledge that invents and sustains grindhouse cinema as a discrete object of devotion.

Cultist viewing practices—such as reading what was hitherto dismissed as trash as a kind of counterculture—arguably furnish contemporary grindhouse fans with a safely "knowing" perspective from which to enjoy exploitation cinema's ambivalent fascination with images of otherness. But wistful longing for the "original" grindhouse experience is not necessarily, or only, reactionary; as Huyssen remarks, nostalgic desire may involve resistant impulses.[9] Grindhouse cult rhetoric may, for example (however disingenuously, ambiguously, or inconsistently), present itself as resistant to censorship, to globalized mass entertainment conglomerates, or to normative representations. In any case, the ideological ramifications of grindhouse cultism cannot simply be read through a generalized theory of grindhouse or exploitation cinema; it depends on what aspects of the present are opposed, and what supposed aspects of the irretrievable cinematic past are idealized, why, by whom, and through which cultural intermediaries. The academic field of memory studies demonstrates that acts of remembering are staged at an intersection of discourses both personal and public.[10] Where performed memories of grindhouse cinema are concerned, this intersection includes: the images and texts presented in grindhouse-focused books, fanzines, blogs, and websites; grindhouse ranges on DVD and Blu-ray; grindhouse film trailer compilation discs; fan conventions; neo- or meta-grindhouse films; and documentaries such as *Schlock! The Secret History of American Movies* (Ray Greene, 2001) and *American Grindhouse* (Elija Drenner, 2010). Faced with all this grindhouse revivalism, we should ask, as Paul Ricoeur does in a very different context, "of *what* are these memories? *Whose* memory is it?"[11]

Confirming Tarantino's influence, *American Grindhouse* is narrated by Robert Forster, one of the stars of Tarantino's *Jackie Brown* (1997), a film replete with nods to 1970s American exploitation films. According to the blurb on the back of its DVD sleeve, Drenner's film provides a "hidden history" of "illegitimate cinema." Such hyperbole is designed to attract cultists for whom disreputability is a badge of honor, but, far from clandestine or out-of-bounds, the field has long been legitimate and "overground." Indeed, as one of a virtual subgenre of documentaries throwing light on once-obscure corners of low popular cinema, *American Grindhouse* contributes to the ossification of a cult-exploitation canon. The film's entertaining historical account (written by Drenner with British horror genre commentator Calum Waddell) offers a standard run-through of subgenres and reheats many familiar anecdotes. Just as classical exploitation films often used educative formats as pretexts for the partial display of "shocking" spectacle, so *American Grindhouse* uses authoritative talking heads to frame a cavalcade of clips from what the back cover optimistically calls "salacious and uproarious" films. In addition to Forster's narration, the clips are contextualized by a combination of eyewitness testimony from veteran industry insiders—such as the filmmakers Herschell Gordon Lewis and John Landis—and scholarly reflection, notably from Eric Schaefer, the preeminent historian of classical American exploitation cinema.

These textual strategies exemplify the tensions involved in any attempt to circumscribe grindhouse as both a type of film and a type of venue. A montage early in the film mixes clips of gimmick king William Castle with, among others, horror, beach party, drug warning, and juvenile delinquent films. The DVD sleeve similarly collages together publicity images for an assortment of items from *The Incredible Two Headed Transplant* (Anthony M. Lanza, 1971) to *Truck Turner* (Jonathan Kaplan, 1974) and even *Psycho* (Alfred Hitchcock, 1960). Schaefer appears on screen to bring taxonomic order to the generic chaos, insisting on the distinction between "grindhouse" and "exploitation," just as in *Bold! Daring! Shocking! True! A History of Exploitation Films, 1919–1959*, where he draws a clear line between classical exploitation cinema and the more protean variants that filled drive-ins and inner-city venues in the 1960s and 1970s. But he is fighting a losing battle: grindhouse and exploitation are used interchangeably, and the field's "evolution" is presented as a sequence continuing smoothly from the 1920s to the 1970s. If this wide compass increases *American Grindhouse*'s potential audience, it also illustrates the methodological trouble that can be stirred by the cultural mobility of the films themselves, many of which cross venue, cultural category, and audience.

Siting (the) grindhouse

Since others have mapped the history of North American grindhouse cinema far more extensively than I am able,[12] I touch on it here only to highlight some of its classificatory frictions and uncertainties. The grindhouse/exploitation nexus is problematic because grindhouse is often used as a shorthand label for otherwise heterogeneous films; the ambiguities are compounded by the fact that, depending on what definitions are brought to bear, not all exploitation films played only at grind houses and not all grind houses exclusively showed exploitation films. Schaefer points out, for instance, that reputable cinemas would sometimes "run an exploitation program to generate some extra action at the box office."[13] Contrary to the mythology surrounding them, grind houses were often nothing more or less prosaic than second-run cinemas: besides exploitation films, many also showed art films, Poverty Row efforts, and larger-budgeted Hollywood features after they had completed their first run (whether such categories mattered to contemporary audiences remains for now a moot point). Meanwhile, movies and theaters changed hands; some venues showed different genres at different times of the day; and box-office failures would be pulled without warning and replaced without fanfare. If most grind houses steered clear of the films of the American underground, they would show "adult" foreign art films, while viewers shy of grind houses could see erotic films at more respectable art houses. *Freaks* (Tod Browning, 1932) exemplifies such cultural mobility. Defined by *American Grindhouse* as a classical exploitation film, Browning's film has a cult reputation attributable to its controversial subject matter and its one-time outlaw status. Having been disowned by Hollywood, *Freaks* was rereleased on the exploitation circuit in the 1940s and 1950s by Dwain Esper. It then enjoyed a new lease of life as part of the Midnight Movie cult of the 1970s, gradually being canonized as a major work by one of the horror genre's auteurs.[14] That categories such as exploitation, Midnight Movie, and "classic horror" are not mutually exclusive reminds us that the overarching term "cinema" belies a diversity of sites, practices, and modes of attention.

Given this diversity and fluidity, it is perhaps inevitable that claims about impact and affect are inconsistent. At some points *American Grindhouse* echoes industry self-mythologization by assuming a model of consumer demand and producer supply, whereby grindhouse cinema is guilty of nothing worse than "giving 'em what they want" (as the tagline has it) by showing allegedly taboo images. The supposed needs and wants of a seemingly uncritical audience foreclose further analysis of the films' aesthetic interest or social significance. At other moments, the very *failure* of grindhouse exploitation to satisfy desire seems to be the cause for a possibly vaguely camp but unquestioned celebration of the relationship between cultural production and the market; Schaefer points out that the exploitation trade "never delivered" the goods, while John Landis delights in the "sheer hucksterism" of the "shysters" in the business, whose products fell short of audience expectations. Indeed, the very abundance of edited moments of bodily spectacle, while demonstrating cultist fetishization of cinematic fragments, may remind some viewers of how dismal many of the films are when seen in their entirety.

Thus cultist texts tend to vacillate between overblown and self-serving declarations of the subversiveness of grindhouse exploitation and disingenuous claims about its joyous vacuity. Although these two positions are not incompatible, *American Grindhouse* is typical in lurching arbitrarily from one to the other, so that "absurd and ridiculous" sexploitation films are applauded for reveling in a "true exploitation spirit" held to be "completely devoid of any socio-political subtext," while a select group of American horrors of the 1970s are revered (in terms that have become axiomatic) as angry, "guerrilla-style" responses to the war in Vietnam. John Landis takes the incontrovertible view that "movies are certainly influential, but ... it's called 'the business.' They want to sell tickets, so they will make anything ... if it makes money," but there is little enlargement on the issue of how social commentary flourishes under exploitation cinema's nakedly market-driven economy. Instead, the cultural memory of grindhouse is cherished nationalistically (the presence of European films on the American exploitation circuit is often assiduously marginalized) as part of the tradition of carnival attractions and ballyhoo most famously associated with P.T. Barnum's showmanship. Tales of the misadventures and sharp practices of "pioneer" filmmakers at popular cinema's lurid fringes also resonate with a combination of Wild West fantasies and the myth of the American Dream. While Frankfurt School critics like Adorno disdainfully compared Hollywood genre output to Fordist and Taylorist modes of production, grindhouse mystique, by contrast, often includes semi-ironic, national pride in a supposed pre-corporate stage of entrepreneurial capitalism that enabled the self-made, rugged individualism of the exploitation shyster-as-auteur. By blithely conflating the red-in-tooth-and-claw profit motivation of the Forty Thieves and other industry characters with a discourse of subcultural oppositionality and lawlessness, grindhouse cultism makes an ideological equation between free enterprise and creative freedom, as though exploitation cinema's economically determined conditions unproblematically gave rise to direct expressions of desublimated desire.

It is not surprising, in light of the mercurial quality of grindhouse cinema, that many cult texts have an equivocal relationship to a supposedly mainstream Other against which they are often pitched. On the one hand, despite the formulaic character of narrative and spectacle in most exploitation films, they usually subscribe to the delusion that grindhouse was "a stark 180° from the mainstream ... the insane anything-can-happen answer to the predictability of a studio picture."[15] On the other hand, *American Grindhouse* illustrates the fringe interference between these fields by citing films as dissimilar as *Easy Rider* (Dennis Hopper, 1969), *Jaws* (Steven Spielberg, 1975), and *The Passion of the Christ* (Mel Gibson, 2004) as examples of "mainstream" exploitation. A comparison between Lewis's *Blood Feast* (1963) and *Psycho* is meant to reveal both how exploitation influenced (or was co-opted by) Hollywood and how exploitation's graphic gore provided more direct, confrontational thrills than dominant cinema could dream of. Blurring distinctions further, Schaefer appears on screen to point out that, at least as far as the promise of forbidden spectacle is concerned, "exploitation is as old as the movies themselves." Such category confusion is justified, but contradicts the cultist insistence on grindhouse as a form and experience of cinema that inherently diverges from a purported Hollywood norm. A similar point is made inadvertently in Bill Landis and Michelle Clifford's book *Sleazoid Express*: on page 3, the authors declare that the grind houses in and around Times Square in the 1970s and 1980s "were showcases for the wildest and most extreme films in cinematic history"; on page 2, an illustration of the area at night shows (nestled among video rental stores, live sex shows, and fast-food outlets) a marquee sign advertising the barely "wild" Arnold Schwarzenegger sword-and-sorcery epic *Red Sonja* (Richard Fleischer, 1985).

Similar category issues bedevil the relationship between grindhouse cinema and other forms of erotic entertainment; a necessarily brief discussion of burlesque, stag films, and hard-core pornography will indicate the tensions and slippages involved in trying to construct grindhouse as a clearly bounded cultural category. There are several reasons why burlesque and grindhouse sometimes overlap in the cultural imagination. Many erotic shorts were shot in burlesque theaters in the 1940s, as producers increased their profit margins by distributing films rather than touring live shows.[16] As *American Grindhouse* points out, performers would put on a show for the camera, after which their services were often no longer required: by the 1960s, many burlesque houses showed films rather than live performances, and burlesque reels were sometimes projected at single-screen theaters in American towns that lacked a specialist burlesque venue. The two kinds of establishment also had similar profit-maximizing strategies. The term "grindhouse" originally referred not to "bump 'n' grind" dancing—although this association was commonly made later—but to a programming policy of the 1920s, according to which films would be shown, or ground out, continuously while the price of tickets increased throughout the day.[17] Likewise, all but the top-billed artistes had to perform "three, four, or even five or more shows per day."[18] The grueling, alienated labor of nonunionized performers suggests Marxian as well as feminist connotations of "exploitation" downplayed by most exploitation fan texts.

Stag films are normally included in American histories of pornography, sometimes in histories of grindhouse cinema and only rarely in accounts of exploitation film, but they occasionally migrated from brothels and private clubs to be edited in with burlesque shorts and strip films as loops in peep booths—locations that, according to some fan publications, constituted part of the metropolitan experience of "original" grindhouse consumers. Yet, despite trumpeting the transgressive and graphic qualities of exploitation fare, many fan and academic cult film texts keep hardcore at arm's length. Among the few grindhouse publications to have stretched their "cult" remit as far as hard porn are *Sleazoid Express*; *Fleshpot*;[19] and, perhaps in cognizance of the rise in "porn studies," *Peep Shows*.[20] *Sleazoid* in particular celebrates a kaleidoscopic urban collage of art houses, strip bars, adult bookstores, arcades, massage parlors, and what Stevenson calls "old inner-city grindhouses ... decrepit vaudeville barns and opera palaces ... converted to exhibit porno,"[21] and other enticements that manifest a fluid, multimedia proliferation of sexual entertainment. D.N. Rodowick has asked whether "moving-image media have special affinities with specific viewing environments,"[22] and where exploitation films are concerned, the answer is affirmative: memories (or memories by proxy) of insalubrious establishments are important to the fantasies of many grindhouse cult texts. This is not, however, to say that particular films have always been exclusively attached to particular apparatuses. For Klinger, "home theater acts to displace the specificity of the film being screened,"[23] and Rodowick agrees that the consumption of films via digital media constitutes a "decentring of the theatrical film experience,"[24] supplanting the "pure" cinema of big-screen projection. But the urban experience of adult entertainments in the supposedly halcyon 1960s and 1970s was in many ways already ex-centric and impure. The cornucopia of bodily spectacles promised by the marquees, booths, and arcades of 42nd Street and similar sites suggests the coexistence of old and new viewing apparatuses, environments, and technologies rather than an unbroken procession of obsolescence and novelty.

The geographic, if not affective, proximity of grindhouse to pornography makes the borders circumscribing the "home" of grindhouse cinema ever more indistinct, but similar category problems have long been bones of contention. Joan Hawkins[25] and Mark Betz[26] have looked at how, in the 1960s, "art" and sexploitation films often appeared at the same cinemas and sometimes on the same bills. In fact, a degree of border-crossing between sex and art cinemas was acknowledged, albeit disapprovingly, by the middlebrow film establishment of that decade. For example, in 1969 *Films and Filming* published "Underground USA and the Sexploitation Market," in which James Lithgow and Colin Heard debated crossovers between the American underground and sexploitation cinema. (Apart from a few sites like the Cameo-Royal in Leicester Square, or ciné clubs like the Compton and the Dilly in Soho, Britain had no equivalent scene, which may be why some Britons are fascinated by American grindhouse memories.) Lithgow observes that sexploitation producers mobilized the word "underground" as a lure, but maintains that while the avant-garde refuses "to knuckle under to the commercialism of the 'studios,'" sexploitation filmmakers—for all their similarly raw production values—take advantage of the new "permissiveness" in the mindless pursuit of profit,[27] an assessment with which few sexploitation filmmakers or fans would disagree. Heard more sympathetically wonders whether the inexplicit "titillation film," as distinct from "the indoor sports practised on the Times Square circuits," might have some value as expressions of sexual permissiveness. Predating the work of Hawkins and Betz, Heard notes how advertisements for sexploitation and underground films not only shared pages in the countercultural press but were alike enough to cause "confusion" between, say, *Flaming Creatures* and "42nd Street 'skin trade' films."[28]

Grindhouse cultism demonstrates that "temporality and spatiality are necessarily linked in nostalgic desire"[29] by yearning for a mythological lost place situated in an abject entertainment "underbelly" beyond the mainstream purview and prior to a fantasized "Disneyfication" of culture. But attempts to define the nature of the exhibition site touch on a "geography of the practices of viewing"[30] and generate a psychogeography of film consumption. Schaefer points out that "if there was a regular 'home' for exploitation movies it was in grindhouses in the skid row sections of cities across the country"[31] but that "if" implies that this home is built on shifting sand, the discursive construction "skid row" is at once vague and value laden. As Schaefer and others discuss, in its original—and some would therefore say correct—usage, "grindhouse" (or "grind house") is a North American term for a low-rent, single-screen, independent cinema, which from the 1930s to the 1980s (periodizations vary) specialized in showing exploitation films at all hours. Although smaller towns had also hosted independent cinemas where—rather like drive-ins—exploitation films, B-movies, and second-run major features might be shown, venues clustered in urban districts such as Hollywood Boulevard (Los Angeles), Times Square (New York City), First Avenue (Seattle), Canal Street (New Orleans), and Market Street (San Francisco). Frequently located near bus or railway stations, these shoestring operations were sometimes also known as "flop-houses," perhaps because they showed films that flopped elsewhere, or perhaps because they sometimes provided unofficial overnight accommodation for nighthawks, transients, and the poor. This coming together of transient audiences, interstitial exhibition sites, and risqué or marginal genre films enables grindhouse cinemas to be framed as "memory places"[32] that bolster contemporary cultists' sense of their own alterity.

In many ways the idealized memory of grindhouse cinema transcends geographic particularity, not least because the "true" place of the object of nostalgic desire is unstable. In *American Grindhouse*, John Landis reminds us that different narrations of the past point to different locales as the "spiritual home" of grindhouse when he says that, for him, the term "grindhouse" most strongly evokes memories of 1970s Hollywood Boulevard. Nevertheless, as the title of the book you are now reading attests, West 42nd Street on Times Square in the 1970s has become the paradigm of grindhouse cinema, partly because of its notoriety as a red-light district, and its traditional association with gaudy attractions. As a string of cinemas known in fan publications as "the Deuce," this area has often been represented as "beyond the beaten path" of Times Square's legitimate theater district, while the market-capitalism-on-parade licentiousness of its "spectacularization of urban space"[33] has long attracted curiosity-seeking tourists, theater-goers, and filmmakers. In filmic terms, its accumulation of neon signs and garish billboards serves as an instant signifier of the city as a theater of distractions offering commodified sex, metropolitan decadence, and glamorous alienation, hence its iconic place in the mise-en-scène of *Midnight Cowboy* (John Schlesinger, 1969) and, especially, *Taxi Driver* (Martin Scorsese, 1976). Additionally, New York City was in the 1960s and early 1970s a center of sexploitation filmmaking by the likes of Doris Wishman, Michael Findlay, and Andy Milligan, whose films sometimes directly portrayed the 42nd Street environs in which they would be shown. One scene in Findlay's *Wet and Wild* (AKA *Virgins in Heat*, 1976) provides a snapshot of how dominated by porn the area was. Accompanied on the soundtrack by the Harry Warren and Al Dubin song "42nd Street" (from the 1933 Warner Bros musical of the same name), a mock-portentous voiceover delivered by the director invokes the mythic opposition between the bright lights of Broadway and "the seamier 42nd Street," a stone's throw away. In a piece of self-aggrandizing reflexivity we see one large marquee sign advertising *Snuff* (1976), partly made by Findlay himself, and another promoting *The Story of Joanna* (Gerard Damiano, 1975). The Rialto 2 plays *Nympho's Divine Obsession* (Lloyd Kaufman, 1976), the Victory advertises a hardcore triple-bill, and the Joy 42nd theater offers no fewer than "five porno hits." Other establishments glimpsed in the sequence include adult bookstores, the "all nude" Roxy Burlesk theater, and The Harem with what it promises is "a steamy jungle of unfettered sex." Amateur footage of the area in the same period, sometimes uploaded by YouTube users, similarly documents a miscellany of mini-cinemas: 16 mm storefront cinemas advertising all-night quadruple bills of erotic shorts, and other adult entertainment outlets. Both touristic and cinematic representations of 42nd Street contribute to its role in mediated memory as grindhouse cinema's quintessence, and are testament to its attraction as a photogenic icon of disreputability and of the blatant commodity fetishism of market capitalism in the raw.

Narratives of decline, revival, and recollection

The haziness of its contours is such that grindhouse cinema can be given no precise date of death. The establishments petered out at different rates in different places, but even by the early 1980s many exploitation films were reissued on home video, and are still sometimes revived for theatrical release on cult networks, raising the question of the difference between contemporary cult viewing practices and "original" viewing protocols. Depending on where borders between exploitation and pornography are drawn, the finger of blame is pointed at many culprits: everything from home video to crack cocaine, mainstream co-optation, hardcore porn, feminist anti-porn protests, "political correctness," Reagan-Bush New-Right moral crusades and gentrification are said to have contributed to grindhouse's demise. In an elegy to 42nd Street penned in 1989, Jack Stevenson noted ruefully that a combination of "herpes and Aids," billionaire property development and crime crackdowns at the behest of Mayors Ed Koch and Ray Flyn had fatally sanitized "the atmosphere" of the district.[34] Other commentators differ from Stevenson in regarding hard X as a nail in the culture's coffin, and propose teleologically that "porno chic," followed by adult video rental outlets and preview booths, destroyed the "softer" sexploitation market. Muller and Faris, for example, see the rise of porn in the 1970s as the start of a slow death completed later by the VCR, which "rewound and erased all traces of grindhouse."[35] In 1986, Frank Henenlotter similarly saw hardcore as villain rather than victim, and bemoaned the fact that "when I was growing up on Long Island … there used to be lots of sleaze theaters that played horror films. One of my favourite ones is now just hardcore porn."[36]

If videotape ushered in a shift from public (if furtive) spectatorship to home viewing, the transformation of urban sleaze flâneurs into domestic consumers and collectors was no overnight occurrence. Embryonic forms of "home cinema" had long existed in both television broadcasts and abridged versions of films on 8 and Super-8 mm reels for home projection. Indeed, the possibility of the home as a site for watching sex films was discussed even in the early days of "porno chic." An article in a 1973 edition of the UK *Penthouse* investigated Teldyne Packard Bell's new Cartrivision TV cartridge system, a "long-awaited technological breakthrough" thanks to which "erotic movies can appear on your own TV set in the privacy of your own home."[37] Despite its potential, too few consumers were prepared to part with £400 for the necessary equipment, so Cartrivision never caught on. Rodowick asserts that for analogue-era cinephiles, "the only way to see a film was to see it projected,"[38] yet the manufacturer's investment and the porn trade's interest in technologies of home viewing suggest that as early as what is often sentimentalized as porn's golden "age of irresponsibility,"[39] the industry was keen to venture into markets beyond theatrical display. Although the eventual rise of home video played its part in the demise of what is now seen as grindhouse culture, by the mid-1980s many fans conceded that, while armchair viewing was a comparatively impoverished experience, the availability of old exploitation films via "mom and pop" video stores or mail order catalogues, rather than "erasing" grindhouse films, thankfully made them available again. In *Incredibly Strange Films*, Henenlotter ruminated on "what 42nd Street *used* to be—now they're getting rid of it," and suggested that his *Basket Case* (1982) was conceived partly as a tribute to that milieu just as its gentrification was becoming imminent. Henenlotter declares that exploitation reissues on tape are his only solace and implies that the act of collecting videos is haunted by a kind of cultural morbidity: "I hate going back to Long Island because everything I used to love is *dead*."[40]

Whether the agent of destruction was hardcore, new technology, or moral campaigning, it is widely agreed that grindhouse cinema was extinct by the end of the 1980s. New York-based fan publications began celebrating, commemorating, and mythologizing it somewhat earlier, as Times Square appeared endangered. Since Times Square was the most spectacular (and therefore most represented) icon of the adult entertainment trade, its "clean-up" came to stand for the victimization and ultimate extinction of grindhouse cinema *tout court*. Looking back on the area in its pomp, Bill Landis recalls how determined he had been in the early 1980s to "document it all" in *Sleazoid*.[41] Other publications, like Michael Weldon's *Psychotronic* and Jim Morton's *Trashola*, had a similar air of preemptive melancholia; their editorial voices all routinely expressed a cultist combination of defiance and wistfulness in their sense of an era passing into yore and a lifestyle under siege. Pondering the incipient decline and equally ruinous "rehabilitation" of his favorite entertainment area, Weldon suggested that it would be "great if we could start a 'save 42nd Street Committee.'"[42] At the same time, the self-designated exponent of the "cinema of transgression" Richard Kern made his elegiac travelogue *Goodbye 42nd Street* (1986). Naturally, processes of documentation, preservation, and fetishization often begin as absence looms.

Narratives of grindhouse's extinction are often connected to narratives of passing youth. Puchalski looks back to a time "before the drive-ins I used to haunt during my college years were turned into mini-malls."[43] *Psychotronic* was founded when Weldon was in his late teens, and the publication concentrated on films he first watched when he was "growing up in Cleveland"; a family friend owned a cinema, and Weldon often played "hooky" to see films there, with the result—so he felt compelled to recount in the updated *Psychotronic Video Guide*—that he failed his exams;[44] Bill Landis was forever "skipping classes" at university to get his "real education" from 42nd Street.[45] Missing school or sacrificing education for cinema is a common refrain because as well as locating grindhouse experience in the remembered affective intensities of adolescence, it resonates with notions of misdemeanor. This entwining of grindhouse memories with recollections of youthful erotic epiphany is doubtless connected to the fact that exploitation cinema capitalizes on fetishistic curiosity about "forbidden" sights, a connection that reminds us that, as Svetlana Boym puts it, the bittersweet pangs of reminiscence can involve "a romance with one's own fantasy."[46] Bill Landis, for example, recalls visiting Times Square as a teen in the mid-1970s. Detaching himself from his bourgeois parents (according to Freud, juvenile sexual investigations are carried out with a sense of alienation from the family), the young Landis explores the seamier side of the cinema district while they watched "tourist trap plays" on Broadway. Landis presents his youthful self as an adventurer, whose voracious spectatorship took him far from the sightseer's perfunctory gaze; seeking out the exploitation films he had seen advertised in the *New York Post* in his youth, he instead found himself overwhelmed by posters for hard-core films like *The Devil in Miss Jones* (Gerard Damiano, 1973).

Traces of places

References to grind houses, flophouses, art houses, drive-ins, and so on evoke distinct spaces of exhibition and consumption but they are also architectural figures for a classed hierarchy of taste. Similar strata come into play when cult texts navigate the topographic nuances of downtown, midtown, inner city, skid row, poverty row, red-light districts, and the rest, with the grind house projected as a site of otherness with which fans may align themselves. The totemic value of grindhouse cinema therefore lies in the mediated memory of a marriage of film type, place, and experience, as much as in the professed qualities of the films exhibited there. The memories narrated in cultist publications are often almost Proustian in approach: dank lobbies, sticky floors, sweating but distracted patrons, and the odor of disinfectant are as likely to be evoked as the movies themselves. In an attempt to ground the grindhouse image in the real, one text waxes romantic about 42nd Street's "unsurpassed array of porno booths, convulsive junkies and gorgeous old theatres stinking of Lysol and vomit,"[47] while another summons "spilled malt liquors, piss, smoke, BO, and Pinesol,"[48] thereby suggesting extracinematic corporeal and ambient effects distinct from but enmeshed with the mental afterimage of the films. Other tropes try to stabilize the slippery grindhouse referent through narratives about spectatorial risk. In *American Grindhouse*, the director William Lustig recalls how grind houses always carried "an ever present sense of danger." Perhaps Lustig imagined this air of threat to be the ideal atmosphere in which to absorb the grimy misogyny of his slasher film *Maniac* (1981). The air of menace felt to permeate Times Square and its environs was similarly played upon, and similarly displaced onto, the bodies of female characters, in Lucio Fulci's slasher film *The New York Ripper* (1982); Fulci's film offers several contemporary glimpses of the area's cinemas and "live sex" theaters (among them the Lyric, Cine 42, and the New Amsterdam) as sites of sordid allure, especially for the Ripper's female victims. In a similarly grubby vein, the author of *Sleazoid Express* aspires to a blend of Hubert Selby Jr. and Travis Bickle in his descriptions of audiences made up of "depressives .... sexual obsessives, inner-city people seeking cheap diversions ... people getting high ... pickpockets,"[49] while the casually homophobic fanzine *Grindhouse Purgatory* creates a vivid picture of "ominous darkness" filled with an "army of winos, dustheads, faggots, pick pockets and other assorted lowlifes."[50] In *American Grindhouse*, Joe Dante fondly remembers sitting in a grind-house audience one night in the 1970s as a murder was committed: "the police came in and turned on the houselights," but the screening continued and Dante's enjoyment of the film was not spoiled.

Foregrounding edginess enables grindhouse cult discourse to project an image of down-at-heel or lawless audiences, while diverting attention from the middle-class film cultist also sitting in the auditorium. Thus grindhouse intermediaries associate themselves with the passion of the "obsessives" and the transgressivity of the "lowlifes," while situating themselves as astute observers of the grindhouse milieu, not unlike Walter Benjamin's evocation of the flâneur who perceives the modern city as a fragmented "theatre of purchases" full of encounters with strangers.[51] This self-presentation as resident of a liminoid site both inside and outside the "original" audience allows the cultist to present grindhouse cinema simultaneously as a bastion of counter-normative impulses, and a wretched shelter for the dispossessed. The notion of grindhouse cinema as a space for misunderstood mavericks (in the auditorium as well as on screen) is of course a ritual of distinction for a "paracinematic" taste discourse that paints itself as an affront to both bourgeois aesthetic norms and avant-garde elitism. As Sconce argues of the classed subject-position of paracinematic audiences, the current grindhouse cult is not simply a "bottom up" phenomenon, even in an age of media convergence that has supposedly seen "the withering of traditional gatekeepers."[52] It has gatekeepers of its own. If in the late 1970s and early 1980s the grindhouse gatekeepers were fans who could covertly use office photocopiers, today it includes documentary filmmakers, academics, festival programmers, and others with the requisite cultural capital.

Bill Landis personifies the intricate relationships between social position and reading protocol. Between 1977 and 1982, Landis divided his time between working as a projectionist for cinemas in Times Square, editing his *Sleazoid* fanzine, and arranging exploitation screenings at Manhattan's 8th Street Playhouse, and "hipster nightspots like Club 57."[53] Landis negotiates his plural access to cultural space by suggesting that his involvement in "the Times Square universe" rendered him both an uncouth "outsider to straight society"[54] and a swashbuckling troublemaker for the cultural elite. Landis reviles the "snobs who populated the art/underground film world,"[55] reporting that Jonas Mekas was "livid that I'd once left *Sleazoid* flyers at a screening of *Chelsea Girls* at his Anthology Film Archives."[56] As well as displaying his membership of that community by name-checking everyone from Warhol to Fernando Arrabal, Landis remembers distributing his fanzine at *Artforum* magazine events and the Times Square Show of 1980.[57] Although Landis fashions himself as a gate-crasher in the art world, the bohemian consecration of "trash" was already a firmly established tradition. Fanzines like *Sleazoid* and *Psychotronic* built on a fondness for "grade z" cinema, whose roots can be found in the surrealist love of "delirious" low culture, Sontag-style camp aesthetics, Warholian pop, the work of film critics like Manny Farber and Parker Tyler, the Midnight Movies cult, and many other factors. At the same time, "B movie," exploitation and drive-in cinema—already often self-parodying—was widely referenced in pastiches and tongue-in-cheek homages like *Hollywood Boulevard* (Allan

Arkush and Joe Dante, 1976) and *The Rocky Horror Picture Show* (Jim Sharman, 1975). All of this meant that the cultural conditions were in place for The Times Square show to have welcomed copies of *Sleazoid* into its gift shop. The art critic Kim Levin described the exhibition as a seminal statement of what the doyen of modernist art criticism, Clement Greenberg, called postmodernism's "new-fangled philistines of advancedness,"[58] a description equally befitting the grindhouse cult. The show also chimed with burgeoning grindhouse cultism by being installed in an "abandoned massage parlor"[59] (the building also housed a stationery shop, a fast-food retailer, and an adult bookshop), and exhibiting art which reflected the frisson of "urban decay" and "Forty-second Street come-ons and other assaults."[60]

The interconnectedness of exploitation, porn, and art worlds should not be overstated; but their coexistence in the same urban environs entailed some sharing of personnel, management, and audience, and sometimes made them joint targets of both right-wing and feminist censorship campaigns. Anti-porn marches in Times Square in the late 1970s, along with Andrea Dworkin's conflation of pornography and snuff,[61] were galvanized by the cheek-by-jowl availability of hard-core and sexploitation films, "snuff" loops, sadomasochistic live acts, and prostitution in the same zone. Apart from occasional snide references to "the feminists, with their endless yakking,"[62] such protests are largely excised from grindhouse cult discourse, but are part of the fabric of grindhouse cinema history, including the history of its representation and self-representation. At any rate, if nocturnal strollers like Landis were fascinated by the gaudy "come-ons" and "assaults" of a Dionysian, carnivalesque marketplace, anti-porn protesters took a different view: one installation at the Times Square Show consisted of the feminist slogan "women—take back the night" scrawled through the site in lipstick.[63]

The grindhouse afterimage

According to Nora, memorial acts and objects are motivated by a dread of amnesia, while Jacques Derrida proposes that the archival impulse to collect, itemize, and preserve is bound up with the death instinct or "destruction drive."[64] Something similar can be said of contemporary grindhouse cultism, from the making of documentary paeans to the building of home exploitation film libraries. The packaging, marketing, and mythologization of grindhouse ascribe relevance and vigor to the field by self-consciously reproducing the florid tone of exploitation cinema advertising. Yet these proclamations of vitality are haunted by a discourse of death and disappearance. As David Church explores, although many grindhouse DVD and Blu-ray ranges are no-frills, other more prestigious fan-oriented products are loaded with supplements, touted as definitive transfers, and marketed through a rhetoric of connoisseurship and auteurism that is alien to the throwaway practices of an opportunistic industry; pristine, supposedly complete editions similarly run counter to the tatty condition in which many exploitation films were originally screened. In recognition of this contradiction, grindhouse disc packaging, menu design, and so on often emulate the look of the original film publicity materials and the imperfections of degraded film stock. Many discs include scratched trailers suffering from frame loss and replications of "old style" intermissions, while their sleeves imitate the texture of creased movie posters. In *American Grindhouse*, scene and chapter transitions are accompanied by simulated projector noise and faded, even melting celluloid. Manifesting what Wolfgang Ernst has described as "media awareness of different modes of textually or visually processing the past,"[65] such "decay" compensates for digital media's perceived lack of physical presence by hypostatizing a lost moment of authenticity. Faux patina connotes a tangibility felt lacking in digital images.

In as much as it reifies film's past through a digital poetics of arrested entropy, grindhouse mystique echoes film theorists from the "prevideo cinephile generation," for whom the analogue-to-digital shift is tantamount to the death of "cinematographic specificity."[66] For Rodowick, pre-digital film theorists—not unlike grindhouse cultists—treasured the particularity of cinema's haptic qualities and signifying practices because prints "had to be chased down in commercial theatres, repertory houses, and film societies."[67] Much as the thrill of this "chase" hints at pleasures beyond the immanence of "film itself," so cult grindhouse texts often eulogize the urban film fan's ambulatory gaze, which includes but also extends beyond the "celluloid strip with its reassuring physical passage of visible images."[68] In a process of technological disavowal, digital emulations of projector noise and celluloid frangibility function like artificial ruins, memorializing—or retrofitting—a structure of feeling thought absent in private home viewing. One fanzine editor muses, "I miss the raincoated perverts … I miss seeing Times Square grindhouse patrons impatiently flick lit cigarettes at the screen … and coming out of the theater squinting into the blazing sunlight," before inviting his readers to "hurry into your seats. The lights will be going down soon."[69] The "home" of grindhouse is, then, discovered in a fetishized notion of "cinema" itself. (This passion for seemingly lost presence has recently embraced obsolescent VHS tapes, and vanishing video retailers, now seen in hindsight less as threats to, and more as part of, grindhouse's cultural space.) Thus grindhouse's disappearance, alongside its continued, supposedly derealized, digital life, equates in the cultist imagination to the death of "real" cinema understood as a multidimensional, even multisensual corporeal encounter between spectator, audience, image, city space, and material apparatus. As one cultist text puts it, "battered, burned and riddled with splices, these films were the lifeblood of the grindhouses and they are all that remain of the wildest era we have ever known"[70]; simulations of the cinematic apparatus both produce and compensate for a sense that the (remembered) experiential plenitude of grindhouse's "original" moment is irrecoverable.

According to Pierre Nora, "memory is constantly on our lips because it no longer exists,"[71] which is to suggest that recollection brings memories into being in the very act of narrating them. In its clinging to idealized memories of sticky floors and cultural detritus, grindhouse cultism involves a sense of "the irreversibility of time: something in the past is no longer accessible."[72] Both the interiors of specific venues and street views of urban spaces become symbolic loci of a cinematic heritage around which cultists can perform their taste affiliations. Hence Steven Puchalski describes the collection of exploitation film reviews in *Slimetime* as "a glimpse into a time long gone,"[73] and Josh Hadley, a conflicted contributor to *Grindhouse Purgatory*, laments the fact that "we have lost a culture as well as a significant piece of film history. No one who was not actually there ... can appreciate what this era of film was, myself included," while confronting the makers of "kitschy" grindhouse "throwbacks"—such as *Death Proof* (Quentin Tarantino 2007), *Machete* (Ethan Maniquis and Robert Rodriguez, 2010), and *Disco Exorcist* (Richard Griffin, 2011)—with what he sees as a harsh truth: "the grindhouse is gone, accept it."[74] One such revivalist is Jeremy Katzen, a filmmaker who shot a remake of Herschell Gordon Lewis's *Wizard of Gore* in 2007. In *American Grindhouse*, Katzen suggests that he can "remember" something about the exploitation scene of the 1960s and 1970s, then corrects "remember" to "imagine," since he "wasn't there." Katzen explains that "it's hard for us to imagine, those of us who weren't alive, what it must have been like to see people eviscerated in a movie ... Herschell was the genius that first did this." Hadley similarly muses that "by the time the grindhouse was over I was not even out of high school yet, so I missed most of this."[75] In these ways, grindhouse cultism almost acknowledges the phantasmic nature of its own references to "lost" times "long gone" being "missed" by fans who "weren't there," suggesting not simply that grindhouse cinema left behind an ersatz shadow of its former self in Tarantinoesque pastiches and revivals but also that the grindhouse era as presently understood and marketed is a product of collective desire.

To this extent, grindhouse memories are, to borrow a Lacanian phrase about trauma, a missed encounter with the real, and that "real" often takes the form of a chimeric "home" assembled from mediated recollections of cinema experience. Hadley extravagantly compares what he imagines was the thrill of original grindhouse cinema to the disappointment of contemporary pastiches: "the redo is never as good as the first time. Fuck all your life and it will never feel as intense as that very first orgasm."[76] The further the "first time" recedes into memory and myth, the more significant it appears. Yet it was never unproblematically present in the "first" place: there is no original moment of plenitude unmediated by fantasy, representation, and self-presentation. For example, the exploitation producer David F. Friedman may have published his autobiography, *A Youth in Babylon: Confessions of a Trash-Film King*, in 1990, shortly before his back catalogue was rereleased on tape by the Seattle-based Something Weird Video, but he had begun curating his legacy and managing his reputation considerably earlier. Around the same time that Findlay's *Wet and Wild* captured the marquees and storefronts of 42nd Street, Friedman was documenting the pre-hard-core exploitation scene in an unfinished film called *That's Sexploitation*.[77] In *Psychotronic*, Weldon remembered old drive-in and 42nd Street movies through the filter of having watched them again on cable TV. When the intrepid young Bill Landis first entered Times Square, it "looked just like I wanted it to,"[78] having seen sensational cinema admats in the press in his youth, and having seen it represented in *Midnight Cowboy*; such mediated afterimages may intensify rather than diminish the potency of the grindhouse myth in the cultist imagination. Perhaps if we approach grindhouse on the basis that it never uncomplicatedly existed, we might arrive at a fuller understanding of why we wish that it did.

Notes

1. Michael Weldon, *The Psychotronic Encyclopedia of Film* (London: Plexus, 1983), x.
2. Andrea Juno, "Interview: Frank Henenlotter," in *Re/Search: Incredibly Strange Films*, ed. Jim Morton (San Francisco: Re/Search Publications, 1986), 8.
3. Jeffrey Sconce, "'Trashing' the Academy: Taste, Excess and an Emerging Politics of Cinematic Style," *Screen* 36:4 (1995): 371–393.
4. Barbara Klinger, *Beyond the Multiplex: Cinema, New Technologies, and the Home* (Berkeley and Los Angeles, CA: University of California Press, 2006).
5. Jacinda Read, "The Masculinity of Cult: From Fan-Boys to Academic Bad-Boys," in *Defining Cult Movies: The Cultural Politics of Oppositional Taste*, eds Mark Jancovich, Antonio Lázaro Reboll, Julian Stringer, and Andy Willis (Manchester: Manchester University Press, 2003), 54–70.
6. David Church, "From Exhibition to Genre: The Case of Grind-House Films," *Cinema Journal* 50:4 (2011): 1–25.
7. Andreas Huyssen, *Present Pasts: Urban Palimpsests and the Politics of Memory* (Palo Alto, CA: Stanford University Press, 2003), 17.
8. Klinger, *Beyond the Multiplex*, 67.
9. Andreas Huyssen, "Nostalgia for Ruins," *Grey Room* 23 (2006): 6–21.
10. Jacques Le Goff, *History and Memory*, trans. Steve Rendall and Elizabeth Claman (New York: Columbia University Press, 1992), 23.
11. Paul Ricoeur, *Time and Narrative*, Vol. 1 (Chicago: University of Chicago Press, 1984), 3.
12. See, especially, David Church's *Grindhouse Nostalgia: Memory, Home Video and Exploitation Film Fandom* (Edinburgh: Edinburgh University Press, 2015). It is a matter of regret that Church's informative and theoretically astute book only came to my attention just as I was completing this chapter.
13. Eric Schaefer, *Bold! Daring! Shocking! True! A History of Exploitation Films, 1919–1959* (Durham and London: Duke University Press, 1999), 119.
14. J. Hoberman and Jonathan Rosenbaum, *Midnight Movies* (New York: Da Capo Press, 1983), 295–297.
15. Josh Hadley, "Burning Down the Grindhouse," *Grindhouse Purgatory* 1:1 (2013): 3.
16. Church, "From Exhibition to Genre," 201.
17. Ibid., 202.
18. Andrea Friedman, *Prurient Interests: Gender, Democracy, and Obscenity in New York City, 1909–1945* (New York: Columbia University Press, 2000).
19. Jack Stevenson, ed., *Fleshpot: Cinema's Myth Makers and Taboo Breakers*, 2nd edn. (Manchester: Headpress, 2002).
20. Xavier Mendik, ed., *Peep Shows: Cult Film and the Cine-Erotic* (London and New York: Wallflower Press, 2012).
21. Stevenson, *Fleshpot*, 243.
22. D.N. Rodowick, *The Virtual Life of Film* (Cambridge, MA and London: Harvard University Press, 2007), 33.
23. Klinger, *Beyond the Multiplex*, 48.
24. Rodowick, *Virtual Life*, 39.
25. Joan Hawkins, *Cutting Edge: Art-Horror and the Horrific Avant-Garde* (Minneapolis: University of Minnesota Press, 2000).

26. Mark Betz, "Art, Exploitation, Underground," in *Defining Cult Movies: The Cultural Politics of Oppositional Taste*, eds Mark Jancovich et al. (Manchester: Manchester University Press, 2003), 202–222.
27. James Lithgow and Colin Heard, "Underground USA and the Sexploitation Market," *Films and Filming* (August 1969): 19.
28. Ibid., 25.
29. Huyssen, "Nostalgia," 7.
30. Mike Crang, "Rethinking the Observer: Film, Mobility, and the Construction of the Subject," in *Engaging Film: Geographies of Mobility and Identity*, eds Tim Cresswell and Deborah Dixon (New York and Oxford: Rowan and Littlefield, 2002), 18.
31. Schaefer, *Bold!*, 119.
32. Pierre Nora, *Realms of Memory: Rethinking the French Past*, ed. Lawrence D. Kritzman, trans. Arthur Goldhammer, 3 Vols. (New York: Columbia University Press, 1996–1968), xvii.
33. Crang, "Rethinking the Observer," 19.
34. Stevenson, *Fleshpot*, 234.
35. Eddie Muller and Daniel Faris, *That's Exploitation! The Forbidden World of "Adults Only" Cinema* (London: Titan Books, 1996), 8–9.
36. Juno, "Interview," 8.
37. Jeffrey Robinson, "Good Evening—Here Are the Nudes," *Penthouse* 7:12 (1973): 88.
38. Rodowick, *Virtual Life*, 26. Thorough histories of the "home cinema" industry can be found in Joshua Greenberg, *From Betamax to Blockbuster: Video Stores and the Invention of Movies on Video* (Cambridge, MA: MIT Press, 2010), and Paul McDonald, *Video and DVD Industries* (London: BFI, 2008).
39. Robert C. Sickels, "1970s Disco Daze: Paul Thomas Anderson's *Boogie Nights* and the Last Golden Age of Irresponsibility," *Journal of Popular Culture* 35:4 (2002): 49–60.
40. Juno, "Interview," 8.
41. Bill Landis, and Michelle Clifford, *Sleazoid Express* (New York and London: Simon and Schuster, 2002), xvi.
42. Weldon, *Psychotronic Encyclopedia*, xi.
43. Steven Puchalski, *Slimetime: A Guide to Sleazy, Mindless Movies*. Revised and updated edn (Manchester: Critical Vision/Headpress, 2000), 9.
44. Michael Weldon, *The Psychotronic Video Guide* (London: Titan Books, 1996), x.
45. Landis and Clifford, *Sleazoid Express*, xii.
46. Svetlana Boym, *The Future of Nostalgia* (New York: Basic Books Press, 2001), 132.
47. Puchalski, *Slimetime*, 9.
48. Pete Chiarella, ed., *Grindhouse Purgatory* 1: 1 (2013): 7.
49. Landis and Clifford, *Sleazoid Express*, 3.
50. Chiarella, *Purgatory*, 8.
51. Anne Friedberg, *Window Shopping: Cinema and the Postmodern* (Berkeley: University of California Press, 1993), 49.
52. Henry Jenkins, *Convergence Culture: Where Old and New Media Collide* (New York and London: New York University Press, 2006), 21.
53. Landis and Clifford, *Sleazoid Express*, xiii.
54. Ibid., xv.
55. Ibid., 5.
56. Ibid., xiv.

57. Ibid., xii–xiii.
58. Kim Levin, *Beyond Modernism: Essays on Art from the 70s and 80s* (New York: Harper Collins, 1989), 197.
59. Levin, *Beyond Modernism*, 198–199.
60. Ibid., 197.
61. Andrea Dworkin, *Pornography: Men Possessing Women* (London: The Women's Press, 1981), 71.
62. Landis and Clifford, *Sleazoid Express*, 137.
63. Levin, *Beyond Modernism*, 198.
64. Jacques Derrida, "Archive Fever," in *The Archive*, ed. Charles Merewether (London: Whitechapel Gallery/MIT Press, 2006), 77.
65. Wolfgang Ernst, *Digital Memory and the Archive* (Minneapolis: University of Minnesota Press, 2013), 37.
66. Rodowick, *Virtual Life*, 19.
67. Ibid., 26.
68. Ibid., 8.
69. Mike Accomando, "Editorial," *Dreadful Pleasures* 11 (1996): 3.
70. 42nd Street Pete, "A Lost Saturday Night at the Venus," *Grindhouse Purgatory* 1:1 (2013), 9.
71. Nora, *Realms*, 1.
72. Huyssen, "Nostalgia," 7.
73. Puchalski, *Slimetime*, 9.
74. Hadley, "Burning," 5.
75. Ibid., 3.
76. Ibid., 3.
77. David F. Friedman, Untitled interview with Doris Wishman, *Something Weird Video* Catalogue # 1, 1995–1996.
78. Landis and Clifford, *Sleazoid Express*, xi.

2

"This Is Where We Came In": The Economics of Unruly Audiences, Their Cinemas and Tastes, from Serial Houses to Grind Houses

Phyll Smith

The unique thing about a motion picture theatre is that in and out of it there is continual traffic. To any other type of auditorium, patrons come at a certain hour before the performance begins, and there is only one performance. But most motion picture theatres operate on a policy of more than one performance during a certain period of the day, the so-called "grind policy" which is common enough to be considered the important characteristic. Patrons arrive at any time following the beginning of the first show, assured of witnessing an entire performance.[1]

Better Theatres, 1933

The term "grindhouse"—along with "drive-in" movies or "serials"—is a genericized term constructed around a past exhibition context; continuous *grind* programming; and its location, "grind houses." David Church has charted the construction and validity of "grindhouse" and "drive-in" as retrospective generic and marketing terms that "nostalgically recall past times and spaces of consumption," questioning the "underground cultural formation" aligned with an "othered" cinematic experience, which itself *"perhaps never truly existed."*[2] Contrary to the received understanding that "grind" represents a desperate lowering of standards in reaction to the demise of popular cinema-going in the 1950s and 1960s, in the *Better Theatres* epigraph above, it is used to denote an already common 1930s exhibition practice. The article, on how cinema designers and architects can best accommodate and facilitate "grind-policy," illustrates an institutionalizing of the practice in new and refurbishing theaters. It does not signify the image of deteriorating locations and dilapidated theaters, which later commentators and scholars have ascribed to grind houses.

These exhibition terms were used contemporaneously to define a set of practices, marked as aberrant, and denote products suitable for audiences imagined to prefer (or tolerate) such practices, and Church has also analyzed the *Oxford English Dictionary* (*OED*) etymology of the terms and their correspondence to generic tropes and promotional tactics in the post-studio era.[3] In describing this subcultural alignment of "grindhouse" fans to an apparently marginal series of exhibition practices symbolic of the degradation of studio era cinema and its audience, the questions Church raises are how marginal were these practices, these audiences, and when and why were they so figured?

Constructing a new, more comprehensive and accurate etymology for "grind" and "grind house" than the *OED* provides allows us to see not only the nuances of the term's use and development but also how it was constructed in opposition to other cinematic forms. The industry used first serial then grind audiences and theaters to offset negative criticism of more prestigious cinema products, a rhetoric marking a middle-class first-run ideal as "normal" and grind and serial practices (and audience behavior) as exceptional, economically marginal, and industrially insignificant, and creating a notion of an audience that respectable audiences and critics could define themselves against. As Richard Maltby identifies, even prior to the studio era "the industry grouped audiences, theatres and pictures according to interrelated generic classifications," so films could be described as of a "serial" or "grind" type regardless of their form or exhibition history, reflecting instead an imagined audience and questions of filmic address, with audience, theater, and picture becoming discursively interchangable.[4] The othering discourses around grind audiences, making distinctions or judgments, often of a moral or class nature, and the exceptionalizing of the commonplace exhibition preferences that defined it—serials, seriality, continuous exhibition, double-features, late-night, and early morning performance—were then used by the majors to police the access of independent and marginal cinemas and producers to wealthier and more lucrative audiences.

By the end of the 1910s the formally lucrative and prestigious serial was at odds with the industry's idealized vision of itself, as Shelley Stamp summarizes:

> Serial pictures represented a marked departure from increasingly normative trends: issued in two reel installments usually over a period of months, serials were neither feature films nor traditional shorts; their multifaceted tie-in publicity encouraged intertextual viewing practices that were distinctly at odds with models of spectatorship becoming standardized in classical narrative; and challenged the decorous promotions to would-be female filmgoers.[5]

These normative trends, acceptable viewing practices, and standardized models of spectatorship codified the behavior of middle-class audiences and dovetailed with the practices of first-run exhibition, while simultaneously policing what, where, and how cinematic consumption occurred and denigrating all exceptional behavior. This normative ideal, and the serial and grind house's construction as oppositional and threatening to it, has far more relevance to the industry's generic discourse around grind house and its nostalgic gentrification than the prevalence, longevity, or viability of its practices.

While rolling performances of shorts were common in fairs and nickelodeons, the emergence of the multi-reel feature facilitated a more theatrical style of presentation, with the quality connotations of legitimate theater over the vaudeville-style mixed bill of films that had preceded it.[6] The non-normative perception of grind houses is intrinsic to the evolution of the terminology through which it is labeled and discussed, and while grind may for the whole of the classical studio period have been the most common form of cinema experience, the apparently non-normative descriptions of its audience's behavior, taste, and economics maintained this perception of anomalousness.

Church's analysis places "grindhouse nostalgia" in the context of "morally and politically charged stigmatizing discourses about grind houses that had appeared since the early years,"[7] in order to "reveal its debt to exhibition institutions," as Altman puts it.[8] However, the discourse and practice of grind as both critical bête noir and economic threat to first-run cinemas not only presages the end of the studio system and vertical integration as Church describes but exists in both, as practice and discourse predating the studio system as an ever-recurring oncoming threat. The discursive associations that both grind house and the serial shared demonstrate how these exhibition/distribution practices are constructed as restricted to certain marginal sectors of the industry and their marginal audiences by social and cultural distinctions around their audiences' viewing choices and habits, distinctions which resonate in the labels by which they are discussed. Both serials and grind pictures become generic industry shorthand for unacceptable audience and exhibition behaviors, while industrially institutionalizing those behaviors in production, distribution, and even architecture. The imagined grind house, whose audience and exhibitor choose the aberrant, can be found to be at odds with the actual economics and institutions of grind exhibition.

While cultural, moral, and psychological arguments around seriality, repetition, overexposure, and narrative disruption central to criticisms of the serial in the 1910s are then transferred to discussions of grind house audiences and their apparent transgressions. Understanding those roots opens new interpretations of work on the series and sequential film and genericism that flourished under the generic "grindhouse" banner through the 1950s and 1960s, with the demise of the serial and the recapitulation of its practices, and audience, in grind houses and the films exhibited therein.[9]

The grinder's angle: Story mills in the dream factory

The phrase "grind house," as a simile of "mill," long predates the invention of cinema.[10] During the 1800s, less formal, pejorative uses of the words referred to factory processes lacking in skill or art, symbolic of the mechanization of creative or higher processes and both dehumanizing and homogenizing, and the hard work and long hours therein became "grind." In early cinema, "grinder" and "grinding" were used as terms for camera operators and projectionists (the jobs initially being a dual role) and their skills. Initially a neutral term, the scornful meanings of "grind" inflected its use, particularly as operators sought to differentiate their job as a skilled role. In other mechanizing creative industries, writers who used typewriters were decried as hacks by referring to their keyboards as "mills" (and ultimately to their writings, as the ground product of the paper mill—"pulp fiction").[11] Ultimately "grind" referred to exhibitors who scheduled an extended day's work on a production line of continuous screenings, but in exhibition the term develops negative associations once alternative screening practices are promoted in contrast to it.[12]

The complex relational frames between mill and grind, crushing and devaluing, unstimulating cyclic labor and low-value culture were all current, long-standing, and commonplace by the point that the notion of grind house cinema is coined in the cinema industry and becomes widespread. The serial, with its long overall print length, was then a medium where the practical and laborious connotations of "grind" might meet, and "the grind" of a film might refer to its shooting period or running time. So the producer Theodore Wharton might be "off again on another long serial grind" with little hint of objection.[13] Similarly a "grinder" might be a nuts-and-bolts description of a daring camera operator, so when "a camera was mounted on the front of a racing car, George 'Tripod' Hill was appointed grinder"—a trooper's badge of honor.[14] However, when Hollywood stills photographers discuss the practice of camera operators, not specialists, taking production stills, their moving picture colleagues are invariably referred to as "grinders" rather than, say, "cameramen," "cinematographers," or "photographers," in a disparaging differentiation of skills.[15]

The terms "grind," "grinding," "grinder," and "grind house" proliferate in projectionist's trade magazines and advertising; the documents of their professional associations and union (the International Alliance of Theatrical Stage Employees (IATSE)) are peppered with examples and are commonplace by the 1910s. The "long grind" of an extended performance—borrowed from all-day pitches at fairgrounds where many camera and projection operators would have had experience as projectionists or barrel organists (whose work had required similar steady cranking skills)[16]—is associated with continuous cinema performance.[17] The ideas of cinema "grind" and "grind houses" and arduous grinding labor or physical milling are distinct enough for the two ideas to be used against each other in wordplay jokes in the trade press from the early 1910s onwards.[18] While nonstop exhibition in this period is usually referred to as "continuous," the term "grind house" is used in projection contexts to differentiate between emerging models of exhibition:

> Continuous shows run about an hour and a half with less than five minutes intermission. 5000ft of film twice weekly is supplied to the grind houses, which are open from 11 A.M. to 11 P.M., while a full program consists of just double that amount of film to the one-a-night class of theatres, where it is common to see the audience in full evening dress (1913).[19]

While there is surprise at the emergence of a middle-class audience here (in this instance an Australian one), both "grind house" and theatrical exhibition are being promoted as new and progressive models for the emerging, larger, purpose-built cinemas.

A more derisive rhetoric was employed during attempts by projectionists to unionize, in order to differentiate themselves from the untrained non-union labor recruited to lower wages or break strikes. In a dispute in 1920 between IATSE union and Los Angeles cinema managers seeking a differential for grind shows, the existing term was forced into wider regular print. The union defined what the industry termed *Class C* and *Class D* cinemas as "grind houses,"[20] and the term became key in differentiating between cinemas' and projectionists' terms and conditions. The Motion Picture Operators (Local 150) asked for an increase in salaries over first-run one- or two-show-a-day houses and a six-day week; the Los Angeles Theatres Association representing all of the downtown theaters including "the Gore and Lesser houses, known as grind houses, against whom the fight was principally directed," acquiesced on wages, but not Sundays.[21] Already in use orally, the term is used in this public dispute to associate the continuous conditions in the downtown houses with unprofessional exhibition, and, as such, "grind house" becomes identifiable as a space and practice.

By 1924 the term had moved from a technician's term to being used by industry in legislative debates defending tax exemptions on 10¢ theaters, already with negative audience connotations ("what we call a grind house opens up early in the morning and perhaps runs until midnight, catering to a strictly transient trade, or people who drop in to rest more than they do to see the picture"),[22] and by 1929 it appears, and is apparently self-explanatory, in the more public sphere of *Vanity Fair* ("There were men who wandered in by mistake, assuming it to be some sort of cheap grind house, who jumped when they saw the price card").[23]

As much as the term "grind house" is fitting—as a filmstock-grinding, culture-damaging, audience-harming, industry profit mill—the term is of course a back transformation. The "grind" here (usually in quotation marks in this period) is the exhibition method: performance after continuous rolling performance of the same handful of films. Widespread use and familiarity of the term in the 1920s is an indicator of its widespread practice, as much as the acceptance of the denigrating and economically segregating connotations of the term.

The story so far: Serials, double bills, continuous houses, and the beginnings of grind

The rechristened *grind* model and its houses fell into a pattern of price and class segregation. As the feature film superseded the serial, those theaters still screening serial products became less attractive, second-class, venues, and needed a name: "serial houses." Through the 1920s, however, as the profile of the serial diminished and it no longer provided the main opposing structure to first-run one- or two-a-night presentation, the continuous theaters of these same audiences, and the newly emergent and derogatory term "grind," became the locus for the same defining discourses.

These debates are ostensibly about the quality of the films, but this is frequently judged through the reactions and behavior of the audience to those films, which are far less indicative of the quality of the films than they are as indicators of the class, race, and nationalities of the presumed patrons they attracted. Behavioral distinctions set these groups apart from the middle-class milieu, to which most critics and social reformers belonged and which many companies saw as an ideal.

In what Maltby identifies as an emergent overlapping taxonomy of "class" and "mass," the discourse around grind and serial exhibition/distribution through the 1930s and 1940s fuses marginal audiences,[24] theaters, and pictures into a single seemingly coherent entity: "grindhouse." Initially industry journals predicted and argued for a two-tier exhibition system:

> Productions will divide themselves into two classes, the good ordinary kind and the monumental productions in the million dollar class ... and the representative key cities will establish two kinds of theatres for two classes of productions: One the usual, grind house to take care of the good product and the two-a-day house to take care of the unusual productions, charging legitimate attraction prices therefor.[25]

While this prediction would perhaps take thirty years to come to its dualistic apogee, already in place are the key areas of rhetoric: that grind houses are cheaper at the box office; they show smaller, older, lower-budget pictures; their lower-class managers and patrons are less cultured than those of "legitimate" cinemas; and that the films shown are usual (i.e. generic) and lack appeal.

While "grind" exhibition suffered from class and taste distinctions in this way, it did not yet attract the same moral opprobrium as the serial, at least while the serial maintained its social and critical currency. As notions of "grind" as a policy and the grind house as an imagined social space gradually separated to define a model of economically marginal independent exhibition and production for a similarly marginal audience, the moral opprobrium became similarly appropriated. By 1922, grind policies began to typify degraded theaters for the trade paper *Film Daily* as new, middle-class cinemas replaced former opera houses and storefront shows:

> The Pan house in Salt Lake is one of the finest houses I ever visited, makes the Los house look like a Main Street grind house and the managers are of a different class, they are well read and on their toes for something new that will appeal.[26]

Fellow trade paper *Variety* five months later uses the term again to describe a superseded cinema building:

> Grauman's Los Angeles house at Broadway and 3rd St since the opening of the new Metropolitan at 6th and Hill streets is likely to become a grind house at a flat 25-cent admission price while the big presentations will be given at the new theatre.[27]

From this point, the term and the policy become synonymous with distinctions between the grand and the squalid—"From the palatial loop houses to the smallest 'Grind house' on the South Side"—and with decline, from one to the other.[28] This trope, equating grind with decline, continued through the Depression, impacting ever-larger theaters, from large towns like Akron, where a "1,500 seat de luxe neighbourhood spot, dark for some time, reopened with a grind policy at 25 cents top," to cities like Los Angeles, whose "Million Dollar theatre, dark for two weeks, to reopen as a 15¢ grind house."[29] Far from being seen, like the serial, as a survival policy in hard times, the lower grind houses were accused of being the cause of the decline of first-run and upper loop cinemas. As *Variety* recognized, "10¢ pictures [were] blamed by managers for the almost entire collapse of their business. Many 10¢ grind houses are doing profitable business while the larger deluxers suffer."[30] Others, recognizing the economic marginality of their patrons, defended their practice on those grounds:

> A ten-cent grind policy in normal times may tend to cheapen the business but ... to take the pictures out of the reach of the people in times of industrial depression and unemployment is economic folly.[31]

The term "grind house" is deployed across the trade press in this early period usually in relation to some quality marking its economic or social aberrance. At a time when first-run box office was between $2 and $2.50, too low an entry cost in the case of "a 10¢ grind house" or "dime grind" was a marker of both the quality of the theater and that of the product shown.[32] A film that "opened and closed in a 10¢ grind house" was a film with no value, and suggested that local patronage was of high enough quality to know better than to see it.[33] Equally, the age of a film could invoke the phrase "Second-run grindhouse" when referring to independent theaters, something that rarely occurs in discussions of second-run houses belonging to integrated chains.[34]

Opening hours also marked lower grind houses as apparently non-normative, so opening too early, too late, or too long indicated patrons untrained in appropriate theatrical scheduling and distracted by 9 a.m. or 10 a.m. opening, or theaters that "grind till 5" or are "grinding till 3" in the morning are notable demarcations of the grind house.[35] Similarly the physical deterioration of the building often prompts use of the term in the event of fire or building collapse.[36]

Finally the double or triple feature that had gained popularity in the 1920s was a key indicator of grind exhibition through the decade, and terms such as "duallers," "double 'grinds,'" or "dual grinders" become synonymous in discussions of grind exhibition[37] but only become noteworthy or dangerous when in the lower rung of theaters. First-run and major chain second-run theaters rarely get described as grind houses, though many clearly operated a grind policy: these are openly referred to as "continuous" or showing a "continuous bill," or "five-" or "six shows a day"; they are described as having bottom and top price (the incremental rises of cost through the day), often only 10 or 15¢ higher than those of the lowest class of cinemas, and may be discussed as screening a particular film "on grind,"[38] yet they do not get tarred with the term "grind house." However this does not indicate that integrated houses were immune from being termed "grinders." Majors such as Lowes' and Publix owned third-run theaters as poor as any indie, and the term "grind house" was applied freely to them.[39] While "grind house" did refer to a mode of exhibition, by the coming of sound the term already had far more to do with differentiating the class of audience (and therefore as Maltby argues, what is shown to them) than the exhibition model being used.

Audience behaviors and non-normative viewing: Class and cultural capitals

As cinemas and studios became economically and socially institutionalized, they became subject to serious backlash and moral outrage. In response, cinema-going became more codified. In the 1910s, theatrical/roadshow exhibition aligned itself with the feature film as middle-class entertainment, and did so in opposition to an imagined working-class audience onto whom any moral opprobrium was deflected. Films consumed inappropriately were claimed to have the seductive powers "of the drug habit, of alcohol, of the Saturnalia and other orgies" and similarly lead to crime, depravity, and disease— such consumption both stemming from and being the cause of mental illness/weakness.[40] Serial products, with their overt advertising tie-ins dominated by the massively popular "Serial Queen" exploitation films featuring New Woman action heroines, were immediately key candidates for such opprobrium and a model for respectable cinema to position itself against.[41] The serial house was then a site of social anxiety, where both on-screen and in the auditorium, crime, delinquency, and deviance could be found and where film content and audience behavior each fed the other:

> The "movie" world, built—not only in the serial but throughout—upon the traditions of the "dime novel." It is crime, violence, blood and thunder, and always obtruding and outstanding is the idea of sex. We shall continue to criticize the business until our pictures shall be an orderly dramatic development of life.[42]

The hypothetical working-class audience in whose minds this "idea of sex" existed were more widely understood as "unbalanced and extremely susceptible mentally" to the dosing effects of cinema, as they were "untrained" in correct cinema-going.[43] That their lives, behavior, and tastes were not "orderly" was evidence of this:

> The "crime serial" is perhaps, the most astounding development in the history of the motion picture. The imagination of men running riot for years in these continued film stories. They are sui generis. Meant for the most ignorant class of the population with the grossest tastes, and it principally flourishes in the picture halls in mill villages and in the thickly settled tenement houses and low foreign speaking neighbourhoods in large cities.[44]

While the content and the form of the serials are criticized here, it is the unsavory audiences they attract that render these films dangerous; the uneducated with their "ignorant" and "gross tastes," the rural and working classes of "mill village" or crowded "tenement," and poor "foreign speaking" immigrants, tapping into media panics around immigration, the unionization of foreign labor, and the use of cinemas as congregation and recruitment centers.[45] Critics constructed what Stamp describes as a "pathology of viewing" by conflating naïve or unsophisticated tastes and behaviors pejoratively to that of impressionable children.[46] The very seriality of chapterplays, or extended periods of viewing through double bills or staying in through continuous performances, apparently *stressed* and *hyperstimulated* the susceptible,[47] dovetailing with arguments that films shown in cheaper cinemas were particularly attractive to, and damaging for, children themselves, regardless of whether children formed the intended or actual audience.[48]

A concern to curb the psychological and physical harms that films may have on children masks a desire to police the behavior of the wider audiences of rural and urban working-class grind houses. The discourse surrounding the serial, its content, cinemas, and grind exhibition are constructed around keeping both audiences and differing film products appropriately segregated. Keeping recent, fashionable, or quality films, and their audiences, in respectable theaters at higher prices was just as important in the rhetoric as ensuring substandard products played only on grind.

By 1919 the preferred audience normativity and the imagined audiences of the working class were codified and stereotyped enough to be satirized. In a *Motion Picture Magazine* article, "At the Movies," the horrors of unruly audiences are lampooned, as the writer describes fleeting glimpses of Serial Queen action sequences caught between the many distractions of mobile grind audience members: latecomers asking what is going on in the film; those who saw the previous screening précis the ending complete with spoilers; one's view being blocked by early leavers getting up, adjusting hats, and putting on coats; people moving past with "sharp knees"; people seating themselves in the dark and sitting on one's hat, or digging their knees into the back of your chair, leaving in the row behind hitting your head, or catching you with their elbow/umbrella/bunches of flowers, all accompanied by the cry of "this is where we came in."[49] These clear delineations of what is not acceptable about grind performance are interspersed (along with hyperbolic exploitation-serial content) with indicators of the audience's class via a lack of cultural capital: the illiterate asking what inter-titles say; the (barely) literate reading them aloud in a variety of inappropriate styles; people reacting loudly to the plot with gasps, cheers, appeals to the screen, or voicing their fears to companions; people eating peanuts and cracking the shells noisily; people smelling of cheap perfume; people dropping food; people with colds and other illnesses; and those who may have come to the cinema for reasons other than watching the film: for shelter, under-supervised children, and courting couples. They denote not only the pitfalls of continuous exhibition but also the class of audience whose lack of cultural capital made this a problem.

Critics aside, the industry itself was happy enough with unruly audience behavior as long as it occurred in the correct place: the independents and former serial houses. The exhibitor-friendly *Motion Picture Herald* was explicit in designating where the voluble serial audience belonged: "a grind house, where people accustomed to shouting and stamping their approval let them selves go."[50] Critics and psychologists shifted their locus from serial house to grind house, adapting their fears of overstimulation to the habit of "staying in" (watching the same program on rotation all day) the supposed strains of volume and repeatedness of exposure on weak and distracted audiences, a pathologized discussion of the social conventions of grind as disease.[51] As Jeff Klenotic and Thomas Doherty have recognized, such behavior was commonplace and catered for in those independent cinemas that formed the lower-half of the grind house circuit and a vast swathe of cinema-going practice.[52]

Double bills were too long, "a strain on the average screen fan,"[53] which, tapping the fear of new media, was "particularly true since the introduction of talking which necessitates closer attention on the part of the audience" (closer presumably than paying attention to both sound and vision in everyday life),[54] while mid-entry moviegoing was "not only a strain on the audiences, but is also uncomplimentary to producers and artists."[55] That "patrons do not desire to be in the theatre on starting times, but seem to come in during the program" was a "defect" that should be "remedied" in order to "develop the correct habit of seeing movies from the start."[56] Not that such concerns were wholly psychological. The Canadian Women's Council "condemned the 'double-feature' as being harmful to the physical being," citing "Extenuated emotional tension and eye strain" as being "definitely harmful to the child." Having medicalized the effects of grind and dualing as physical, both symptoms and causes are explained solely in moral and social terms, just as they had been argued around serials.[57]

Reports on the full midday houses of flourishing grind houses "noted that the audiences were almost entirely men," while a review of *Flash Gordon's Trip to Mars* (1938) defined its venue as "the Rialto theatre, New York, patronized chiefly by men and partial to thrill and unusual films."[58] These homosocial spaces are painted by outsiders as bastions of (prohibitive) male behaviors. In a jokey article on a golf tournament rivalry, *Film Daily* suggests the golfer "that cusses the loudest and longest wins a season pass to any grind house on Forty-second St. That ought to teach him a lesson," lessons presumably that female and respectable middle-class audiences would not wish to learn.[59] Just as Shelley Stamp found female serial patrons subject to a normative prohibition when exceeding the bounds of middle-class exhibition practice, so Tim Snelson finds wartime women castigated for attending Times Square grind houses and fraternizing with male patrons, while implicating the sequential/serial nature of the bill as an attraction.[60] The presence of women, so key to the legitimizing feminized discourse of first-run cinemas, does not raise these theaters' status but marks those patrons as the wrong kind of women: Victory Girls, patriotutes, and children seduced by seriality and corrupted into harlots and delinquents.

Distractions from normative viewing came in several overlapping sources: extratextual interactions from both outside the cinema (the film inappropriately breaking the bounds of the diegetic space—into home life, magazine, radio, or pornographic adaptations, into narrative speculation or imitative play)[61] as well as theatrical distractions from the text (food/games/narrative disjuncture/late night, early morning or Sunday screening), and in the audience's behavioral interactions with the text (vocal interactions in the cinema, and pursuit of narrative/characters/stars outside the cinematic space or lack of attention, disjointed attendance, incomprehension).

Medicalized and psychologized prejudices around serials proved no less contentious when those easily reproduced generic structures and intertextual exploitation angles were incorporated into what became known as "grindhouse" cinema. The psychological claims and discursive structures made around exploitation cycles from juke box jazz to rock 'n' roll delinquents, drag racing and motorcycle gangs, by critics and social commentators through the 1950s and 1960s, are precisely those Eberholtzer was making in the 1920s about similar audiences, but with general issues of seriality succeeding those specifically of the serial.

The economics and language of independence in the studio era

The generic understanding of marginal theaters and producers who serviced marginal audiences was institutionalized in an economic structure, which Douglas Gomery identifies as established by the 1930s, with smaller exhibitors "scrambling" for cheap independent films:

> The Big Five granted their own theatres first-runs and soaked up as much of the box-office grosses as possible, [leaving] independently owned theatres to scramble for the remaining bookings sometimes months or years after a film's premiere.[62]

As sound became an inherent part of that standard model of normative spectatorship, distinctions developed in the 1930s between good and bad sound film consumption. Former grind houses that wired for sound in the initial days of transition were seen as "trading up" to become first-run houses—though there is little suggestion that they abandoned continuous exhibition to achieve this. With the industry's overwhelming drive to promote sound as the premium product, no discussion of "second class" sound exhibition could be tolerated, so grind houses were excused their exhibition strategy with emphasis being placed upon their shedding of other *grind* associations. By dint of the paucity of available sound material, many exhibitors moved from dualing to a single sound feature with sound shorts and perhaps a silent serial. Others retained a silent B-picture, even the most prestigious of which were relegated in this way—in either case those sound features were naturally some of the latest products as there was no back catalogue to exploit. These two factors were enough for these theaters to throw off their grind house stigmas in the trade press, at least in the short term.

Grind theaters that could afford to wire early were already better heeled than those that couldn't, being parts of chains or serving the high turnover downtown communities. Smaller, poorer, rural, and more marginal theaters that were clinging to silent exhibition turned more and more to the still-silent serial producers for new product, in some cases into the early 1930s. Immediately prior to the Wall Street Crash, the poorer serial and grind houses were the last to wire for sound.[63] Following the Crash, serial houses were unable to borrow the wire that was required, and became more and more unviable, allowing them to be bought up by the integrating majors and opened as lower clearance circuit chains on "grindhouse" models.

Many theaters that were still silent opened irregularly, only for easily exploited pictures sold on lurid and sexual themes (often, ostensibly medical exposé documentaries), "operat[ing] as a 15¢ grind house, but open[ing] only occasionally for sensational sex pictures." Such policies indicated a cinema "becom[ing] a grind house. Outside of sex films shown recently the house has nothing."[64] The final silent houses became the cheapest spaces with the most disreputable films, and with a reputation less as entertainment houses than mere shelters for transients and social outcasts.

Independent exhibitors who had managed to wire for sound faced either draconian contracts for poor films with the major distributors or reliance upon the faltering states' rights system, but were saved mid-decade by the National Recovery Administration rulings and the resultant consolidation of Poverty Row production and distribution with the formation of companies such as Herbert Yates' Republic Pictures, Sol Lesser's Principle Distribution Corporation, and later Producers Distribution Corporation (PDC).

While the negative discourse around serial products never disappeared, the grind policy came to define their demonized audience more universally than serials, and the currency of the "serial house" as a site of opposition declined. The new lower rung of independent distribution and exhibition both typified—and *were typified by*—"grind house," associations that mirrored their former "serial house" status, in a way that major chain grind theaters were not, while serials become associated with the daytime screenings of grind houses.

Grind and double-feature presentation could no longer be redeemed by sound, and the earlier biases against grind and the "grind house" returned. Grind theaters quickly reverted to models of dualing pictures as soon as enough product was available to do so, so when "all the near-Loop grind houses have gone double-feature" this typified "grindhouse," and the bulk of popular exhibition by 1931.[65] Simultaneously theaters showing new features inside the clearance system instituted talkie revival nights with reissued sound "classics" as their second features.[66] By the mid-1930s, grind exhibition, often in a shorter program of "A" feature and serial during the day and double feature for evening shows, had become standard practice in most—albeit not in prestige metropolitan—cinemas.

This became ever more necessary during the Depression, when middle-class audiences traded down for their entertainment en-masse. Calls emerged for quality banding in cinemas, with higher-class films for higher-paying audiences, and no access to these films for grind theaters:

> A picture is shown at a first-run theatre for 60¢ ... then it goes to a local downtown theatre (which was a 50¢ house a few months ago) at 15¢, and still a little later to another former first-run house for 10¢. The result is that the 10¢ house is playing capacity, and the general public has gained contempt for the neighborhood theatre that tries to get more than the lowest admission grind house ... competes against the lower admission grind house playing the same pictures, sometimes at even lower matinee admission.[67]

The emergence of the "B" picture following the National Industrial Recovery Act led not to the twin-tier theater system with two separate and distinct sets of products as initially imagined, but rather to a two-tier double-bill system, in which the upper half of the bill would still trickle down from roadshow and large first runs through a zoning and clearance system, while the lower half of the grind bill would rarely show in more expensive theaters. Further, the B-films of the major studios played on continuous "grind" in cinemas that would rarely be decried as "grind houses," while the independent cinemas and poorer chain houses, which relied on the serials, series films, and B-pictures of the Poverty Row and the minor studios were characterized as grinds, even when, in the cases of rural cinemas using these films, they were unlikely to have held more than a couple of screenings a day. The mature cinema hierarchy in a single town is typified by the cinemas of the Baker/Malco theater company, where single-feature non-grind exhibition makes "the Malco stand out, the Strand and Seville follow as double-feature houses, and the Bleich trails the others as the final subsequent run outlet, two features and a serial."[68]

Institutionalizing double features in this way, combined with the sort of clearance zoning that created the grind house "scramble" for films and returns made dualing a matter of distribution than of exhibition. While Gomery describes the little three and Poverty Row independents as "cozying up to the big five to secure bookings" as B-films to the majors' A-s,[69] this meant smaller and indie producers were "left only the rural markets where little money was made," but it is easy to overlook the scale of those markets and audiences, just as it is easy to overlook the scale of grind exhibition. A sample from a census of cinemas in major cities—the heartland of first runs—and smaller cities in the late 1930s gives some idea of where this scramble may occur (see Table 2.1).[70]

These seat figures do not equate directly to patrons, and of course many first-run theaters ran grind programs, while some clearance houses did not. These inconsistencies aside, given the higher number of screenings per day (6–10) compared to first-run style presentation (1–3), and the rapid change of bill (often three times a week) compared to the apparently normative model of the premier houses (each film a week or more), in the subsequent grind house run the volume of films screened

Table 2.1 *Motion Picture Daily* survey of first run and clearance cinemas, seats and their prices, by city, 1939

City	No. of cinemas	No. of cinema seats	Entry price
Chicago	10 first runs*	20,500 seats	25¢–75¢
	304 clearance houses	298,336 seats	10¢–55¢
Philadelphia	10 first runs*	17,160 seats	25¢–75¢
	198 clearance houses	195,503 seats	10¢–40¢
Los Angeles	10 first runs*	26,380 seats	30¢–65¢
	171 clearance houses	135,161 seats	10¢–40¢
Detroit	5 first runs*	15,000 seats†	20¢–65¢
	132 clearance houses	132,000 seats†	10¢–35¢
Cleveland	6 first runs*	15,300 seats†	30¢–50¢
	98 clearance houses	100,000 seats†	10¢–30¢

*First run single program and "quality" grind exhibitors.
† Extrapolated from average theater capacity.

and opportunity for attendance was immense. Across the survey extracted from here, major cites had around ten times the number of second-run grind seats, showing at least twice the number of screenings compared to first-run seats. Similarly lower seat prices are artificially lower in the upper category of theater by the presence of respectable first-run grinds. Gomery's integrated first runs are clearly making easier money, at higher ticket prices with lower overheads (as a cost-profit ratio, rather than per-theater). Outside the cities where the big first runs were located, Gomery is again right; independent cinemas, showing Poverty Row product, on grind timetables were even more prevalent. However, illustrated in this sample are the vast audience (or at least the seats for them) and their small but cumulative revenues in clearance grind houses, screening re-runs and films of marginal producers. "When business in point of admissions is checked with theatres charging legitimate house prices it will be found the grind policy 'pop' houses are far ahead."[71] These narrower profits kept a swathe of cinemas open and people employed, and provided the experience of cinema to what is likely to have been at least 90 percent of the cinema-going public, maintaining the structure and habit of exhibition needed for the larger, occasional breakout successes that Gomery locates as the powerhouses of Hollywood profits.

The late-night screenings of grind houses, which become a staple of later "grindhouse" mythology and their association with transients, sleepers, and sexual pick-ups,[72] are also neither economically irrelevant nor restricted to lower houses. When toward the end of World War II a national midnight curfew was placed upon theaters (effectively meaning 1 p.m.) it was estimated that 10 percent of theater revenues were lost rising to 20 percent on Saturdays.[73] However, this was not restricted to poorer theaters, with first-run cinemas estimating that their single cancelled late performance lost the venues 15 percent.[74] Just as legitimate cinemas used after-midnight screenings, the curfew highlighted the range of late-night performance strategies in the eighty-three affected grind houses operated by eleven different indies in New York and New Jersey: fifty had screenings that began after midnight, typically running till 2 a.m. weekdays and 5 a.m. weekends, the others having performances that overran curfew by up to an hour.[75] Curtailing these various strategies lost grind theaters between $50 and $750 a night.

Again the discourse surrounding after midnight opening had far more to do with the motivations and classes of the different audiences. Exhibitors seeking to exploit this profitable market niche are only made visible and criticized for doing so to lower-paying patrons within the imagined grind house. Infractions of decorum police grind exhibition and remain comically noteworthy, so late-night audiences are inappropriate when "Saturday midnight shows get play from recuping [sic] benders and folks who remove new shoes to ease pained puppies," and variations of undressing and imbibing typify the distractions.[76]

The grind theaters, then, constituted the bulk of exhibition, and in the lower clearance houses exhibited at a fraction of the first-run or roadshow price. While their profit margins were far slimmer, their audiences—across these lower exhibition sectors—were far larger, with the size of the audience growing in inverse proportion to its ticket price.

Conclusion: The long grind

The grind house and its products have been sidelined in the cultural and economic history of cinema as Gomery states:

> Films by marginal, small producers consisted almost entirely of low-budget features, cheap westerns and serials. Such low cost fare played rarely in the first-run houses of the Big Five [whose] features helped generate 90 per cent of the box office revenues, while marginal producers had to scramble for the rest.[77]

But while that handful of pictures showing to a relatively small but lucrative audience may have been the Holy Grail chased by most producers, first-run exhibition was not the common experience of the majority of cinemagoers throughout the studio period. The cultural experience of cinema-going for the bulk of the audience took part within the "scramble" Gomery describes: watching marginal films in marginal cinemas (serials, series, and "grindhouse" products in serial and grind houses). It is here, possibly, that the bulk of the cultural influence of cinema was felt. More certainly it is where the influence of the audience was felt most keenly upon cinema products, and where the cultural value of cinema was most keenly and divisively debated.

Far from being a minority screening practice, grind—that is, continuous—exhibition strategies have been commonplace from the inception of cinema. While the rise of longer feature films, and the move to purpose-built exhibition spaces in the transformative era of the mid-1910s also saw the rise of proscribed ideas of preferred screening and viewing practices based on middle-class theatrical models, if these exhibition and audience behaviors were ever typical, certainly within a few years grind was again the most common exhibition mode.

While the industry promoted and reinforced a series of social distinctions that marked grind and grind houses as aberrant, it did so to protect the economic interests of the more profitable and respectable cinemas and the reputation of the industry itself. In marking initially the "serial" and later "grind" as the diametric opposite of deluxe, roadshow, or first-run cinema, industry discourse and cultural commentators obscured the bulk of middle-tier grind practice and insinuated it into the poorest (technically and economically) exhibition practices. The imagined audience and location of grind was used to mask the prevalence and profitability of mass audiences and lowbrow taste. These cinemas and practices were homogenized by the typifying of their audiences' class through degenerate or culturally incompetent behavior. As such the norm was portrayed as abnormal and undesirable, in order to secure the exclusivity of a lucrative cinema-going elite.

In seeking to segregate their audiences economically in this way, to guarantee the best returns, the industry scapegoated audiences and cinemas already made pariahs in anti-cinema witch-hunts. This insulated the industry's preferred forms from such criticism, but also laid grind houses open to moral outrage previously aimed at serials. The transfer of these medicalized moral and psychological concerns to continuous performance and double bills was as tenuous and flimsy as the original charge against serial exhibition, but in consistently insinuating that the mythically debauched "grind house" and its grind, dual, and round-the-clock screenings were marginal practices, the industry deflected criticism that it encouraged delinquent or harmful processes, and masked the institutional facilitation and utilization of them. Beyond the financial concerns of the trade press in reinforcing the stereotypes, the wider media concern with grind houses was hereafter primarily moral rather than economic.

The defining features of "grindhouse" exhibition strategies from the 1920s to the 1940s (double features, serials, continuous entry, stepped admission prices, reruns, midnight screenings), all of which are used as denigrating frames for poorer and independent cinemas, and are cited as economically or popularly dubious, prove commonplace across all cinemas, including in some cases first-run theaters. Midnight screenings and all-night performances, often offered as evidence of an uneconomic practice continued for immoral rather than cinematic purposes, prove to be significantly profitable to grind houses (where audiences may or may not be chastely watching the screen), and also to first-run cinemas (whose audiences at one or two o'clock are presumably ethically spotless). The poorest of cinemas, however, the rural theaters, rarely served populations large enough to warrant grind performance, and where successive houses were cleared to segregate audiences along gender, race, age, and class lines, despite the *grind* appellation of these cinemas and audiences.

The apparent rise of "grindhouse" in the 1950s is well understood as the failure of more respectable cinemas and the deserting of middle-class audiences for other suburban entertainments. Conversely the "grindhouse" "boom" of this period, and the critical concern around it, is no boom at all, merely business as usual for a raft of workhorse cinemas. Similarly the concerns around the rise of double bills in the depression of the 1930s, and of serials in the depression of 1922, illustrate this same reliable audience, going about their cinema-going business at times when first-run cinemas struggle. As an exhibition practice, continuous grind is perhaps the longest standing and most widespread model of programming throughout cinema history. Overshadowed by more socially prestigious and financially lucrative models, it remained the norm, during periods where smaller, higher paying, middle-class audiences generated larger receipts.

While the grind houses were key to the survival of the serial through the 1920s to the1950s, serials were only a small feature of grind house exhibition. Sharing the disreputability of grind house models, and similarly marginalized, serials remained lucrative and widespread as long as those independent, rural, neighborhood, and grind house cinemas that supported them remained operational. As the grind model, being the dominant exhibition form, absorbed the serial, double features, and twenty-four-hour opening, all features that the industry found financially unsettling, and critics found culturally distasteful, the common troubling tropes around these exhibition choices and their audiences, became the key discursive elements that relationally framed grind houses, and the emergent generic conception of their products.

It is easy to see Gomery's "scramble" in both independent production and exhibition as an irrelevant surface froth on top of the industry as a whole, a semi-parasitic entity feeding on the leftovers of the real players in Hollywood, and creatively at least there is probably some validity to this view. But when thinking, as Gomery is, of the economics of Hollywood, a far more apposite analogy for the marginal cinemas and audiences over whom the small producers are scrambling is as the bedrock of the Hollywood industry, a sedimentary bedrock made of tiny creatures but vast in number; and in their ubiquity comes reliability, underpinning Hollywood, giving it a foundation, not making its great profits, but paying its bills.

Notes

1. "Observations," *Better Theatres* (July 1, 1933), 7 (supplement to *Motion Picture Herald*—précis of article by Leslie C. Kinley in *Better Theatres* June 3, 1933).
2. David Church, *Grindhouse Nostalgia: Memory, Home Video and Exploitation Film Fandom* (Edinburgh: Edinburgh University Press, 2015) 3, 13, 8, 4 (emphasis in original).
3. David Church, "From Exhibition to Genre: The Case of Grind-house Films," *Cinema Journal* 50:4 (2011): 2–4. Also, Church, *Grindhouse Nostalgia*, 77–78.
4. Richard Maltby, "Sticks, Hicks and Flaps: Classical Hollywood's Generic Conception of Its Audiences," in *Identifying Hollywood's Audiences: Cultural Identity and the Movies*, eds Melvyn Stokes and Richard Maltby (London: BFI, 1999), 23–25.
5. Shelley Stamp, *Movie-Struck Girls: Women and Motion Picture Culture after the Nickelodeon* (Princeton, NJ: Princeton University Press, 2000), 102–103.
6. In those specialist theaters that never adopted feature-length film—most significantly, newsreel theaters—grind programs of news, cartoons, serials, and factual shorts were always the accepted norm.
7. Church, *Grindhouse Nostalgia*, 87.
8. Rick Altman, *Film/Genre* (London: BFI, 1999), 91, acknowledged in Church, above.
9. See, e.g., social and textual histories of Sam Katzmann's evolution from exploitation serials to feature production in Thomas Doherty, *Teenagers and Teenpics: The Juvenilization of American Movies in the 1950s* (Philadelphia: Temple University Press, 2002) and Wheeler Winston-Dixon, *Lost in the Fifties: Recovering Phantom Hollywood* (Carbondale: Southern Illinois University Press, 2005), or the fertile interplay between the serial factories of Republic and Columbia and the ubiquitous B and series Westerns in Peter Stanfield's *Hollywood, Westerns and the 1930s: The Lost Trail* (Exeter: University of Exeter Press, 2001) and *Horse Opera: The Strange History of the 1930s Singing Cowboy* (Urbana: University of Illinois Press, 2002).
10. "Sheffield Our Great Grindhouse," *Mechanics Magazine* 14:369 (September 4, 1830), 169.
11. See *OED* "Mill" n. III 8b (*Pacific Monthly* 1911).
12. The notion of an extended day's work as a *grind* exists in any profession but particularly where extended hours are less usual. As such, it exists in theater but not in the specific sense of rolling performance where it only gets applied to theatrical or musical employment after its commonplace usage in cinema (though is often applied to retrospective practices when "three-a-day" or "five-a-day" theaters were typical terms).
13. "Screen Gossip," *Pictureplay* 7:6 (February, 1918), 296, see also *Pictureplay* 6.5 (August, 1917), 263.
14. "Reel Tales about Reel Folk—Diamond in the Sky," *Reel Life* (June 12, 1915), 18.

15. Shirley Vance Martin, "The 'Still' Camera Man," *Photo-Era: The American Journal of Photography* 52.24 (February 1924), 80–85.
16. See adverts for fairground pitches 1900–1910, e.g. "Last Call Great Lake County Fair," *Billboard* 30 July (1910).
17. Braun, "The Problems of the Operating Room," *Motography* (March 1912), 127.
18. See the humorous story about a hypnotized operator in *Moving Picture News* 4.1 (January 7, 1911), 13; or the grind house that grinds up film in, John M. Joy, "Film Mutilation," *Transactions of the Society of Motion Picture Engineers* 26 (November, 1926), 19.
19. Anon. "W. H. Bell Back from Australia," *Moving Picture World* (June 28, 1913), 1344.
20. Schader, "Coast Film Notes," *Variety* (January 28, 1921), 44.
21. Anon. "LA Operators Raised; Big Strike Is Averted," *Variety* (January 21, 1921), 47.
22. *Revenue Revision, 1924 Hearings before the Committee on ways and Means* (House of Representatives, US Government Printing office, 1924), 44–45.
23. Samuel Grafton, "And Now the Yearning Celluloid," *Vanity Fair* 33.3 (November 1929), 124. This article introduces the new concept of "art cinema" and uses the familiar "grind house" as a reference point, a comparison that has resonances in modern scholarship, e.g. Mark Betz, "Art, Exploitation, Underground," in *Defining Cult Movies: The Cultural Politics of Oppositional Taste*, eds Mark Jancovich, Antonio Lázaro Reboll, Julian Stringer, and Andy Willis (Manchester: Manchester University Press, 2003), 202–222; and John Cline and Robert G. Weiner, eds *From the Grindhouse to the Arthouse: Highbrow and Lowbrow Transgression in Cinema's First Century* (Lanham, MD: Scarecrow Press, 2010).
24. Maltby, "Sticks, Hicks and Flaps," 25.
25. "Aronson Looks Forward to 1924," *Exhibitors Herald* (January 19, 1924), 34.
26. "Praises Small Town Houses," *Film Daily* (September 12, 1922), 2.
27. "Turner-Dahnken Deal Makes Lessers Strong," *Variety* (February 1, 1923), 46.
28. Mort Blumenstock, "Playing the Favorites," *Exhibitors Herald* (November 29, 1924), 63.
29. "Akron, O., July 13.—The Miles-Royal," *Motion Picture Daily* (July 14, 1934), 4; "L.A.'s Hippodrome Folds after 25 Years," *Variety* (June 14, 1939), 47.
30. "Dime Grinds Ruining Minn's Loop Houses," *Variety* (May 31, 1932), 29.
31. "Allied Defend Ten-Cent Shows," *Motion Picture Herald* (August 22, 1931), 16.
32. "$2 Pictures on B'way Slipping Into Discard; Grind Policy at Popular Prices Seen Prevailing," *Motion Picture News* (December 14, 1929), 21.
33. "'Topsy's' 10¢ Limit," *Variety* (June 27, 1928), 8.
34. "Open Second-Run Grind House," *Motion Picture Herald* (June 16, 1934), 94.
35. "Orpheum Grinds 'Till 5 A.M," *Variety* (January 9, 1929), 8; "Three B'dway Deluxers in late Grinds," *Variety* (May 15, 1935), 2.
36. "Bldg. O.O. after Mishap," (Collapse) *Variety*, Tuesday (June 7, 1932), 27; Les Rees, "Times Square Chatter" (Fire), *Variety* (April 11, 1933), 53.
37. "Zis Boom bah," *Showman's Trade Review* (November 17, 1941), 31; "Pioneers of the West," *Variety* (January 29, 1930), 62; "Lone Horseman," *Variety* (February 26, 1930), 39; "30 Chicago Houses Show Triple Bills," *Motion Picture Daily* (April 4, 1940), 1.
38. "Three B'dway Deluxers in Late Grinds," 2; "Denver, Isis–15-cent Fox House," *Motion Picture Herald* (December 24, 1932), 57.
39. "Film Leads Broadway: All Houses Open," *Motion Picture Daily* (October 21, 1939), 1, 12.

40. Georgre Humphry, "Do the Movies Help or Harm Us," *Colliers* (May 1924), 5.
41. On the global rise of the Serial Queen genre, see Marina Dahlquist, *Exporting Perilous Pauline: Pearl White and the Serial Film Craze* (Urbana: University of Illinois Press, 2013); for information about campaigns against exploitation serials and advertising, see Ben Singer, *Melodrama and Modernity: Early Sensational Cinema and Its Contexts* (New York: Columbia University Press, 2011) and Stamp, *Movie Struck Girls*.
42. Ellis P. Oberholtzer, *The Morals of the Movies* (Philadelphia: Penn Publishing, 1922), 56–57.
43. Hazzard, "The White Slave Films: A Review," *Outlook* 106 (1914): 347–350; Stamp, *Movie Struck Girls*, 96.
44. Oberholtzer, *The Morals of the Movies*, 55.
45. See Raphael Vela, *With the Parents' Consent: Film Serials, Consumerism and the Creation of the Youth Audience*, PhD thesis (University of Wisconsin-Madison, 2000); and Richard Abel, *The Red Rooster Scare: Making American Cinema* (Berkley: University California Press, 1999).
46. For the pathologizing campaigns in silent serial exhibition see Singer, *Melodrama and Modernity*, and Stamp, *Movie Struck Girls*; for the sound period, see Phyll Smith "'Poisoning Their Daydreams': American Serial Cinema, Moral Panic and the British Children's Cinema Movement," *Iwu: Literatur in Wissenschaft und Unterricht* XLVII:1/2 (2014): 39–54.
47. See also Church, "From Exhibition to Genre," 12.
48. So prevalent is this discourse that it remains stubbornly ingrained in academic film history, with scholars claiming that serials and series films were "a cartoonish children's genre" (Ben Singer, "Serials," in *Oxford History of World Cinema*, ed. Geoffrey Nowell-Smith (Oxford: Oxford University Press, 1996), 110); or "clearly intended for children" (Richard Koszarski, *An Evening's Entertainment: The Age of the Silent Feature Picture, 1915–1928* (Berkeley: University of California Press, 1990)), 183). However, such claims around audience composition for these films, and so for grind houses, through the 1930s and 1940s are robustly challenged at length in more recent work. See, e.g., Guy Barefoot, "Who Watched that Masked Man? Hollywood's Serial Audiences in the 1930s," *Historical Journal of Film, Radio and Television* 31:2 (2011), 167–190; and in Stanfield, *Horse Opera*.
49. Charlotte Mish, "At the Movies," *Motion Picture Magazine* (February 1919), 6.
50. Weaver, "The Gallant Defender," *Motion Picture Herald* (September 26, 1936), 42.
51. Ibid.
52. Jeff Klenotic, "'Four Hours of Hootin' and Hollerin': Moviegoing and Everyday Life Outside the Movie Palace," in *Going to the Movies: Hollywood and the Social Experience of Cinema*, eds Richard Maltby, Melvyn Stokes, and Robert Allen (Exeter: University of Exeter Press, 2007), 130–154; also Thomas Doherty "This Is Where We Came In: The Audible Screen and the Voluble Audience of Early Sound Cinema," in *American Movie Audiences: From the Turn of the Century to the Early Sound Era*, eds Melvyn Stokes and Richard Maltby (London: BFI, 1999), 143–163.
53. "Larry Kent Says Double Bills Prevent Relaxation," *Variety* (November 10, 1930), 1.
54. "Double Feature Bills a Strain on Audiences," *Film Daily* (November 10, 1930), 2.
55. "The End Was Not Yet," *Motion Picture Herald* (January 23, 1932), 26.

56. Don Bloxham, "Seeing Films from Start Important," *Motion Picture Herald* (August 25, 1934), 57; see also, "The End Was Not Yet," 26; and "That Continuous Programming," *Motion Picture Herald* (May 19, 1934), 25.
57. H. E. Hastings, "Better Pictures for the Child," *Cinema Progress* 2.2 (June 1937), 11; see also Hastings "'Better Films for Children' Canadian Cry," *Cinema Progress: The Film and Life* 2.4 (October 1937), 22.
58. "$2 Pictures on B'way Slipping into Discard; Grind Policy at Popular Prices Seen Prevailing," 21; "Flash Gordon's Trip to Mars," *Motion Picture Herald* (May 4, 1940), 5.
59. "Get Set for the Dual of the Duffers at Rye, N.Y.," *Film Daily* (June 6, 1939), 6.
60. Stamp *Movie Struck Girls*; Tim Snelson, *Phantom Ladies: Hollywood horror and the home front* (New Brunswick, NJ: Rutgers University Press, 2015).
61. For domestic and magazine intertexts, see: Stamp *Movie Mad Girls* and Singer *Melodrama and Modernity*; radio: Frank Krutnik "'Be Moviedom's Guest in Your Own Easy-Chair': Hollywood Radio and Movie Adaptation," *Historical Journal of Film, Radio and Television* 33.1; pornography: Phillip Smith and Ellen Wright, "A Glimpse behind the Screen: Tijuana Bibles and the Pornographic Reimagining of Hollywood," in *Tabu~Trend~Transgresja tom 2 Skandal w Tekstach Kultury*, ed. Marian Ursel (Uniwersytet Wrocławski Academia Medyczna im. Piastów Śląskich/Wydawnictwa DiG.; Wroclaw, Poland: 2013); speculation and play: Scott Higgins, *Matinee Melodrama: Play and the Art of Formula in the Sound Serial* (New Brunswick: Rutgers University Press, 2015). Vela, *With the Parents' Consent: Film Serials, Consumerism and the Creation of the Youth Audience*.
62. Douglas Gomery, "The Economics of the Horror Film," in *Horror Films: Current Research in Audience Preferences and Reactions*, eds James B. Weaver and Ron Tamborini (New York: Routledge, 1996), 51. For the key differences in major and minor studios' approach to B film distribution between first-run and lower grind theaters, see Mark Jancovich, "'Hot Profits Out of Cold Shivers!' Horror, the First-Run Market, and the Hollywood Studios, 1938–42," in *Merchants of Menace: The Business of Horror Cinema*, ed. Richard Nowell (London: Bloomsbury Academic, 2014).
63. See, e.g., Harold Cohen, "Pittsburgh," *Variety* (July 10, 1929), 53.
64. "Another F. & R. House Closes in Minneapolis," *Variety* (May 30, 1928), 22; "Milwaukee: The Garrick; Dark Most of the Time," *Variety* (January 29, 1930), 93. See also "Sexer Films," *Variety* (January 28, 1930); "Sex Film Docs Panning," *Variety* (June 27, 1928), 48.
65. "Circuits Extend Double Features," *Motion Picture Herald* (May 9, 1931), 20.
66. "Revival Nights!" *Managers' Round Table Club* (*MPH* supplement) (April 25, 1931), 89.
67. Ike Geller, "Hopes Lichtman Idea Will Succeed," *Motion Picture Herald* (June 4, 1932), 52; see also "What Is Happening to Downtown Theatres," *Hollywood Reporter* (March 3, 1931), 1–2; "Depresh Public Waits Until Price Is Right; 10¢ Houses' Competish Socking First Runs, Chains Complain," *Variety* (July 5, 1932).
68. "Owensboro, Ky., Puts Stress on Newspaper Ads," *Motion Picture Herald* (February 28, 1948), 46.
69. Gomery, "The Economics of the Horror Film," 51.
70. All data here are drawn from a single survey of giveaways and gambling games in cinemas published in *Motion Picture Daily* across January and February 1939.
71. "$2 Pictures on B'way Slipping into Discard; Grind Policy at Popular Prices Seen Prevailing," 21.

72. See Bill Landis and Michelle Clifford, *Sleazoid Express: A Mind-Twisting Tour through the Grindhouse Cinema of Times Square* (New York: Fireside, 2002). See also Glenn Ward's contribution to the present volume.
73. "Curfew Cuts 10–15% from Grosses at N.Y. Theatres," *Motion Picture Daily* (March 6, 1945), 10.
74. "Late Showings Return as Midnight Curfew Ends," *Motion Picture Daily* (May 10, 1945), 10.
75. "Theatres Quick to Comply in Curfew, Revenue Loss Indicated as Duals Are Hit," *Motion Picture Daily* (February 21, 1945), 19.
76. Joe Kolling, "Times Square Chatter: Cincinnati," *Variety* (March 25, 1931), 52.
77. Douglas Gomery, *The Hollywood Studio System* (London: BFI/MacMillan, 1986), 9.

# 3

Temporary Fleapits and Scabs' Alley: The Theatrical Dissemination of Italian Cannibal Films in Melbourne, Australia

Dean Brandum

Between 1974 and 1981 a cycle of nine exploitation features, in which western protagonists encounter indigenous cannibalistic tribes in the rain forests of Asia and South America, were produced by Italian film companies. Such "cannibal films," which include, most famously, a number of films directed by Umberto Lenzi such as *Man from Deep River* (1972), *Cannibal Ferox* (1981), and *Eaten Alive* (1980), and a number directed by Ruggero Deodato such as *Last Cannibal World* (1977) and *Cannibal Holocaust* (1980), have attained critical notoriety for their crude and often racist representations of indigenous tribes as exotic, barbaric, and uncivilized. Today, over three decades since the last of the cycle was released, this horror subgenre has acquired a cachet in horror and cult film fan communities, due to the nostalgia triggered by their associations with what is often loosely referred to as "grindhouse" cinema.

As industry parlance "grindhouse" referred to the exhibition practice of screening low-budget genre films as double or triple features at a low ticket price. Generally the theaters engaged in this practice were located in urban areas and the venues often in disrepair and poorly maintained. As described in 1947, they were "cheap theaters in the downtown areas of large cities featuring horror pictures and sex thrillers for transients."[1] It was New York City's 42nd Street and its surrounds (often referred to as "the Deuce") that became synonymous with America's grindhouse precinct (a search of the *New York Times*' online archives finds mentions of "grind house" venues in the area as early as 1937). However, more than just a form of exhibition practice, "grindhouse" has become equated with a particular form of consumption experience.

It was in the New York grind houses that many of the Italian cannibal features received their first American screenings. Bill Landis and Michelle Clifford have situated the Italian cannibal features as belonging to a particular theater, The Liberty on 42nd Street:

> The Liberty specialized in intensely erotic and violent movies from across Europe, which lent it a distinct status on the Deuce. The content of these films was so graphic that they often wouldn't be distributed to theaters in the rest of New York City, effectively making the Liberty their exclusive showcase.[2]

Landis (and later, Clifford) produced *Sleazoid Express*, a self-published zine (that evolved into a book) that acted as a journal of record for New York's grindhouse circuit during its most recognized period of 1964 through the 1980s (when the zine was first published). Landis worked as a projectionist in a number of grind house venues, and both the zines and the book are filled with reminiscences of the films screened, the grind house theaters, and the personalities who frequented the area. Never a homogeneous chain of venues, each grind house theater was a unique entity, distinct in product, décor, staff, hygiene, and patronage. Clearly a labor of love for the writers, *Sleazoid Express* allowed readers encumbered by age or distance a vicarious taste of the grindhouse experience. In 2015, a quarter of a century after the last of the genuine grind houses closed, David Church has investigated the nostalgic desire for the period that has only increased with the greater accessibility of the once-obscure films to screen in these theaters. For many fans available releases of these titles exist not only as texts but as cultural artifacts that "[spur] longing for a sense of subcultural community that *perhaps never truly existed* but which persists as an object of nostalgia in itself."[3]

For American fans of such films the term "grindhouse" appropriately reflects the exhibition model through which the Italian cannibal films were disseminated into the United States. However, "grindhouse" is a term specific to that country and any acceptance of its usage on an international basis negates the other distribution trajectories that these and other exploitation films experienced as they were released across the world. The problematic context is intensified when "grindhouse" is applied to non-American products, such as Italian exploitation films, in that it decides that it is the American theatrical experience that determines the paradigm of context through which these films are remembered, recognized, and discussed. Indeed—and to illustrate this point—the US home media distributor Grindhouse Releasing—which specializes in repackaging foreign exploitation films for the US home media market—very recently reissued "deluxe" and "definitive" editions of both *Cannibal Ferox* and *Cannibal Holocaust* on region-free Blu-ray to much fanfare.[4]

Exhibiting exploitation in Melbourne

This chapter explores the distribution and exhibition strategies of the Italian cannibal cycle in the city of Melbourne, Australia. Other than *Cannibal Holocaust* (which was banned by the censor) all of the Italian cannibal films received Australian releases, and apart from the first film in the cycle—*Man from Deep River*—each was cut by the censor in order to receive the strongest censorship classification of an R-rating. As an English-speaking market and one that was dominated by Hollywood studio product, it would seem that the natural course of exhibition evolution would allow for a grind house model to exist in the Australian screen-space.

However, "grind houses" did not *per se* exist in Australia and nor was the term common usage within the industry. Among the reasons for the lack of these styles of distribution outlets were the strong government-imposed censorship restrictions in place until 1971 that either banned or heavily cut many exploitation titles. Even after these restrictions were loosened, what was deemed permissible in Australia still fell short of that allowed on an American screen. Additionally, most exploitation products still came to Australian screens via the distribution channels of major companies. With a small population (in 1980 Australia had a population of 14 million) and limited screening space (829 screens at 713 theatrical points that year[5]), it left many independent distributors forced to deal with majors to ensure their films' exposure. The 1970s–1980s was also a period of major flux in the exhibition industry in which the traditional space of the city picture palace transitioned to that of the multiplex, with numerous "pop-up" style venues cashing in on the exhibition void for more adult fare. Exhibition outlets in Melbourne, for instance, ranged from reputable picture palaces owned by major chains to less salubrious, independent, shop front, and basement theaters. The major chains "retained high standards while the rest of the operators, the independents, offered anything to very high quality to quite awful. The latter became known as 'fleapits.'"[6] And, whereas the American grind house was, strictly speaking, a sub/urban phenomenon, the city center of Melbourne was not the main space of consumption for the cannibal cycle. Rather, it was the suburbs in which these films thrived through the popularity of drive-in theaters: exhibition points that, by the late 1970s, had tailored their programming with a preference for exploitation features.

For the purpose of context it is necessary to discuss the history of exploitation exhibition in Melbourne's central business district (CBD), beginning in the 1930s, when two "fleapit" theaters began a policy of genre double features.[7] These were the Greater Union (GU) chain's Liberty that operated until 1951, when it was gutted by fire and the Hoyts company's Lyceum that continued a successful double-feature policy until 1963. GU also had a smaller theater—the Grosvenor—that spent its final years screening weekly genre changeovers, before closing in 1968.

The popularity of television dented the profitability of major chains operating venues specializing in double features of B-films. It also caused the five "hour-show" theatrettes (all with seating capacities below 250), which had operated on a diet of newsreels supplemented with cartoons and shorts, to move to a feature film policy in the 1960s. These theaters focused on screening independently distributed features, often from Europe and mostly of a salacious nature. At the time Australia's censorship laws were so restrictive that all nudity was forbidden, while violence, drug taking, and homosexuality were among the content that was heavily edited for local consumption.[8]

In 1971 the censorship laws were loosened to reflect changing moral standards including a ratings system that would classify films based on their audience suitability. The most restrictive was the R-classification that allowed viewing only to those over the age of eighteen. Twelve months after its introduction, nine of the twenty-six screens in the city were exhibiting R-certified engagements.[9] While four of these screens were former newsreel theatrettes, the others were popular screens catering to a mainstream audience. By late in the decade a number of converted shop fronts and basements also took to sex films and in 1979 there were as many as eleven dedicated soft-core sex theaters operating in the CBD.

These venues were close approximations of American grind house theaters. However, for all their similarities—continuously running double or triple features, shop front and basement locations, lurid front-of-house advertising—there was a notable difference: these Melbourne theaters (with rare exceptions) screened *only* sex films. Other genres that are nowadays typically associated with grindhouse, including horror, action, blaxploitation, martial arts and European westerns, were screened elsewhere in the CBD, and although some city theaters would devote months to consecutive screenings of exploitation, no theater would maintain an ongoing policy of American-style grindhouse programming. There is no clear reason for why no theater would attempt to differentiate its business in a busy market by appealing to the genre audience, as several theatres (the Liberty, Lyceum, and Grosvenor) had found a comfortable niche exhibiting genre double features in the pre R-classification period. However, a study of the theater listings of the 1970s and 1980s shows that exploitation films received numerous bookings in Melbourne's twenty-two suburban drive-in theaters.

The drive-ins (of which Village controlled twelve, Hoyts nine, and the small Dendy group one) operated in a manner similar to that of the chain-run suburban theaters (the numbers of which had been decimated since the arrival of television in 1956) by serving as the second-run suburban distribution point for films that had ceased their city engagement. However drive-ins also offered an alternative experience to that of the suburban theater in that they were more inclined to program exploitation material as support to mainstream releases and to also screen exploitation films as first-run releases either simultaneously with the city or (quite regularly by the late 1970s) as exclusive first-run releases, bypassing the city completely. The drive-in also offered something the city theaters could not: all night marathons of up to five films (almost always of the exploitation variety) that were programmed for weekends or the nights before public holidays. It should be noted that sex films were also regular staples on the suburban drive-in screens, often existing alongside horror features in double feature and marathon pairings. While "grindhouse" may have retained a place in the American vernacular, the term "scab's alley" referred to those drive-ins that had parkland alongside where a car could park with a view of the screen and radio reception (for the screen audio) without paying an admission fee (often due to the passengers being below the age restriction of the R-rated entertainment). Although few drive-ins exist today, the term remains in use.

For the release of Italian cannibal films in Melbourne, the drive-in theaters of the suburbs played a crucial role. As Melburnian Michael Helms, editor of the seminal exploitation culture magazine *Fatal Visions*, explains:

> There was no single distributor behind the release of Italian horror films. The only way you could keep informed was by diligently poring over daily newspapers that were then filled with giant display ads for the best, sleaziest and wildest horror films. Drive-in audiences were borne out of our love for car culture and appreciation for these films was always demonstrated by the car horn.[10]

Due to the exhibition practices of the times, most films were required to be provided with an exclusive first-run booking at a city theater before being unleashed in the suburbs. In terms of a cultural hierarchy within the CBD's theaters, the sex theaters occupied the lowest rungs. Commonly referred to as "porno" (or, more diplomatically, as "adult") theaters, their fare was rarely reviewed by the press and their advertising kept distinct from that of the major chains. As there were no true art house venues in the city center, the top position within the hierarchy was taken by the four sleek multiplex venues that screened the most viable mainstream product. Holding the middle ground were the aging, once-popular, large capacity venues that had lost their audiences and broad-appeal films to the multiplexes. It was this stratum of venue that became the initial exhibition point for most Italian cannibal films in Melbourne.

In 1974, when the first of the Italian cannibal features was released in Melbourne, the CBD of the city housed thirty-two screens in twenty-five theaters. Nineteen of these venues were controlled by three major exhibition chains—Greater Union, Village, and Hoyts—with the smaller Dendy group also operating two single screens. The carefully established terms of film-to-theater relations were discarded with the introduction of the R-certificate. The abundance of films now available for exhibition and their immediate popularity with audiences resulted in theatrical chains toying with their venues' long-established natural order. Theaters that were once the domain of prestige productions were now screening Scandinavian sex comedies or violent martial arts spectacles. The hierarchical boundaries of high and low art were, for some years, blurred, and other than the quality of the seating, décor, and service, there was little to distinguish between certain established mainstream theaters and the once lowly regarded venues that had dwelt on titillation as their mainstay. The experience of the cannibal cycle of films in Melbourne illustrates this period of flux.

Independent distributors and major exhibitors

Eric Dare, the son of one of Australia's radio technology pioneers,[11] moved into film distribution in the 1960s and, with his sister Patricia, formed the company House of Dare. The films Dare imported into Australia were often provocative and infiltrated both the high and low culture, from the art house favorite *The Pawnbroker* (Sidney Lumet, 1965) to the feminist biker-revenge flick *Bury Me an Angel* (Barbara Peeters, 1972). Dare faced controversy when he gained the rights to a number of Andy Warhol productions; that *Heat* (Paul Morrissey, 1972) made it past the censors unscathed (after having been cut for its British release) surprised many,[12] but the permissive decision was a reflection of the audience's embracing of the new R-certificate classification.

In 1973 Dare had managed to get the first entry in the cannibal cycle; Lenzi's *Man from Deep River* passed uncut by the censors, classified "R." Telling of a wildlife photographer captured and then sexually humiliated by an indigenous tribe in the jungle near the Thailand-Burma border, the film features many of what would become familiar tropes within the genre, including ritualistic torture, animal cruelty, female nudity, and, naturally, cannibalism. It opened in Melbourne on March 8, 1974, at GU's Forum Theatre, which, having been established in 1963, had enjoyed long runs of popular fare supplied by major companies such as Universal and Columbia until the late 1960s, when, following the opening of a rival theater, engagements became shorter and less prestigious. *Man from Deep River* was one of several exploitation films to screen at the venue in 1974.

According to the print advertising (see Figure 3.1), one is called upon to witness the film's exotic and peculiar events as if they were documentary evidence of rarely filmed cultural practices within a genuine ethnographic presentation: "It goes beyond the primitive. Beyond the savage. Beyond the grotesque. To sights unseen before. DOES IT GO TOO FAR?" Such promotion recalls the patter utilized for *Mondo Cane* (Jacopetti, Prosperi, Cavara, 1962), the promotion of which, as David Kerekes and David Slater note, drew on its exoticism and a promise to shock and titillate[13]—a mix which had proven very popular with audiences in Melbourne when the film screened for six weeks in 1963 at GU's Odeon Theatre.

Of all the cannibal features released in Melbourne, *Man from Deep River* was the only entry to be reviewed by the local press, where papers such as *The Herald*, the broadsheet *The Age*, and the sensationalist tabloid *The Truth* ran mostly negative reviews. Nevertheless, the film ran for six weeks at the Forum. With the following films at the theater including a mafia thriller, a martial arts spectacular, and a biker drama, it appeared that the menu at the Forum was aimed squarely at a "low art" audience. In 1974, with such once-forbidden cinema both popular with audiences and in surfeit supply, GU was moved to channel these films into venues with reputations at odds with such fare. As a consequence several theaters, including the Forum, were lured into a downmarket period of programming, competing with the extremely successful drive-in theaters that were delivering this product directly

Figure 3.1 *Man from Deep River* advertisement, *The Herald*, March 8, 1974, 23.

to the suburban audiences. Indeed, as an aging, once-respectable theater reduced to a diet of exploitation features, the Forum at this time did bear resemblance to an American grind house (albeit one still well maintained and owned by a major chain). A factor that differentiates the Melbourne theatrical experience to that of the American grind house is the fact that, in the mid- to late 1970s, venues screening such material could easily transition to the screening of mainstream fare. In the case of the Forum, by late August 1974 it was chosen to screen the highbrow literary adaptation *The Great Gatsby* (Jack Clayton, 1974) and several months later the Academy Award–winning *The Godfather Part II* (Francis Ford Coppola, 1974). That such high and low culture could mingle at Melbourne's first-run theaters at this time suggests the desire of audiences to sample as many offerings as possible from the R-rated buffet, whether it be *Man from Deep River* or *The Godfather* and its sequel. It would take until late in the decade for demarcations of taste and reputation to be re-established, after which exploitation of the cannibal kind would rarely fraternize with Hollywood fare. Until that time, though, a venue such as the Forum could operate on a "temporary grind house" basis, although in the Australian parlance, "temporary fleapit" may be a more suitable description.

Man from Deep River had its suburban release at seven Village drive-ins on June 20, 1974, supported by *The Hot Rock* (Yates, 1972) and *Valley of the Dolls* (Robson, 1967) among others: the major studio-produced fare reduced to the role of anonymous second features on a double bill on which an Italian exploitation film was the star attraction. The advertising for this suburban release was generally identical to its first-run promotion except for the addition of a small text box, which included the following lines: "You may call it perversion—but to them it's just middle class morality!"[14] "You" would be the suburban viewer. "Them," we can presume, were the tribespersons, the perpetrators of the various acts of savagery listed within the rest of the ad copy. Whether it is the customs of the tribe or the judgmental nature of the viewer that is being accused of harboring "middle class morality" is undefined. Ambiguous and possibly throwaway the copy may be, but in addressing suburban Melburnians that this platform of release was directed toward, it also posed questions regarding the content of the R-certificate and the attitudes it encountered. If one were to be offended by what is seen in *Man from Deep River*, is the offence legitimate or is it a product of the outdated standards once enforced through the adherence to Melbourne's middle-class mores? In the context of the period, one may read the first drive-in release of *Man from Deep River* as issuing a challenge. Ostensibly it dares the viewer to see the film but on a broader level it challenges the audience to question their own preconceived notions of R-rated cinema, its content and social acceptance.

Generally a wide drive-in release would be the final noteworthy exhibition point for any exploitation film. However, *Man from Deep River* defied this trend by being reissued by Eric Dare as a support for his latest release, *Addio Zio Tom/Farewell Uncle Tom* (Jacopetti & Prosperi, 1971). Compared to the breathless claims plastered onto the admats for *Man from Deep River*, for *Farewell Uncle Tom* Dare kept the copy to a minimum: "The first motion picture, based on historical facts, about the rise and revolt of slavery in America" (see Figure 3.2).

Figure 3.2 *Farewell Uncle Tom* advertisement, *The Sun*, April 10, 1975, 56.

It would seem that Dare wished to convey that this film would present a sobering and historically accurate depiction of slavery in the United States. Yet, recognizing that controversy could be good publicity, he was happy to add a quote from Sydney's *The Sun* critic Robin Ingram that read simply "The most offensive movie I've ever seen." In this case (and in that of publicity for all films discussed here), the promotional angle is a form of the time-honored "ballyhoo": "that noisy, vulgar spiel that drew audiences to circuses and sideshows ... a hyperbolic excess of words and images that sparked the imagination."[15] Utilizing Ingram's quote, with neither context nor balancing opinion, was a deliberate form of ballyhoo intended to ignite *Farewell Uncle Tom*'s sensitive yet incendiary subject matter. Coupled with *Man from Deep River* the engagement was a harsh cauldron of African and Asian stereotyping created by Italians and curated by Dare for an Australian audience.

This double feature was released through Hoyts's Athenaeum Theatre on April 10, 1975 (almost a year to the day since *Man from Deep River* had premiered at the Forum). Hoyts took over the lease on the theater in 1932, and until 1948 it operated on a strictly British-only policy. In later years, coinciding with the opening of Hoyts's Cinema Centre complex, the Athenaeum was relegated to the company's least preferred city theater and was rarely supplied with popular product. Instead, the company funneled through the theater what may be termed "difficult" material that gained a loyal following of students and counter-culturalists. In June 1973, the Athenaeum introduced "supper shows" late each Friday and Saturday night, comprising a mix of studio classics, art house favorites, and recent New Hollywood releases.

Farewell Uncle Tom and *Man from Deep River* ran for four weeks at the Athenaeum, with the theater screening the sexual habits of animals documentary *Birds Do It, Bees Do It* (Noxon & Rosten, 1974) and *Bring Me the Head of Alfredo Garcia* in between (Sam Peckinpah, 1974). Following this was a reissue of two George Bernard Shaw film adaptations: *Pygmalion* (Anthony Asquith, 1938) and *Major Barbara* (Gabriel Pascal, 1941). With Italian exploitation and George Bernard Shaw coexisting in the same space, temporally separated by a matter of weeks, the apparent "art house" policy of the Athenaeum dispensed with the imposition of high- and low-art distinctions, the concept of taste, and any adherence to middle-class morality. Hoyts maintained the Athenaeum until closing the venue in January 1977, its eclectic programming emulated by new hip theaters such as the Valhalla in the nearby suburb of Richmond (opening in 1976) that mixed the repertory with the art house and transformed the supper show into the midnight movie.

Farewell Uncle Tom and *Man from Deep River* received a suburban release through nine Hoyts drive-ins on April 28, 1976 (see Figure 3.3). Hoyts used Lenzi's film as a support feature in June 1978 for the drive-in release of the futuristic sex comedy *2069: A Sex Odyssey* (Georg Tressler, 1974), with Village also issuing the same combination the following year. On October 26, 1978, the double returned to the city for a week at the 319-seat Albany Theatre, a former newsreel house now mostly specializing in sexploitation. In September 1980 Village reissued *Man from Deep River* at five of their drive-ins with the sex comedy *The Case of the Smiling Stiffs* (Sean S. Cunningham, 1973), a film that had been a popular drive-in staple. Village acknowledged the durability of the films in its ad copy:

> 2 GIANT BLOCKBUSTERS. We know you've seen them AGAIN and AGAIN and AGAIN but now see them TOGETHER for the FIRST TIME!

Figure 3.3 *Man from Deep River* and *The Case of the Smiling Stiffs* advertisement, *The Herald*, September 18, 1980, 20.

Six years after its release *Man from Deep River* therefore remained a viable product for Melbourne's drive-in operators. Theater programmers also viewed the film as a worthy staple to plug gaps in the release schedule. In March 1979 a double feature of *Man from Deep River* and *Flesh for Frankenstein* (Paul Morrissey, 1973) was hastily booked at the Chelsea Theatre to replace the expensive thriller *Sorcerer* (William Friedkin, 1977) after it had failed to impress in its sole week. In 1981 Village was still able to package the film as a support for a reissue of *Emmanuelle* (Just Jaeckin, 1974) at eight drive-in sites. Even after its home video release and first television screening, *Man from Deep River* would continue to turn up for often bizarre one-night theatrical engagements throughout the 1980s including in 1985 at the elegant Astor theater—a suburban repertory house—paired with Derek Jarman's *Sebastiane* (1976), a British art house feature. Such incongruous programming is explained (to a degree) by both films being House of Dare imports.[16]

The enduring popularity of *Man from Deep River* with Australian audiences during this 1970s and 1980s is not as easy to qualify as, say, the popularity of other films during his period, such as the G-rated staples *Gone with the Wind* (Victor Fleming, 1939) and *2001: A Space Odyssey* (Stanley Kubrick, 1968)—which MGM had refused to make available to TV companies—or R-rated films with big promotional campaigns from major distributors, such as *A Clockwork Orange* (Stanley Kubrick, 1972), *The Godfather* (Francis Ford Coppola, 1972), and *The Exorcist* (William Friedkin, 1973). While it is not within the scope of this chapter to speculate on the mind-set and tastes of Australian drive-in audiences in the 1970s, a possible reason for *Man from Deep River's* enduring popularity at this time is potentially due to the fact that, similar to other low-budget films with little-known actors that had proven popular with contemporary audiences—such as the Australian *Stone* (Sandy Harbutt, 1974)—Lenzi's film was innovative, insofar as it was an early originator of the violent cannibal adventure film (just as *Stone* was a formative Australian biker film). That many subsequent imitators were unable to emulate *Man from Deep River*'s Australian box-office success indicates, perhaps, that, for the time, the quality of originality had a lasting effect on the potential of repeat viewings.

As has been heavily documented elsewhere, *Man from Deep River* spawned a number of imitators, such as *Last Cannibal World* (Ruggero Deodato, 1977), which not only features two of the stars of Lenzi's film (Ivan Rassimov and Me Me Lai) but also shares a similar narrative progression and tropes that would become standard for the cycle. It premiered in Italy on February 8, 1977, and, quite unusually for the period, appeared less than five months later in Melbourne. In current practice this time frame may seem unremarkable; however, in the 1970s, the process of an independently produced European horror feature locating an Australian distributor, being classified by the censor and then receiving an exhibitor's booking, often took years to complete. The rapid delivery of the film to Australian audiences was due to the work of its distributor, Franco Zeccola, and his company, Unitalia Films Australia. In 1969 Zeccola, an Italian immigrant, purchased a former Hoyts cinema in the inner suburb of Brunswick and successfully screened Italian language films for the area's large migrant population. He also dabbled in promotion, bringing Italian musical and comedy performers to Australia. Zeccola's intimacy with the Italian industry may have allowed for the second of the cannibal horrors to be fast-tracked to Australia. In order for *Last Cannibal World* to achieve a mainstream booking, Zeccola found agreeable terms for Cinema International Corporation (CIC), a company formed to distribute the titles of Paramount, Universal, and MGM internationally, to handle the film in Australia. The CIC connection allowed for the film to be placed into GU's 810-seat Chelsea Theatre in Melbourne.

Opened in 1912 as the Majestic, the theater was renovated in 1960 and relaunched as the Chelsea, the company's venue for 70 mm presentations, including a number of long-running roadshow spectacles. As these extravaganzas fell out of favor with audiences, so too did the Chelsea, and in 1974 the theater's programming turned decidedly downmarket. Horror and sex films screened at this time at the Chelsea in a manner similar to the programming policy adopted by the Forum and the Athenaeum and continued for several years, yet extending to more eclectic fare. That the programming at the Chelsea in 1977 was diverse is evidenced by the theater screening four of the Disney Studios' children's films, a disaster thriller, a disco musical, an Italian western, and a pair of horror double features, as well as hosting a Marx Brothers festival. Among these, beginning on 24 June, was *Last Cannibal World*. CIC and GU did not deviate far from the advertising strategy employed for *Man from Deep River* three years earlier (see Figure 3.4).

Once again the appeal lay in the film's exotic, and supposedly veracious, content. An alternative advertisement placed in the press the day before the film's premiere attempted a more subtle approach. Featuring the photograph of a single-engine airplane at the top of the ad and a near-silhouette image of a tribesperson in side profile drinking from a cup, the remainder is 180 words of text, detailing the supposed "true" story on which the film is based and the efforts undertaken by the filmmakers to recreate it. That verisimilitude has been achieved is suggested by the ad's claim that "The film crew had to work under the protection of a detachment of soldiers—but even

Figure 3.4 *Last Cannibal World* advertisement, *The Herald*, June 24, 1977, 31.

so a technician disappeared and was never found. The locals were convinced that his disappearance was due to the practice of cannibalism."[17] The response to Deodato's film was lukewarm, with only three weeks on the Chelsea Theatre screen. *Last Cannibal World* could not repeat the success of *Man from Deep River*.

Last Cannibal World appeared in twelve Village drive-ins (and the same company's Australia 2 cinema) for a week beginning November 24, 1977, with the disaster thriller *Black Sunday* (John Frankenheimer, 1977) as its support. For this engagement the pretence of investigative reportage alluded to in the advertising for *Last Cannibal World*'s first theatrical run was dispensed in favor of grindhouse-style ballyhoo, daring the audience to attend if they were brave enough. *Last Cannibal World* would turn up in 1981 at four Village drive-ins as support for *The Island* (Michael Ritchie, 1980), but would not emulate the repeat viewing success of *Man from Deep River*, limiting its later screenings to filling slots within drive-in sex film marathons, including in 1983, when it appeared within a quartet packaged as "Unbelievable and erotic passions of untold lust and wanton women!!!!"

Mountain of the Cannibal God (Sergio Martino, 1979) opened on September 12, 1980, with the title changed to *Slave of the Cannibal God* (the title it also used in the United States) and its distributor listed as Garland Productions (an Eric Dare owned company) at the Forum Theatre in Melbourne, where the House of Dare release of *Man from Deep River* had begun its long theatrical life. The Forum's position in the GU stable of theaters had been downgraded since the company had opened its six screen Russell Street complex less than two blocks away in late 1978. That year the company's Odeon and Times theaters were closed and demolished, and in 1980 the Chelsea would follow. With the majority of "quality" product being channeled into its Russell Street cinemas, the leftovers were sent to the Forum and adjoining Rapallo. As a result the Forum's 1980 exhibition slate included a number of moveovers from the Russell complex and reissues of previous favorites. Yet the theater also managed some high-profile first runs, including *American Gigolo* (Paul Schrader, 1980) followed by Disney's live action *The Last Flight of Noah's Ark* (Charles Jarrott, 1980). Once this film ended its four-week run, GU replaced it with *Slave of the Cannibal God*, Sergio Martino's tale of adventurers in New Guinea who encountered a cannibalistic tribe. Although it had the advantage of including two well-known performers (Ursula Andress and Stacy Keach) in its cast, little effort was made to promote the film, with the admat art taken directly from the Italian poster (focusing heavily on a bound and scantily clad Andress) and the generic tagline "Their cult was death … their lust was for blood" (carried over from the US promotion) lacking the marketing hype of previous cannibal titles (see Figure 3.5). It would appear that the film was only scheduled for a two-week engagement as the opening-day print promotion noted that it would open at Village drive-ins on 25 September, which it did, with the House of Dare's *Blood for Dracula* (Paul Morrissey, 1974) as support. Oddly, GU appeared to have been at a programming loss at the time, replacing the film in the Forum with a week of *Citizen Kane* (Orson Welles, 1941) paired with *Elvira Madigan* (Bo Widerberg, 1967) followed by a triple feature of 1960s biker features for a week. Such programming advances the impression that the theater was in its death throes, yet in June 1981 both the Forum and Rapallo would undergo refurbishment and reopen as (respectively) the Forum 1 & 2 Theatres and remain viable venues for the company. As a sign of this faith, both were granted the exclusive day and date release of *E.T.* (Steven Spielberg, 1982) with great success. The theaters finally closed in June 1986. *Slave of the Cannibal God*'s engagement at the Forum came at a time when the theater's positioning within the GU chain was uncertain and its programming resembling that of the Chelsea which had closed a year earlier. After the renovations and rebranding, exploitation appearances were rare among the high-profile Hollywood releases at the Forum and the period that contained Martino's cannibal exercise seemed to be from another theater and another time entirely.

None of the final four entries in the cannibal cycle to be released in Melbourne were exhibited in the older, larger houses that had proved so receptive for the earlier entries. *Emanuelle and the Last Cannibals* (Joe D'Amato, 1977) was distributed in Australia by Blake Films. Sid Blake began importing a mixture of art house and exploitation features in the 1950s, but by the 1970s the content was almost exclusively sexploitation with the Roadshow corporation taking a financial interest in the company late in the decade. *Emmanuelle* had enjoyed a thirteen-week season at Village's East End 2 screen, followed by a wide suburban release and numerous reissues. The numerous cash-ins (altering the spelling of the titular character's name) mostly played in the city's burgeoning sex theaters, and although several in director D'Amato's strand in the series

Figure 3.5 *Slave of the Cannibal God* advertisement, *The Herald*, September 12, 1980, 21.

starring Laura Gemser delved into darker and often violent territory, the promotional emphasis remained on the promise of the films' sexual content.

Emanuelle and the Last Cannibals opened on November 16, 1978, with *Black Emanuelle Goes East* (D'Amato, 1976) at the Penthouse, a 150-seat theater located in the basement of the aging Nicholas Building in Swanston Street, the city's main thoroughfare and, at this time, the location for four adult cinemas. The Penthouse had opened as a Village cinema in March 1977, with *Vices and Virtues* (Miklós Jancsó, 1976) as its premiere feature. Soon the pretence to art house was dropped in preference to a slate of mostly sex features, many of which combined elements of violence within their narratives including *Emanuelle in America* (D'Amato, 1977), *Love Train for the S.S.* (Alain Payet, 1977), and *Jack the Ripper* (Jesús Franco, 1976). It was due to the often sordid content of the Penthouse's films that although Village retained a stake in the theater it was listed as an independent venue. *Emanuelle and the Last Cannibals* features an uneasy blend of soft-core sex sequences, both heterosexual and lesbian that, although kept distinct from the acts of horror, caused anguish for the censor, with the film initially banned for "indecency" and "excessive violence" until two and a half minutes were excised from the print.[18] D'Amato's film ran for five weeks at the Penthouse and then next appeared on screen on June 7, 1979, for a week at eight Village drive-ins with a selection of anonymously advertised supports. It then reappeared for a week beginning March 12, 1981, as the first billed feature at five Village drive-ins on a triple bill with *Emanuelle in America* and *Girls with Open Lips* (Edward Dietrich, 1972). From that point, its theatrical exhibition was reduced to drive-in marathon slots.

Eaten Alive! (Umberto Lenzi, 1980) was another Eric Dare release (once again via Garland Productions). Bypassing a hard-top release, it opened directly at six Village drive-ins on July 2, 1981, with two Dare-distributed, Italian-produced features as supports: *Autopsy* (Armando Crispino, 1975) and *The Cheaters* (Sergio Martino, 1975), each at three screens. *Eaten Alive!* appeared again over twelve months later at nine Village drive-ins for a week as the first support to the slasher horror *Maniac* (William Lustig, 1980) (another Dare release), with *Autopsy* filling out the second support slot.

Within the space of two months the final two cannibal releases would appear on Melbourne's screens. *Cannibal Apocalypse* (Antonio Margheriti, 1980) (its title a deliberate attempt to capitalize on Coppola's *Apocalypse Now* of the previous year) told of Vietnam veterans who develop a hunger for human flesh after being bitten in combat. It opened on August 12, 1982, at eight Village drive-ins, with the martial arts feature *The Naked Fist* (Cirio H. Santiago, 1981) as its support. From that point there are no further instances of the film screening in Melbourne through to the end of 1985.

The last of the Italian cannibal film cycle to receive a theatrical release in Melbourne was *Woman from Deep River* (Umberto Lenzi, 1981). It is notable that in a number of countries this film retained its original Italian title of *Cannibal Ferox* in order to capitalize on the notoriety of *Cannibal Holocaust*. In the United States the film was given the more lurid retitling of *Make Them Die Slowly* (possibly due to the film being released in 1983 in that country, before *Cannibal Holocaust* was unleashed there in 1986). As *Cannibal Holocaust* continued to be banned in Australia the path of association was traced back to *Man from Deep River* by the distributor. Thus, while much of Europe was led to consider the film within the lineage of *Cannibal Holocaust*, Australian audiences experienced *Woman from Deep River* as a relative of Lenzi's first foray into the cannibal cycle. Eventually *Woman from Deep River* (retitled in Australia in order to reference the earlier film) was released through AZ distribution, a company named after Antonio Zeccola (brother of Frank) that would evolve into Palace Films, now one of Australia's most successful production, distribution, and exhibition companies. Lenzi's film opened on September 23, 1982, at Village's Capitol 2 Cinema. Originally the Century Newsreel theatrette, it was renamed the Swanston in 1970, and until new venues were built or acquired, it was one of the chain's premier sites. In 1979 it was rebranded (as an adjunct to the neighboring, larger Capitol Theatre) and had slipped down Village's hierarchy of city screens. By 1982 it alternated between films moving over from other theaters and first runs of martial arts, slasher, and sex comedy features. *Woman from Deep River* screened at the Capitol 2 for a week, assisted by a promotional print campaign that included imagery of a woman strung up by hooks through her breasts and another butchered by a machete. The ad copy delivered promises of barbarity with relish:

GRUESOME! GROTESQUE! HORRENDOUS!
The Goriest Orgy that ever bloodied the screen!
DOES IT GO TOO FAR?[19]

The question of "Does it go too far?" had also been posed by the promoters of *Man from Deep River* and *Last Cannibal World*. For this latest film the ads also felt the need to remind the audience that the film was "All New!" in case it all felt too familiar. Upon leaving the Capitol 2, *Woman from Deep River* spent a week in nine Village drive-ins, heading a triple feature bill also containing *Behind the Door* (Oliver Hellman, 1974) and *Emmanuelle 3* (Jean-Marie Pallardy, 1980). It was not unusual for a popular film to move over to a second (generally smaller) city screen once its initial engagement concluded. Generally this would be an immediate move, with the extended city stay delaying the suburban release. *Woman from Deep River* managed that achievement *after its suburban release*, which was rare for any film and virtually unheard of for exploitation fare.

Once it finished its drive-in engagement *Woman from Deep River* was picked up by the city's Dendy Collins Street cinema for a four-week run. The 250-seat Dendy had opened in 1972 as an art house but quickly abandoned that policy in favor of sex features. In 1980 the cinema attempted a mainstream approach of moveovers of popular titles and first releases of mostly horror features, but sex soon crept back into the schedule. Lenzi's film was replaced at the Dendy Collins Street with a single-week engagement of the German vice drama *Christiane F* (Uli Edel, 1981) and then a successful season of the critically acclaimed Australian romantic comedy *Lonely Hearts* (Paul Cox, 1982), which had moved over from Hoyts Cinema Centre. In February 1984 the cinema would present the Australian premiere of *Texas Chainsaw Massacre* (Tobe Hooper, 1974), finally passed by the Australian censor. Shortly afterwards it would revert to a sex-film policy that remained for its final years. Although the early 1980s was a boom period for exploitation films—with a vast number receiving theatrical releases in Melbourne—the experience of the Dendy suggests that although certain titles could deliver an audience, no theater could sustain exclusive (nonsexual) exploitation programming. Whereas in the 1970s the suburban drive-ins of Melbourne would function as alternative second-run release points for mainstream attractions with exploitation as supplementary programming, by the 1980s it was exploitation cinema (such as the cannibal features and the abundant slasher horrors) that comprised the majority of drive-in fare and often as first-run items. Traditional "grindhouse" exploitation was consumed in the suburbs, leaving the CBD fleapits to concentrate on sex material. *Woman from Deep River* was also granted a second suburban life as it then landed a six drive-in release with Hoyts for a week toplining a bill of "3 Gut-Churning Chapters" with *Dawn of the Mummy* (Frank Agrama, 1981) and *Hell of the Living Dead* (Bruno Mattei, 1980).[20]

Conclusion

Eventually all of the discussed titles would turn up on video format in Australia, with *Man from Deep River*, *Last Cannibal World*, and *Cannibal Apocalypse* all broadcast on television (albeit in heavily censored form).[21] None would receive a legitimate DVD release in this country except for the long-banned *Cannibal Holocaust*, which was finally granted a DVD release in 2005, completely uncut, with the stronger R18+ rating, and then on Blu-ray by Siren Visual in 2014 with a wealth of extras spread over its two discs.[22] The passing of time and the relaxing of censorship had granted the most notorious of the Italian cannibal releases the widest potential audience in the digital era. It is with some irony that *Man from Deep River* has not been deemed worthy of a digital release in the country where it was the most theatrically popular of the cannibal titles. Instead, the only exemplar of the genre available for interested viewers is the one that never graced a cinema screen or video rental store shelf.

In contrast, each of these films has received a substantial digital release in the United States and the films collectively have been the subject of a documentary (*Eaten Alive!: The Rise and Fall of the Italian Cannibal Film* (Calum Waddell, 2015)). In 2015 (after distribution difficulties), Director Eli Roth's *Green Inferno* was released to cinemas. A homage to the Italian cannibal subgenre, Roth filmed on location in Peru and employed a local tribe as extras for the production. As preparation, he screened *Cannibal Holocaust* for the tribe—reportedly the first film they had ever seen.[23] Roth also contributed a fake "trailer" to the film *Grindhouse* (2007). Directed by Quentin Tarantino and Robert Rodriguez, this project attempted to replicate the grindhouse experience by comprising two features with additional imaginary trailers. For the touch of authenticity, the films were purposely made to look scratched, worn, and incomplete. For overseas territories (including Australia), the two features were released separately (with prints pristine and complete). Tarantino explained: "They don't really have this tradition. Not only do they not really know what a grind house is they don't even have the double feature tradition."[24]

Tarantino was only partially correct, at least in reference to Australia: for the double feature *was* a tradition in Australia, however, not in the context of the American grind house. For exploitation films (including the Italian cannibal titles), the collective memory (and associated nostalgia) is more likely of a suburban drive-in experience rather than a hardtop. That was the continuing, near-permanent exhibition space in Melbourne. In terms of the content, at least there were moments when particular theaters took on the approximation of the American grind house, yet never for any lasting period (sex cinemas aside).

The history of the cannibal film cycle in Melbourne did not mirror its experience in the United States. Neither the historical modes of consumption nor the embrace of the R-certificate allow for such similarities in history. Instead, in their theatrical life these films enjoyed their initial success in belonging to a wave of material that was no longer verboten and channeled through venues previously identified for their reputable entertainment. To a degree this was similar to what occurred in traditional grind houses, except that the US theaters rarely returned to mainstream status. For the majority of the Melbourne theaters, their fleapit periods were temporary caterings to audience demands before normal transmission resumed. The second life for the cannibal films—found in the drive-in—is where the shared experience has retained a nostalgic glow in Australian culture.

Notes

1. Ruth Inglis, *Freedom of the Movies* (Chicago: University of Chicago Press, 1947), 42–43.
2. Bill Landis and Michelle Clifford, *Sleazoid Express* (New York: Fireside, 2002), 177.
3. David Church, *Grindhouse Nostalgia: Memory, Home Video and Exploitation Film Fandom* (Edinburgh: Edinburgh University Press, 2015), 4.
4. Grindhouse Releasing, "Cannibal Ferox," available at grindhousereleasing.com/?page_id=28 (accessed December 12, 2015); Grindhouse Releasing, "Cannibal Holocaust," available at grindhousereleasing.com/?page_id=30 (accessed December 12, 2015).
5. Screen Australia, "Total Screens, Seating Capacity and Theatres in Australia: 1980–2014," available at www.screenaustralia.gov.au/research/statistics/cinemasttotal.aspx (accessed August 17, 2015).
6. Simon Brand, *Picture Palaces and Fleapits* (Sydney: Dreamweaver, 1983), 189.
7. Trevor Walters, *The Picture Palaces of Melbourne: A History of Melbourne's Picture Theatres* (Melbourne: Trevor Walters, 2003), 230–260.
8. Phil Edwards provides a comprehensive overview of Australian film censorship and classification in this period (Phil Edwards, *Shocking Cinema: The Breaking of Movie Taboos* (Beaconsfield: Mentmore Press, 1987), 66–85).
9. "Theatre Listings," *The Herald* (November 23, 1972).
10. Michael Helms, personal email communication with the author, June 14, 2015.
11. "Radio Pioneer Dies Suddenly," *The Sydney Morning Herald* (December 29, 1954), 6.
12. Michael Smith, "The Heat Is On and Without a Cut," *The Age* (April 5, 1973), 2.

13. David Kerekes and David Slater, *Killing for Culture: An Illustrated History of Death Film from Mondo to Snuff* (London: Creation, 1994), 107–108.
14. "*Man from Deep River* Drive-in" advertisement, *The Herald* (June 20, 1974), 27.
15. Eric Schaefer, *Bold! Daring! Shocking! True! A History of Exploitation Films, 1919–1959* (Durham: Duke University Press, 1999), 103.
16. *Sebastiane* and *Man from Deep River* advertisement, *The Age* (July 18, 1985).
17. *Last Cannibal World* advertisement, *The Herald* (June 23, 1977), 33.
18. Refused Classification: "Emanuelle and the Last Cannibals," available at www.refused-classification.com/censorship/films/e.html#emanuelle-and-the-last-cannibals (accessed November 22, 2015).
19. *Woman from Deep River* advertisement, *The Herald* (September 23, 1982), 19.
20. *Woman from Deep River*, *Dawn of the Mummy*, and *Hell of the Living Dead* advertisement, *The Herald* (November 4, 1982), 23.
21. The database www.refused-classification.com provides an excellent overview of the censorship and various releases to each of the individual titles discussed.
22. Siren Visual, "Cannibal Holocaust—Blu Ray Special Edition," available at sirenvisual.com.au/index.php/cannibal-holocaust-blu-ray-special-edition.html (accessed December 4, 2015).
23. Ali Plumb, "Eli Roth Talks the Green Inferno," *Empire Online*, available at www.empireonline.com/movies/news/eli-roth-talks-green-inferno/ (accessed December 7, 2015).
24. Peter Sciretta, "Interview with Grindhouse Directors Quentin Tarantino and Robnert Rodriguez," *Slash Film*, available at www.slashfilm.com/interview-with-grindhouse-directors-quentin-tarantino-and-robert-rodriguez/ (accessed December 7, 2015).

4

Run, Angel, Run: Serial Production and the Biker Movie, 1966–1972

Peter Stanfield

The novelist and essayist Joan Didion watched nine biker films in seven days before publishing an account of the experience in a May 1970 edition of her regular *Life* magazine column. In the manner of an anthropologist, she sets out to explore a dark continent of moviegoing, which only a "few adults have ever seen." For her, the cycle constitutes a sort of "underground folk literature for adolescents" and a fabricated mythology to "express precisely that audience's every inchoate resentment, every yearning for the extreme exhilaration of death." The biker movie is, she claims, a "perfect Rorschach of its audience."[1]

Watching the movies in Bakersfield and Tarzana drive-ins and in a Hollywood Boulevard theater, Didion ponders the fascination these films hold over her, especially given that they are all the same: "To see one is to have seen them all," she writes. Each film meticulously observes the rituals of "getting the bikers out of town and onto the highway, of 'making a run', of terrorizing innocent 'citizens' and fencing with the highway patrol and, finally, meeting death in a blaze … of romantic fatalism."[2] Her concise description of generic elements grasps the basics of the formula: bikers terrorize a small town or community, have run-ins with the police, and ride to their certain sentimentalized death. "There is always that instant," she observes, "in which the bikers batter at some psychic sound barrier, degrade the widow, violate the virgin, defile the rose and the cross alike, break on through to the other side and find, once there, 'nothing to say.'"[3] It is not the narrative repetition that fascinates her, and keeps her returning to these films, but the thought that she is getting an insight into contemporary America that cannot be found in the *New York Times*. The biker film provides her with an ideogram of the nation's youth, one that offers a far from edifying vision.

Didion perceives the mute bikers as mirror images of the films' audience of undereducated working-class youth. Her symptomatic reading of the cycle as representative of a generalized social malaise prefigures scholarly accounts of the biker movie specifically and exploitation films more generally. Similarly, Didion's identification of narrative repetition as a sign of a filmmaker's flawed aspirations is a commonplace in critical reactions. To contend with and to offer a challenge to these received perspectives, I shift the focus on to a consideration of the mode of assembly, circulation, and consumption of the biker movie. I do this in order to better understand the function of repetition and the practice of serial production in commercial cinema.

In her study of the recurring figure of Fu Manchu, Ruth Mayer writes, "Seriality relies on iconicity, on emblematic constellations, and on recognizable images, figures, plots, phrases, and accessories that, once established can be rearranged, reinterpreted, recombined, and invested with new significance and thus constitute major parts of the serial memory that upholds complex serial narratives and representational networks in the first place."[4] Her conception of seriality does not rest here, but is based on the proposition that it is self-generating. The context and process involved in the fabrication and consumption of a serial form are paramount. Seriality, she argues, arises from "concrete formal, material and institutional foundations."[5] Silent film historian Rudmer Canjels notes that serial forms of movies are "dependent on production and distribution possibilities and conventions that are often directly linked with the perceptions of the film industry itself on how a feature could function best."[6] He claims that the narrative conceits and the formal devices of serial film—its repetitions—are imbued in their production, distribution, and reception. Seriality is never just a question of form and content.

Within and outside of the cycle, actors and character types, stories and sequences, formal and stylistic elements are shared and repeated, borrowed and stolen. This process of interchange is part of the concept of seriality, but it is only a part. Following the direction taken by Mayer, I contend with the mechanics of serial production and the aggregate of its many parts. It is not just the films that are of significance but also the demands of the marketplace and the ability of filmmakers to work within this context and supply a particular type of picture in an effective and economic manner, one that meets the need of exhibitors and satisfies the intended audience.

The Wild Angels (1966), a Roger Corman production distributed by AIP, was the film that kick-started the biker cycle. With its subject and story line evoking recent news stories, the film fastidiously exploits the contemporaneous subculture of Californian motorcycle gangs.[7] The run of movies that followed in its wake quickly gathered intensity—seven in 1967, six in 1968, nine in 1969, and seven in 1970, peaking with ten in 1971, and then declining and finishing with four in 1972. The serial titling of the films is indicative of the process of maximizing repetition within a cycle. Originally seeking to benefit from the notoriety of the Hells Angels, Corman's film was developed under the working titles of *Fallen Angels* and *All the Fallen Angels*, but the release title went for a broader reference set when it invoked the seminal outlaw motorcycle picture, *The Wild One* (1953), effectively fusing the past and present.

Films in the cycle all confected variants on "wild" and "angel," and *The Wild Angels* begat *Devil's Angels*, *Hells Angels on Wheels*, *Wild Rebels* (all 1967), and *Angels from Hell* (1968). Having "angel" in the title remained almost obligatory right up and until the end of the cycle. In 1969 there was *Hell's Angels '69*, *Naked Angels*, *Nam Angels* (aka *The Losers*), *Run, Angel, Run!*, and, with barely a pause into 1970, *Angel Unchained*, *Angels Die Hard* (aka *Violent Angels*), *Black Angels*, before thinning out in 1971 and 1972 with *Angels Hard as They Come*, *Bury Me an Angel*, *Pink Angels*, and *Angels' Wild*

Women. In between, the Devil is further given his due with *Hell's Belles*, *Satan's Sadists*, *Hell's Chosen Few*, and *Hell's Bloody Devils*, while "savage" replaces "wild" in order to provide some variety with *Savages from Hell*, *The Savage Seven* (both 1968), and *Cycle Savages* (1969).

Repetition in titling helps delineate the cycle and points toward a concept of seriality defined by Umberto Eco as a repetitive art form and practice. There is, he contends, a number of distinctive serial types, which include the retake, the remake, the series, the saga, and the intertextual dialogue. The latter "is a didactic work that takes account of the idealized rules of its own production."[8] Intertextual dialogues are often parodic as in *Angels from Hell*, which is partly set in Hollywood and features a caricature of a Jewish producer, Saul Joseph. After meeting a gang of bikers, Joseph has the idea of making a motorcycle picture: "Find out," he says to a minion, "what these gangs are about. You know the sex, the orgies; all that stuff. Give us a chance to capture some of that dialogue we hear here." In his review of *C.C. and Company* (1970), *Los Angeles Times* movie critic Kevin Thomas suggests parody is a given within any cycle of films: "It probably isn't essential to the enjoyment of [the film] to be familiar with all the bike pictures that have followed in the wake of *The Wild Angels*. But it sure helps in recognizing this raunchy, hilarious movie for what it is: a lovingly precise send-up of the entire motorcycle genre."[9]

Intertextual dialogue can also help authenticate a film by playing it off against another example. *Angel Unchained* (1970) tacitly evokes *Easy Rider* (1969) and, for those with longer memories, *The Wild Angels*. The hero is a one-time member of an outlaw biker gang who tries to dissuade the leader of a commune from getting cyclists involved in his battle with local rednecks: "Listen to me will you. These guys are not like Peter Fonda. They play rough. It's like asking for trouble. It's like asking a maniac to baby sit your kid brother."[10] But regardless of whether or not it is parodic or authenticating in its intent, intertexuality in serial productions depends and comments on repetition as formula. *Los Angeles Times* editor Charles Champlin, in his review of *The Glory Stompers* (1967), one of the first half-dozen films to follow *The Wild Angels*, writes,

> The cycle is over. The law of diminishing returns has been ratified, you might say, by the American International release, *The Glory Stompers* now vrooming city-wide and kicking up dust but no excitement … formula has taken over from immediacy and you get that curious but not unfamiliar feeling of being in the presence of a film based not on life but on other films.[11]

Self-reflexivity—films referencing films—and intertextuality—the shaping through exchange of one film by other films and other texts—are essential components of seriality within the biker movie cycle, but repetition here is also subject to drivers and influences ignored by Eco: industrial and market forces are equally profound in their impact on the interchange between films.

Variety describes the credo of Sid Frazer and Dan Kennis, producers of the outlaw motorcycle picture, *Satan's Sadists* (1969), as "Plan ahead, cast medium high, shoot fast and furious and on a low budget, aim for the action market and never stop to look behind you."[12] These producers had a keen eye on the youth audience, one that had been redefined three years earlier beginning with *The Wild Angels*. AIP used the film to help make the break from the beach and horror movie cycles that had dominated production at the company. *Variety* reported on the company's putative plans in March 1966 when it noted that it "cannot romp around forever in invisible bikinis, or dress up in Edgar Allan Poe glad-rags to play spooks."[13]

Three months later, in June 1966, the trade journal continued the story: "From Sand in Bikini to Sand in Machinery: AIP on 'Protest' Kick," noting that the producer was "Swinging to the other end of the teenage cycle now that the 'beach' brand has used up most of its potential," and it was gearing up for "a series of 'protest' films."[14] As the company's director of development Louis M. "Deke" Hayward explained to the *Los Angeles Times*, the "protest" tag was little more than an expedient exploitation of the generation gap: "Among the movies we are planning for the coming season are subjects about stock-car racing, *Fireball 500*, and one about Hell's Angels—a type of motorcycle club, both of which represent a protest against society." AIP "always assumes the teenagers' viewpoint," he said, but also added that the protest films will be "moral tales."[15] Both films feature stories of mobile youth, but there the comparison ends. *Fireball 500* stars Frankie Avalon and Annette Funicello, and the context of stock-car racing represents no more than a change of location in creating a break from the couple's earlier beach party movies. *The Wild Angels* is, by comparison, a radical departure for AIP.

Among the papers left to the Margaret Herrick Library by the screenwriter Howard R. Cohen, a man responsible for *Young Nurses* (1973), *Vampire Hookers* (1978), and *Emmanuelle 5* (1987) are his notes on a 1970 treatment for an unproduced outlaw motorcycle movie, *Bikers in Outer Space*—a science fiction comedy musical wherein Frankie Avalon tries to bed Annette Funicello. Avalon's amorous intentions are blocked, because his object of desire is "totally imbued with the Madonna-Whore complex" and she decides that a virginal image is the more marketable attribute. Meanwhile, the outlaw bikers—big coats, Davy Crocket hats, Nazi insignia, and so forth—are searching for The Hole in the Universe, the ultimate nirvana.[16] The concept is beach movie meets biker movie—the corruption of an innocent age of exploitation picture by a gnarly, sexually promiscuous, and predatory present. Like actual examples of the motorcycle film, *Bikers in Outer Space* lacks originality, even as it employs an acute self-awareness of its antecedents. Such self-consciousness had been apparent from the beginning of the cycle.

From wholesome beach movie to offensive biker film, the shift in genre and tone undertaken in AIP's production plans would prove to be economically canny. In March 1967, *Variety* reports that *The Wild Angels* has taken $6 million domestic gross on a $300,000 investment, and had just realized $30,000 in its Paris opener over a February weekend.[17] In an attempt to capture further exceptional box-office returns, AIP had ready for release or in production *The Trip*, *Riot on Sunset Strip* (both 1967), *Psych-Out*, and *Wild in the Streets* (both 1968). This tranche of forthcoming "protest" films from AIP was augmented in 1967 alone with three biker movies: the *Devil's Angels*, *Glory Stompers*, and *Born Losers*, which the company either produced or part financed.[18]

Trade press and other reviews of *The Wild Angels* stress the film's topical appeal and apparent authenticity: "For thematic motivation, Corman, who produced in almost documentary style, has chosen a subject frequently in the headlines," notes *Variety*.[19] The *Los Angeles Times* considers the film to be an "exciting, original film that captures an authentic slice of contemporary life."[20] The *Los Angeles Herald Examiner* thought it "well made and astonishingly honest."[21] But the film also dismayed and upset critics; the reviewer for the *Motion Picture Herald* writes, "no one will leave the theatre without feeling he has seen a slice of life—dirty stupid and appalling as it is."[22] This point of view is echoed in the *Hollywood Reporter*: "even necrophilia, the most loathsome of perversions, is presented with detachment."[23] The *Hollywood Citizen News* underscored the generally held distaste by reviewers for a film that "concentrated on orgiastic behavior and wanton destruction."[24]

AIP's and Corman's defence was that *The Wild Angels* was true to the world it depicted, but a columnist in the *Saturday Review* thought this a spurious justification. Citing AIP's beach party specialties, he writes: "Bikini beaches exist, too, but no one takes movies about them seriously. Their appeal is to adolescents, and they are made for 'exploitation' purposes only, for a fast buck, in other words. And this is the use to which the same firm is putting *The Wild Angels*." Gang members are all portrayed as being on the "low-side of intelligence ... a few were homosexually inclined ... and behaved as they did for psychopathic reasons as well as because of parental and social neglect." But, "with social excrescences such as these, it is not enough, ever, to merely show the surface." Instead, he argues, "an umbrella of meaning is required."[25] By not giving an explanation for his characters' actions, Corman, the columnist argues, is being morally derelict.

The lack of compensating moral values and the display of nihilism were something entirely new for AIP, going beyond what even Deke Heyward would consider an acceptable teenage "protest against society." Though it corrupts the moral certainties of a beach movie, the cycle's break with earlier AIP fare is neither as decisive nor as absolute as *The Wild Angels* might suggest it would be. Kevin Thomas's *Los Angeles Times* review of *Devil's Angels* calls it a "sequel" to *The Wild Angels*, though not as good as the "first instalment." "Actually," he writes, "it is more like a remake, a variation on the theme of the first film." The *Devil's Angels* lacks the qualities of its forerunner, because repetition diminishes the impact of the original and the director is not as accomplished as Corman, but for Thomas the film's real failure is its "self-consciousness." This aspect diminishes any claim it might make for an authenticity in its portrayal of outlaw bikers, as had been made for *The Wild Angels*. The film knowingly and determinably tries to make itself a "little more attractive, a little more likable, and ... appealing." In the process "history repeats itself," echoing the Dead End Kids's transformation into the Bowery Boys. The "sequel" exploits and softens the impact of its predecessor, presenting the outlaw bikers as cartoon figures who "act like Beach Party cut-ups in Halloween costumes."[26]

Whether *Devil's Angels* was conceived as a pastiche, sequel, remake, instalment, or variation, it breaks with *The Wild Angels* by returning the lost voice of morality (however compromised). Typically for an AIP picture, morals are ventriloquized by the female lead. In the first cycle of biker movies, she was cast, costumed, and groomed as if playing a part in a beach party movie. The casting of Nancy Sinatra, with her blond

Figure 4.1 *The Born Losers* (1967): bikini beach blanket party versus beer, grease, and bikers.

backcombed hair, in *The Wild Angels*, or Elizabeth James, shod in white kinky boots and matching bikini ensemble, in *Born Losers* (Figure 4.1), or Beverly Adams, wearing a mod outfit and boyish short hair, in *Devil's Angels* are all designed to appeal to the girls in the audience, who the producers assume look at films as fashion guides. Like the distorted and overamplified instrumental surf music—Dick Dale on steroids—that defined the first run of biker movie soundtracks, the female lead accentuates the cycle's uncertain break with its beach movie antecedent.[27]

Sinatra, James, and Adams may seem out of place and stylistically at odds with the grease and beer biker culture, but female characters in American formulaic cinema rarely carry the weight of imparting authenticity. John Wayne's costume in Westerns, for example, was remarkably consistent throughout his career, with only minor modifications made from film to film and within any given film. The costumes worn by his female costars change between scenes and, as vogue dictates, between films.[28] Wayne represents stability, the women faddishness. Relative to the men's, the description of women's costumes, bodies, and hair in the screenplay for *The Glory Stompers* is detailed and substantive; descriptions of both men and women are gendered and generic:

> Nancy, a slender, elegant-looking girl in her early 20's with flowing blonde hair, dressed in hip-huggers, blouse and white boots ... Joanne, a slender girl in her early 20's, with long dark wind-blown hair. She is attractive but has a hard look about her, and it is evident that she knows her way around. Her costume consists of a sexy black outfit; skin-tight denims, blouse, and knee length high-heeled boots ... Darryl Hudson, a tall, muscular youth in his mid-20's, wearing jeans, cowboy boots, T-shirt, and a sleeveless denim jacket with the words "Glory Stompers" and the club emblem on the back ... Chino, a lean, bearded youth in his mid-20's, dressed in denim jacket, leather pants, and motorcycle boots.[29]

Equally gendered and generic is the dialogue, which reads like the kind of patter Shadow Morton might have molded for a Shangri-Las recording session or, more appositely, like something from a beach movie:

> Nancy: ... I want something better than being a Stomper's girl ... (she notices his hurt expression) Darryl, I still love you ... but I want a man I can depend on, not someone who runs around with a pack of over-aged delinquents.
> Darryl: (shrugs helplessly) But you don't understand ... Nancy, they're my friends ... They're like family.[30]

These sentiments contrast sharply with the following kidnap scene, with its threat of selling Nancy to a Mexican pimp, and subsequent rape scenarios. A review of *Hell's Angels on Wheels* in *Variety* supports a reading of the first tranche of films in the cycle as somehow throwbacks to earlier exploitation types, even as they proffered the novelty of corrupting the beach movie's innocence: "As is now expected of these cycling pix, the girls are too clean and too pretty. One new gimmick is the suggestion of perversion among both the cyclists and their girls ... The film will make money but it's not likely to make many friends."[31] Later films in the cycle, like *Satan's Sadists*, would disclaim any correspondence with beach movies or at least the pretence to have a direct appeal to teenage girls, but by then the cycle was firmly established.

The Wild Angels's marketing broke with a romance and comedy approach used for the beach movie and returned to a form of ballyhoo and sensational imagery that had been a mainstay in the promotion of juvenile delinquent pictures during the mid- to late 1950s: "They come like a wolf pack on wheels ... Dirty, deadly and dangerous. Their badge is the swastika, their colors black and red. They are a living legend of violence and strange excitements for they hate everything—and everyone—but each other."[32] In its distribution and exhibition, the film followed an established pattern of screenings in urban neighborhood cinemas or in drive-in circuits that AIP had been using and had developed since the company's inception.

Figure 4.2 The abundant use of swastikas in *The Wild Angels* (1966) was a major source of the controversy it generated.

In the *New York Post*, Archer Winsten's review of *The Wild Angels* paid little heed to the film's break or otherwise with beach movies, or to the potentially disruptive, inauthentic presence of Sinatra; instead he comments on the debt the film owes to *Scorpio Rising* ("Kenneth Anger did it a lot better") and concentrates on the film's play dates in the grind houses along 42nd Street, where it opened without fanfare at the Selwyn, before jumping to the better appointed Lyric and then the larger Liberty theater.[33] On the West Coast, *Citizen News* announced a late September run for the film in thirty Southland theaters and drive-ins.[34]

Two AIP programmers, *Hell's Angels '69* and *Angel Unchained*, can stand as examples of how seriality works in terms determined by context as much as by content. The former picture opened in Detroit in July 1969 and racked up grosses of $172,486 in the first seven days, showing in ten of the region's drive-ins. With play dates over five days at three drive-ins in Louisville, Kentucky, it made $24,680, and on the east coast, in Washington, DC, across the same number of days, it topped $42,000, and it had equally strong returns in open-air theaters in the Midwest.[35] These figures are impressive on a film with production costs of $375,000, which has as its main attraction, or point of distinction, participation from "The Original Oakland Hell's Angels."[36] The movie was something of a vanity project for the actor Tom Stern, who starred, wrote, produced, and bought in AIP to part finance the production. Stern's deal with AIP was outlined in *Variety*:

> a case study of independent financial agility. Actual production costs ran about $375,000, although it was never in hand at any given moment. However, as is required in independently financed deals like this, there was a completion bond guarantor, in this case Del Webb, whose associate Pat Rooney was named exec producer. With bond, AIP's guaranteed pickup for £175,000 was bankable for a loan at Bank of America. An outside private industry putting up another $50,000, plus deferments of $100,000, completed the budget. Within eight months of release *Hell's Angels '69* paid off everyone and was in profits.[37]

In its publicity materials the film is sold as offering "one of the wildest robbery plots ever conceived, two wealthy brothers play a deadly game by infiltrating the ranks of the Hell's Angels with the ultimate purpose of using them for a cover in the spectacular holdup of Caesar's Palace in Las Vegas." Marketing tags rely on an audience's knowledge of the film's antecedents and suggest that it maximizes those repeat attractions: "Makes the others look tame … The latest is the lustiest of all!" Reviews of the film responded to its distinctive elements: "Somewhat different from most of the roaring motorcycle films, this one at least involves a robbery of the Riviera Hotel casino in Las Vegas," but they were not generally convinced that these novelties made the effort of watching worthwhile: "How many more cycle films can there be without hopelessly diminishing returns? There is always room for a great one, but the motor does seem run down by now."[38] The review in the *Motion Picture Herald* saw a similar play between the old and the new: "in the endless cycle of bike films, *Hell's Angels '69* takes a sharp turn out of its genre midway through the running time."[39] The reviewer for *Box Office*

Figure 4.3 Left to right: actor Jeremy Slate, and Hells Angels Terry the Tramp and Sonny Barger in *Hell's Angels '69* (1969).

thought that whatever shortcomings the cycle as a whole had, it has "lasted longer than most industry prognosticators expected, due in no small part to the fact that many of these low-budget action programmers have more life and excitement than any number of stillborn multi-million dollar epics."[40] Michael Ross in the *Los Angeles Herald Examiner* somewhat concurred: "*Hell's Angels '69* takes the utmost trouble to find the right way to tell a very simple story. But, nevertheless, the film bristles with more raw excitement and vitality than many other pseudo-hip, semi-virtuosic cycle films."[41] "The unwashed, mangy, illiterate itinerants who straddle their bikes and roam the country, are back with us again," writes Nadine M. Edwards for the *Hollywood Citizen News*. "This time, however, their celluloid capers are less violent, far less revolting and more suspensefully orientated than in the past."[42] In total, the reviews are just as repetitive as the film they lambast for being repetitive: "Latest wheeler, another trip to tedium, limps along with silly plot, weak direction and weaker performances."[43]

Hell's Angels '69's similarity to *Ocean's 11* (1960), or some such recent caper movie, and to *Treasure of the Sierra Madre* (1948) is noted in review after review. Kevin Thomas in the *Los Angeles Times* thought the picture to be "completely preposterous, blatantly contrived and punctuated with credibility gaps big enough to race through … The first third is pretty much like any other motorcycle movie. Then it takes a *Thomas Crown Affair* (1968) twist and winds up with a *Treasure of the Sierra Madre* climax."[44] With the same cavalier attitude that *Hell's Angels '69* has to originality and its story lines, *Angel Unchained* stole from *The Magnificent Seven* (1960) the trope of outlaws defending a peasant community. This time the film was wholly produced by AIP and was conceived as the company's primary contribution to the following season's cycle of biker movies.

Angel Unchained opened in the summer of 1970, five months after Jeffrey Alladin Fiskin submitted his final draft of the screenplay (he would be retained on a week-by-week basis for rewrites until principal filming commenced on 13 April). The film returned $23,000 in its opening weekend Los Angeles run.[45] Programmed in seven Kansas theaters, playing with second-run biker movies *Born Losers* and *The Losers* (aka *Nam Angels*), it took $21,000.[46] In four Minneapolis drive-ins, it was paired with *Devil's Angels*.[47] In Ohio, the picture was shown at five "ozoners" and pulled a "lively" $15,000.[48] Teamed with *Cry of the Banshee*, *Angel Unchained* played thirty houses in the New York region and gathered $165,000.[49]

The film was shot over three weeks, with Sundays off, which was a standard AIP schedule for a programmer. A production office was set up in Superstition Inn, Apache Junction, Arizona, with the surrounding countryside providing the exteriors. Cost was pegged at $410,000 and the film came in on time and on budget. Five to six setups per day were completed, which equates to roughly six pages a day, as dictated by the tight and always demanding timetable. Fiskins's script is 112 pages long, and when broken down, it represents eighteen days of principal photography. Forty thousand feet of Eastman color stock was ordered and a running time of ninety minutes was planned, which allowed for a little under a three-to-one ratio of wasted-to-used film. *Angel Unchained* was meticulously planned and executed.

Grasping a sense of the temporary alliances, creative relationships, and business partnerships—the employment of personnel across a cycle—provides insight not

Figure 4.4 Left to right: Don Stroud, Larry Bishop, Bill McKinney play members of The Nomad motorcycle club, in *Angel Unchained* (1970).

only into filmmaking practice at this point in time but also into the process of serial production. The director Madden is the key figure straddling both *Hell's Angels '69* and *Angel Unchained*.⁵⁰ AIP clearly considered him to be a crucial part of the creative process; he not only directed *Angel Unchained* but also had a hand in the story and a producer's credit. After his period of employment with AIP, Madden moved on from directing features to working on industrial films for his own production company, which specialized in making shorts and commercials for automobile manufacturers—analogous employment that cannot be entirely poetical coincidence. His coproducer was Norman Herman, who had recently worked on AIP's *Bloody Mama*, which showcased *Angel Unchained*'s new star lead Don Stroud: a "Brandoesque performer of extreme competence."⁵¹ Bud Ekins did the bike stunts (as he had also done on *Hell's Angels '69*), and the cinematographer, Irving Lippman, had made a reputation for himself by working on fifty-six episodes of the *Monkees* TV show; he surely knew how to lens for the youth market.

Supporting actors Luke Askew and Larry Bishop had appeared in *Easy Rider* and *The Savage Seven* respectively, and the latter would make another biker movie appearance in *Chrome and Hot Leather* (1971). Bishop was the son of Rat Packer Joey Bishop, and publicity for the film makes much of this fact along with the presence of Tim Ryan, son of Robert Ryan. What was emphasized here, beyond the exploitation potential of familiar names, like Fonda and Sinatra in *The Wild Angels*, is youth. In contrast and in order to accentuate the generation gap, the casting agent used Hollywood veteran Aldo Ray as a disinterested, elderly sheriff. He was employed for a single day's filming.

The screenwriter Fiskin was a novice, but that too could be used. In publicity notes for the film he is described as "26 years young." Those same notes suggest marketing should draw attention to the film's social message: "the search for identity so apparent in so many young people throughout the world."⁵² That message was but an echo of earlier films in the cycle. *Born Losers*'s press book, for example, similarly stresses the youthfulness of the filmmakers and the movie's protest angle: "*Born Losers* was created by young people who become increasingly angry at simply standing by and watching the spreading decay at the root of society. As the condition seemed to become more prevalent, they had to do something about it. And they pulled no punches."⁵³

On the basis of the script submitted on March 31, 1970, the Motion Picture Association of America, which classifies films for exhibition, considered *Angel Unchanged* to be a potential "GP" story, but any extensive use of profanity, plus nudity and unacceptable levels of violence, could bring the film in to an "R" or "X" category. In order to attract a younger audience than was typically the case with earlier examples in the cycle, AIP worked to ensure it maintained a GP rating. *Hell's Angels '69* had received an "M" category. Though still suggestive of adult content, a reviewer noted that this represents something of a curb on the usual fare of vulgar, violent, and sexually explicit content: "One strange aspect of the film is its lack of violence and the lack of offensive language. This new restraint may puzzle audiences who may be expecting an entirely different sort of movie." He also suggests that the film does not meet "the new high standard of bike films set by ... *Easy Rider*." Dennis Hopper's film was an "R," which perhaps pushed the producers of *Hell's Angels '69* and *Angel Unchained* to be more inclusive in an appeal to a youth audience who want to see *Easy Rider* but were excluded due to its adult-only rating.[54]

The first cut of *Angel Unchained* was completed by May 20, 1970. Editing notes for amendments generally specify the need to tighten up sequences, scenes, and moments: for example, "First riding sequence is too long. Eating sequence is too long. Trim scene of hippies running." Notes from 25 May are along the same perfunctory lines, suggesting "trims and reversing cuts," alongside the comment that a "'ballad' should be used if riding shots are kept long" and, in order to maintain the GP rating, recommendations were made to cut back on explicit indicators of rape. By early June, post-production was complete and the film premiered in Minneapolis on 19 August, followed by a Los Angeles opening on 2 September.

Marketing slogans were drafted:

"His name was Angel, but he was running a devil's race"
"... playing it alone, without his Pack at his back, against the Freaks and the Straights that ruled this slaughterhouse suburb of Hell!"
"Hang loose ... when you make the slaughterhouse run"
"This is the hell run that you make all alone"
"He cut out from the pack to make his blood run alone"
"... against the straights and the freaks—and the weirdoes that rule Hell's Back Alley."[55]

The actual poster taglines were a variation on these drafts—"This is the slaughterhouse run that you make alone ... When you've cut yourself off from the pack to go flat out against the Freaks and the Straights who rule this cozy corner of Hell!" The repetition in the tags, saying the same thing differently, encapsulates the cycle's serial nature, just as surely as the repetitive titling.

Press reception was neither enthusiastic nor unduly negative, and tends to stress the film's generic and formulaic elements. "*Angel Unchained* takes itself too seriously for its own good. Ideally motorcycle flicks should be outrageous, preposterously sure of their purpose. This latest offer from AIP suffers, like its hero, from an identity crisis."[56] The film reviewer for the *Los Angeles Times* echoes those thoughts:

Like all the better bike pictures *Angel Unchained* fulfils the action requirements of its genre, yet goes on to make a social comment. The story of a Hell's Angels-type trying to drop out is pretty familiar by now, but AIP has freshened up the formula by adding hippies to the scene ... *Angel Unchained* has its awkwardnesses, and some of its plot contrivances would draw snickers from sophisticates, but on the whole it's a satisfying, pertinent effort.[57]

"Okay dual exploitation programmer ..."[58] is the best *Variety* could say of the picture.

In her account of seriality, Mayer acknowledges that popular culture is produced collectively, but she argues that such activity needs to be understood "within a larger network of cultural meaning making."[59] She is wary of assigning the dynamics of serial production to substitutes for an author, such as publishing houses, studios, readers, or fans. Across the cycle of biker movies, filmmakers formed creative alliances and partnerships, where knowledge and experience are traded, exchanged, and put to work, but they are not the sole authors of these films. In the collective process of making a film, interchangeable and standardized parts are modified, customized, by skilled workers. Like the designers and the mechanics who build custom motorcycles, these filmmakers find value in working with and modifying preconceived forms and they do so within an institutional framework that provides services and materials.

Film is an industrial art, but it is not a conveyor belt product designed to be indistinguishable from others in the run, as if each movie was struck from the same template. Discussing the issue of management and the division of labor within a studio system that is conceived as a producer of regulated narratives, Janet Staiger stresses the need to understand that this does not presume that Hollywood was an assembly line operation.[60] It was instead a "collective mode of manufacture": "Serial manufacture of a standardized product resulted in a collaborative work situation in which craftspeople jointly mass produced a great number of remarkable (and admittedly, not so remarkable) films."[61]

As represented by the biker movie, serial production carried out by middling (e.g. Crown) and large (e.g. AIP) independents was a collective mode of manufacture, but it was also distinct from other types of collaborative film production; it was not the in-house studio-defined operation that Staiger discusses that resulted in such outputs as Universal's horror pictures, MGM's Tarzan films, or Republic's Gene Autry horse operas. Division of labor is more flexible in an independent context than in any studio operation, but it is still important. Dedicated networks of specialist providers supply the products and services to filmmakers that would otherwise be beyond their resources. These networks offer significant support, for example, insurance, transport, and catering; equipment hire, such as lights, sound gear, and cameras; the processing and printing of the film stock; and the marketers, distributors, and exhibitors, who provide financing, promotion, and access to audiences.

Figures 4.5 and 4.6 *Naked Angels* (1969): cruising the neon strip in Las Vegas, the bike gang pass in front of a run of cinemas, a moment of heightened self-consciousness, especially in the refracted image with "GORE" superimposed alongside the outlaws.

Neither studio nor independent films should be conceived as if they are this season's model of car with an offering of a number of standardized, predefined configurations and specifications. Distinctiveness matters even for exploitation films, though it matters a whole lot less than it does for a mainstream film with pedigree actors, high production values, access to first-run houses, and a marketing strategy designed to sell its individuality. Nor are films such as biker movies craft objects created by artisans who work with raw materials. Neither mass-produced nor bespoke, exploitation filmmaking is instead analogous to forms of customization, where enthusiasts and highly skilled individuals work together in temporary creative alliances to reconfigure stock parts into a novel whole. Similarly, networked, exploitation filmmakers assembled biker movies not to the order of a fixed preconceived ideal but to a norm that, at a superficial or stylistic level, is open to modification.

Automobile customizers, like exploitation filmmakers, work within prescribed limitations—a custom motorbike still needs to be rideable and an outlaw biker movie still needs to tell its story. Move too far away from a given framework and you have a pile of unconnected parts. Planning is paramount; little is left to chance. During assembly elements can be modified, even individualized, but what's possible will be constrained by time, materials, skill, budget, and convention. The end result should promote the subject's unique features, but the framework and alignment of parts will in effect differ little from other examples. A movie's component parts are the conventions drawn on to produce sequences such as chases or fights. These conventions may be as fixed in their form and function as a V-twin engine, unsusceptible to a radical overhaul, but adaptable to the surrounding parts that can be modified, like a fuel tank, which is open to surface decoration, resizing, and shaping so long as it can still contain liquid and be fitted to the bike and perform its key function.

Though the mode of production in 1960s and 1970s exploitation movies emulates some aspects of earlier forms of low-budget, non-studio filmmaking, such as that documented by Eric Schaefer, it also differs in a number of important ways. Schaefer notes that the "classic era" exploitation film—1919–1959—can be distinguished from the dominant, studio, model of production in terms of labor and financing, but also through four unique aspects: recycling, padding, square-ups, and hot and cold versions.[62]

In biker movies content is recycled but there are few, if any, instances of film elements being reused from earlier productions, nor is stock imagery from specialist film libraries much on view. Around the more spectacular action-oriented scenes significant padding is apparent, most notably in the use of liberal footage of motorcycles moving languorously through vast empty landscapes, though here "padding" might be seen as an attraction in and of itself, rather than something to be endured. The choice of landscapes also ensures that the sequences become in their own way spectacular, reinforced through the syncing of a rock soundtrack. Didion wrote that many of the biker films are "extraordinarily beautiful in their instinct for the real look of the American West, for the faded banners fluttering over abandoned gas stations and the bleached streets of desert towns."[63] There are no square-ups—hypocritical apologies or excuses, a moral message to justify prurient imagery; the biker film instead revels in a coarse amorality, in a disruptive, antisocial, animalist behavior. Outside a nominal number of films, title variations were not in circulation at any given moment, at least not until these films found new audiences through their distribution on VHS tape. Neither on original nor subsequent release were radically distinct censored or uncensored versions, hot or cold iterations as Schaefer calls them, put into circulation.

The social problem, sex, and titillation movies that Schaefer so valuably covers were not conceived as being part of a production cycle. With the biker movie, cyclicality and seriality are production principles. The film cycles of the 1960s and 1970s are distinctive in their strategy of reiteration that pertains not just to their content and form but also to their production, circulation, and consumption. There was undoubtedly a financial incentive behind this strategy because, for the cycle's producers, the biker movie held the allure of realizing profits that far exceed the returns that earlier exploitation filmmakers could have ever dreamed of achieving.

When Joan Didion describes the biker movie as a "perfect Rorschach of its audience," she means that it amply delineates the inchoate desire, frustration, and resentment of its youthful viewers—filmgoers she defines as drive-in regulars who "majored in shop and worked in gas stations and later held them up." They are the children of "'hill' stock," who hold an "obscure grudge" against the world. "It is," she writes, "in the commercial cultivation of this grudge that bike movies reveal their rather spellbinding venality." As true as this might be, and I do not doubt for a moment that the core audience for these films were working-class youth, even if I find her description of them demeaning, the correspondence between how the movies are fabricated, distributed, sold, and consumed and the class, age, employment, leisure activities, and interests of its audience expresses something far more interesting than their venality.

Didion's particular disdain for, and fear of, the audience is something shared by critics writing for trade and popular press alike. They consider the cycle of motorcycle films as essentially illegitimate and its audience as unruly: "At best, *Cycle Savages* is a film without talent, a credible story line, subject matter of interest, or anything else which might save it from being simply a horrible film. It might do well in a drive-in situation where most people don't watch the film anyway."[64] The view of the drive-in audience and of the bikers portrayed in the films they are watching (or not watching as the case may be) is that of a young, easily distracted, motley crew of undereducated, disengaged, narcissistic malcontents. No one seems to be gainfully employed, yet all seem to have disposable income. They are mobile but loop only in circles without direction or ambition, so too the movies and their characters:

> At their low-budget best, a couple of the earlier motorcycle flicks had a raw, awkward vitality which the budget limitations enhanced rather than defeated. They gave you some insights into what made some basically sad cats go. If there were big chunks of sex and violence, there were also glimpses of loneliness, alienation, a real enough, if misplaced idealism, the forlorn use of speed and daring as sexual substitute.[65]

Youthful bravado, however, soon becomes boorish and boring, tedious in its repetitions, just as with the films themselves:

> *Cycle Savages* comes at end of Motorcycle Series … Boldly limping into the theatres after the motorcycle craze has all but been put to bed. Trundling along with near flat tires to a dispersed box office line sliced even thinner with its R rating … an unintentional "parody of the motorcycle breed."[66]

Satan's Sadists and *Hell's Bloody Devils* were double-billed during their initial theatrical run, and as such they were reviewed as a pair. Neither thrilled the critics: "It is amateur night by professional money-makers, with these two films which look and smell alike, have been produced and directed by the same person (Al Adamson) and even have overlapping in the cast … Both films are absolutely unmitigated garbage."[67] Interchangeable and thereby indistinguishable, made for profit by inept personnel, both in front of the camera and behind the scenes, who travel between productions and thereby further ensure an undifferentiated product, biker films are trash—devoid of any appreciable cultural capital. While the uniqueness of individual films and the professionalism of the filmmakers can be debated, the films' lowly cultural status is unarguable, not least because they were conceived as products to be sold on their vulgar, uncouth, and brutish appeal. The biker film was assembled in order to offend, that is, to appeal to a youth audience because it provoked their elders and betters. Unlike the products of the classic Hollywood studio system, the biker film was rarely imagined as being inclusive and universal in its appeal; quite the opposite.

Like the hot rod film before it, the biker film was produced to meet the needs of a specific market. It was not chance, serendipity, or simple temporal simultaneity that took these films about mobile youths into drive-ins; they were expressly designed to circulate within economic border regions and to move through rundown inner-city theaters and edgeland open-air theaters.[68] Biker pictures were shown in cinemas that require a steady flow of product to satisfy their habitual patrons, who pay for a type of film that serves their purposes. In so much, then, the films provide an uncertain reflection of their primary consumers, not because characters and audience are equally venal, but because the youthful viewers treat movies with the same lack of respect an outlaw biker in the film shows to law enforcement figures or bourgeois citizens. The disorderly and distracted audience refuse an authoritarian appeal to be fixated on and respectful toward the projected images and amplified sounds. They turn, as their want demands, toward their companions, to look at themselves, ignoring the screen, which is even then displaying unruly motorcyclists, equally self-absorbed.

In defining seriality, Mayer placed her emphasis on reconfiguration rather than on novelty, and suggests that the devaluing of originality is one reason for the form's taint of illegitimacy: "It is no accident that the lexicon of the serial mode in popular culture is replete with such terms as sprawl, growth, dispersion, and excrescence rather than exclusively relying on associations of linear unravelling, careful design, or microstructural complexity."[69] Like its featured characters, the biker film can be said to revel in a lack of cultivation, in low pleasure, and in disrespect toward figures of authority. As a film genre with an uncertain lineage, commentators and reviewers alike responded to it as if it were an unloved stepchild, symptomatic, I would argue, not of the nation's lost youth as Didion thought, but of an atrophied Hollywood production system that had long lost the ability to regulate and promulgate itself.

Notes

1. Joan Didion, "Nine Bike Movies in Seven *Vroom!* Days," *Life* 68:17 (May 8, 1970), 4.
2. Ibid.
3. Ibid.
4. Ruth Mayer, *Serial Fu Manchu: The Chinese Supervillain and the Spread of Yellow Peril Ideology* (Philadelphia: Temple University Press, 2014), 11.
5. Ibid., 12.
6. Rudmer Canjels, *Distributing Silent Film Serials: Local Practices, Changing Forms, Cultural Transformation* (New York: Routledge, 2011), 7.
7. For example, William Murray, "Hell's Angels: Outlaw Motorcycle Club in California," *Saturday Evening Post* (November 20, 1965), 37–40; Hunter S. Thompson, "The Motorcycle Gangs: Losers and Outsiders," *The Nation* (May 17, 1965), 521–526; "Hell's Angels Called Threat on Wheels" *Los Angeles Times* (March 16, 1965), 1–2; "California Takes Steps to Curb Terrorism of Ruffian Cyclists," *New York Times* (March 16, 1965), 15.
8. Umberto Eco, *The Limits of Interpretation* (Bloomington: University of Indiana Press, 1994), 84, 90.
9. Kevin Thomas, "Namath in Debut as Cyclist," *Los Angeles Times* (October 16, 1970), E1.
10. Transcribed from *Angel Unchained* screenplay. Margaret Herrick Library special collection
11. Charles Champlin, "*Glory Stompers* and *Teen* Screen," *Los Angeles Times* (June 5, 1968), C7.
12. Robert B. Frederick, "Action Credo of Frazer, Kennis: Eye on Youth," *Variety* (September 17, 1969), 3, 20.
13. "*Wild* Producer Roger Corman Called in Senate Juve Delinquency Probe," *Daily Variety* 135:16 (March 27, 1967), 1, 4.
14. "From Sand in Bikini to Sand in Machinery: AIP on 'Protest' Kick," *Variety* 243:3 (June 8, 1966), 4.
15. Bob Thomas, "Tide Running Out for Beach Films, In for Protest Movies," *Los Angeles Times* (February 12, 1966), B7.
16. Howard R. Cohen papers, Margaret Herrick Library.
17. "Swastika-Symbols Help?" *Variety* 246:1 (February 22, 1967), 29.
18. "Quick Marketing of AIP's *Devil's Angels*," *Variety* 246:6 (March 29, 1967), 21.
19. Review, *Daily Variety* 132:22 (July 6, 1966), 3.
20. *Los Angeles Times* (September 29, 1966), *Wild Angels* cutting file, Margaret Herrick Library.
21. *Los Angeles Herald Examiner* (September 30, 1966), *Wild Angels* cutting file, Margaret Herrick Library.
22. *The Motion Picture Herald* (July 6, 1966), *Wild Angels* cutting file, Margaret Herrick Library.

23. *Hollywood Reporter* (July 6, 1966), *Wild Angels* cutting file, Margaret Herrick Library.
24. *Hollywood Citizen News* (September 1, 1966), *Wild Angels* cutting file, Margaret Herrick Library.
25. "SR Goes to the Movies: A Director Strikes Back," *Saturday Review* (September 10, 1966), *Wild Angels* cutting file, Margaret Herrick Library.
26. Kevin Thomas, "Motorcycles Return in *Devil's Angels*," *Los Angeles Times* (June 7, 1967), F17.
27. Post-1967 biker movies tended to feature leaden rock and blues, though *Run, Angel, Run!* has an immaculate contribution from Tammy Wynette. Country music, bikes, and leather never sounded and looked so right.
28. For an account of Western costume and authenticity, see Peter Stanfield, *The Cool and the Crazy: Pop Fifties Cinema* (New Brunswick: Rutgers University Press, 2015), 162–187.
29. *The Glory Stompers*—undated script, pp. 1–2, Margaret Herrick Library special collection.
30. Ibid., 6.
31. "Hell's Angels on Wheels," *Daily Variety* 136:1 (June 6, 1967), 3.
32. For a discussion of AIP and other companies' sensational marketing of earlier film cycles, see the chapter on hot rod movies, "Intent to Speed," in Stanfield, *The Cool and the Crazy*, 112–134.
33. Archer Winsten, *New York Post* review (August 29, 1966), *Wild Angels* cutting file, Margaret Herrick Library.
34. *Hollywood Citizen News* (September 16, 1966), *Wild Angels* cutting file, Margaret Herrick Library.
35. Box-office data are taken from AIP marketing materials for *Hell's Angels '69* cutting file, Margaret Herrick Library.
36. The Hells Angels had previously received screen credit in *The Wild Angels* and *Hell's Angels on Wheels*.
37. Stern's deal with AIP is outlined in *Variety* (January 17, 1971), 3, 27.
38. *Cue* (September 20, 1969), *Hell's Angels '69* cutting file, Margaret Herrick Library.
39. *The Motion Picture Herald* (August 13, 1969), *Hell's Angels '69* cutting file, Margaret Herrick Library.
40. *Box Office* (August 18, 1969), *Hell's Angels '69* cutting file, Margaret Herrick Library.
41. Michael Ross, *Los Angeles Herald Examiner* (August 15, 1969), *Hell's Angels '69* cutting file, Margaret Herrick Library.
42. *Hollywood Citizen News* (August 15, 1969), *Hell's Angels '69* cutting file, Margaret Herrick Library.
43. Review: "Hell's Angels '69", *Daily Variety* 144:37 (July 29, 1969), 3.
44. Kevin Thomas, *Los Angeles Times* (August 15, 1969), *Hell's Angels '69* cutting file, Margaret Herrick Library.
45. *Variety* (September 9, 1970), 9.
46. *Variety* (September 16, 1970), 10.
47. *Variety* (August 26, 1970), 14.
48. *Variety* (September 2, 1970), 28.
49. *Variety* (December 23, 1970), 10.
50. The cycle's key figures are the producer Joe Soloman (six films), the actor Adam Roarke (four films), the actor/director Jack Starrett (six films), the cinematographer Laszlo Kovacs (five including *Easy Rider*), the music soundtrack Davie Allan (five

films), Mike Curb, the soundtrack and producer (six films), and the character actor Robert Tessier (six films), but these, and other, individual contributions need to be seen in the context of the fact that around half the films in the cycle were produced and distributed by three companies and one quarter by a single firm: Crown International (five films), Fanfare Film Productions (six films), and American International Pictures (twelve films).

51. "*Angel Unchained* Stars Hard-hitting Newcomers," *Entertainment Today* (September 2, 1970), 7.
52. *Angel Unchained* materials, Margaret Herrick Library special collection.
53. *Born Losers* press book, Margaret Herrick Library special collection.
54. *Motion Picture Examiner* (August 27, 1969), *Angel Unchained* cutting file, Margaret Herrick Library.
55. James Raker papers, Margaret Herrick Library special collection.
56. Bridget Byrne, *Angel Unchained* review, *Los Angeles Herald Examiner* (September 4, 1970), *Angel Unchained* cutting file, Margaret Herrick Library.
57. *Los Angeles Times* (September 4, 1970), *Angel Unchained* cutting file, Margaret Herrick Library.
58. *Angel Unchained* review, *Variety* (August 19, 1970), 16.
59. Mayer, *Serial Fu Manchu*, 12.
60. David Bordwell, Janet Staiger, and Kristin Thompson, *The Classical Hollywood Cinema: Film Style & Mode of Production to 1960* (London: Routledge & Kegan Paul, 1985), 82–83.
61. Ibid., 329.
62. Eric Schaefer, "*Bold! Daring! Shocking! True!*" *A History of Exploitation films, 1919–1959* (Durham: Duke University Press, 1999), 42–95.
63. Didion, "Nine Bike Movies," 4.
64. *Film TV Daily* (May 7, 1970), cutting file, Margaret Herrick Library.
65. Champlin, "*Glory Stompers* and *Teen* Screen."
66. *Hollywood Reporter* (May 21, 1970), cutting file, Margaret Herrick Library.
67. Donald J. Mayerson, *Cue* (January 23, 1970), cutting file, Margaret Herrick Library.
68. In Stanfield (*The Cool and the Crazy*) the correspondence between the content and form of the hot rod movie and the primary venue for its exhibition, the drive-in, is examined and explained. This was no idle link.
69. Mayer, *Serial Fu Manchu*, 7.

5

"The Smashing, Crashing, Pileup of the Century": The Carsploitation Film

Robert J. Read

The term "carsploitation," like other subgenres that fall within the parameters of the grindhouse mythos—such as blaxploitation, nunsploitation, nazisploitation, Canuxploitation, and Ozploitation—denotes a body of cinematic production organized around a unifying theme or a national cinema within the context of exploitation film production. In its broadest sense, "carsploitation" might represent any film in which an automobile is central to the narrative.[1] This catchall term could account for a wide variety of disparate films and genres, including stock car racing films: *Thunder in Carolina* (Paul Hemlick, 1960) and *Fireball 500* (William Asher, 1966); drag racing films: *Dragstrip Riot* (David Bradley, 1958) and *Fast Company* (David Cronenberg, 1979); and track racing films: *Roadracers* (Arthur Swerdloff, 1958) and *Pit Stop* (Jack Hill, 1969). The term also extends to include youth culture films about hot rods, juvenile delinquents, and cruising the streets: *The Choppers* (Leigh Jason, 1961), *Supervan* (Lamar Card, 1977), *The FJ Holden* (Michael Thornhill, 1977), and *Van Nuys Blvd.* (William Sachs, 1979); as well as major Hollywood auto-oriented films like *Two-Lane Blacktop* (Monte Hellman, 1971), *America Graffiti* (George Lucas, 1973), and *Corvette Summer* (Matthew Robbins, 1978). The elasticity of carsploitation also includes films that are otherwise non-car narratives, but include break-neck car chase action sequences, such as crime films: *Bullitt* (Peter Yates, 1968) and *The Master Touch* (*Un uomo da rispettare*) (Michele Lupo, 1972); and comedies: *What's Up, Doc?* (Peter Bogdanovich, 1972) and *Freebie and the Bean* (Richard Rush, 1974); as well as such extreme examples of automotive carnage as the musical *The Blues Brothers* (John Landis, 1980) and the dystopian thriller *The Road Warrior* (George Miller, 1981); however, despite their emphasis on car culture, car chases, and car crashes, these various car films are peripheral to the carsploitation cycle discussed in this chapter.[2]

Unlike other car-oriented films, the cycle of carsploitation films emerged in the mid-1970s when low-budget exploitation film was undergoing a process of "unprecedented mainstreaming."[3] Low-budget independent film producers were not only benefiting from wider exhibition potential, but they also began to explore new film cycles in relation to greater social events. As Peter Stanfield has outlined, film cycles rise and fall in accordance with topical social issues and popular trends. As a form of cinematic production, film cycles are organized by associations made between the serial production of movies and the public sphere; therefore, the historical analysis of a film cycle must consider that "contiguous events and activities inside and outside the institutions of filmmaking form film cycles," and a descriptive analysis of a cycle must be understood through its relationship to the topical. The topicality of a film cycle is, however, difficult to determine; one determinant is to examine "the incorporation of everyday objects into the mise-en-scene."[4] The topicality of the carsploitation film is not simply the car, the chase, or the crash but a combination of shifts in film production and exhibition; the changing relationship between the American consumer and the production of automobiles; and the astounding, gratuitous destruction of cars—not just the principle vehicles of a car chase but the wholesale destruction of every possible car that can be destroyed within a film's budget. Thus, the topicality of carsploitation is situated within the events of the period and represented through the excessive demolition of automobiles as pure destructive sensation. As the hyperbolic rhetoric of the trailer for *Cannonball* (Paul Bartel, 1976) stridently declared: "It's the smashing, crashing, pile up of the century!" (Figure 5.1)

The carsploitation cycle was the result of two distinct trends inside and outside the filmmaking institutions of the exploitation film industry. In the mid-1970s, many small-scale independent film producers began to move outside of Hollywood in order to take advantage of regional film production opportunities. Many exploitation film productions were relocated to various regions across the United States, primarily in the South, Southwest, and Midwest, and to communities immediately outside the Los Angeles city limits. These independent productions benefited greatly from various incentives, including tax cuts, supportive local governments, and local financial backing, as well as production resources, technicians, local actors, bit players, and wide-open landscapes.

Figure 5.1 The pile up of the century: *Cannonball* (1976).

In a 1977 article the *New York Times* noted that "one of the more interesting phenomena in recent years has been the survival of the low-budget program picture and its transformation, almost accidentally, into something that might be classified as the regional film":

> There are as many different regional films as there are regions, but because the vast majority of them are produced in the south, future anthropologists studying these movies of the 1970s, could well get the idea that everything outside New York City and Los Angeles was redneck country inhabited by corrupt sheriffs and inhabited by repressed middle-age parents of hell-raising teen-age children who left their automobiles from time to time to sleep and eat and sometimes to make love.[5]

The article discusses many regional exploitation films such as *Walking Tall* (Phil Karlson, 1973), *Macon County Line* (Richard Compton, 1974), *The Great Texas Dynamite Chase* (Michael Pressman, 1976), *Grizzly* (William Girdler, 1976), and *Jackson County Jail* (Michael Miller, 1976). "Though these locales are easily recognized, they are often disconnected to any plot point as the denatured studio setting of the B-films of the 1930s and 1940s," further noting that Georgia, one of the busier states, promised technical and financial cooperation.[6] Thus, the move of independent film producers to regional film production was financially motivated through the subsidizing of film production by local financiers and state tax incentives to lower production costs.

Beyond these financial incentives, the move to regional film production was also linked to exhibition and audience. Although low-budget independently produced films made the low-end grindhouse exhibition circuits of big cities, their largest exhibition in the United States was in the drive-ins—the open-air grind house equivalents of the South and Southwest—precisely where these films were shot. "They are the kinds of movies that do best in drive-ins," stated the *Times*, which wondered if there is "some kind of automatic association between the movie and the drive-in setting that enhances the action on the screen; [s]ince 90 percent of the action in these films has to do with one automobile's pursuit of another."[7]

More than just teens sitting in cars watching teens sitting in cars, these exploitation films incorporated the relationship of regionalism, audience, and automobile. Vincent Canby of the *New York Times* called this trend "country movies":

> They are movies supported—almost exclusively—by people who live in the rural South, Southwest, and Middle West, people who see most of their movies in drive-ins, and respond, I suspect, to the non-stop action (which is often just movement), to the colorful heightened vulgarity of the language and who feel most at home in the country movie's principle setting: the automobile.[8]

The growing mid-1970s trend for "country movies" played upon many issues and stereotypes of everyday life in the South and Southwest, including regional vernacular and slang, rural poverty, moonshine production, local criminality, government corruption, and most importantly car culture.

Noting the standardization of these "country" films, Canby states: "They raced down the road in a souped-up automobile following a macadam trail that is eventually revealed to be a figure eight. Speed, not space, is the medium. The kids land back where they started." Moreover, "for reason one can only speculate on, audiences respond to this particular kind of hugely romantic space-age pessimism."[9] In reference to *Dirty Mary, Crazy Larry* (John Hough, 1974), the *Times* article questions, "Do the Saturday night patrons at a rural Texas drive-in watch characters like Dirty Mary and Crazy Larry burn up at the end of a movie and think how tragic it is? Do they take it with a grain of salt? Do they simply enjoy all the running around in cars and wish their lives were as exciting?"[10] Although the *New York Times* critics may have pondered the relationship between the audience and the "space-age pessimism" and whether or not films like *Dirty Mary, Crazy Larry* are indeed tragic, the volume of carsploitation films produced throughout the cycle suggests that it was the "running around" and the pleasure of massive automotive carnage that appealed to audiences.

Produced independently under the banner of Academy Pictures Corporation with financing and distribution provided by Twentieth Century Fox, *Dirty Mary, Crazy Larry* employed many of the elements of regional film production and "country films." Larry the driver (Peter Fonda) and Deke the mechanic (Adam Rourke) are two failed stock car racers who attempt to regain entry to the race circuit with money from a grocery store robbery. Unfortunately their plan goes awry, partly because of the appearance of Dirty Mary (Susan George) and partly because of a relentless police pursuit executed by the ruthless, obsessive, and vulgar state police detective (Vic Morrow). After the robbery, the hapless trio escape in a drab everyday Chevrolet sedan, souped up by Deke, but the Chevy is quickly replaced with a faster getaway car: a limelight yellow 1969 Dodge Charger R/T. Once the miscreants switch to the muscle car—a car considered so fast that no one can catch them—the film begins its climactic car chase. The Charger was intended to give the trio the horsepower needed to outrun any police car; however, its appearance only escalates the situations as the police respond with helicopter surveillance and an untried, unfinished, high-powered police interceptor. As the pursuit escalates, the open road becomes a confusing maze, but escape is still at hand. The police interceptor collides with another motorist and the helicopter runs out of fuel. The trio get their chance to "bust out" and make their way to freedom. But as the Charger speeds around the next bend in the road, it collides head-on with a freight train. The car crumples and explodes, enveloping them, and the end credits roll over the tragic image of the burning wreckage (Figure 5.2).

Dirty Mary, Crazy Larry exemplified the move of small-scale independent film producers to regional film production. Although the *New York Times* critics assumed the film was shot somewhere in the South, the exact location of the story is never disclosed. The film employs many of the characteristics of Canby's "country films," including the endless rural landscape, the omnipresence of law enforcement complete with southern drawls, and most importantly the fixation on car culture. Larry and Deke are purposefully depicted as driver and mechanic, which not only explains their exceptional automotive skills but also immediately creates associations with drive-in audiences and car culture. But the film, like many other "country films," was actually

Figure 5.2 The burning Charger: *Dirty Mary, Crazy Larry* (1974).

shot in the small towns, farmyards, country roads, and non-descript state highways of Southern California.[11]

Regional film production provided independent producers with more than just financial incentives. It also provided cooperation with local and state authorities, natural lighting (eliminating the need for costly studio shooting), and vast open landscapes for car chases. Like *Dirty Mary, Crazy Larry*, many carsploitation films were shot outside the Los Angeles area including *Cannonball*, *Moving Violation* (Charles S. Dubin, 1976), *Eat My Dust* (Charles B. Griffith, 1976), *Grand Theft Auto* (Ron Howard, 1977), *Double Nickels* (Jack Vacek, 1979), and *Smokey and the Hot Wire Gang* (Anthony Cardoza, 1979). These films took advantage of the countryside to create a generic "country" landscape with endless roadways, highways, and freeways. For example, the producer/director H.B. Halicki completely avoided Hollywood institutions and shot *Gone in 60 Seconds* (1974) on city streets and freeways with permission granted by the cities and police departments of Long Beach, Torrance, Carson, and Redondo Beach, along with the California Highway Patrol, the Los Angeles Police Department, the L.A. County Sheriff's Department, and the L.A. County Fire Department.[12]

But many other carsploitation films were actually shot in various regions throughout the United States in order to exploit their southern "country" stereotypes of redneck sheriffs, moonshine running, and car culture: *The Great Lester Boggs* (Harry Z. Thomason, 1974), later retitled *Redneck County*, was shot entirely in Arkansas; *Thunder and Lightning* (Corey Allen, 1977) was filmed in Florida; and *The Georgia Peaches* (Daniel Haller, 1980), despite the title, was filmed in South Carolina. The best example of independent film production taking advantage of its regional production was *The Polk County Pot Plane* (Jim West, 1977).[13] The film was shot entirely in Georgia and took full advantage of its setting by sensationalizing local news headlines. On August 4, 1975, a cargo plane loaded with drugs landed on a runway bulldozed out of the trees atop of Treat Mountain in Polk County, Georgia. The smugglers were eventually arrested and 3,000 pounds of marihuana and 74 ½ pounds of hashish were confiscated. The abandoned plane became a local tourist attraction, and, in order to capitalize on its infamy, Jim West, a former State Representative, pilot, and real-estate investor, purchased Treat Mountain and the stranded plane. West, who had no previous experience in the film business, thought the story had "the ingredients for a spectacular motion picture." He hired a film crew and locals to act in the film including the county sheriff and himself as the pot plane pilot. Although his intention was to produce a film about daredevil drug smugglers, *The Polk County Pot Plane* became little more than three extended car chases—three spectacularly thrilling and insanely destructive car chases. The film was enormously popular in drive-ins, especially in Georgia.[14]

The regional imagery of *Dirty Mary, Crazy Larry* and *The Polk County Pot Place* placed them within the trend toward "country films," but these films were much less interested in presenting an authentic regional image as they were preoccupied with speed and destruction. As Vincent Canby stated of *Dirty Mary, Crazy Larry*, "at least half of [the film] is devoted to semi-spectacular examples of trick driving and multi-vehicle smash-ups"[15]—a point echoed by the review in the *Independent Film Journal*:

> The virtues of *Dirty Mary Crazy Larry* lie almost entirely with its elaborate chase-sequence, a doozie of an effort taking more than half the film's running time and involving no more than 18 ingeniously demolished cars and a variety of well-played stunts.[16]

The *Journal* also described the film as the "ultimate made-for-drive-in movie," noting that it proved exploitable in Western and Midwest areas where stock car racing has the status that surfing once did on the West Coast. There is no doubt that the film's producers were well aware of their market and, despite its bleak ending, *Dirty Mary, Crazy Larry* was hugely successful with an estimated twelve-million-dollar profit.[17]

Concurrent with the trend toward regional film production, American car culture was undergoing a significant historical shift. Concerns over gas prices and automotive safety brought government intervention and a rapid reengineering of American cars from large powerful "gas-guzzlers" to compact fuel-efficient "econobox" cars. This shift resulted in the decreasing commodity value of older outmoded cars as consumers quickly turned toward new economy models. The loss of commodity value of older, less-efficient cars was a boon for low-budget film producers. Once valuable automobiles were now outmoded and unwanted and, most importantly, could be purchased cheaply for the sole purpose of destruction. Unlike earlier car chase action sequences in which a car could be damaged and destroyed as a result of a thrilling chase, the now-affordable spectacle of the destruction of cars could become the central focus of a film's action. As Canby noted of *Dirty Mary, Crazy Larry*, there is a point in which the audience becomes "perfectly aware that the actors have been replaced with stuntmen."[18] Indeed, the narrative gives way to the extended car chase and the characters fade into the background as speed and destruction monopolize the remainder of the film.

The limelight yellow 1969 Dodge Charger was an immediately recognizable icon of the muscle car period, which was initiated in the mid-1960s, when American automobile manufacturers began placing oversized, high-performance engines into everyday mid-size automobiles. The muscle car was, however, largely an innovation of marketing, as automobile manufacturers offered American drivers a seemingly unlimited combination of performance options and decorative badging. These nearly infinite combinations created a new sense of automotive individuality that drove its popularity and fashioned the muscle car's iconic cultural status. As automotive historian David Gartman has noted:

> What was new about the muscle car was not its horsepower but its individuality—it was a new category of car that advertised its difference from run-of-the-mill models. Not social superiority but being different—just like everyone else—was the appeal.[19]

The muscle car further reinforced its mythology of individualism by offering consumers the opportunity to customize their own cars by choosing their own performance options. "By cultivating connotations of difference and defiance, muscle cars sought blatantly to commodify the youthful rebellion against [assembly-line uniformity of] Fordism," thus the production of the muscle car was able to provide consumers with a sense of power, individuality, and rebellion. By the late 1960s, the muscle car became a symbol of individual freedom and social power. But as Gartman explained, "the American rebellion had surged over the containing walls of consumerism and begun to challenge the core of Fordist institutions." The muscle car era, by the early 1970s, had become a "bad trip" and "it was quietly cancelled as the country moved into the sobering 1970s."[20]

In 1973, the Organization of Petroleum Exporting Countries (OPEC) began an embargo on the exportation of oil to Western countries. The resulting oil crisis created fear among consumers as rising prices and gas shortages threatened the general economic system. At the same time, and driven by Ralph Nader's very public condemnation of the American automobile industry, consumer advocacy groups began raising issues over automotive safety.[21] The automobile became the focus of a great deal of social discontent with American consumers. The unsafe, inefficient car became the symbol of all that was wrong with American consumerism and the subject of mounting pressure for "the government to mandate changes in Detroit's dinosaurs." In 1974, the National Maximum Speed Law was passed in the United States limiting highway speed to fifty-five miles per hour; this was followed by further legislation for five-mile-an-hour safety bumpers (1974), the regulation of fuel economy (1975), and mandatory seat belt legislation (1984). Within a few brief years, the American consumption of automobiles had changed from that of individual choice and social rebellion to that of concerns over well-being and efficiency, and the "socially responsible" consumption of car commodities.[22] Outcries for safety and economy brought a massive public intervention that culminated in a shift within "America's automotive consciousness away from the fantastic dreams of escape and individuality towards the sober reality of efficiency and functionality."[23] The American automotive industry began retooling its automotive production to create the appearance of European-copied fuel efficiency and pseudo-functionalism.[24] In 1973, Ford discontinued production of the original Mustang, and, in 1974, Chrysler stopped production of the original Dodge Charger, thus marking the end of the muscle car era.

The choice of cars represented within the carsploitation film was not a critical statement with regard to the relationship between consumers and the automotive industry, nor was it intended to mark the demise of the muscle car. But these films did incorporate these social changes into the mise-en-scène by representing the destruction of the everyday objects of mass-produced and mass-marketed cars. The destruction of large quantities of pre-1974 cars became the hallmark of the carsploitation film that featured dozens of crashes and collisions though extended chases and crash sequences, with a particular emphasis on outmoded muscle cars: *Gone in 60 Seconds* (H.B. Halicki, 1974) featured a 1972 Ford Mustang Mach II; *Cannon Ball* (Paul Bartel, 1976) featured a 1971 Pontiac Trans Am, a 1967 Ford Mustang, and 1969 Dodge Charger; both *Polk County Pot Plane* and *Crash!* (Charles Band, 1976) featured late 1960s Camaros; *Speed Trap* (Earl Bellamy, 1977) featured a Mark II Jensen Interceptor; and *Hi-Riders* (Greydon Clark, 1978), which was essentially a biker film with muscle cars replacing motorcycles, featured a fleet of aging muscle cars.

Similarly, police vehicles were also made up of an array of older decommissioned Dodge, Plymouth, and Ford sedans, built between 1967 and 1974—with *Moving Violation* having the unique distinction of destroying a fleet of obsolete 1974 AMC Ambassadors—bought cheaply at surplus auctions (Figure 5.3). These sacrificial vehicles were not only cheap to obtain but they also came equipped with high-powered pursuit engines capable of keeping up with the muscle cars as well as being sturdy enough to be used in dangerous stunts and crashes. In addition to these featured chase cars, the carsploitation film also relied heavily on the availability of cheap outmoded cars of 1950s and 1960s vintage for the sole purpose of roadside destruction. For the "pile-up of the century" featured in *Cannonball*, the filmmakers accumulated a dozen or so mid-1960s cars to crash and burn in an orgy of destruction, and H.B. Halicki bought ninety-three used cars, decommissioned police cars, and a garbage truck for a total cost of $160,000 to destroy in *Gone in 60 Seconds*.[25]

The car stunts, crashes, and demolitions of the carsploitation film were entirely real: real cars, real speed, and real danger. There were no camera tricks or optical effects to augment stunts and heighten the thrills. For better-financed, independent productions, all of the destruction was performed by professional stunt drivers. This was true of *Eat My Dust* and *Grand Theft Auto*, both of which used the professional drivers of the Joie Chitwood automotive thrill show to perform elaborate stunts and destruction. But for many carsploitation films, the stunts were performed by non-professional stunt performers. In the closing credits of *The Polk County Pot Plane*, for instance, the producers proudly boast that "no stunt men were used in this film," and H.B. Halicki performed all of his own driving stunts for *Gone in 60 Seconds* and his later films. The filming of these car stunts and crashes was incredibly dangerous and sometimes fatal. While filming *Gone in 60 Seconds*, there were several accidents, including an unintended collision with a lamppost, the near miss of supporting players, the accidental damaging of several brand new Cadillacs, and Halicki receiving a spinal injury during the final jump. Tragically, while filming *Hi-Riders*, stunt coordinator Vic Rivers was killed when his jump in an old pickup truck fell short of its landing. All of these mishaps and Rivers' ill-fated jump are visible in the films.

Despite the spectacular stunt work and the massive automotive carnage, destruction in the carsploitation films was presented as comedy. The *Independent Film Journal* review of *Dirty Mary, Crazy Larry* described the numerous collisions as "an assortment of amusing demolitions."[26] As the film historian Eileen Bowser has noted, the relationship between automobiles and comedy can be traced back to the origins of cinema, but the comedic potential found in the this relationship was an essential element of slapstick:

> These [slapstick] comedies generally show man defeated by the machine because he doesn't understand how it works or because he doesn't know how to handle the frightening new power and freedom of movement. Yet he survives after all because he is never really injured, even when the vehicle runs him over or blows him to pieces.[27]

The carsploitation cycle works within a similar relationship of human, machine, and survivability. Within the carsploitation film, the local police force, corrupt or not, is equipped with overwhelming workforce, surveillance, and seemingly endless supply of old patrol cars, but despite this enormous show of force, they are unable to apprehend the outlaw driver of the outmoded muscle car. Police cars skid off the road, collide with other cars, splash into bodies of water, and are unceremoniously decapitated as car roofs are sheared off. But despite the life-threatening destruction, the drivers always emerge physically unharmed; *Moving Violation* even features the use of an experimental airbag as a police car is driven head-on into a brick wall. The representation of the demolition of cars as comedy, rather than the result of reckless endangerment, served many purposes, including diminishing the futility of the chases and the pessimism of fiery conclusions.

The emphasis on harmless comedy also earned a number of carsploitation films a PG rating—unlike most exploitation films that were rated as R or X for adult audiences—that allowed for wider exhibition potential and later television sales. The violence, mayhem, and destruction of carsploitation were presented in such an innocuous manner that in his review of *Thunder and Lightning*, Canby likened it to Bugs Bunny cartoons stating that the "buoyantly slapdash comedy" of the film becomes a "benignly peaceful experience."[28] The repetitive destruction of police car after police car echoes the relationship between human and machine presented in slapstick, but the comedic destruction of authority also becomes the focus of the humorous indignity. As Rob King argues, within slapstick the challenge to class difference appealed to the working-class poor of early cinema audiences.[29] Similarly, within carsploitation, the humorous

Figure 5.3 The decapitation of an AMC Ambassador in *Moving Violation* (1976).

destruction of police cars and the humiliation of their officers, who safely emerge from their wrecks, were designed to appeal to younger audiences and their rebellious fantasies of upending authority figures.

As the high-speed impacts and amusing demolitions motivated by pursuit and escape became increasingly transformed into staged comedy gags, the carsploitation film began to lose the dark pessimism of earlier films. The destruction of chasing police cars, as well as other pursuant vehicles and collateral damage, was stretched beyond the simple inability to handle the machine to become comic humiliation and emasculation as vehicles are demolished solely for amusement. In *Eat My Dust*, for example, Hoover (Ron Howard) steals a stock car in an attempt to impress a girl and then leads the local constabulary on a riotous chase through the small town and neighboring farmland. "What follows is a demolition derby with little bloodshed in an atmosphere of humor," stated Lawrence Van Gelder of the *New York Times*.[30] Indeed, during the first chase, they destroy several police cars; collapse a Chinese Restaurant in a false-front gag; crash a police car in a pig sty; and leave another cruiser upside down in a ditch, with its officer requesting assistance from Strategic Air Command. The film presents its chase solely as a comedic joyride complete with old-time gags of manipulating film speed and hillbilly fiddle music. Moreover, *Eat My Dust* has no hint of real consequence from the police pursuit as the "space-age pessimism" of earlier films has been diffused with humor, idiocy, and humiliation; and, despite all the mayhem, Howard's character is rewarded with a chance to become a real stock car driver.

Similarly, *Grand Theft Auto* presents its gratuitous destruction of automobiles within the parameters of teen comedy. Ron Howard and Nancy Morgan star as a young couple who elope in her father's Rolls-Royce. The girl's father is presented as a morally corrupt gubernatorial candidate, who is more concerned with his Rolls than the virtue of his daughter. He places a bounty on the couple, which initiates an eighty-five-minute car chase across the Southern California and Nevada landscapes. Stated *Boxoffice*: "Ron Howard's first directorial stint may have some sort of record in the car crash genre, and movie fans who enjoy chases and sight of smash-ups will get more than their fill in this light-hearted actioner,"[31] while *Variety* called the film "the last word in the car crash genre, a non-stop orgy of comic destructiveness."[32] Although the film's narrative focuses on the tribulations of the young couple on the run, it also revels in the comic destruction of cars as the inept pursuers wreck car after car. At the center of the film is the impending destruction of the Rolls-Royce. Throughout the film, the audience is taunted and teased as the Rolls has a jousting match with pursuers, duels with a helicopter, and performs a spectacular jump, landing seemingly unscathed. But eventually the Rolls, as symbol of the corrupt authoritarian father, must be destroyed. Howard and Morgan make a wrong turn into a demolition derby where the Rolls-Royce, along with every other car in the film, is systemically destroyed by the Chitwood stunt drivers to the uproarious cheers of the crowd. Again, in spite of the destruction, Howard's character emerges triumphant, earning both the girl and her father's respect.

Eat My Dust and *Grand Theft Auto* not only marked the escalation of destruction for the sake of comedy, but they also demonstrate the declining cultural importance of the muscle car as symbol of individuality and freedom. The social rebellion once associated with the muscle car has been replaced by the stock car and the Rolls-Royce, and the individualized outlaw status associated with the muscle car had been replaced with the social conformity of a racing career and marriage. The verve of the carsploitation cycle was further worn down by big-budget Hollywood car chase comedies like *Smokey and the Bandit* (Hal Needham, 1977) and its sequels, *Used Cars* (Robert Zemeckis, 1980), *The Cannonball Run* (Hal Needham, 1981) and its sequels, and the mainstreaming of automotive destruction in television programs such as "CHiPs" (1977–1983), "The Dukes of Hazzard" (1979–1985), and the short-lived "B.A.D. Cats" (1980).

The carsploitation film began to lose its novelty through repetition and imitation, but the cycle was also weakened as the social discontent over the severe downsized functionalism of the 1970s was increasingly accepted by consumers and cars were being restyled with positive and futuristic streamlining and aerodynamic body styles. As Gartman explained, "the sleek, slippery shape of automobiles connoted a promise of salvation through the application of the latest science and technology."[33] The effects of this shift in attitudes are evident in later carsploitation films and subsequent car chase comedies: *Smokey and the Bandit* featured a 1977 Pontiac Firebird; *The Last Chase* (Martyn Burke, 1981) featured a can-am racer; *The Cannonball Run* had a Ferrari 308; and *Speed Zone* (Jim Drake, 1989) featured a Lamborghini Countach. The re-enchantment of cars through the mainstreaming of safety and, more importantly, new aerodynamic design concepts further distanced the carsploitation film from its initial relevance, and the excessive destruction of cars was losing its ability to draw audiences.

By the early 1980s, the social and industrial events that drove the carsploitation cycle had been exhausted. This, however, did not stop H.B. Halicki, who at the dearth of the cycle released two car crash films. *The Junkman* (1982) was the semiautobiographical story of a film producer/director (Halicki) making a film about a car thief relentlessly chased by the police. The film begins with the filming of a sequence in which the car thief (also played by Halicki) crashes a Bricklin SV1 into a police barricade. After shooting is completed, the producer/director finds himself the target of hired assassins, which begins the first of two extended car chases with an unprecedented level of automotive destruction.[34] As *Variety* commented:

> Cars screech crash, turn over and explode throughout "*The Junkman*." That's good for people who like to watch cars screech, crash, turn over and explode. Bad for everyone else.[35]

Boxoffice echoed these sentiments: "*The Junkman* is a mindless piece of homemade filmmaking that should entertain those folks who rate a film by the number of car crashes it presents."[36] Although the car chases and crashes were entertaining, they were also bereft of obsolete muscle cars. Instead, the first extended car chase featured contemporary automobiles—Halicki in a luxurious 1980 Cadillac El Dorado with the assassins driving a 1977 Dodge Magnum and a 1977 Ford Thunderbird—all three cars imitated European style. But without the individualized rebellion and subsequent pessimism of the late muscle car era, or the teen audience appeal of Ron Howard's inconsequential delinquency, *The Junkman* had little to offer other than its unceasing destruction of cars, trucks, boats, and airplanes, most of which were intentionally and ham-fistedly staged as comedy. The potential of *The Junkman* was further hampered by considerable distribution problems. In some major markets, the film's distributor mistakenly advertised it with an R rating instead of its proper PG. This error drastically limited the film's audience and potential revenue, and Halicki sued several major national distributors claiming breach of contract and slander.[37]

Halicki's next effort was *Deadline Auto Theft* (1983). The film was conceived as an improvement on the original *Gone in 60 Seconds*, but was little more than a cobbling together of footage from Halicki's two earlier films. It begins with the Bricklin crash taken from *The Junkman*, but this time, the sequence is presented from the perspective of the car thief and not the film crew. The footage of the theft and crash was then tacked on to the 1974 film, with the brief inserts from the 1982 film. The footage was obviously mismatched and *Deadline Auto Theft* received negligible theatrical distribution (probably as a result of the earlier lawsuits) and faded into obscurity as the cycle came to an end. But, in 1989, Halicki returned to production with another car crash spectacle: *Gone in 60 Seconds 2*. For the film, he acquired 400 cars and 80 police cars to be destroyed.[38] In addition, he built a wedge-shaped aerodynamic race car called "the slicer" designed to maximize destruction. "The slicer" was able to slide under police cars at high speeds and flip them over. The film was intended to destroy as many cars as possible and it included one stunt in which a watertower was to collapse, crushing dozens of police cars. Unfortunately, the stunt went wrong when one of the tower's guide wires snapped, killing Halicki instantly. *Gone in 60 Seconds 2* was never completed.

The carsploitation cycle of films fluctuated as low-budget independent film producers tried to anticipate audience approval. Initially, the carsploitation film exploited the trend for regional film production and countrified themes to appeal to regional drive-in audiences, and at the same time, these films indirectly confronted the false romanticism of car commodification and harsh realities of unsafe and inefficient automobiles with a frenzy of demolition and destruction. But in order to dilute the poignancy of its discontent and maximize box-office potential, producers formulated the automotive violence within a discourse of comedy. While this strategy earned these films a more democratic PG rating, the growing emphasis on comedy led to repetition and imitation. Moreover, the cycle was further weakened as the once discredited automobile industry was able to revitalize its image with the marketing of new space-age aerodynamic styling. As a result, the carsploitation film lost its appeal with audiences and film producers looked to new topical issues to exploit.

Notes

1. I would like to express my appreciation to Martin Poulin for allowing me access to his exceptional collection of carsploitation films.
2. For more information on the greater scope of carsploitation, see the Grindhouse Movie Database, at www.grindhousemoviedatabase.com.
3. David Cook, "Movies and Political Trauma," in *American Cinema of the 1970s*, ed. Lester D. Friedman (New Brunswick, NJ: Rutger's University Press, 2007), 116.
4. Peter Stanfield, *The Cool and the Crazy: Pop Fifties Cinema* (New Brunswick, NJ: Rutger's University Press, 2015), 8–13.
5. "Where Have B-Movies Gone? They've Moved to the Country," *New York Times* (March 20, 1977), 83.
6. Ibid.
7. Ibid.
8. Vincent Canby, "Why Smokey and the Bandit Is Making a Killing," *New York Times* (December 18, 1977), 109.
9. Vincent Canby, "A Surprise Movie that Charts Our Disintegration," *New York Times* (June 20, 1976), 73.
10. "Where Have B-Movies Gone?"
11. Information on filming locations for *Dirty Mary, Crazy Larry* and other films was obtained from DVD commentaries and the Internet Movie Database.
12. Whit., "Gone in 60 Seconds," *Variety* (July 31, 1974), 19.
13. *The Polk County Pot Plane* was retitled *In Hot Pursuit* for home video release.
14. "'Polk County Pot Plane' Set for Early Release," *Boxoffice* (March 14, 1977), SE-6; reprinted on March 28, 1977, W-6; "'Polk County Pot Plane' Opens in Atlanta Area," *Boxoffice* (August 22, 1977), SE-7.
15. Vincent Canby, "Screen: Auto Racers and a Girl Adrift in 'Dirty Mary,'" *New York Times* (July 11, 1974), 27.
16. "Dirty Mary, Crazy Larry," *Independent Film Journal* (May 29, 1974), 13.

17. Figure taken from imdb.com, "Dirty Mary, Crazy Larry."
18. Vincent Canby, "Screen: Auto Racers and a Girl Adrift in 'Dirty Mary.'"
19. David Gartman, *Auto Opium: A Social History of American Automobile Design* (London and New York: Routledge, 1994), 196.
20. Ibid., 183.
21. The consumer advocate Ralph Nader published *Unsafe at Any Speed* (1965). The book was a condemnation of the American automobile industry that decried negligible safety standards on the part of manufacturers and demanded increased government regulations.
22. Gartman, *Auto Opium*, 213.
23. Ibid.
24. Ibid., 215–216. The redesign of American automobile style was largely copied from two European cars: the sleek body style of the Mercedes SL class coupe introduced in 1971 and the compact boxy shape of the Volkswagen Golf introduced to North American markets as the VW Rabbit in 1975.
25. Whit., "Gone in 60 Seconds."
26. "Dirty Mary, Crazy Larry."
27. Eileen Bowser, "Mack Sennett vs Henry Ford," in *Slapstick Comedy*, eds Tom Paulis and Rob King (New York: Routledge, 2010), 108.
28. Vincent Canby, "Film: 'Thunder' from King of Bees," *New York Times* (November 17, 1977), 73.
29. Rob King, *The Fun Factory: The Keystone Film Company and the Emergence of Mass Culture* (Berkeley: University of California Press, 2009), 65–104.
30. Lawrence Van Gelder, "'Eat My Dust' Is Demolition Derby," *New York Times* (May 26, 1976), 34.
31. "Grand Theft Auto," *Boxoffice* (June 27, 1977), 4960.
32. Mack., "Grand Theft Auto," *Variety* (June 15, 1977), 20.
33. Gartman, *Auto Opium*, 219.
34. For many years, *The Junkman* held the Guinness record for the most cars destroyed in one film. According to the IMDB, the record was first broken by *The Matrix Reloaded* (The Wachowski Brothers, 2003) with 300 cars donated by General Motors for the sole purpose of destruction. This record was then surpassed by *Transformers: Dark of the Moon* (Michael Bay, 2011), when an insurance company donated 532 flood damaged cars to be destroyed in the film.
35. Berg., "The Junkman," *Variety* (September 1, 1982), 8.
36. "The Junkman," *Boxoffice* (December, 1982), 119.
37. "$450-Mil Suit Filed by H.B. Halicki vs Exhibs Re 'Junkman,'" *Variety* (September 14, 1982), 7.
38. The data on the number of cars obtained for the film are from the DVD commentary.

6

Cars and Girls (and Burgers and Weed): Branding, Mainstreaming, and Crown International Pictures' SoCal Drive-in Movies

Richard Nowell

A scene from the youth-centered comedy *Pick-Up Summer* (George Mihalka, 1980) depicted moviegoers enjoying the leisure opportunities available at the drive-in: making out in cars, stocking up on snacks, imbibing intoxicants, watching the film. Amid these clichéd activities, two pranksters relay a sound recording of an amorous couple over the speaker system, leading action on the screen to merge with that taking place in front of it. This self-reflexive sequence did not just advance a romantic vision of the film's intended exhibition sites. It also laid bare the textual, industrial, and social functions of its inspiration: four tales of fun-loving Southern California teenagers around which the American producer-distributor Crown International Pictures had built its brand identity.

Crown positioned these films—*The Pom Pom Girls* (Joseph Ruben, 1976), *The Van* (Sam Grossman, 1977), *Malibu Beach* (Robert J. Rosenthal, 1978), and *Van Nuys Blvd.* (William Sachs, 1979)—as a cohesive product line set apart from the stand-alone exploitation staples supplementing its output. The production head Marilyn Tenser emphasized continuity by reusing Los Angeles locations like Malibu Beach, performers like Bill Adler, characters like the hotheaded Dugan, character-names like Bobby and Sally, and songs like "You're gonna find love." What is more, irrespective of the talent involved, each installment boasted a distinctive structure, loosely arranging elements of youth-oriented genres into almost self-contained episodes linked by young characters. "A virtually plotless [sic] collection of scenes calculated to amuse the youth audience," as the trade paper *Variety* called it.[1]

Crown positioned these in-house productions as a flagship product intended to represent the company in the marketplace. For example, in an article on female exploitation filmmakers, Marilyn Tenser—billed as a "trend-setter in the youth market"—emphasized how the series helped her cultivate this niche.[2] Crown also differentiated the films for exhibitors. Thus, Mark Tenser's team of marketers emblazoned trade ads and exhibitor manuals with a hallmark infusing the company name with an air of shrewd assembly and savvy promotion: Crownsmanship.[3] Derived primarily from these films and their marketing campaigns,[4] the company's brand centralized four intersecting, complementary facets: vehicles, female youth, fast food, and marijuana.

Crown's brand strategy represented an attempt to fortify the supply chain that linked this producer-distributor to the prime ticket-buying audience via the drive-in theaters mainly responsible for showing the series.[5] Crown's flagship product and its brand therefore self-reflexively promoted the leisure activities from which the company and its exhibition partners earned their money. As Andrew Horton has observed, in principle "the drive-in provides a social function … the drive-in audience enjoys the totality of the outdoor experience including the people, cars, food, music, open air … and films."[6] Accordingly, this strategy imagined the films' seventeen- to twenty-one-year-old target audience as multitaskers switching between the various recreational opportunities made possible by their semiprivate, largely unsupervised exhibition sites. "Five years ago we were making pictures basically for the drive-in," confirmed Mark Tenser half a decade after the fact.[7]

Based on the sense of innocuousness, middle-class-ness, and recreation of its facets—the illegality of marijuana use notwithstanding—Crown's flagship product and its brand projected an unmistakable sense of anodynity. The company dubbed *The Van* "a light-hearted fun-fest," *Malibu Beach* its "new fun film," and *Van Nuys Blvd.* "a fun filled romp."[8] Industry-watchers agreed, describing *The Van* as "noteworthy for its wholesome vivacity," *Malibu Beach* as "pleasant as a summer holiday," and *Van Nuys Blvd.* as a "good natured summer-season comedy."[9] In branding terms, Crown sought to self-anthropomorphize.[10] It overwrote the mainly unseen creative, commercial, and logistical operations constituting the company with a public image based on the associations projected by the personalities and actions of the individuals featured in and around its media texts.

With these points in mind, this chapter argues that such qualities enabled Crown to maneuver itself toward an imagined cultural mainstream constructed around notions of commerciality, conformity, and conservatism.[11] By extension, they also permitted the company to distance itself from some of the more economically compromising aspects of exploitation cinema, especially the perceived luridness, proletarianism, and threats of the grind house.[12] The second section of the chapter posits Crown's strategy developed out of the company's negotiations to the conduct and heritage of that talismanic embodiment of the mainstream: Hollywood. From there, subsequent sections detail the specific logics and practices undergirding the individual facets of the Crown brand, beginning with vehicles, before moving on to female youth, and finally to fast food and cannabis. Before doing so, however, it is imperative we consider how such an historical case study promises to broaden conceptualizations of 1970s exploitation cinema in a manner that might reorient understandings of this under-researched aspect of audiovisual culture.

Crown International Pictures, 1970s exploitation, and the mainstream

A schism exists between, on the one hand, Crown's position in the history of American cinema and, on the other, its historiography. This company may have been a stable if undistinguished distributor of lowbrow fare in the first decade and a half following its establishment in 1959 by industry journeyman Newton P. "Red" Jacobs.[13] What is more, before its eventual demise in the early 1990s, the fleeting success Crown enjoyed in the youth market of the mid-1980s with films such as *My Tutor* (George Bowers, 1983) certainly pales in comparison to contemporaneous Hollywood hits like *Wargames* (John Badham, 1983) and *Risky Business* (Paul Brickman, 1983). However, it needs stressing that, facilitated by its mid-to-late 1970s brand, Crown did briefly transform from an unremarkable independent into a pre-home video exploitation powerhouse of a magnitude comparable with American International Pictures and New World Pictures.[14] It also precipitated the late 1970s' institutionalization of the Hollywood teen film,[15] a development *Variety* proclaimed the most industrially significant of the decade.[16] Yet, despite being relatively prominent, profitable, and influential, Crown occupies a marginal position in histories of 1970s American exploitation.[17] This marginality, I submit, is in large part a product of the company's calculatedly anodynous and mainstream brand identity rendering it anathematic to two discourses that have structured diachronic understandings of the period's exploitation cinema.

In this respect, scholars have understandably focused on salacious examples of exploitation—particularly violent, sexually explicit, or profane material[18]—and on connections between exploitation and art cinema.[19] These tendencies converge in arguably the most widely discussed developments of the period. The first spotlights New World's demands for creative personnel to fulfill quotas of sensational material, as well as the company's connections to directors of Hollywood Renaissance pictures and international art cinema.[20] The second casts exploitation as an unsupervised space permitting socially engaged, left-liberal filmmakers to craft brutal, progressive horror movies including *The Hills Have Eyes* (Wes Craven, 1977) and *Dawn of the Dead* (George A. Romero, 1978).[21] As these examples suggest, both tendencies are united in an elitist cultural politics that works toward legitimizing an oft-disparaged conceptual hub by linking it to prestigious cultural formations, especially to cult, indie, and art cinema.[22] Thus, where associating exploitation with critically celebrated works imbues it with cultural capital derived from purportedly sincere intention and distinctive execution, emphasizing salaciousness implies transgression, thereby investing it with subcultural capital.[23] Yet, such tendencies also risk either divorcing exploitation from an imagined mainstream—or better still mainstreams—with which it was deeply intertwined or reducing the mainstream to little more than a conceptual foil maintaining exploitation's purported superiority.[24]

The extent to which the American exploitation cinema of the 1970s was characterized by aspirations to anodynity and not just sensation is nonetheless indicated—however obliquely—by a small body of work focusing on its more prosaic output. Exemplary in this respect is Frederik Wasser's (1995) analysis of the lengths to which regional producer-distributors like Sunn Classics went to provide rural Christians with wholesome fare advancing traditional lifestyles, such as *The Life and Times of Grisly Adams* (Richard Friedenberg, 1974).[25] Yet, however brilliant it might be, Wasser's study still furnishes readers with an additional example of exploitation companies pursuing product differentiation from an imagined cinematic mainstream represented, as it typically is, by a caricature of Hollywood. Only this time, their conduct derives from efforts to monetize purported moral—as opposed to aesthetic or critical—superiority.[26] As a foil, Hollywood is imagined here to be a hotbed of secular-liberalism profoundly out of touch with conservative values, rather than the corporate monolith spewing narcotizing banalities onto the undemanding masses so often invoked by oppositional cultural or subcultural formations.[27] Perhaps because of this conceptual underpinning, Wasser frames his study in terms of independence rather than exploitation, foregrounding his subjects' institutional distinction from the Hollywood trade organization the Motion Picture Association of America over their location within the broader field of production.[28] That these companies' output owed much to a bygone vision of a cultural mainstream equated primarily with Hollywood and that their economic achievements inspired several major studios to reintroduce such fare to their release slates are issues left largely unaddressed.[29]

By contrast, in the 1970s, stakeholders conceptualized exploitation cinema in ways that accommodated calculatedly anodyne fare like Crown's SoCal drive-in movies. This perspective reflected their belief in the emergence of a new cinematic order distinct from the self-contained field of 1919–1959.[30] It was generally accepted at this time that modes of production, content, distribution, exhibition sites, and audiences had come to be increasingly shared between the Hollywood companies and the undercapitalized independents traditionally associated with exploitation.[31] Industry-watchers usually based their views on those films they believed to occupy low positions in contemporaneous cultural hierarchies, on the grounds that they did not evince the hallmarks of rarified cultural forms.[32] In effect, they conceptualized exploitation as the inverse of the proto-indie currents traversing the American culture industries, which, as Michael Z. Newman argues, seemed to offer a credibly "authentic, autonomous alternative" to the imagined mainstream of Hollywood.[33] Exploitation was therefore seen *not* to transcend profit-seeking, *not* to eschew formulae and accessibility, and *not* to aspire to surpassing mainstream modes of reception and consumption. Rather, it was seen to represent an extreme manifestation of these exact—devalued—characteristics, characteristics invariably centralized in conceptions of the mainstream.[34] As such, exploitation was thought of as unequivocally commercial in motivation; unashamedly derivative and unchallenging in execution; and unapologetically tailored for venues, viewers, and modes of engagement boasting little cultural or subcultural capital. Industry-insiders and industry-watchers overlaid these abstractions onto the historical specificities of American audiovisual culture. They therefore largely conceived of exploitation films as inexpensive, undemanding potboilers handled mainly by independent companies, and primarily screened at rundown rural, urban, or drive-in theaters to animated audiences devoid of discerning college-educated adults.[35] Those companies with a reputation for handling such fare were seen collectively to constitute the exploitation sector.[36]

The more holistic view traversing critical and industrial circles at the time situated Crown and its flagship product firmly within conceptions of 1970s American exploitation cinema. Thus, a *Los Angeles Times* article on the subject opened with exemplary titles including the horror film *Point of Terror* (Alex Nicol, 1973), the women-in-prison opus *Terminal Island* (Stephanie Rothman, 1973), and Crown's flagship series.³⁷ Similarly, while dubbing the notorious *Don't Go in the House* (Joseph Ellison, 1979) "gruesome exploitation," *Variety* labeled *The Pom Pom Girls* "basic exploitation," *Malibu Beach* "summer exploitation," and *Van Nuys Blvd.* a "slick, attractive exploitationer."³⁸ Moreover, Kurt Wollner of Dimension Pictures categorized *Hellcats* (1977) as "terror exploitation," Stephen Bremner of Joseph Bremner Associates called *Ginger* (Don Shain, 1971) "sex exploitation," and Marilyn Tenser described her productions simply as "exploitation."³⁹ Capturing its devalued status and its mainstream aspirations with a term typically reserved for Hollywood's most marketable and accessible fare,⁴⁰ Mark Tenser later called his company's one-time flagship "high concept exploitation."⁴¹ Crown did not derive its brand identity from distinguishing itself from an imagined mainstream represented by Hollywood though, but rather from negotiating its relationships to the conduct and history of this institution.

The genesis of Crownsmanship

In the mid-1980s, the film historian Ed Lowry cautioned against treating New World as a quintessential 1970s exploitation company, suggesting instead that its competitor Dimension Pictures furnished readers with a more representative example.⁴² Lowry's position hinged on New World's fairly unusual relationships to art cinema and on the fact that Dimension mainly handled exploitation standards like monster movies and car chase films.⁴³ While one can do well to heed Lowry's calls about the oft-cited New World, it is equally important that one avoid homogenizing exploitation companies by isolating their similarities. New World's relationships to international auteurs were indeed somewhat atypical but its motivations for publicizing them were anything but; it transformed such dealings into a facet of a brand expected conceptually to set apart the company from its peers. Whereas Dimension may have struggled to forge an equally clear-cut identity, others did so with some success. Crown of the mid- to late 1970s represents arguably the most prominent example of such practice.

Changes in the structure and conduct of the American movie business encouraged independent distributors like Crown to associate themselves with a distinctive aspect of their output. In the early 1970s, the Hollywood majors were in a financial tailspin, having incurred huge losses on over-budgeted fare and having failed to reverse declining attendance.⁴⁴ One way they responded to these crises was by jettisoning riskier projects, thereby reducing their output.⁴⁵ This step initially benefited smaller companies because it generated a shortfall of new films these outfits could fill.⁴⁶ "An independent producer, if he's really smart, can cash-in," Crown president Mark Tenser told *Variety*.⁴⁷ However, such incentives soon led supply to outstrip demand, allowing theater operators once again to pick and choose the films they booked. That Crown responded through branding is unsurprising given Mark Tenser's view that exhibitors needed to prioritize sector heavyweights over smaller concerns.⁴⁸ Receiving the 1976 Independent Motion Picture Company of the Year from the National Association of Theater Owners, Tenser reportedly pressed exhibitors to "begin buying indie product by label."⁴⁹

Crown's brand can be traced back to the confidence this company placed in an audience-targeting/content-tailoring strategy that previously spanned the American movie business: crafting films specifically for youth. Amid claims of the wholesale juvenilization of American cinema at this time,[50] it is easy to forget that few films were being made primarily for and about young people in the mid-1970s.[51] In fact, the Hollywood companies had all but abandoned this niche by 1973 owing to reservations about the political viability of the counterculture pictures they and others released after *Easy Rider* (Dennis Hopper, 1969).[52] Their concern evidently ran so deep that no major studio attempted to capitalize on the anomalous *American Graffiti* (George Lucas, 1973), a youth-centered megahit all but devoid of the social critique rendering the counterculture pictures so problematic.[53] The commercial decline of the once-preeminent teen film genre also prompted many independent distributors to replace specifically youth-oriented fare with output aimed squarely at blue-collar urbanites or southerners.[54] Only Crown truly bucked the trend by continuing to support youth market fare year after year after year. The company's persistence would pay off. Crown stumbled on a lucrative model when *The Pom Pom Girls* became one of the highest grossing non-Hollywood releases of 1976, and Crown's biggest hit to date, when it generated rentals of $4.3 million to place inside the top fifty earners that year.[55] "The scarcity of contemporary teen pix," noted *Variety*, "may account for the film's appeal."[56]

Crown positioned *The Pom Pom Girls* and its successors as loose updates of a dormant youth market standard: the "unabashedly wholesome entertainment" that was "the clean teenpic."[57] Jettisoning these older films' heavy-handed moralizing, Crown retained their distinctive sun-soaked California settings, young casts, and scenes of outdoor leisure.[58] "Not much has changed with the beach bunny picture since its inception in the late 1950s," noted one reviewer, concluding *Malibu Beach* "repeats the excesses of American International's interminable string of 'beach blanket' epics."[59] Although industry-watchers typically compared Crown's films to AIP's onetime tentpole, the clean teenpic had also been a Hollywood staple, as evinced by Columbia's *Gidget* series of 1959–1963. Updating this genre also invited parallels to the biggest youth-centered picture of the day: Universal's pastiche of the earlier period's fare, *American Graffiti*.

Invoking the clean teenpic inflected Crown's flagship output—and its brand—with a talismanic regional brand rooted very much in conceptions of the mainstream. As Kirse Granat May details, the 1950s and 1960s witnessed cultural agents posit a vision of the films' Southern California settings shorn of race and class inequalities, and generational conflicts.[60] During this time, musicians, advertisers, politicians, and others framed the southern part of the Golden State as a glimpse into an idealized national future—"not a region, but the mainstream, America only more so."[61] "These representations," Granat May suggests, "celebrated young Californians as a white, suburban, middle-class cohort enjoying consumer opportunities and pursuing happiness."[62] Epitomized by beach life, custom cars, fast-food joints, and teenagers—and exemplified by Disneyland, the Beach Boys, and the clean teenpics—this discourse undergirded Crown's flagship product and its brand. "The America we see pictured in 'The Van' has been effectively reduced to a strip of highway that seems to run between

Los Angeles and Santa Monica," noted Vincent Canby of the *New York Times*. "Its wonders are filling stations, automobile salesrooms, Pepe's Pizza Parlor, car washes, side roads for drag racing, at the end of which is the Pacific Ocean and a beach where one can park one's van and make out."[63] As Canby's comments make clear, a key facet of the Crown brand derived from one thing young people needed to access this company's preferred exhibition sites, consume its products, and enjoy the activities these screenings made possible.

Cars

Automobiles have been a recurring presence in and around American exploitation cinema, especially in the 1970s, when Crown's flagship series exemplified this phenomenon. "So much of the action takes place in or adjacent to vehicles," wrote Canby of *The Van*, "[y]ou might have assumed [the protagonist] Bobby had been bred in a glove compartment."[64] Where Horton speculated that such content may have been driven by nostalgia and escapism, Tico Romao argues the production and textual features of the period's car films were a product of Hollywood and independents jockeying for market share.[65] However, Peter Stanfield recently linked a spate of 1950s hot rod films to a broader range of phenomena, including press interest, concerns about juvenile delinquency, entertainment value, marketability, and—crucially— drive-in theaters.[66] An analysis of Crown's flagship series permits consideration of why this venue incentivized one company to centralize vehicles in its output, albeit two decades later. The commodification of topicality, along with the pursuit of product differentiation and personal investment, emphasized in existing studies only partially explain this facet of the Crown brand. Granted, at the time, two forms of vehicular leisure commanded public attention, evinced some box-office potential,[67] and furnished filmmakers and marketers with potentially attention-grabbing content. Yet, more important still, I contend, was the material's endorsement of those pleasures the young target audience could anticipate from the drive-in experience and from which Crown and its exhibition partners earned their living.

Crown sought to thematize this notion by positioning vehicles as a bridge linking film content to everyday life. Stressing that the pleasures characters derived therefrom were available to audiences as well, the company suggested exhibitors imbricate the series within automotive culture, by disseminating bumper stickers, advertising at auto dealerships, and sending stickers to car magazines.[68] Crown also advised theater operators to stage stunts involving vehicles like those in the films, recommending they publicize *The Pom Pom Girls* with cabriolets filled with cheerleaders and with vans bearing the film's title.[69] The company also proposed sites screening *The Van* and *Van Nuys Blvd.* would benefit from displaying customized vans and hot rods outside their entrances.[70]

Rather than sensationalizing vehicular leisure, as stakeholders had done with 1950s hot rod films, Crown framed cruising and customizing in ways that reflected the cultural rehabilitation of the two. In the mid- to late 1970s, interested parties suggested these intersecting pastimes were the subjects of mainstreaming, stressing their reputations as West Coast subcultures were being diluted by uptake among older, wealthier, Middle Americans. These formerly contentious fads were therefore seen to have lost some of their aura of youthful rebellion, as the speeding hot rods of yesteryear gave way to lavish "road rods" or "street rods" seen parading down thoroughfares like Van Nuys Blvd. "Along with its resurgence is a desire for a cleaner image," noted *Chicago Tribune* writer Richard Phillips, "one that won't raise eyebrows in a grocer's parking lot, or even worse, bring on the police squadrol."[71] Beyond evincing a personalization of Fordist production, the interstitiality of vans rested on their permitting activities prohibited from the public sphere while simultaneously evoking domesticity through the installation of beds, chandeliers, and other furnishings. "Born a decade ago in California, where it was once disparaged as a sin bin of young marijuana smokers," wrote the *New York Times*' Georgia Dullea, "the custom van has since travelled eastward and upward on the scale of respectability."[72]

Picturing vehicles as vantage points, status symbols, and liminal spaces enabled Crown to orient to its commercial objectives three pleasures devotees often claimed to derive from this leisure pursuit: public validation, manifest scopophilia, and semiprivate licentiousness. "It's an identity thing," one fan explained to the *Boston Globe*, "[w]hen I [customized] mine I was just looking to make it unique ... so that everyone can sort of put you together with your truck."[73] Another enthusiast detailed his investment in a van as a means of seeking out romantic partners and hosting casual liaisons. "There's something about a good-looking man in a good-looking van that women just can't pass up," he explained to the *Washington Post*, "[t]hey know he's gonna show them something ... [y]ou're not going to some motel."[74] The dim, communal, automotive environment of Crown's preferred exhibition sites offered an ideal staging ground for these activities. "The 'van revolution' has spread to the drive-in opening new possibilities for many who might not otherwise attend," noted Horton; "... the van of the seventies makes watching a movie that much more exciting for the proud owners."[75]

By celebrating vehicles as sites from which characters enjoyed visual pleasures, Crown allegorized the drive-in patron's encounter with its films and with extra-diegetic objects. In so doing, the company promoted the location's provision of both enclosed consumption space and opportunities to imagine or experience social interaction. Crown pictured in-car scopophilia as an innocuous amusement and as a springboard from which to pursue relations with the opposite sex. Each film featured scenes of male youths wooing young females they spot when cruising, with two seniors in *The Pom Pom Girls* trawling a beachside road until they find girls to pick up. Similarly, print advertising boasted images of groups gathered in, on, or around vehicles, gazing forward as if captivated by an object in the distance. For example, posters advertising *The Van* showed a young man sitting atop this vehicle and three female youths leaning against the hood, looking not at each other but straight ahead (see Figure 6.1).

Crown also pictured vehicles as objects of a solicited gaze, which increased an owner's sense of self-worth by garnering the approval of courted parties. This practice endorsed an exhibitionistic dimension of drive-in attendance whereby patrons displayed their

Figure 6.1 Crown pictured vans and cars self-reflexively as vantage points in order to endorse the spectatorial and social dimensions of the vehicular patronage characteristic of the drive-in (*The Van*, Crown International Pictures, 1977).

vehicles as a sign of their taste, resources, and eligibility. Nowhere was this approach more apparent than in *The Van*, in which a young man curtails his sexual failures when his newly customized vehicle proves irresistible to women. "Bobby couldn't make it ... until he went fun-truckin'!" read print advertising. Crown's SoCal drive-in movies also emphasized homosocial approval, with, for example, *Van Nuys Blvd.*, and its theatrical trailer, opening to exchanges between awestruck pedestrians and exultant cruisers. Moreover, the notion of the automobile as a source of self-esteem underpinned the chicken runs and car races featured in each film, sequences that concluded with a young man either proud in victory or maturing upon recognizing his infantility.

Lastly, presenting vehicles as liminal spaces allowed Crown to highlight the drive-in's provision of a retreat in which patrons might surreptitiously enjoy activities likely to provoke censure if indulged publically. Chief among these were romantic activity and the consumption of marijuana. Given the restrictions placed on advertising MPAA-rated films on sexual content and illegal drugs,[76] audiovisual marketing materials usually limited such depictions to teenagers making out in cars—or "love boats" as *Van Nuys Blvd.*'s exhibitors' manual called them.[77] However, the organization's more liberal stance toward rated motion picture content did ensure these activities were showcased in the films themselves. Thus, a nighttime tracking shot from *Malibu Beach* surveys a line of steamed-up parked cars filled with amorous couples, which, while shot on a bluff, echoed parking arrangements at drive-ins. Moreover, *The Van* shows Bobby sharing a joint, sipping a beer, flirting, being rebuffed, and finally having sex in his customized vehicle. Scenes such as these pointed to another important facet of Crown's flagship product and brand identity.

Girls

Discussion of exploitation cinema often emphasizes sex and gender, with charges of misogyny routinely leveled at the makers and distributors of exploitation films, the materials they produce, and the audiences consuming them.[78] Yet, several studies have shown that the production, content, and marketing of some low-prestige films are shaped by efforts to counter such claims. They suggest that maximizing returns from white slavery films, horror movies, women-in-danger thrillers, teen sex comedies, and others sometimes hinges on making these appear attractive to female and male moviegoers.[79] Economics, public relations, symbolic capital, and entertainment value thus converge here on the back of two forms of industry logic: one dictating that audiences tend to gravitate to films that foreground their own demographic, the other that feminization elevates low-prestige, masculine forms toward an imagined mainstream.[80]

Crown was well versed in these strategies because it had made the cultivation of both sexes a centerpiece of its production and distribution operations for some time. In the early 1970s, this company sought to stimulate attendance by bowing to what management considered to be the power dynamics of mixed-sex consumption: "[m]ore than half the tickets purchased are influenced by women," stressed Marilyn

Tenser.[81] Unsurprisingly, given the masculine connotations of exploitation, Crown framed its products as specifically female-friendly. With Marilyn Tenser convinced that "[w]omen like to see themselves in lead roles,"[82] and with Mark Tenser convinced that they had "sharp memories for promo campaigns,"[83] Crown re-titled acquisitions to suggest female-centeredness. "Impulsion" became *The Stepmother* (Howard Avedis, 1972), "Rectangle" *The Sister-in-Law* (Joseph Ruben, 1974), and "Friends" *Couples* (Noel Nosseck, 1975).[84] Crown's early in-house productions also represented efforts to balance the company's view that "women can identify with women characters" with its evident belief that male audiences enjoyed watching female characters wearing and shedding tight clothes.[85] Crown reworked prominent action movies by adding conventionally attractive heroines who demonstrated professional, platonic, and romantic mastery. *Superchick* (Ed Forsyth, 1973) was effectively a woman-centered Bond film, *Policewomen* (Lee Frost, 1974) a distaff *Dirty Harry* (Don Siegel, 1971), and, as Marilyn Tenser herself admitted, *Las Vegas Lady* (Noel Nosseck, 1975) a "female 'Ocean's 11' [Lewis Milestone, 1960]."[86] The heroines of these films embodied the "neofeminism" exemplified by the single-girl phenomenon of the 1960s, *Cosmopolitan* editor Helen Gurly Brown, and Tenser herself.[87] As Hilary Radner explains, advocates of this philosophy-cum-lifestyle pursue security within existing power structures while also valuing apolitical and egalitarian sisterhood and embracing varnished femininity as a means of realizing economic security, sexual fulfillment, and self-esteem.[88]

Crown recalibrated its established approach to account for the composition and conduct of the younger mixed-sex audiences of its new flagship series. Portraying female youths as budding neofeminists allowed the company to transform the industry standard of pitching youth-oriented fare to both sexes into another means of leaning the films toward an imagined mainstream.[89] As Gregory A. Waller has suggested of a comparable feature of teen sexploitation like *Revenge of the Cheerleaders* (Richard Lerner, 1976), this form of characterization was remarkably similar to that prevalent in contemporaneous television advertising and in an extremely high-profile television series. "Cute, white, athletic, and hip without being too jaded or sophisticated," writes Waller, these youths recalled "[*Charlie's Angels* (1976–1981) star] Cheryl Ladd and the women featured in TV ads for soft drinks and yoghurt."[90]

Crown's depiction of female youths promoted the dynamics of an exhibition site where young people were imagined performing gender in order to initiate and sustain mixed-sex interaction. The company presented these characters as soliciting an innocuous diegetic male gaze akin to the one a young woman might herself experience at screenings. Crown emphasized that for better or worse, conduct of this sort was part of everyday life when it encouraged exhibitors to use beauty pageants and swimsuit models to promote the films.[91] The notion of alluring female youths magnetizing their male peers was encapsulated in the promotional tagline for *The Pom Pom Girls*: "They Were the Girls of Our Dreams …". The films and their marketing campaigns were awash with images of female youths who—not unlike their "peacocking" male friends—showcased their conventional attractiveness to garner the attention of a desired party when the mood took them. The exhibitionism these well-liked, respected, self-determining young women performed served to preempt cries of onscreen objectification that threatened to alienate female viewers from the product and its conditions of consumption.

Crown's SoCal drive-in movies also used scenes of young women steering heterosexual interaction to address female youth in a manner resonant with their potential circumstances of consumption. As the social historian Kerry Seagrave explains, drive-ins had a reputation as teenage "passion pits" for a good reason.[92] This material emphasized the right of a female youth to manage her sexual life as she saw fit. Repeatedly staging such action in and around vehicles reminded viewers of both sexes that this position also applied to events taking place in front of the screen. "Some girls do it, and some girls won't," proclaimed the female voiceover to *The Pom Pom Girls* trailer, gesturing to the fact that this and subsequent installments depicted young women rejecting, forestalling, or cultivating advances, as well as embracing flings and steering relationships. Quotidian rather than sensational, Crown's depiction of female heterosexuality reflected Mark Tenser's hope that this material be received as lighthearted rather than menacing or sleazy. "Sex can be treated from the stand point of young people—with fun," he explained to *Variety*.[93]

Crown bolstered its attempts to normalize the notions of young women as a source of innocuous visual pleasure and as active agents by presenting female characters as fun-seekers who embraced leisure. Spotlighting the significance of this material, Mark Tenser emphasized that *The Pom Pom Girls* "[i]s not a sex film. Sex is very minor to the film. It's [about] young people having fun."[94] Accordingly, promotional materials highlighted scenes of young women behaving in a hedonistic but ultimately conformist fashion.[95] Such content typically featured their participation in activities showcasing the body in motion and displays of exhilaration: volley ball, surfing, jet-skiing, motorcycling, and so on (see Figures 6.2 and 6.3). When complemented with scenes of young females playing fairground amusements, toking, and snacking, such scenes positioned heterosexual interaction as one of myriad leisure activities young women might enjoy. This content allowed the company to suggest that the pursuit of gratification driving female youths on the screen was realizable through a narrow

Figures 6.2 and 6.3 To appeal to both sexes, Crown pictured female youths soliciting an innocuous male gaze and as seeking pleasure from leisure pursuits similar to those available at drive-in theaters (*Malibu Beach*, Crown International Pictures, 1978).

range of activities similar to those available at the drive-in. In effect, Crown suggested what a girl really wanted was vehicular leisure, romantic interaction, and recreational imbibification—the last of which reflected the remaining facets of the Crown brand.

Burgers and weed

When highlighting the extratextual dimensions of exploitation cinema consumption, scholars typically prioritize the communicative dimensions of engaging with such fare in public. Exemplary in this respect are the sociosexual dynamics of young drive-in patrons discussed above, attention-seeking outbursts among audiences of scary movies,[96] and the performativity of cinephiles attending exploitation films as "midnight movies."[97] However, significantly less attention has been paid to those extratextual dimensions of exploitation film consumption that lean more toward personal gratification than communication, even though they may involve or facilitate some human interaction. Chief among these are two aspects of drive-in culture that occupied prominent albeit secondary locations in Crown's flagship series and its brand identity: fast food and marijuana.

Crown emphasized the junk foods central to the mainstream branding of Southern California in order to encourage young people to purchase these snacks, both as a means of enriching their moviegoing experience and maximizing the revenue exhibitors generated from the films. Such conduct promised to strengthen the company's relationships to drive-in operators by showing them that Crown was not only a reliable supplier of lucrative product but that it actively advanced the commercial interests of partners. Concessions was a growth industry by 1977, with its annual revenues of $400 million typically determining profitability in the exhibition sector.[98] "[C]ash flow from hunger and thirst appetites of entertainment-seekers comprise the 'difference' on occasions between break even and profit," noted *Variety*.[99] Sales were strongest in summer and at drive-ins, thanks to younger audiences, intermissions, and larger menus boasting "hot dogs, hamburgers, pizza, chili, steak sandwiches, hero sandwiches and other dishes."[100] Estimates suggested that almost 90 percent of drive-ins made more from these treats than the box office.[101] "Movies may get people into theaters," noted Barbara Isenberg of the *Los Angeles Times*, "but popcorn and other snacks pay the bills."[102]

Which specific types of film helped best pay the bills was a question preoccupying the concessions industry at the time Crown was pushing out its flagship series. Perhaps because the company's founder and chairman cut his teeth in concessions,[103] Crown was slightly ahead of the curve in recognizing that "[e]xhibitors say that given the choice between two films of equal box office appeal, they'll go with the one expected to do the biggest business at the snack bar."[104] Naturally, above anyone else, it was the concessionaires operating franchises at theaters and drive-ins, along with their suppliers, who were most invested in the issue. After all, they could not fall back on solid ticket sales if a well-attended film failed to electrify the refreshment stand. Yet, regardless of whether drive-in operators outsourced this aspect of the business or ran it themselves, they too had a vested interest in ensuring their films energized such a decisive profit center. Understandings of this phenomenon may have been in their infancy, with the National Association of Concessionaires only bankrolling research into the matter in 1979,[105] but stakeholders suspected escapist fare generated significantly higher returns than cerebral releases.[106] Their view was based not only on the former usually drawing bigger crowds and the younger people who mainly consumed the types of food on sale but also on their excitement transforming snacking into something of a coping mechanism.[107] With its standardized textual model strategically geared to numbing rather than accentuating thrills (see below), Crown adopted a more direct approach to encouraging viewers to stock up on treats.

Effectively engaging in voluntary product placement, Crown reflected one concessionaire's view that moviegoers "buy impulsively and it's our responsibility to make everything look … as appetizing as possible."[108] As with the aforementioned facets of its brand, Crown sought to bridge film content and consumption, this time by encouraging exhibitors to collaborate with eateries. The company recommended advertising *The Pom Pom Girls* at fast-food joints selling drinks and sandwiches named after the film, and encouraged operators to promote *Malibu Beach* with "weenie roasts" catered for by a "teen restaurant."[109] The links such events were designed to foster were stressed in audiovisual marketing materials and the films themselves, both of which fetishized concession-stand goods and showed them complementing other facets of the Crown brand. "Their favorite foods are pizza and hamburgers," joked Vincent Canby about this content, "but their teeth are so perfect they look capped."[110] Thus, where a male youth converses at length with a server making his sandwich in *Van Nuys Blvd.*, *The Pom Pom Girls* included an otherwise redundant scene of a young man ordering a burger, watching it being prepared, and then discarding it. Moreover, the films and their trailers often showcased drive-in restaurants as settings, allowing for shots of characters enjoying meals in vehicles, and pictured eating places staging heterosexual interaction. For example, Bobby's favored stomping ground in *The Van* was a pizza parlor. Similarly, carhops hook up with customers in *The Pom Pom Girls* and *Van Nuys Blvd.*, with the latter even integrating a hamburger into foreplay; all of which featured in their respective trailers. Shots from *Malibu Beach* of a glazed-eyed young man transfixed to a grilled frankfurter gestured to one of the roles food played vis-á-vis the final facet of the Crown brand.

Upon speaking about the company's updating of the clean teenpic, *Variety* noted that "the only new wrinkle Crown International's 'Malibu Beach' introduces is the shift from beer guzzling to pot smoking."[111] Marijuana's presence in the Crown brand epitomizes the challenges of analyzing media branding strategies. As Alisa Perren explains, the analyst ultimately seeks to illuminate a practice characterized by misrepresentation, misdirection, and obfuscation, executed by parties incentivized to withhold their logic and strategies from their competitors and consumers (and thus from scholars as well).[112] This situation is compounded, however, when public acknowledgment of the strategy in question threatens to provoke censure. Crown's public silence on the matter exemplified a wholesale reticence on the part of industry-insiders publically to discuss the roles they envisaged this widely used contraband playing in the assembly and consumption of some of their output. Although Crown clearly spotlighted and teased marijuana consumption, public acknowledgment thereof risked exposing the company to charges of inciting illegal activity, and exhibitors to accusations of breaking drug laws by encouraging cannabis use on their property.

A rare insight into the industry's engagement with marijuana users at this time is provided, however, by a major Hollywood hit that mainstreamed the drug by romanticizing it and all but encouraging audiences to consume it before and during screenings. Paramount's *Up in Smoke* (1978) featured the pro-cannabis double act of Cheech Marin and Tommy Chong in a comedy about dope trafficking and taking, which was sold on the taglines "Don't go straight to see this film" and "You'll be rolling in the aisles." Aimed squarely at what Chong called "the dope crowd,"[113] the film jettisoned the depiction of marijuana consumption as the politicized act of rebellion and enlightenment showcased in early counterculture films such as *Easy Rider* and Crown's own *The Young Graduates* (Robert Anderson, 1971). Instead, it portrayed the drug as anodyne youthful recreation devoid of negative side-effects apart perhaps from an innocuous bout of short-term memory loss or a sudden urge to snack.

Beyond its romanticization of cannabis, *Up in Smoke* bore additional hallmarks of complementing the state of mind its marketing campaign encouraged patrons to achieve. The film utilized a meandering, dream-like narrative punctuated by moments of spectacle that reflected the intoxicated protagonists' oscillation between intense focus, spontaneity, and distraction. A *Variety* reviewer said as much of one of the film's follow-ups. "[*Nice Dreams* (Tommy Chong, 1981)] stands as a collection of set pieces … so that if one keys into the reefer-induced frame of reference from the beginning (as millions of fans are inarguably able to do) it's pure enjoyment from there on."[114] Given the incitement for moviegoers to attend Cheech & Chong's output in this state, such a structure suggests an effort to tailor the films specifically for audiences under the influence. *Variety* even reported that this conduct was prevalent at the exhibition sites Crown targeted. "Drive-in biz was particularly heavy," noted the paper, "in that patrons are free to mimic the on-screen action in the privacy of their vehicles."[115] In effect, structurally and thematically, *Up in Smoke* transformed a facet of Crown's flagship product into an organizing framework.

Crown pictured marijuana complementing the other facets of its brand and thus the drive-in experience.[116] In lieu of an extra-filmic bridge conflating content and consumption, the company used the films themselves to ensure its depiction of the drug "should find lots of empathy from ozoner patrons."[117] Thus, in *The Van*, Bobby celebrates his first cruise in his new vehicle by watching the sun set with a joint. In *Malibu Beach*, marijuana is shown catalyzing an unspoken bond between a female youth and a police officer who break bread over joints on the sands. And, the sight of the taciturn sausage-gazer noted above flagged up the relationship between this drug and the comfort foods available at the drive-in concession stand. As such scenes made clear, this venue provided patrons with an ideal site for imbibing the substance, with a sense of imagined community based on its consumption, and with requisite relief should they succumb to the desire to devour the snacks pushed on the screen.

Crucially, Crown presented marijuana as capable of enriching consumption of its SoCal drive-in movies themselves. For example, in *The Pom Pom Girls*, two football players are pictured sitting in adjacent restroom cubicles smoking a joint, an unusual composition clearly intended to invoke the placement of car passengers watching the film. The two are shown later, once again seated next to one another, exchanging knowing glances as they watch every other character participate in a mass brawl. Much like the *Variety* reviewer noted of Cheech & Chong's movies, the unusual organization of Crown's films evinced a calculated effort to entertain a spectator whose engagement with the screen was apt to be intense but fleeting, a glancing, occasionally spellbound moviegoer rather than a protractedly captivated one. Their modular structure and loose narration enabled patrons pursuing other forms of recreation related to their vehicles, the opposite sex, or the concession stand intermittently to follow the action on the screen;[118] however, more than anyone else, viewers likely to be enthralled by a crackling sausage could derive pleasure from the spectacle of cars and girls and burgers and weed.

Conclusion

Crown's branding strategy and its brand identity suggest that painting a fuller picture of 1970s American exploitation cinema will likely hinge on moving beyond the relevant but limiting notion that this sector was characterized by salacious fare. Recognizing that exploitation was seen as output that occupied extremely low positions within cultural hierarchies opens up the possibility for a broader perspective—one that takes into account devalued rather than simply lurid films. Such a position in turn suggests that rather than accentuating profanity, sexuality, or violence, as is commonly assumed, numerous companies operating in this sector are likely to have also tailored and framed at least some of their output in ways which distanced it—and, by extension, themselves—from the tawdrier aspects of exploitation. Given that this sector was responsible for the majority of films released on the American market in the 1970s,[119] we can expect their approaches to have been manifold. By broadening our perspective in such a way, scholarship on this underexamined aspect of American culture promises to reinstate conceptions of the mainstream into understandings of exploitation, not merely as a foil summoned to underscore product differentiation at the industrial or critical level but as a multifaceted and mutable discourse constructively informing both the conduct of the sector and the texts it generated.

Arguably the most prominent example of such practice of the mid- to late 1970s, Crown's brand represented a multidirectional engagement with various visions of the mainstream. It derived from updating an industry-wide audience targeting/content tailoring strategy rooted in an innocuous production trend of yesteryear and a regional branding strategy. What is more, its individual facets exemplified the rehabilitation of a once-sensational subculture, representational practices drawn from television and advertising, everyday foods, and a romanticized vision of a recreational intoxicant. Articulated in and around a flagship series of SoCal drive-in movies, this brand was designed to bolster the supply chain linking Crown to the consumer, by promoting the leisure pursuits on offer at these films' principal exhibition sites.

The Crown brand of the mid- to late 1970s captured the liminality and ephemeral nature of its subject matter. Where Kevin Thomas of the *Los Angeles Times* proclaimed *The Pom Pom Girls* "embodies what most teenagers wish their lives were like," three years on, a *Variety* reviewer sensed a "curiously mirthless quality" to *Van Nuys Blvd*.[120] With the success of the series around which Crown had branded itself incentivizing the production of Hollywood youth market fare like *Corvette Summer* (Matthew Robbins, 1978), *Grease* (Randal Kleiser, 1978), *Animal House* (John Landis), and *Up in Smoke*, it was clear that this company's salad days were over. It is perhaps fitting then that the final frames of *Van Nuys Blvd.*, of the series as a whole, and of the most successful chapter in the company's history would involve passing self-reflexive comment on Crown's sense of self and place. Upon concluding an obligatory chicken run, this time on a newly laid stretch of highway, the film's young characters find themselves having quite literally reached the end of the road.

Notes

1. Mack., "The Pom Pom Girls," *Variety* (September 16, 1976), 16.
2. Linda Gross, "A Woman's Place Is in … Exploitation Films?" *Los Angeles Times* (February 12, 1978), 34.
3. See Crown International Pictures, "*The Pom Pom Girls* Exhibitors Manual" (Crown International Pictures, 1976), unpaginated; Crown International Pictures, "*The Van* Exhibitors Manual" (Crown International Pictures, 1977), unpaginated; Crown International Pictures, "*Malibu Beach* Exhibitors Manual" (Crown International Pictures, 1978), unpaginated; Crown International Pictures, "*Van Nuys Blvd.* Exhibitors Manual" (Crown International Pictures, 1979), unpaginated.
4. Crown occasionally used its Crownsmanship label to position other youth-centered releases closer to its flagship product. The films in question were the high-school romance *Coach* (Bud Townsend, 1978), the drag-racing drama *Burnout* (Graham Meech-Burkestone, 1979), and the crime film *Malibu High* (Irvin Berwick, 1979).
5. Will Tusher, "Crown: Drive-ins Losing Impact," *Variety* (November 30, 1981), 1.
6. Andrew Horton, "Turning On and Tuning Out at the Drive-In: An American Phenomenon Survives and Thrives," *Journal of Popular Film* 5:3/4 (1976): 239.
7. Mark Tenser quoted in Tusher, "Crown," 1.
8. Crown, "*The Van*," unpaginated; Crown "*Malibu Beach*," unpaginated; Crown "*Van Nuys Blvd.*," unpaginated.
9. Linda Gross, "Rite of Passage in a Cruising Van," *Los Angeles Times* (April 20, 1977), E10; Kevin Thomas, "'Malibu Beach': A Farewell to Youth," *Los Angeles Times* (May 5, 1978), H19; Kevin Thomas, "'Van Nuys Blvd.' a Summer Cruise," *Los Angeles Times* (May 11, 1979), G26.
10. See Terry Hanby, "Brands—Dead or Alive?" *Journal of the Marketing Research Society* 41:1 (1999): 7–18; Fabian Faurholt Csaba and Anders Bengtsson, "Rethinking Identity in Brand Management," in *Brand Culture*, eds Jonathan E. Schroeder and Miriam Salzer-Mörling (Abington: Routledge, 2006), 118–135.

11. See Mark Jancovich, "Cult Fictions: Cult Movies, Subcultural Capital, and the Production of Cultural Distinctions," *Cultural Studies* 16:2 (2002): 315.
12. See Joanne Hollows, "The Masculinity of Cult," in *Defining Cult Movies: The Cultural Politics of Oppositional Taste*, eds Mark Jancovich et al. (Manchester: Manchester University Press, 2003), 35–53; David Church, "From Exhibition to Genre: The Case of Grind-house Films," *Cinema Journal* 50:4 (2011): 1–25.
13. Richard Klein, "Crown OK's Two More Youth Pix for '84 Prod'n," *Variety* (February 21, 1984), 1, 22.
14. See, e.g., Todd McCarthy, "Bright Outlook for Indies: Less Blue-Collar Fare from Majors Could Open Market," *Variety* (June 19, 1980), 20.
15. See Richard Nowell, "There's More than One Way to Lose Your Heart: The American Film Industry, Early Teen Slasher Films, and Female Youth," *Cinema Journal* 51:1 (2011): 123–128.
16. Dale Pollock, "Mega-Pix Push Filmbiz into '80s: B. O. Champs-A-Chargin'," *Variety* (January 3, 1980), 3.
17. See Suzanne Mary Donahue, *American Film Distribution: The Changing Marketplace* (Ann Arbor: UMI Research Press, 1987); Nowell, "There's More," 123–128.
18. See, e.g., Eithne Johnson and Eric Schaefer, "Soft Core/Hard Gore: *Snuff* as a Crisis in Meaning," *Journal of Film and Video* 45:2/3 (1993): 40–59; see also Stephen Thrower, *Nightmare USA: The Untold Story of the Exploitation Independents* (Godalming: FAB Press, 2007).
19. See, e.g., Mark Betz, "Art, Exploitation, Underground," in *Defining Cult Movies: The Cultural Politics of Oppositional Taste*, eds Mark Jancovich et al. (Manchester: Manchester University Press, 2003), 202–222; Mark Betz, "High and Low and in Between," *Screen* 54:4 (2013): 495–513.
20. See, e.g., Jim Hillier and Aaron Lipstadt, "The Economics of Independence: Roger Corman and New World Pictures, 1970–1980," *Movie* 31/32 (1986): 43–53.
21. See, e.g., Robin Wood, *From Vietnam to Reagan ... and Beyond: Expanded and Revised Edition* (New York: Columbia University Press, 2003), 63–85. For a critique of this perspective, see Joe Tompkins, "Bids for Distinction: The Critical-Industrial Function of the Horror Auteur," in *Merchants of Menace: The Business of Horror Cinema*, ed. Richard Nowell (New York: Bloomsbury, 2014), 203–214.
22. See Jancovich, "Cult Fictions."
23. Ibid.
24. Ibid.
25. Frederick Wasser, "Four Walling Exhibition: Regional Resistance to the Hollywood Film Industry," *Cinema Journal* 34:2 (1995): 51–65.
26. Ibid.
27. Ibid.
28. Ibid.
29. See also Justin Wyatt, "Revisiting the 1970s' Independent Distribution and Marketing Strategies," in *Contemporary American Independent Film: From the Margins to the Mainstream*, eds Christine Holmund and Justin Wyatt (London: Routledge, 2005), 229–244.
30. See Eric Schaefer, *Bold! Daring! Shocking! True! A History of Exploitation Films, 1919–1959* (Durham: Duke University Press, 1999).
31. See, e.g., Charles Schreger, "20 Feature Films on New World's Release Slate," *Variety* (November 23, 1977), 1.8.

32. The conceptual utility of such a rubric allowed interested parties to discount critical challenges to their position posed by the para-cinematic recuperation of such fare, including the Museum of Modern Art's acquisition of *The Texas Chain Saw Massacre* (1974). See Jeffrey Sconce, "'Trashing' the Academy: Taste, Excess, and an Emerging Politics of Cinematic Style," *Screen* 36:4 (1995): 371–393; see also Ellen Farley, "Impresarios of Axploitation Movies," *Los Angeles Times* (November 13, 1977), O1, 48.
33. Michael Z. Newman, "Indie Culture: In Pursuit of the Authentic Autonomous Alternative," *Cinema Journal* 48:3 (2009): 16–34.
34. See, e.g., Frank Segers, "New York More Turbulent than Ever," *Variety* (June 5, 1979), 26, 28.
35. Ibid.
36. Ibid.
37. Gross, "A Woman's Place," 34.
38. Step., "Don't Go in the House," *Variety* (June 11, 1980), 22; Mack., "The Pom Pom Girls," 16; Poll., "Malibu Beach," *Variety* (May 18), 3; Cart., "Van Nuys Blvd.," *Variety* (May 8, 1979), 171.
39. Kurt Wollner, quoted in Farley, "Impresarios," 49; Stephen Bremner quoted in Farley, "Impresarios," 49; Marilyn Tenser quoted in Lilly Lipton, "Sexual Discrimination in Films," *Variety* (October 29, 1974), 74.
40. See Justin Wyatt, *High Concept: Movies and Marketing in Hollywood* (Austin: University of Texas Press, 1994).
41. Mark Tenser quoted in Anon., "Crown Int'l Pix to Peddle 3 Films at Mart," *Variety* (March 8, 1985), 87.
42. Ed Lowry, "Dimension Pictures: Portrait of a '70s Independent," *The Velvet Light Trap* 22 (1986): 74.
43. Ibid.
44. Sheldon Hall, "Tall Revenue Features: The Genealogy of the Modern Blockbuster," in *Genre and Contemporary Hollywood*, ed. Steve Neale (London: BFI, 1998), 17.
45. Ibid.
46. A. D. Murphy, "300 Indie Films Pace Production: Invest $100 Mil Outside Majors," *Variety* (June 9, 1976), 32.
47. Mark Tenser quoted in Joseph McBride, "'Analyze the Sale before Shooting,' Crown Prez' Advice to Producers," *Variety* (July 16, 1975), 3.
48. Another company that responded to this situation through branding was AIP, whose blaxploitation films—*Truck Turner* (Jonathan Kaplan, 1974), *Hell up in Harlem* (Larry Cohen, 1975), and others—imbued the company with the topicality of their themes of class, governance, and anxiety. See Jan Kraszewski, "Recontextualizing the Historical Reception of Blaxploitation: Articulations of Class, Black Nationalism, and Anxiety in the Genre's Advertisements," *The Velvet Light Trap* 50 (2002): 48–61.
49. Schreger, "Twenty Feature Films," 16.
50. Thomas Doherty, *Teenagers and Teenpics: The Juvenilization of American Movies in the 1950s* (Philadelphia: Temple University Press, 2002).
51. Nowell, "There's More," 122–123.
52. See Aniko Bodroghkozy, "Reel Revolutionaries: An Examination of Hollywood's Cycle of 1960s Youth Rebellion Films," *Cinema Journal* 41:3 (2002): 38–58.
53. Nowell, "There's More," 122–123.
54. McBride, "Analyze the Sale," 30.

55. Anon., "Big Rental Films of 1976," *Variety* (January 5, 1977), 14, 44.
56. Mack., "The Pom Pom Girls," 16.
57. Doherty, *Teenagers and Teenpics*, 153.
58. Ibid., 158–159.
59. Poll., "Malibu Beach," 18.
60. Kirse Granat May, *Golden State, Golden Youth: The California Image in Popular Culture, 1955–1966* (Chapel Hill, NC: University of North Carolina Press, 2002).
61. Irving Stone quoted in ibid., 11.
62. Granat May, *Golden State*, 186.
63. Vincent Canby, "Andy Hardy Updated to the Sexy '70s," *New York Times* (June 12, 1977), 83.
64. Ibid.
65. Horton, "Turning On," 242–243; Tico Romao, "Engines of Transformation: An Analytical History of the 1970s Car Chase Cycle," *New Review of Film and Television Studies* 1:1 (2003): 31–54.
66. Peter Stanfield, "Intent to Speed: Cyclical Production, Topicality, and the 1950s Hot Rod Movie," *New Review of Film and Television Studies* 11:1 (2013): 34–55.
67. See Romao, "Engines of Transformation."
68. See Crown International Pictures, "The Pom Pom Girls"; Crown International Pictures, "The Van"; Crown International Pictures, "Malibu Beach"; Crown International Pictures, "Van Nuys Blvd."
69. Crown International Pictures, "The Pom Pom Girls," unpaginated.
70. Crown International Pictures, "The Van," unpaginated; Crown International Pictures, "Van Nuys Blvd.," unpaginated.
71. Richard Phillips "Custom Cars: Today's Hot Rods Cruise with More Style than Speed," *Chicago Tribune* (August 22, 1979), E1.
72. Georgia Dullea, "Van Décor: Strictly Deluxe," *New York Times* (April 20, 1978), 1.
73. Ken Brown quoted in Anon., "Makers See No Limits to Van Fan Explosion," *Boston Globe* (February 20, 1977), 70.
74. Larry Palacky quoted in Kathy Sawyer, "Spangled Vans: Beds, Beers, and Fun on Four Wheels," *Washington Post* (September 7, 1975), 1.
75. Horton, "Turning On," 238.
76. See Motion Picture Association of America, "The Code of Self- Regulation (Revised Edition, 1977): Declaration of the Principles of the Code of Self-Regulation of the Motion Picture Association." Reprinted in Jon Lewis, *Hollywood vs. Hardcore: How the Struggle over Censorship Saved Hollywood* (New York: New York University Press, 2002), 307–314; Anon., "MPAA Gets Par to Clean 'Up' Ads," *Variety* (November 16, 1978), 5.
77. Crown International Pictures, "Van Nuys Blvd.," unpaginated.
78. See, e.g., Johnson and Schaefer, "Soft Core/Hard Core."
79. See Shelley Stamp Lindsey, "Is Any Girl Safe? Female Spectators at the White Slave Films," *Screen* 37:1 (1996): 1–15; Tim Snelson, "'From Grade B Thrillers to Deluxe Chillers': Prestige Horror, Female Audiences, and Allegories of Spectatorship in *The Spiral Staircase* (1946)," *New Review of Film and Television Studies* 7:2 (2009): 173–188; Richard Nowell, "Targeting American Women: Movie Marketing, Genre History, and the Hollywood Women-in-Danger Film," *InMedia* 3 (2013), available at http://inmedia.revues.org/600; Richard Nowell, "'For Girls': Hollywood, the Date-Movie Market, and Early-1980s Teen Sex Comedies," *Post-Script* 33:2 (2014): 16–32.

80. See, e.g., Mark Jancovich, "'Hot Profits Out of Cold Shivers!' Horror, the First-Run Market, and the Hollywood Studios, 1938–1942," in *Merchants of Menace: The Business of Horror Cinema*, ed. Richard Nowell (New York: Bloomsbury, 2014), 165.
81. Marilyn Tenser quoted in Anon., "His and Hers Fantasies in the Dark Keep the Box Office Glowing," *Variety* (June 19, 1975), 16.
82. Ibid.
83. Mark Tenser quoted in Anon., "Crown Gearing '75 Releases to Women," *Variety* (December 18, 1974), 10.
84. See Mcbride, "Analyze the Sale," 3.
85. Marilyn Tenser quoted in Lipton, "Sexual Discrimination," 74.
86. Marilyn Tenser quoted in Dick Kleiner, "David Carradine Tells Movie Plans," *Sumter Daily Item* (June 22, 1974), 17.
87. Hilary Radner, *Neo-feminist Cinema: Girly Films, Chick Flicks, and Consumer Culture* (New York: Routledge, 2011), 6–25.
88. Ibid.
89. See Nowell, "There's More."
90. Gregory A. Waller, "Auto-Erotica: Some Notes on Comic Softcore Films for the Drive-In Circuit," *Journal of Popular Culture* 17:2 (1983): 138.
91. Crown International Pictures, "The Pom Pom Girls," unpaginated; Crown International Pictures, "Van Nuys Blvd.," unpaginated. Marilyn Tenser even suggested such practice influenced casting. "The performers in these movies are like the kids the audience goes to school with," she explained; "[w]e go for a natural look." Marilyn Tenser quoted in Gross, "A Woman's Place," 34.
92. Kerry Segrave, *Drive-in Theaters: A History from Their Inception in 1933* (Jefferson, NC: McFarland, 1992), 148–152.
93. Mark Tenser quoted in Will Tusher "Dangers of Non-Major Filming: Drift from 'Sex' and 'Violence'; Bad Guesses Never Hit Market," *Variety* (June 22, 1977), 46. Evidence suggests Crown successfully walked the line. Where Linda Gross claimed *The Van* was "entirely free from malice" (1977) and Vincent Canby emphasized it was "not pornographic nor even dirty" (1977), Kevin Thomas suggested *Malibu Beach* featured "sex, nudity, and salty talk—none of which is carried to excess" (1978). See Gross, "Rite of Passage," E10; Canby, "Andy Hardy," 24; Thomas, "Malibu Beach," H19.
94. Mark Tenser quoted in Tusher, "Dangers," 46.
95. See also Waller, "Auto-Erotica," 138.
96. See Wood, *From Vietnam to Reagan*, 84.
97. See, e.g., Bruce A. Austin, "Portrait of a Cult Film Audience: The Rocky Horror Picture Show," *Journal of Communication* 31:2 (1981): 43–54; J. Hoberman and Jonathan Rosenbaum, *Midnight Movies* (New York: De Capo Press, 1991).
98. Sharon Johnson, "Corn King Coverts 'Wars' and 'Jaws,'" *New York Times* (May 14, 1978), F7.
99. Robert J. Landry, "Edible and Portable Showmanship: Up from the Oranges of Nell Gwyn," *Variety* (April 17, 1974), 5.
100. Vernon Scott, "Popcorn Keeps the Movies Popping," *Boston Globe* (October 20, 1976), 32.
101. Michael Blowen, "Movie Munchies: A Moviegoer's Guide to the Tastiest Concessions" (March 1, 1979), A12.

102. Barbara Isenberg, "Movie Snacks: 'Pop' Goes the Cash Register," *Los Angeles Times* (July 11, 1976), 54.
103. Anon., "Service Sunday for Red Jacobs, Crown Founder," *Variety* (November 7, 1980), 30.
104. Isenberg, "Movie Munchies," A12.
105. Anon., "Book Pix that Stimulate Food and Drink: Argue Stands Are Sites Salvation," *Variety* (February 28, 1979), 7, 38.
106. Johnson, "Corn King," F7.
107. Ibid.
108. Leonard Lowengrub quoted in Isenberg, "Movie Snacks," 54.
109. Crown International Pictures, "The Pom Pom Girls," unpaginated; Crown International Pictures, "Malibu Beach," unpaginated.
110. Canby, "Andy Hardy," 15.
111. Poll., "Malibu Beach," 3.
112. Alisa Perren, "A Big Fat Indie Success Story? Press Discourses Surrounding the Making and Marketing of a Hollywood Film," *Journal of Film and Video* 56:2 (2004): 18–31.
113. Dale Pollock, "Cheech & Chong Riding High on 'Smoke,' Prep 2d Feature," *Variety* (October 20, 1978), 2.
114. Cart., "Cheech and Chong's Nice Dreams," *Variety* (June 3, 1981), 14.
115. Anon., "New Pix Blitz L.A. B.O.; 'Smoke' 260G; 'Nile' 175G," *Variety* (October 3, 1978), 3.
116. The company rarely alluded to marijuana in promotional materials. Aside from two fleeting references in the trailer for *Malibu Beach*, a trade ad placed in *Boxoffice* magazine represented something of an exception. Advertising a double bill of *The Pom Pom Girls* and *The Van*, it employed a thinly veiled double entendre throughout. Across a trio of taglines, it highlighted a marijuana-themed term in three ways: capitalizing, underlining, and with a larger font than surrounding words— "Together for a California <u>HIGH</u>," "<u>HIGH</u> WAY TRUCKERS," and "<u>HIGH</u> SCHOOL GIRLS." *Boxoffice* (March 6, 1978), cover.
117. Poll., "Malibu Beach," 3.
118. See also Nowell, "'For Girls.'"
119. Murphy, "300 Indie Films," 1, 6.
120. Kevin Thomas, "Teen-Age Hijinks in 'Pom Pom Girls,'" *Los Angeles Times* (September 10, 1976), F16; Cart., "Van Nuys Blvd.," 2.

7

From "Sex Entertainment for the Whole Family" to Mature Pictures: *I Jomfruens Tegn* and Transnational Erotic Cinema

Kevin Heffernan

Near the beginning of Finn Karlsson's 1973 Danish hard-core film *I Jomfruens Tegn* ("In the Sign of the Virgin," US title, *Danish Pastries*), Mr. Armand (Ole Søltof, star of major studio Palladium's hugely popular *Bedside* series), a visiting administrative superintendent of a provincial girls' academy who has mistaken a town brothel for the school, and the husband of the brothel Madame (Benny Hansen) engage in a minutes-long conversation at cross purposes. Armand believes he is discussing the astrological foundations for the strict psychological discipline that underlies the school's teaching method, and the Madame's husband (unnamed in the dialogue of the film) thinks that the astrological signs Armand is discussing are code words for the female employees of the establishment and the services they offer to clients. After Armand asserts that he is a Virgin (*jomfruen*, both the astrological sign of Virgo and Danish for a female virgin, which in Armand's case appears to be half true), the Benny Hansen character expresses annoyance at Armand's supposed use of euphemism ("Is all this crap really necessary?"), and the conversation, flawlessly performed in two extended single takes with perfect comic timing by two well-known mainstream comic actors, devolves into a sexual "Who's on First" set of misunderstandings ("[Astrological] balance? Nah, we just call it a three way … Geminis ('*tvilingenes*', the Zodiac sign of the twins, which is complementary to Virgo)? We'd like to have a pair of those [to offer male clients], but they're hard to get these days," etc.), before Armand asks to see the "headmistress" and is taken upstairs to meet Gine, the Madame.[1]

How did this scene featuring one of Denmark's most popular mainstream comic actors find its way into a sexually explicit film that in two years would be playing in porn theaters in American inner-city neighborhoods? The film historian Jack Stevenson has identified the "folk comedy" as one of the dominant subgenres of Danish erotic cinema. This production trend can be seen as far back as the 1962 release of Gabriel Axel's *Det tossede paradis/Crazy Paradise*,[2] but it reached critical mass in 1970 with Director John Hilberd's *Mazurka på sengekanten/Bedside Mazurka*, the first installment of Hilbert's soft-core *Bedside* series very loosely based on the work of the comic novelist Erik Soya. Both soft-core and hard-core films that followed in the wake of this series (which itself began to incorporate hard-core inserts in 1975 with *Der må være en sengekant/Come to My Bedside*) developed a highly successful formula that included recognizable film and television actors in stylized comic roles, brief scenes of explicit sex performed by extras or body doubles for the name performers; plots derived from the farce or New Comedy that included mistaken identity, chase sequences; and a mockery of middle-class propriety and sexual repression. The bubbly, anodyne quality of these and other sex films—which were collectively known by the Americanized neologism *glad porn*—was later described by Danish critics as "sex entertainment for the whole family."[3] Perhaps the most successful series of hard-core Danish folk comedies was the six *Tegn* or "Zodiac" films that began in 1973 with *I Jomfruens Tegn*, produced by Anders Sandberg's Con Amore, the company that also produced Ole Ege's groundbreaking hard-core feature *Bordellen* in 1972. The *Tegn* films deployed a repertory company of Danish character actors including *Bedside*'s Ole Søltoft, Sigrid Horne-Rasmussen, and Benny Hansen and played to huge crowds in Denmark's largest theater chains.

In the United States, such crossover between porn and mainstream film comedy was impossible, if not unthinkable. Still, the first of the *Tegn* films, *I Jomfruens Tegn* ("In the Sign of the Virgin"), played a crossover role of sorts for Mature Pictures, an ambitious distributor in the ghettoized world of hard-core cinema. Mature dubbed the film into English, retitled it *Danish Pastries*, and used its aspirational or upscale elements to move the company from its previous status as the provider of low-budget program pictures to the more profitable realm of booking crossover adult hits into first-run porn theaters and, eventually, releasing soft-core cuts of porn films into drive-ins and other situations.

Palladium and Ole Søltof, Danish everyman of sexual desire

In 1968, the arched eyebrows of the world turned to Denmark, where recommended changes to censorship laws by the newly appointed justice minister Knud Thiestrup were approved by the Danish Parliament and almost all forms of commercial pornography became legal in the summer. Previously underground businesses such as sex cinemas and Peter and Jans Theander's Rodox Corporation (publishers of *Color Climax* magazine) became tourist destinations and hot international commodities. Soon, Copenhagen was home to dozens of live sex establishments such as Club Venus, where uncomfortable-looking businessmen, as well as a growing smattering of women, sat silently and watched couples, women, and threesomes copulate on mattresses onstage while rock music blared through overmodulated speakers. The following year cemented Copenhagen's reputation as the epicenter of pornography and commercial sex when the Theanders organized an international trade show for the sex industry, Sex 69, which became an international media circus and was attended by rock stars and other celebrities.[4] American filmmaker Alex DeRenzy brought a documentary crew to the convention, and the film that resulted, *Pornography in Denmark* (1970), became one of the first widely released films to show explicit sex on American commercial theater screens. Sweden's Torgny Wickman and Germany's Phyllis and Eberhard Kronhausen also brought film crews to Copenhagen to document Denmark's bold approach to the media and sexual freedom.[5]

This international obsession with Denmark presented an opportunity for the mainstream Danish film industry to move decisively into the international market and to profitably make and release more than the twenty-five or so annual features that the domestic market could bear.[6] The major company that took the lead in this trend was Palladium, the oldest motion picture company in Denmark. Palladium began as the Swedish company Skandinavisk Filmscentral, which was founded in 1915, owned a chain of very successful theaters in Sweden, and operated a major production studio in Denmark. In 1919, the company changed its name to Palladium and began making comedies and historical costume pictures for the world market.[7] Danish interests controlled the company after 1922, and because of their reserving a portion of their release slate for artistically significant films, particularly those of Carl Theodor-Dreyer, Palladium was able to acquire a cinema license that exempted them from 1922 and 1938 restrictions against production companies owning movie theaters. Palladium continued to operate profitable theaters in Copenhagen and other major cities throughout the cinema license period, which ended in 1972.[8]

Palladium had, in fact, begun their erotic comedy trend before the 1968 changes to censorship laws in 1965 with their production of *Sytten/Soya's 17*, a coming-of-age comedy that made a star out of the young Ole Søltof, whose humiliating quest to lose his virginity would become one of Palladium's most successful premises well into the 1970s. In 1968, *Sytten*'s director, Annalise Meineche, teamed with the screenwriter John Hilbard to make *Uden en trævl/Without a Stitch*, a nudity-filled comic drama that copied the Swedish sex film formula of the picaresque sexual adventures of a young woman from the provinces (Anne Grete) in the big city, in this case one whose anorgasmia is "treated" by a hands-on male gynecologist (Ib Mossin) and who is then released into the wilds of Copenhagen to practice what she has learned. In 1970, Palladium found the golden formula when it teamed the screenwriter Hilbard, the stories of the comic novelist Erik Soya, and masculine *naïf* Søltof in *Mazurka på sengekanten/Bedside Mazurka*. Søltof plays a Max Mikkelsen, a virginal but popular teacher at the repressive *Krubbesögårds* (Crab Lake) boys' school who is next in line to become principal when the current administrator, Mr. Bosted (Axel Strøbye), resigns to become the minister of culture. Since the school charter states that the principal must be married, the students, constantly plotting against and subverting the school's authority through the use of spies and walkie-talkies, attempt to engineer Max losing his virginity lest the job fall to the repressed and authoritarian Mr. Holst (Paul Hagen). Max attempts to learn about sex in short order by looking at ancient Greek erotic art and visiting one of Copenhagen's sex shops, but neither the boys' setting him up with a local stripper nor the aggressive pursuit of him by the wealthy Erica (Anne Grete from *Without a Stitch*) gets him any closer to his goal.

The daughter of one of the school's directors, Lena (Birt Tove), is the object of his affections, but she is not interested in deflowering him just to qualify him for a promotion. Eventually, he finds sexual initiation in Eva (Annie Birgit Gade), the frustrated wife of Mr. Bosted. At the end of the film, he has become a suitable partner for Lena, and the two become engaged after being caught *in flagrante* at the annual school picnic. The confusing array of roles into which women can be cast leave Max confused about their desires and intentions throughout the film, and a rhyming series of shots contrast women as trophy portraits on a bureaucrat's desk, two-dimensional images on a pornographic trading cards, figures on glazed *objets d'art*, and disembodied artificial vaginas in sex shops.

The film was a huge hit and spawned an entire series from Hilbard and Palladium, which brought back the repertory cast and repeated and refined the narrative and comic formula. In the second film, *Tandlæge på sengekanten/Bedside Dentist* (1971), Søren Stømberg, who played a small role as a hippie protester in *Bedside Mazurka*, was cast in a much larger part as Søltof's licentious and promiscuous friend Michael, and the contrasting of the two parodic inflections of contemporary Danish masculinity became one of the richest comic veins that ran throughout the series.

Bordellos and girls' schools: The hard-core *lystspils* and *I Jomfruens Tegn*

As the first two installments of the *Bedside* series were playing to packed houses, the producer Anders Sandberg with American partner Transamerica (by then, the "adult" division of American International Pictures) produced the soft-core comedy *Dagmars Hetta Troser/Dagmar's Hot Pants, Inc.*, the story of a young call girl tying up lose ends on her last day at work. On hand for a romantic subplot was the now-ubiquitous Ole Søltof as Dagmar's shy client and romantic interest. With the money from this hit, the producer Sandberg formed Con Amore, a company to produce hard-core films to be screened outside of red-light districts in major theaters. Con Amore's first film was a collection of short films written and directed, and shot by the highly eccentric pinup photographer and maker of 8 mm sex loops, Ole Ege, titled *Pornografi—en musical/Pornography, a Musical* (1971), which featured a short musical performance by American jazz pianist Dexter Gordon. In 1972, Sandberg and Ege returned with *Bordellet/Bordello*, the first full-length pornographic feature made in Denmark. *Bordello* tells the now-familiar story of Ingrid (Lonny Federsen), a young woman from the provinces at the turn of the century who comes to Copenhagen and joins the staff of an upscale brothel. Her adventures are intercut with the efforts of the repressed Inspector Sørensen (the famous television comic Gotha Anderson) to go undercover as a rich patron of the establishment to arrest the Madame and her employees.

Bordello's poster described the movie as "a good-time girl's memories" (*en glædespiges erindringer*) and a "pornographic farce" (*pornografisk lystspil*). The movie revels in its disunity and artificiality, with both narrative and porn action completely stopping to showcase unusual burlesque performances including a woman whose act climaxes with her setting her pubic hair on fire with a candle. There are undercranked Keystone Cops-style chases, the 1972 hairstyles are deliberately unconvincing in their approximation of *fin-de-siècle styles*, and many of the most erotic sequences are

Figure 7.1 The playful stylization of *Bordellet*'s mise-en-scène was reflected in the design of the film's poster and publicity materials.

intercut with goggle-eyes reaction shots of Gotha Anderson with his glaringly pasted on moustache.

After the success of *Bordello*, which had combined elements of farce and burlesque, the pinup, and the hard-core loop into a winning commercial feature film, the producer Anders Sandberg planned a follow-up for his Con Amore production company, which would humbly claim on its one-sheet poster to be "the biggest, boldest, most exciting Danish comedy" (*det største, fraekkeste, mest forrygende Danske lystspil*) and which would inaugurate an ambitious hard-core series to rival Palladium's spectacularly successful soft-core *Bedside* films. The series' inaugural feature, *I Jomfruens Tegn*, was about the approach of the planet Venus toward the earth-threatening widespread sexual anarchy and the subsequent efforts of both a school for girls and the *bordello* next door to weather the (largely human-made) bacchanal that follows in the planet's wake. Crucial to the series' concept was the participation of the hugely popular Søltof, who, while not participating in the hard-core action himself, would bring to the non-sex scenes his comic execution of many bits of business that had made the *Bedside* films huge hits in Denmark, Sweden, Germany, and the UK. The non-sex cast was rounded out by many other experienced mainstream comic actors, including Sigrid Home Rasmussen in the role of Headmistress Miss Astra, Lone Helmer as Gine, the brothel Madame, and television actor Benny Hansen as Gine's inept husband and assistant in managing the brothel. The male sex roles would be played by Bent Warburg, half of Denmark's porno power couple along with his wife Anne-Bie (also appearing in the film as Geminette, one of the schoolgirls), who was also an ambitious and gifted comic actor in his own right, Bent Rohweder and Keid Holm from *Bordello*, and another couple of more-or-less anonymous players.[9] The female sexual performers are only identified in the film's credits by their first names and include the aforementioned Anne Bie Warburg as well as Vivi Rau (soon to replace Birt Tove in the *Bedside* films as they moved into hardcore), Lena Andersen as Tauretta, the most aggressive and experienced of the girls, Eva Lundberg as Minet, a new arrival to the school and the most psychologically shaded of the schoolgirl characters, and a repertory company of another eight young women who would, with slight variation, appear in each of the series' five follow-ups.

In *I Jomfruens Tegn*, Sandberg and the writer/director Finn Karlsson concocted a hybrid of Danish screen sex as it had been shown and marketed for the previous five years. The dominant register of the film is erotic farce derived from the *Bedside* series and other folk comedies. The oppressive and hidebound social setting of the *Nulpolitterorden* girls' school is a direct descendent of the Crab Lake Boys School of *Bedside Mazurka* and the Dental College of *Bedside Dentist*. As the boys in the Crab Lake School pass unseen through space with their network of walkie-talkies, the girls of *Nulpolitterorden* possess a key that links the subterranean detention dungeon with an alleyway connected to the brothel, where students such as the insatiable Tauretta escape their imprisonment for sexual improprieties to fully indulge their appetites with the patrons of the establishment next door. Like *Bedside Dentist* and the following films in that series, which contrast the Ole Søltof character's sexual naiveté with the indiscriminate promiscuity of his thematic opposite played by Søren Stømberg, *I Jomfruens Tegn* contrasts Søltof's character Mr. Armand, who comes to the Swiss village of Petit Bois carrying a suitcase containing a powder that diminishes the sex drive, with Bent Warburg's manic and libidinous Professor Bomwitz, who arrives on the same day bearing an identical suitcase containing a jar of a powerful aphrodisiac. In a classic farcical plot device illustrating what the literary historian Albert Bermel calls "the object as antagonist,"[10] the two suitcases are exchanged, and Armand dumps the entire jar of aphrodisiac powder into the city reservoir. The already horny students at the school drink pitchers of water at dinner, attempt to ravish Armand in the school's dining room, and flee the school through the underground passageway to wreak havoc on the brothel and the harried Benny Hansen character in a twenty-minute group sex romp, providing perhaps the most vivid example in film history of the "incapacitated victims" of the farcical spell described by Bernel as central to the genre.[11] The school's headmistress, the prudish scold Miss Astra, a character without whom the farce as a mode or genre could never exist, is the next in a long line of characters that include Mr. Holst from *Bedside Mazurka* and Inspector Sørensen from *Bordello* and that stretches back through Malvolio in Shakespeare's *Twelfth Night* all the way to the figures in the *commedia dell'arte* and, ultimately, Aristophanes.[12]

In addition to being the movie's most important commercial asset, Ole Søltof's performance as Armand is the element that most firmly unifies the disparate elements of the film in the comic mode: it even anchors and gives shading to its mirror image, the hyperactive, priapic antics of Bent Warburg's Professor Bomwitz. The most frenzied copulating in the brothel orgy is intercut with Armand trapped atop the armoire with three naked young women trying to grab him by the arms and legs and pull him down into the melée.

I Jomfruens Tegn reprises many of Søltof's signature comic bits from *Soya's 17* and the *Bedside* series: he chokes on the liquor offered him by the brothel manager; he replays the cluelessness of his visit to the sex shop in *Bedside Mazurka* when he encounters a hand-cranked vibrator, flipping it over several times before he is able to turn the crank and tickle himself with its rubber pad; and, in a scene repurposed from virtually every *Bedside* film, he finds himself aggressively pursued by a sexually voracious woman, in this case a nude employee of the brothel who he has watched masturbate through an open doorway (his surprised, delighted, and wonderstruck facial expressions here are one the comic highlights of the film), but unlike in the earlier films, he finds himself on the verge of giving in to her entreaties.

Suddenly, Gine appears at the top of the stairs, grabs him by his tie, and pushes him into an adjacent room where she intends to initiate him into the world of sexual experience. When he tells her that behaving in this way violates the wishes of the board of directors, she angrily replies that hers is an independent business with no board of directors and ejects the aroused and confused Armand from the establishment.

But, this is also porno, as a viewer learns seconds after the opening credits, when another "Virgin," a character played by Vivi Rau, is shown to be the recipient of enthusiastic oral sex performed by Tauretta (Leni Andersen), who manages to coax an orgasm from her just as the school bell rings. *I Jomfruens Tegn* is not just a studio sex farce with the added *frisson* of unsimulated sex. Rather, its sexual explicitness and use of the tropes of Danish moving-image pornography constitute a very nuanced response to and recombination of the commercially successful formulas that preceded its 1973 production. While the balanced plot machinations and intricate formal unity of running gags and motifs characteristic of farce pull the film in one direction, a more inchoate and varied set of elements characteristic of film pornography pull the film away from the rigor of farce toward a more episodic structure.[13] As Linda Williams writes in *Hard Core*, the pornographic feature film showcases a range of "numbers" consisting of varied sex acts (lesbian or "girl/girl," heterosexual couplings, threesomes, solo masturbation, group sex, etc.),[14] whose deployment can interfere with the ruthless efficiency of the New Comedy plot. Also, there are times in which a form of stylized erotic display halts the narrative outright, as had some of the burlesque-derived interludes in *Bordello*. The most spectacular instance of this in *I Jomfruens Tegn* occurs when Professor Bomwitz, in another incidence of the "incapacitated victims" of the farce, is frustrated by the effects of Armand's drive-killing potion and experiences a surreal dream in which women's bodies form a desert-like landscape and he floats in midair surrounded by double-exposed dancing nude women whose bodies are painted green and blue as a synthesizer-driven arrangement of Ravel's *Bolero* plays on the soundtrack. These moments of performative female display would become more elaborate in the dance musical production numbers in later films in the *Tegn* series.

Some of the earliest documentary sex films shot in Copenhagen and environs after the liberalization of censorship laws, such as the Kronhausens' *Freedom to Love* (1969) and Torgny Wickman's *Love Play: That's How We Do It* (1972), saved their scenes of group sexuality and carnality, whether group sex or communal body painting, for the conclusion of the film for both aesthetic and political reasons because they were the most visually intricate scenes in the films, and they appeared to present a utopian alternative to the dominant social norms of mandatory monogamy and the patriarchal family. The brothel orgy that concludes *I Jomfruens Tegn* serves at least one of these functions, presenting a spectacle of maximum comic misrule: the Benny Jensen character screams "Gine! Gine!" throughout, realizing the brothel is being both physically and commercially destroyed, and Miss Astra looks on in panic from a doorway, both replaying the incredulous mugging that had characterized Gotha Anderson's comic reaction shots in *Bordello*.

Of course, the scene also provides the most insistent, varied, and powerful barrage of explicit imagery in the film. Then, Armand, still mistakenly believing that the town's water supply contains the libido-killing chemical, screams, "to the reservoir!" and the sex-crazed denizens of the brothel run through the city streets, many of them fully nude, toward the outskirts of town. When they reach the reservoir, they all jump in and engage in an underwater aquatic orgy that repeats many of the visual motifs from Bomwitz's dream while a choral version of Bert Bacharach's "What the World Needs Now Is Love" plays on the soundtrack. Where neither the constrained space of the school nor the similarly limited and limiting space of the brothel can contain the collective erotic energy, in this magical amniotic realm there seems to be pure communal bliss and the dissolution of individual ego. And, of course, this takes place under the sign of Aquarius, the water bearer and beacon to a new age of empathy and enlightenment. At first glance, the reconfigured monogamous heterosexual couple, which dominated the resolution of all of the *Bedside* films, seems to have been displaced as the figure of narrative closure.

There is another set of narrative and generic norms from the sex film complicating this picture, however. Eva Lindberg's Minet, who wears a Cancer medallion around her neck, emergences as the central female character: she is the school's most recent arrival, and we witness her cruel hazing and integration into the contested hierarchy of the students' world, which is intercut with Armand's disoriented tour around the brothel.

Her efforts to find sexual gratification are repeatedly frustrated in the middle half of the film. In another sex films, such as Joe Sarno's *Inga* (1968), Ole Ege's *Bordello* (1972), or Mac Ahlberg's *Justine and Juliette* (1975), she would be the film's main protagonist. After being brutally assaulted by the girls and forced to give oral sex to Piscetta on the kitchen prep table, she escapes to the brothel only to have Professor Bomwitz, inadvertently drugged with Armand's powder, unable to respond. Then, she attempts to seduce the character played by Ditte Maria in a hot steaming bathtub but is rejected by the sullen statuesque brunette. Finally, during the frenzy at the end of the film, she sneaks into Miss Astra's office, dials home, and has phone sex with her girlfriend Minot. The Ditte Maria character looks longingly at her from the doorway, comes forward, and, in a very lyrical passage with double-exposed overlapping action, the two hesitantly at first, then passionately, make love on Miss Astra's desk before later joining the others in the reservoir.

What happens to Ole Søltof's Armand? He is thrown into the reservoir by the frenzied schoolgirls. Stevenson writes of the different world the actor seems to inhabit from some of the other performers, "underplaying his part marvelously [and] never shed[ding] his clothes,"[15] but he may be mistaken: at the very end of the underwater orgy, Minet, naked but still wearing her Cancer medallion, pulls off Armand's red paisley underwear briefs at the moment the Burt Bacharach-singing chorus lets out a stinger of "Everyone!" and soon the Søltof member (or that of a body double) is billowing freely in the water. This is a strong hint that even at what seems to be the point of maximum pornotopic instability, *I Jomfruens Tegn* is establishing narrative closure by mating its two central protagonists. As Bermel notes, farce is neither nihilist nor utopian, and its inversion and misrule is always circumscribed, often by a return to some version of order at the end of the shenanigans.[16] The movie follows this scene with a decidedly phallocentric and patriarchal epilogue as Armand and Professor Bomwitz look through the gates of the *Nulpolitterorden* school, where the now-pregnant girls are all playing ringtoss. When both men count the expectant students on their fingers and reach the number ten, they slap both hands in the air in pride of ownership. This moment of male privilege for Armand and Bomwitz recalls the credit sequence, where Ole Søltof and Bent Warburg appear with the "legitimate" talent and the female sexual performers all share one title card and are only identified by their first names. As the camera zooms into the penis of the *putto* adorning the fountain in the courtyard, we hear Miss Astra hiss, "Scandalous," and the film ends.

Ordinary Joes and Scandinavian crumpet: Sam Lake, Maturepix, and *Danish Pastries*

In June 1973, one month before *I Jomfruens Tegn* was released in Denmark to spectacular business, US Supreme Court finally agreed on a definition of obscenity in the landmark *Miller v. California* case, and thereafter, films, books, and magazines that failed its "three-prong test"[17] could be prosecuted more easily under obscenity laws of individual American states. After this decision, the Court increasingly refused to overturn or even hear lower court decisions finding films and other forms of media obscene. Within a year, it was clear that "community standards" in the *Miller* test had become local rather than national, and Federal obscenity prosecutors began "venue shopping" to try obscenity cases in conservative communities in the American South and Midwest. The orderly national release of an adult film was now threatened by the possibility of prosecution in local venues irrespective of the result of the film's obscenity prosecution elsewhere. This was one of many factors that led to a major shift in adult film distribution by the middle of the decade in which control of the most profitable sectors of the industry was increasingly consolidated into a smaller number of larger firms releasing a smaller number of 35 mm features with higher budgets and production values (i.e. greater possible "serious literary, artistic, political, or scientific value") in larger print runs. Some of the most successful of these firms prepared R-rated soft-core cuts of their releases for many profitable bookings into drive-in theaters as well.

One company hoping to make this transition from supplying desperate American porn theaters with program pictures to releasing upscale features in both hard and soft versions was Mature Pictures Corporation.[18] Before moving into the hard-core market in the early 1970s, the company, as Sam Lake Enterprises, had distributed low-end soft-core sexploitation product such as Francis Ford Coppola's *Tonight for Sure* (1962), the Yoko Ono-starring "roughie" *Satan's Bed*, and Doris Wishman's *Bad Girls Go to Hell* (1965) to theaters adopting an adults-only policy during the product shortage of the American film industry's severe 1960s recession, eventually financing such modest productions themselves just as the market became glutted in 1967–1969. Company head Lake had also been a member of the partnership that owned New York's World Theater on 49th Street during its transition from an art house showcasing films of the French New Wave to Gotham's flagship adults-only theater.[19] After entering the hard-core market and changing the company name to Mature Pictures, Lake and President Robert Sumner continued financing low-budget features such as *Sex Rituals of the Occult* (1970), the New York-shot *Sexual Customs in Scandinavia*, and *The Morning After* (both 1972). After failing to enter the upper tier of the industry with their ambitious in-house production *High Rise* in 1973, Sumner acquired the American rights to *I Jomfruens Tegn*, produced an English-language dialogue track directed with some flair by Richard D'Antoni,[20] and even secured a license to include the Burt Bacharach song on the movie's soundtrack.

In the years between the "porno chic" popularity of *Deep Throat* (1972), *Behind the Green Door* (1972), and *The Devil in Miss Jones* (1973) and the 1975 Maturepix dubbed release of *I Jomfruens Tegn*, the 1974 success of Just Jaeckin's *Emmanuelle*, released dubbed in the United States by Columbia Pictures, suddenly made a broadly defined European erotica popular in the United States again. Would Americans still have a specifically Danish flavor of erotica in mind, with five years having passed since both the explosion of documentary exposés of "wide open Copenhagen" and the high water mark of US fascination with "Swedish sin?"[21] Stevenson offers a hilarious description of this dilemma:

> Either ... Swedish gals were more desirable, or, more likely, ... many folks in America actually thought Copenhagen was the capital of Sweden (as Danes like to joke). To the average American Joe the two countries were in fact pretty much interchangeable. Copenhagen probably had more star power than Stockholm, and Sweden, as noted, was synonymous with sex to a greater degree than Denmark since "Danish" was inevitably equated with pastries. And any American can toss off a rough approximation of a singsong Swedish accent, but generally they have no idea that Danish sounds completely different. Scandinavia is a jumble of stereotypes to outsiders, so why not for the sake of convenience move Copenhagen across the Øresund Strait to Sweden? Then one would have the best of both worlds. If one can say that a kind of simplified "porno geography" exists parallel to the real thing, then that is where you would find Copenhagen, in Sweden, where all the blonde girls wear long braids and are milk maids—which in itself seems to be more of a German or Swiss cliché.[22]

Thus, *I Jomfruens Tegn* was christened *Danish Pastries* by its American distributor.

It premiered in March 1975 at the World in New York, and Mature Pictures pulled out all of the stops to present it as an upscale release for a crossover audience of women and couples. "See it with someone you'd like to love," purred the ads (in America, the only "whole family" suitable for adult films was, after all, a heterosexual couple), which featured the same picture of Ole Søltof from the film's Danish one-sheet surrounded by the nude repertory company of eleven female sexual performers. The poster featured critical raves, the *sine qua non* of the crossover porn release, and featured Al Goldstein praising "eleven of the most beautiful women I've seen in a sex film," even as both the crossover and raincoat crowds are addressed in a blurb from all-news station WINS and *Swank* magazine film reviewer Bob Salmaggi that praises the film's production values, locations, and (somewhat disingenuously) its content of "sex, sex, and more sex." Although the film would appear ideal for slight trims to remove the hard-core content and gain wider bookings in a soft-core version, there is no indication that such bookings for the film ever occurred. But the movie was a huge hit for Mature Pictures and was constantly in rerelease after the company changed its name to Maturepix later in the decade and even into the 1980s, when the company's catalogue was absorbed into sometime-partner Distribpix. The film's hybrid status as both pornographic feature and general release motion picture, so crucial to its success for Palladium at home, served a similar function for Mature Pictures in their efforts to upscale their release schedule: after the successful release of *Danish Pastries*, the company initiated several in-house productions that could serve as both first-run releases in the hard-core market and, with reedits and a soundtrack remix, do double duty as soft-core drive-in fare, such as *Expose Me Lovely* (1976) and *Take Off* (1978). They also continued to import bigger-budget films from abroad such as the French *Mes nuits avec ... Alice*,

Figure 7.2 Maturepix's advertising art and publicity materials for *Danish Pastries* stressed its potential as a crossover film with appeal to both the raincoat crowd and a broader audience of women and couples.

Pénélope, Arnold, Maud et Richard/Kinky Ladies of Bourbon Street (1976) and the Swedish *Bel Ami* (1977). Films that they did not release include the subsequent five films in the *Tegn* series that were directed by Werner Herdman between 1974 and 1978. In fact, there is no record of any of the later Zodiac films being theatrically screened anywhere in North America, which raises a set of fascinating questions that are, alas, beyond the scope of this chapter.

Conclusion

In the six films in the *Tegn* or Zodiac series, the integration of pornographic and mainstream cinema, something dreamed of by American filmmaker Gerard Damiano, came to pass in Denmark in what could only be described as "erotic entertainment for the entire family." *I Jomfruens Tegn* successfully integrated the elements of many disparate modes of Danish moving-image erotica from the sex loops shown in arcade cinemas to the "sex documentaries" that proliferated in the wake of Denmark's liberation of censorship laws to the *Bedside* and other films produced by Denmark's largest and oldest film studio, Palladium.

Unlike Denmark, where there was a hybrid or reciprocal relationship between pornography and mainstream cinema, hard-core pornographic cinema in the United States was relegated to a system of production, distribution, and exhibition entirely separated from mainstream popular entertainment, especially after the Supreme Court's *Miller* decision in 1973. This did not keep a dubbed version of *I Jomfruens Tegn* from being successfully released in 1975 under the title *Danish Pastries* by Sam Lake's Maturepix company in an effort to move their release schedule from a high-output program feature mode to one of high print runs of fewer films with bigger budgets and an "upscale" gloss. In this context, the hybrid nature of *I Jomfruens Tegn*, which combined elements of the pornographic feature with those of the mainstream motion picture, as well as many of the formal features of the film, including its dubbed soundtrack, numerous sight gags, girls' school premise, and slightly indeterminate Swiss period setting, made it ripe for both crossover success in its initial runs and profitable rerelease. In fact, the current nostalgic craze for "golden age" porn of the 1970s has made a 2009 DVD box set of the *Tegn* films a strong seller in both Europe and the United States. In both countries, the films' popularity now resides in their preserved-in-amber qualities of what Peter Schepelem of the Danish Film Institute calls "time-typical national kitsch."[23] Because of its ability to transcend many generic, commercial, and national-cinema categories, *I Jomfruens Tegn/Danish Pastries* remains one of the signature examples of successful transnational pornographic cinema.[24]

Notes

1. Mariah Larsson explained the Danish astrological and sexual puns deployed in this scene to me during the editing phase of a previous version of this chapter.

2. Jack Stevenson, *Scandinavian Blue: The Erotic Cinema of Sweden and Denmark in the 1960s and 1970s* (Jefferson, NC and London: McFarland and Company Inc., 2010), 28, 30, 37–38.
3. Isak Thorsen, "Family Porn—The Zodiac Film: Popular Comedy with Hard-Core Sex," *Journal of Scandinavian Cinema* 4:3 (2014) attributes the "family porn" moniker to Niels-Jørgen Dinnesen and Edvin Kau, *Filmen I Danmark* (Copenhagen: Akademisk Forlag, 1983).
4. For an account of the Theanders's role in the development of the modern porn industry, see Stevenson, *Scandinavian Blue*, 117 and John Heidenry, *What Wild Ecstasy: The Rise and Fall of the Sexual Revolution* (New York: Simon and Schuster, 1997), 56–57, 215–216.
5. For an overview of Torgny Wickman's sexual documentary films, see Elisabet Björklund, *The Most Delicate Subject: A History of Sex Education Films in Sweden* (Lund, Sweden: Critica Litterarum Lundensis, 2012). The Kronhausens wrote extensively about their experiences filming sex in Denmark in Phyllis in Eberhard Kronhausen, *The Sex People: A Professional View of Sensuous Celebrities and Erotic Entertainers—Who They Are and Why They Do It!* (Chicago, IL: Playboy Press, 1975), 7–8, 41–95.
6. Stevenson, *Scandinavian Blue*, 168, discusses the relationship between the domestic and export market for the *Bedside* series and other mainstream commercial films.
7. Isak Thorsen, "Carl Theodore Dreyer: The Man and His Work: Palladium," *Danish Film Institute*, available at http://english.carlthdreyer.dk/AboutDreyer/Workplaces/Palladium.aspx (accessed March 2015).
8. Peter Schepelem, "Danish Film History: 1920–1929," *Danish Film Institute*, available at http://www.dfi.dk/Service/English/Films-and-industry/Danish-Film-History/1920-1929.aspx (accessed March 2015).
9. Cast names and information for the film are from the International Adult Film Database listing, available at http://www.iafd.com/title.asp?title=Danish+Pastries&year=1973 (accessed March 2015).
10. Albert Bermel, *Farce: A History from Aristophanes to Woody Allen* (New York: Simon and Schuster, 1982), 27–30.
11. Ibid., 24–25.
12. For a historical account of the farce as a dramatic mode from Aristophanes to the Hollywood cinema, see Bermel, *Farce*. Bermel enumerates several of farce's characteristic settings and plots on pages 22–36.
13. Thorsen, "Family Porn," 290–295, discusses some of the generic tensions and overlaps between the farce and porn genres in the *Tegn* films.
14. Linda Williams, *Hard Core: Power, Pleasure, and the "Frenzy of the Visible"* (Berkeley: University of California Press, 1990), 120–154.
15. Stevenson, *Scandinavian Blue*, 216.
16. Bermel, *Farce*, 43–48.
17. Under the *Miller* test, a work was subject to prosecution under state obscenity laws if (1) "the average person, applying contemporary community standards, would find that the work, taken as a whole, appeals to the prurient interest," (2) "the work depicts or describes, in an offensive way, sexual conduct," and (3) "the work, taken as a whole, lacks serious literary, artistic, political, or scientific value." The text of the *Miller* decision can be found at https://supreme.justia.com/cases/federal/us/413/15/case.html (accessed March 2015).

18. A later interview with the company president Robert Sumner outlining the company's strategy for releasing multiple versions of bigger-budget adult films can be found in James Cook, "The X-Rated Economy," *Forbes* 122:6 (September 1978): 84–85.
19. A detailed history of Sam Lake Enterprises, the World Theater, and Mature Pictures was provided by the adult film historian and preservationist Joe Rubin in an interview with the author, March 2015.
20. After watching both versions of the film many times, I have only been able to detect one small change D'Antoni and Sumner made to the film: the voice of Minet's hometown sweetheart during her phone-sex masturbation scene was changed from female to male. This suggests that in the original version of the film, the teenage character was sent to the strict school to "cure" her bisexuality, an aspect of her character that Armand's unwitting deployment of the aphrodisiac was able to contain, at least in appearance, through her pregnancy at the film's end.
21. The role played by Sweden in the American (male) erotic imagination of the 1960s is discussed in Eric Schaefer, "'I'll Take Sweden': The Shifting Discourse of the 'Sexy Nation' in Sexploitation Films," in *Sex Scene: Media and the Sexual Revolution*, ed. Eric Schaefer (Durham, NC: Duke University Press, 2014).
22. Stevenson, *Scandinavian Blue*, 98–99.
23. Peter Schelepem, "Danish Film History: 1970–1979," *Danish Film Institute*, available at http://www.dfi.dk/Service/English/Films-and-industry/Danish-Film-History/1970-1979.aspx (accessed March 2015).
24. I would like to thank Steven Morowitz of Distribpix and Joe Rubin of Vinegar Syndrome for sharing with me their encyclopedic (and in Steven's case, first-hand) knowledge of 1970s adult filmmakers and personalities, Distribpix, Maturepix, and the print runs and booking patterns of *Danish Pastries*, and other porn features. Mariah Larsson and Chris Holmlund gave invaluable feedback on an earlier version of this chapter, and Casey Scott, Laura Helen Marks, Peter Alilunas, and the panel attendees at the 2015 Film and History Conference in Madison, Wisconsin, helped me clarify several aspects of my central argument here.

8

"Bigger Than a Payphone, Smaller Than a Cadillac": Porn Stardom in *Exhausted: John C Holmes the Real Story*

Neil Jackson

He almost has mythic stature to me. He's almost a god. He walked among us with that massive tool ... he was like some huge dinosaur ... you'd hear the thump, thump, thump, but it was his balls hitting the ground.

Al Goldstein[1]

penises are only little things (even big ones) ...

Richard Dyer[2]

This chapter identifies and negotiates the ways in which *Exhausted: John C Holmes the Real Story* (Julia St Vincent,[3] 1981) explores the limits and possibilities of male porn stardom in the twilight of the adult film industry's presumed "golden age." While the film seems upon initial glance to be a hagiographical portrait of its subject, in which bigger is most certainly better, I will argue that it is also a rare example of a pornographic film that (self-)consciously reflects upon the meanings that it generates, an attribute that is largely a symptom of its quasi-documentary form. While the film is ostensibly an articulation of carnal supremacy, it is endearingly naïve as an attempt at image control and media manipulation. And while it was intended for consumption primarily within North American porn theaters, it also communicates directly with the mainstream, focalizing the possibilities and contradictions inherent in the image of this prominent and prodigious male performer.

Any cursory perusal of movie theater listings (or analysis of photographic or film evidence) of select major urban centers of the late 1970s/early 1980s indicates a film exhibition culture that had become truly international in scope and distinctly eclectic in its range of choice. This accommodated a phenomenon in which Hollywood productions played in sites adjacent to buildings projecting domestic or foreign exploitation product, as well as largely homegrown hard-core features. Regardless

With special thanks to Martin Brooks and Oliver Carter for the supply of research material, and Phil Marson, Sarah Thomas, and Thomas Joseph Watson for some valuable suggestions.

of this global celluloid detritus adorning crumbling movie marquees at this point in history, *Exhausted* serves as evidence that equally eccentric and peculiarly ambitious manifestations were being produced by figures operating in the United States's despised subcultural margins. As a consequence, stubborn institutional resistance to pornography allowed transcultural incursions to occasionally occur from within, with both the star of *Exhausted* and the hard-core feature film in general embodying the disreputable underside of heteronormative tendencies within commercial film (and wider show business) culture. However, the chapter will also demonstrate how the attempt to mold and contain Holmes's image is repeatedly frustrated by the persona he affects under questioning, his evasiveness and dishonesty being especially revelatory when he responds to queries designed to be aggrandizing. The subtitle of the film makes explicit reference to a "real story" that it renders impossible, and the interviews with Holmes provide further insights and observations exposing the gulf between his spoken aspirations and their actual realization, subverting the attempt to declare his potency and desirability while enabling a discursive pattern in which he is at once venerated and ridiculed.

Released in 1981,[4] *Exhausted* was by no means the first occasion upon which Holmes appeared as a version of himself onscreen. Both *Superstar, John Holmes* (Alan Colberg, 1979) and *Undulations* (Carlos Tobalina, 1980) were previous attempts to mediate his persona, but in ways that were less obviously personalized and engaged. Consequently, the chapter contends that the film develops a self-reflexive surface that is not part of a deliberate creative strategy, but appears to have been quite accidental, the emergent image of Holmes being a symptom of both pornography's inherent cultural handicap and a haphazard level of authorial control. Ultimately, while the film strives to express Holmes's mystique and magnificence, it also gives voice to the general public's (and even his own colleagues') amusement and detachment from his (and the adult film industry's) ambitions for wider acceptance or legitimacy.

Holmes was born John Curtis Estes[5] in Ashville, Ohio, in 1944, and of all male porn performers, he has had the most significant impact on mainstream perceptions of the US adult film industry.[6] Thus far, he has inspired three biographical accounts,[7] while emerging as a pivotal figure in the oral history of the US adult film industry *The Other Hollywood*.[8] Besides serving as a very loose inspiration for aspects of *Boogie Nights* (Paul Thomas Anderson, 1997), a section of Holmes's life directly influenced *Wonderland* (James Cox, 2003), a speculative account of his involvement in the eponymous crime for which he would be tried. Additionally, he has been the subject of at least two retrospective documentaries, *Wadd: The Life and Times of John C. Holmes* (Cass Paley, 1999) and *XXL: The John Holmes Story* (Dave Hills, 2000).[9] All of these films draw upon the archival wellspring of *Exhausted*: in *Boogie Nights*, porn queen Amber Waves (Julianne Moore) creates what is effectively a direct pastiche; *Wonderland* incorporates images from *Exhausted* into its opening title sequence, and particular mannerisms deployed by Val Kilmer in his portrayal of Holmes are uncannily similar to those evident in the film; and both *Wadd* and *XXL* use footage, including moments that were discarded from the final release version. Despite its relatively limited exposure and consumption in its own right, *Exhausted* has infiltrated the mainstream, affecting perceptions of Holmes's iconic status; understanding of his furtive double life as an errant husband, drug addict, and alleged police informant; his highly publicized acquittal for the Wonderland murders in 1982; and his eventual death from AIDS-related complications in 1988.

At best, Holmes has served as an unreliable narrator in a personal biography that unfurls like a modern porno picaresque; at worst, his life is a cautionary tale on the travails of moral permissiveness, in which an arch-hedonist pays the ultimate price for a lifestyle irreversibly tainted by excess. His ubiquitous status was partly a symptom of his prolific output; Jennifer Sugar and Jill C. Nelson estimate that, from the mid 1960s until his death, he appeared in excess of 1,000 feature-length hard-core films, 8 mm loops and video productions.[10] Of course, his position in the hierarchy of adult film personnel was sealed by the outrageous dimensions of his penis, the exact specifications of which seem to have varied according to whoever was wielding the tape measure, including Holmes himself. Posthumous transformation of Holmes's tumultuous life into "legend" has been characterized by a combination of tarnished nostalgia, ghoulish voyeurism, and historical reappropriation, but regardless of the odd inch discrepancy here and there, it is the unembellished visualization of the length and girth of his member that provides incontrovertible proof of his reputation.

On a broader level, *Exhausted* is an unwitting snapshot of an industry on the cusp of a major cultural and economic transformation, its gradual death throes as a theatrical, communal experience soon to be expedited by the growth of domestic consumption. Chuck Kleinhans has identified the "drastic change"[11] in the industry as a consequence of the impact of home video technology, pointing out that, by 1987, theaters exhibiting 16 mm or 35 mm porn features shrank from a peak of 763 in 1982 to 250 by 1987.[12] Unaware of this imminent sea change, *Exhausted* positions Holmes at the center of an industry still hopeful of a shift from the cultural margins. It combines interviews with Holmes, his colleagues, and members of the public with stage-managed, behind-the-scenes location footage, all of which is interspersed with hard-core sexual content compiled from films directed by Holmes's frequent taskmaster Bob Chinn.[13] The sex sequences comprise several montages that emphasize the sheer quantity of Holmes's onscreen partners over multiple films, along with four longer individual encounters that strive to convey his onscreen chemistry with specific women. This includes an extended rape fantasy encounter and another where it is claimed that the actress had initially refused to perform real sex onscreen, only to lose her inhibitions due to the expert cajoling of her leading man. The final sex sequence provides an extended payoff to a recurrent strategy in which Holmes's interview comments are offset by those of Seka, one of the most prominent female performers in the industry at the time of production. Although Holmes and Seka are seen briefly *in flagrante* in the first hard-core montage, this climactic tryst resembles a familiar *fictional* trajectory: a heterosexual union at the point of dénouement, narratively enthroning porn's reigning male monarch alongside his platinum blonde queen.

Laura Kipnis has argued that there has been very little room to maneuver when it comes to discussing pornography's creative potential, contesting that

> the only expressing it's presumed to do is of misogyny or social decay ... that it might have more complicated social agendas, or that future historians of the genre might generate interesting insights ... are radically unthought thoughts.[14]

In this sense, *Exhausted* is a crucial, if not necessarily "radical," document of the relationship between the hard-core film industry and its potential consumers, as well as between filmmakers and their subjects. In fact, it is a rare beast in the pornographic realm: a promotional publicity vehicle that conducts its own empirical audience research that, for better or worse, posterity has proven to be less than conclusive or complimentary. It is also informed by retrospective knowledge of Holmes's drug addiction and criminal associations at the time of production and distribution, with both physical degeneration and (artificial) stimulation evident in his attitude and demeanor onscreen.[15] Indeed, Chinn has confirmed that the film ceased production only days before Holmes's involvement in a brutal 1981 multiple-homicide that came to be known as the "Wonderland Murders."[16]

Reflection upon Julia St. Vincent's creative role is crucial to any evaluation of the film. Never a sex performer, her involvement within the porn industry came about as a result of her employment at Freeway Films by her uncle, Armand Atamian, the distributor in control of several Holmes films.[17] This led to both a personal and professional involvement with Holmes, and St. Vincent has claimed as follows:

> I started shooting these interviews with John mainly because I realised he was going to die one day ... John would realise he's not a bad guy, and would get out of the dumps. In the case he died, I would have that footage of him and I'd become rich.[18]

Therefore, according to its creator, the film is an attempt at initiating personal rehabilitation while remaining cynically mindful of the value of Holmes's cultural notoriety, documenting his alternately inane and illuminating observations. St. Vincent has admitted that much of the film was motivated by her own misguided infatuation and jealousy, commenting, "I bait him constantly—I'm trying to figure out what's going on ... did you love me or not?"[19] However, long before these comments, the film had already been read as a desperate cinematic love-letter, a notion supported by the sporadic but exceedingly ripe voiceover narration and title song recorded by St. Vincent herself, both of which seem to contradict the later expression of her personal angst during production. In an audio commentary recorded for a specially edited version of *Exhausted* included on the 1998 Criterion laserdisc release of *Boogie Nights*, Paul Thomas Anderson commented:

> When I saw that title "Produced and Directed by Julia St Vincent," that was the moment where I realised what this documentary was. That is, it wasn't a

documentary. It was just a poem. It was just this love story to John Holmes that was like, let me give you two hours to talk about how great you are, let me show clips of your dick, let me just kinda go nuts and present you as this mysterious and wonderful man of the world.[20]

Therefore, the film also expresses the fraught relationship of an inexperienced filmmaker with her wayward subject, their involvement lending extra weight to the sense that, beneath a fragile veneer of celebrity portraiture, the film is also voicing personal disdain and disappointment with Holmes, who comes to embody the limits of both St. Vincent's and the porn industry's hopes and desires while striving vainly to maintain and elaborate the substance underlying his own myth.

Any comprehensive trawl through Holmes's vast (and, in some cases, lost or inaccessible) filmography in an attempt to identify a set of definitive signifying elements would be a thankless task. As with many pornographic film performers, and regardless of any inherent qualities within individual films, there is little that might offer a significant diversion from his primary function. However, *Exhausted* is of particular value in its attempt to come to terms with the very nature of Holmes's elevated status. Retrospective analyses have located him at the center of a phenomenon frequently characterized as "porno chic," a term that was coined by Ralph Blumenthal in the *New York Times* in 1973,[21] and adopted later in the year by Bruce Williamson in a *Playboy* article[22] covering the burgeoning production of adult feature films across the United States. Although he does not refer to either article, Brian McNair has defined "porno chic" as

> not porn [itself] but the representation of porn in non-pornographic art and culture; the pastiche and parody of, the homage to and investigation of porn; the postmodern transformation of porn into mainstream cultural artefact for a variety of purposes.[23]

McNair neglects to properly contextualize "porno chic" as a descriptive category, ignoring the etymology of the phrase and seeing it as a phenomenon that observes pornography from a detached perspective, reformulating and reimagining it with a sense of historical and ironic perspective. However, as conceived in the early 1970s, it was also characterized by the attempt of the industry to refute the ghettoization of real sex on film, and Williamson's article stresses explicitly that the phenomenon was fuelled as much by the ambitions of the filmmaking community itself as any neoliberal cultural consensus. Charting the varied industry travails on the East and West coasts, Williamson emphasizes "a whole new breed of filmmakers doing what they can to dissociate themselves from the stigma of smut."[24] This reach-out for wider acceptance runs consistently through *Exhausted*, and when Holmes is not ruminating upon anatomical dimensions, sexual variations, and female quantities, he articulates a desire to have some kind of significance beyond the world within which the film is systematically framing him, making at least half-sincere proclamations on his First Amendment rights and the social value of his chosen profession. This extends to his claim in one instance that he receives letters from couples who have thanked him for laying "a stepping stone" on the road to their own sexual discoveries. Presented in a tight one-shot that lends a sense of his personal urgency, Holmes exclaims that "it *is* an art now. It *does* have socially redeeming value. It has a place in our society. It teaches. It instructs." This attempt to politicize the wanton hedonism that Holmes frequently espouses is often supported by the comments of interviewees from the general public regardless of their age or gender, momentarily establishing a sense of an industry and society united in support of a liberal (if not necessarily libertarian) agenda. At no point in the film do any of the interviewees renounce Holmes's right to explore and express his sexuality in the public domain.

Thus far, I have avoided using the phrase "porn star" in order to give emphasis here to its peculiar resonance as an analytical paradigm. By the time *Exhausted* emerged, the era of "porno chic" had already played itself out, its "pornotopian" (to borrow Linda Williams's resonant phrase[25]) dreams of mainstream crossover more or less quashed by institutional resistance, a conservative trend that culminated in 1986 with the recommendations of the Meese Commission.[26] The embroilment of the industry's primary male icon in the even-dirtier world of drugs and homicide (and his diagnosis as HIV positive in the same year as the Reese recommendations) merely seemed to justify the realignment of the adult film industry back in the peripheries, and the very notion of the "porn star" immediately invokes its status as an oxymoron, a micro-celebrity manifestation of an oft-despised and, at least for much of the period prior to the 1980s, *criminalized* subculture in which opportunities for the wider dissemination of an industry perceived as both legally and morally dubious were severely limited. Consequently, any established analytical methods of performance, production, distribution, and audience consumption[27] must be modified accordingly to take into account the insularity and isolation of performers working in the adult film industry. Therefore, at least as a starting point, it is much more useful to evaluate such figures from the position of cult stardom, a realm in which renegades and outsiders have found significant cultural capital. Kate Egan and Sarah Thomas emphasize the importance of specialized, committed audiences and their identification of the "authenticity" of particular screen personalities for whom certain appeals lie beyond established conventions. They argue that

> rather than being positioned at the centre of a concealment/reveal narrative around a singular star image, the authenticity of cult lies in the identification of alternative, sub-cultural texts and tastes which have been marginalised through "normal" boundaries of commodification and dominant cultural practices.[28]

In this context, despite lacking what might be deemed conventional movie-star good looks or performative attributes, Holmes's penis effectively became the ultimate visual signifier of his "authenticity." As Stuart Muirhead comments, Holmes has in many ways come to embody "everything you think of when you imagine a caricature 70s porn star: a superfly, open shirted, mustachio'd loverman; a man's vaguely comical idea of a woman's dream."[29]

So, it was *that* organ, unaided by the interventions of creative photography, effects, or special makeup appliances, that served as fundamental textual proof of Holmes's special status, the anatomical size consolidated by his sexual stamina and durability with multiple partners across hundreds of films. Within the technical and economic limitations of porn production, the defining element of Holmes's persona could not be readily fabricated, and its peculiar status as a disembodied icon was regularly confirmed by the authenticating genital close-up, assuming its own mythos while enhancing the star aura of Holmes himself. Effectively, the image of Holmes's erection, coupled with the inevitability of its fundamental role in the enactment of female pleasure, served as the ultimate visual embodiment of the phallocentric dictates of the porn movie, a spectacle of excess in which the revelation and utilization of his penis guaranteed bigger and better visual pleasures.

This is interesting in light of Richard Dyer's contention that "sexuality is on the whole better represented through symbolism."[30] In hard-core films, the sensory and often allusive soft-core pleasures of "colours, textures, effects of light [and] the shape of things"[31] are supplanted by the literalizing effect of physical detail. However, Dyer was dealing predominantly with mainstream media and is fully cognizant of the cultural compartmentalization that affects any understanding of pornography. He emphasizes that pornography has developed its own "devices of symbolism to construct a particular sense of the sex it shows,"[32] wherein the visual rendition of that which is conventionally hidden or repressed begets an alternative system of representation:

> The first thing to say about the symbolism of male sexuality is that it is overwhelmingly centred on the genitals, especially the penis ... Male sexuality is repeatedly equated with the penis; men's sexual feelings are rendered as somehow being "in" their penises.[33]

Of course, this argument is especially pertinent when we reflect upon the demands of male porn stardom. Regardless of Holmes's iconographic value, his status was encumbered by the cultural and aesthetic limitations of hard-core cinema, in which male performers invariably affirm their phallic primacy in the enactment of female pleasure.

Discussing levels of differentiation in the reception of cult stardom, Matt Hills argues that "stardom is typically thought of as manufactured—as a product of industrial processes aimed at naturalising concepts of 'talent' and 'individuality.'"[34] In Holmes's case (as with any male porn star), "talent" and "individuality" once again become qualities intrinsically linked with the visual realization of sexual performance and physical endowment—indeed, the very term "performance" becomes loaded with innuendo, regardless of the dramatic capabilities of the porn actor. A cult actor's public profile is occasionally informed by perceptions of thespianic limitation, and Matt Hills uses the examples of Jean Claude Van Damme in *JCVD* (Mabrouk El Mechri, 2008), Bruce Campbell in *My Name Is Bruce* (Bruce Campbell, 2007), and William Shatner in *Free Enterprise* (Rober Meyer Burnett, 1998) and their attempts to control their image through participation in films that allow them to self-reflexively "engage with their own sub cultural valorisations and personae."[35] Although these films are fictions, they play upon real-life personae and, like *Exhausted*, each is acutely aware of the signifying components of these stars' individual appeal. However, *Exhausted* was merely one part of a process that sought to give a certain shape and coherence to Holmes's career. This was best exemplified by the attempt to associate his star image with Johnny Wadd, a recurring fictional private detective character. Developed throughout the 1970s with Bob Chinn, the character's very existence is testament to the associative value of a star persona amid the franchising of specific performative elements. *Exhausted* makes extensive use of footage from the Johnny Wadd series, to the point where it becomes another exhibit in the range of flimsy evidence upon which Holmes's appeal is founded. This is an extreme, almost pathological case of a screen persona becoming embroiled with the actor, with Wadd's characterization dependent exclusively upon Holmes's ability to supply definitive visual confirmation of the promise embedded in the character's surname. David Black has argued that some actors become intrinsically bound by particular performances. He suggests that "the join between character and actor" is so strong that "[characters become] particularly resistant to abstraction from a given actor,"[36] culminating in the development of "charactor," a fusion of idiosyncratic nuances of performance with scripted elements integral to any critical and audience engagement. In *Exhausted*, Holmes distinguishes his own approach to sexuality and masculine performance from that of the Wadd character, contesting that "[Wadd is] always exuding and portraying masculinity; he's very virile. I'm just very blasé about sexuality." Despite this, it is through footage of Holmes *as* Wadd that the film seeks to affirm the former's status, further convoluting the relationship between star and character through the paradoxical representation of real sexual activity within a fictional form.

Introducing a selection of publicity posters of "golden age" adult films, Robin Bougie points out that

> ignoring the AKAs, for the most part [the cast lists of these posters] are the same 25 names over and over again … the early New York, San Francisco and Los Angeles scenes were very tight knit and dependent upon each other for support.[37]

This image of a mutually supportive group of countercultural outsiders consolidates the sense of a development beyond established theoretical paradigms of stardom. However, just like the Hollywood mainstream, star images became crucial in the marketing and reception of adult films, but it was the commercial emphasis upon *female* performers that provided an obvious indicator of a target audience of heterosexual males devoted to the display and consumption of the female body. Just a cross section including figures such as Linda Lovelace, Georgina Spelvin, Marilyn Chambers, C.J. Laing, Annette Haven, Terri Hall, Constance Money, Serena, and Seka reveals a pronounced emphasis upon particular Caucasian archetypes or physical ideals. Male performers featured very rarely as the focal point of any commercial strategy, and a cursory glance at the promotional posters for scores of the films in which Holmes appeared reveals that he was no exception. Nevertheless, a number of other trusted and equally prolific men emerged in this period, such as Marc Stevens, Harry Reems, Eric Edwards, Jamie Gillis, John Leslie, Joey Silvera, and Paul Thomas, again all variations upon models of white masculinity that met the tastes and preferences of a racially determined demographic.[38] Often absent as an icon within marketing discourses, the textual presence and preeminence of Holmes within *Exhausted* is disproportionate to the value placed upon him as a reliable fulcrum for commercial considerations.

Holmes's career and place within this method of star systemization runs more or less concurrently with the perceived golden age of hardcore, and a canon has emerged encompassing key films, directors, and historical landmarks. His coexistence with a franchised, surrogate onscreen personality sets him apart from his male contemporaries, yet *Exhausted* reveals that he is ultimately denied absolute authorship and autonomy as far as both the Wadd character and his own modes of personal expression are concerned. The film hints at a creative collaboration between Holmes and Chinn through interview footage that presents them seated next to each other in an editing suite, elaborating upon the development of their working relationship. However, in a moment that was transposed directly in *Boogie Nights*, Holmes attempts to convey the creative dimensions of his work, claiming that the director allows him to "block" the sex sequences in which he performs. When St. Vincent questions Chinn on why he would relinquish this control, his amused and only slightly irritated response is to hesitate momentarily before glancing over at Holmes to say "I don't allow you to block your own sex scenes!" Holmes's self-perpetuation as *artiste* is immediately undercut in his presence by his supposed collaborator, his exposure as a fantasist only eliciting a desperate response that accentuates his isolation: "You see! I don't tell him how to edit and he doesn't tell me how to fuck!" Regardless of this, within the parameters of the image he seeks to project, Holmes remains cognizant of his own individuality being enmeshed with the sexual capabilities of an onscreen persona founded on sexual prodigiousness. Shot in a medium close-up, Holmes addresses the deleterious impact upon his personal relationships, alluding to his image as both human caricature and living cartoon:

> It's hard to achieve what I want sexually and mentally from somebody who is trying to fuck a Walt Disney character, which I'm not. I'm just a human being.

Because it remains extremely difficult to disentangle this statement from the brace of outlandish proclamations that he makes elsewhere, Holmes's self-contradictory behavior, in conjunction with the film's own schizophrenic tendencies, ultimately renders him unknowable as an individual.

However, *Exhausted* remains a useful litmus test in defining the boundaries of Holmes's appeal, especially insofar as the audience for theatrically exhibited pornography was largely anonymous and furtive in its modes of consumption. In a film that struggles to articulate Holmes's desirability as a heterosexual icon, the interviews with male audience members outside of the X1 and X2 adult movie theaters in Los Angeles are notable for their expressions of admiration and envy

("We're not all built that way. We wish we were!"). Consequently, the film allows these respondents to express a range of opinions on Holmes's stardom from a gender-specific perspective, shifting the emphasis from the heteronormative consumption of images of femininity into the realm of the homosocial, that is, "social bonds between persons of the same sex ... meant to be distinguished from 'homosexual.'"[39] In this case, verbal proclamations of homosocial identification are far more emphatic in their enthusiasm than with any of the female interviewees drawn from the public, many of whom express reticence or even repellence at the prospect of encountering Holmes sexually. Susanna Paasonen and Laura Saarenmaa argue that retrospective treatments of the golden age of hardcore, such as *Boogie Nights* and *Rated X* (Emilio Estevez, 1999) have

> envision[ed] a homosocial golden age of men, boys and brothers ... porn is represented as "guy stuff" ... The homosocial framework does not accommodate the voices of either women or gay men.[40]

This would certainly allow us to address the film's rendition of female desire through the fictions of the Johnny Wadd footage, which are in frequent juxtaposition with the assertions of the male interview subjects, and allusions by Holmes to a personality removed from the constrictions of pornography are countered by male audience members whose deluded fantasies he has embodied. One repeat interview subject refers to him admiringly as "a machine," a description which is befitting the film's battery of sexual content, but undermines Holmes's occasional claims to ordinariness. However, *Exhausted* more than merely "accommodates" a female voice; this is a film "produced and directed by Julia St Vincent" and, as such, the contradictions that emerge from the film's enactment and fulfillment of desire and identification are the product of an authorial project that is in constant tension with the star persona that it is ostensibly promoting.

Despite its nominal documentary status, the film is still structured in a manner which reflects and fulfills the demands of the hard-core fictional narrative; instead of dramatic exposition, standard conventions of non-fictional film are interspersed with extended bouts of sexual activity. The sum effect of this strategy is to define Holmes's life primarily as a function of pornography—in essence, this is pornography *as* biography: *pornobiography*. The very form of the film conveys a life defined and, perhaps more importantly, *restricted* by pornography, limiting the cultural parameters within which Holmes's persona might resonate. St. Vincent's unsteady authorial control merely bears this out further, and her very first words in the film are spoken off-camera as she questions a range of separate male and female interviewees: "Do you know who John Holmes is?" The very phrase instantly qualifies any claim to genuine stardom, assuming the possibility of ignorance from a randomly chosen subject. The responses, ranging from the affirmative ("Fantastic!"; "Sure! Big John Holmes!") to the nonplussed ("Johnny who?"; "He's a boxer, isn't he?"[41]), point to a general ambivalence, a sense that porn stardom is something that has made only tentative steps into general awareness or acknowledgment. The final interviewee of the opening section merely serves to compound this ambivalence: "Sure! Everyone knows John Holmes, just like everyone knows Kirk Douglas or John Wayne." Evidently, this comment contradicts what the film has already suggested after little less than a minute of running time and provides an immediate structural marker for its discourse on Holmes's brand of celebrity.

The ensuing title sequence reinscribes Holmes's textual authority through two brief shots of him traversing a serene shoreline and an urban space, the latter a static image in which the film's title appears as he approaches the camera until his denim-clad crotch fills the screen. There follows a procession of insert images and credits identifying twenty-three female costars in various states of writhing ecstasy, including headline performers such as Seka, Annette Haven, Jesse St. James, and Georgina Spelvin. This is underscored by a rueful ballad, sung by St. Vincent, its lyric ("He is the passion, he is the dream … He is the man of love, He is the light!") an expression of romantic absurdity that ascribes quasi-spiritual dimensions to Holmes's sexual aura. This ludicrous attribution of deific qualities reaches its zenith later in the film when Seka, with more than a trace of a knowing smile, proclaims that Holmes "has cum like God!".

The process is developed immediately after the title sequence when, accompanied by a short montage of Holmes in public spaces, we hear his voice proclaim that "everything in life is an act … if all the rumours that were spread about me were true, it would wear to a nubbin"—a statement that is particularly disingenuous in light of his complicity in that process of misinformation over the film's duration. However, immediately after this, and regardless of the uncertainties and ambivalence expressed by the interviewees elsewhere in the film, St. Vincent's voiceover states unequivocally that

> John Holmes is the biggest star in the history of the adult film industry. There's a certain intrigue that follows him after working in the heat of lights and the glamour of movies, and being sought after by countless women, does he step out of our fantasies into a life of respect and charm and wealth? Or is he a character of lust and perversion, stalking the night for women and sex?

This provides the film with a discursive base from which its wayward form and structure are developed. The statement itself is subject to debate and modulation, and after proclaiming Holmes's "legend," the voiceover even provides dubious statistics for a filmography numbering 2,500 and sexual partners in excess of 14,000. The latter figure is a pre-echo of something Holmes will articulate himself onscreen only moments later, using a baffling mathematical system that accounts for the accumulation of partners in a personal and professional lifestyle encompassing "the orgy trip, tricks, freebies and girls in films."

Amid all of the allusions and direct references to Holmes's imperious sexuality, there is also a montage later in the film that aligns carnal mastery with the qualities of the conventional action hero. Describing various shoot-outs and tough-guy posturing from the Johnny Wadd films, St. Vincent's voiceover again conflates Holmes with Wadd and positions the character beyond the mere expression of sexual libertarianism as an embodiment of a natural, individualistic justice, recalling the earlier interviewee's reference to John Wayne and Holmes's stated hope that his films might one day play on late-night television "like Bogart":

> John was slick with a gun when he had to use one but only did so in the vein of good and right ... John protected the values of the American ideal and fought for causes that would instil pride in a society where morals seemed hard to come by.

Despite all of this deliberate, but rather quaint mythologizing, one could quite easily make a case for a figure such as Linda Lovelace as having had a more profound cultural impact than Holmes ever had, both through her promotional value in the early days of porno chic and in her later renouncement of the industry and her associations with anti-porn feminist groups.[42] What *Exhausted* suggests implicitly is that Holmes is the biggest *male* star in the adult film industry, but that it is not his tangible sociocultural impact but his very gender, along with the unusual physical manifestation of his masculinity, that privileges him with iconic status. Within this heteronormative discourse, there is a suggestion that St. Vincent is actually mounting an address to female spectators directly and exclusively, through her emphasis upon Holmes's place within "*our* fantasies," and the tension between mystification and *de*mystification is partly engendered by her dual roles as narrator *and* interviewer, in which she adopts and articulates contradictory positions; in short, in her role as the former, she is complicit in the construction of a persona that her role as the latter consistently undermines and critiques.

The line of questioning pursued by St. Vincent also demonstrates how Holmes's star persona is obliged to function, charting subject areas that on the one hand would be basic material for the star/celebrity interview, but on the other would be taken as extreme intrusiveness and impertinence: "how many women?"; "what's the best blow job you've ever had?"; "how did you get started in films?"; "are you like Johnny Wadd/the same person we see on screen?"; "how big is it?"; "are you exploited?"; "what's the difference between your onscreen sex life and your personal life?"; "have you met people who can discern the real man from the screen image?"; "how do you think people will look at your films in a hundred years?"; "would you change anything about your life and career?". Holmes's outward projection of wanton sexuality allows these questions to be accepted as legitimate personal incursions, and many of them are met with fanciful answers, including the suggestion that his entry into the porn industry came about through the necessity of having to pay his fees at UCLA.[43] The questions also allow him to express the blasé approach that he claims to adopt regarding his sexuality, stating that he has never personally measured his own penis but providing the vague, but evocative confirmation that it is "bigger than a payphone, smaller than a Cadillac!" Regardless of the suspect veracity of Holmes's claims, these interview sequences also privilege him with momentary expressions of self-awareness and intelligence, even as he provides sustenance to his own mythology, and the interviews occur in a variety of spaces, ranging from an outdoor film location (during which he is framed seated in a personalized chair amid lighting equipment, occasionally flanked by starlets) to the contemplative setting of an urban interior in which traffic rolls by in the background. In essence, the film strives to address the dichotomy of the ordinary and the extraordinary so often identified as a defining feature of movie stardom, something which is enhanced by the presentation of Holmes fluffing his lines before he gets down to the fundamentals of his star specialism.

The questions posed to the other interviewees tend to imply Holmes's status as a culturally aberrant figure: "what would you do if you encountered something that big?"; "do you think acting in porn is unusual or strange?"; "does the size bother you at all?"; "are people in porn a rare breed." A question specifying Holmes's personal wealth—"do you think he is rich?"—also points to uncertainty regarding his economic worth, again providing doubt as far as perceptions of affluence and financial security common to the successful mainstream show business personality are concerned. Even Seka cannot verify his fiscal status, commenting only that she would hope he has achieved personal wealth because "he has made an awful lot of people an awful lot of money," perhaps a tacit acknowledgment of the relatively low economic status of even the most famous performers in the pornographic food chain. Her own lack of (or, perhaps, withheld) knowledge regarding Holmes's private persona is underlined in the final moments of the film when asked to provide a succinct definition of the man, alluding momentarily to his unacknowledged intelligence just after making a hand gesture approximating the size of his erection.

The sex sequences induce a certain astonishment at the anatomical accomplishments both enacted by and demanded of Holmes's erect penis and its recipients. This ranges from a montage in which various women struggle to orally pleasure Holmes due to the sheer difficulty of fitting the organ in their mouth to another in which some women express their astonishment directly to his crotch through comedic dialogue. The final montage sequence, which places particular emphasis upon extreme genital and anal close-ups set to a rhythmic, repetitive, synthesized score, culminates in a series of money shots, which are accompanied aurally by the electronic approximation of crashing waves, evidence that the film was quite willing to mine any stylistic cliché in the expression of its subject's sexual capabilities. Taken cumulatively, these montages that alternately celebrate and satirize Holmes's physical endowment point to an underlying awareness of an image dependent upon a dual discourse of veneration and mockery, a casual assumption of anatomical aberration that verges perilously close to a contemporary form of sideshow freakery. However, this recurrent fascination and assumption regarding the uniqueness and peculiarity of Holmes's penis is wryly satirized by one of the male public interviewees, greeting St. Vincent's question—"what would you do if you were sized like John?"—with a knowing smile before replying: "what makes you think I'm not!"

In a film rife with contradictions, ruptures, and ironies, the end credit acknowledgment thanking Holmes for "being himself" merely underlines the extent to which the "real story" promised in the title has passed into a legend adorned with his own embellishments and fabrications. Observed with the accumulation of extratextual knowledge three decades after its production, its attempt to mediate a personality in free-fall seems misguided and desperate, its ruminations on its subject's stardom severely hamstrung by his reluctance to allow a breach in the obstacles he lays before his inquisitor. Despite (or perhaps because of) its loose cannon star, the film can lay claim to being one of the most important to have emerged from this golden age of feature film pornography, its accidental revelations and contradictory discourses delineating a subcultural stardom that only achieved sporadic infiltrations of the mainstream but sought to mimic and exaggerate its representational modes. The questionable attempts of *Exhausted* to express not only Holmes's sexual potency but also his agency, energy, desirability, and righteousness embody a modest subcultural assault upon the assumptions and tendencies of the mainstream, mounting a curious alternative to the models of white masculinity that continue to dominate popular Hollywood cinema. Within their own historical frame of reference, various participants in *Exhausted* cite Humphrey Bogart, John Wayne, and Kirk Douglas as paragons of cinematic masculinity, a status that allowed these stars to achieve wealth, adulation, and respect on a global scale unimaginable to Holmes except in his wildest delusional state. However, at least in the terms laid down by *Exhausted*, he was and will forever remain *bigger* than all of them.

Notes

1. Quoted in *Wadd: The Life and Times of John C. Holmes* (Cass Paley, 1999).
2. Richard Dyer, *The Matter of Images* (London: Routledge, 1993), 113.
3. As is common practice within the adult film industry, the name is pseudonymous.
4. According to Jennifer Sugar and Jill C. Nelson, the film replaced *Deep Throat* (Gerard Damiano, 1972) from a "12 year" run at the Pussycat Theater on Hollywood Boulevard, Los Angeles. The release date of *Deep Throat* dictates a theatrical run of nine years at the most, a very significant duration nonetheless. See Jennifer Sugar and Jill C. Nelson, *John Holmes: A Life Measured in Inches* (Albany, GA: Bear Manor Media, 2008), 246.
5. Although Holmes's mother, Mary, was married to an abusive drunk named Edward Holmes, his actual father was named Carl Estes, with whom Mary had a brief affair during her marriage. This adds another layer of sad irony. In an industry in which virtually every performer assumed a *nom de porn*, Holmes used what he assumed to be his actual name for the duration of his career. According to his second wife, Laurie Holmes, he only discovered the truth of his parentage two years before his death. See Sugar and Nelson, *John Holmes*, 19–20.
6. One might argue the case for Ron Jeremy having had a wider impact. However, while his career commenced in the latter part of the 1970s, his transition into mini-celebrity status was achieved when the adult industry had become firmly established as a home consumer phenomenon. That said, he has also inspired a documentary account of his life and career, *Porn Star: The Legend of Ron Jeremy* (Scott J. Gill, 2001), and his own biography *Ron Jeremy: The Hardest (Working) Man in Showbusiness* (New York: Harper Collins, 2007).
7. As well as the Sugar and Nelson book, there has been the posthumous *Porn King* (Albany, GA: Bear Manor Media, 1998), co-credited to Holmes's widow, Laurie. St. Vincent's assessment of the book—"kind of true, but not really" (in Sugar and Nelson, *John Holmes*, 179)—is pithy, but about as accurate an assessment as one is

likely to come up with. This was supposedly transcribed from "cassette tapes and writings" left behind by Holmes, although much of it seems as fanciful as *Exhausted*. Its value as a reliable research resource is debatable, particularly in light of the fact that Holmes's first marriage, which stretched over three decades, is given barely half a page—indeed, most of the narrative unfolds as if she does not even exist. *The Road through Wonderland: Surviving John Holmes* (Aurora, IL: Medallion Press, 2010) by Dawn Schiller is an account of her life with Holmes up to and beyond the events of the Wonderland murders.

8. Legs McNeil and Jennifer Osbourne (with Peter Pavia), *The Other Hollywood: The Uncensored Oral History of the Porn Film Industry* (New York: Regan Books/Harper Collins, 2006).
9. Holmes was also the subject of a tantalizingly unmade Abel Ferrara project (written by Zoe Tamerlis Lund) in the late 1980s, with Christopher Walken in the lead. See Brad Stevens, *Abel Ferrara: The Moral Vision* (Guildford: FAB Press, 2004), 343.
10. The *Porn King* biography provides a figure of "over 2000" (Holmes, *Porn King*, vii).
11. Chuck Kleinhans, "The Change from Film to Video Pornography," in *Pornography: Film and Culture*, ed. Peter Lehman (New Brunswick/New Jersey/London: Rutgers University Press, 2006), 154.
12. Ibid., 156.
13. The opening titles of *Exhausted* privilege Chinn with his own authorial provenance, proclaiming that the footage of Holmes engaged in sexual activity is "from the works of Bob Chinn." His credit at the end of the film is "Director of Production." In the film's DVD commentary, Chinn states that his working relationship with Holmes had already broken down by the time *Exhausted* was being made. The film that is supposedly being shot during the behind-the-scenes footage (*Waikiki Wadd*) was completely fabricated for the purposes of St. Vincent's production.
14. Laura Kipnis, "How to Look at Pornography," in *Pornography: Film and Culture*, ed. Peter Lehman (New Brunswick/New Jersey/London: Rutgers University Press, 2006), 119.
15. The latter is particularly evident in the extended interview excised from the final cut, included as an extra feature on the US DVD release.
16. Chinn isn't specific on the time frame, but reveals that the last footage was shot "about a week" before the killings on July 1, 1981. Sugar and Nelson, *John Holmes*, 181.
17. St. Vincent ran the company following Atamian's death in 1980, but states to Sugar and Nelson that she never owned it outright (ibid., 180).
18. Quoted from November 2012 interview: "Julia St Vincent: From Exhausted to Boogie Nights," *Golden Goddesses*, available at http://goldengoddessesbook.blogspot.co.uk/2012/11/spotlight-on-julia-st-vincent.html (accessed June 18, 2015).
19. Sugar and Nelson, *John Holmes*, 190.
20. Paul Thomas Anderson, audio commentary for *Exhausted* (abridged), *Boogie Nights* laserdisc, Criterion Collection, 1998.
21. Ralph Blumenthal, "Porno Chic," *New York Times* (January 21, 1973).
22. Bruce Williamson, "Porno Chic," *Playboy*, August 1973.
23. Brian McNair, *Striptease Culture* (London/New York: Routledge, 2002), 61.
24. Williamson, "Porno Chic," reprinted in *Flesh and Blood: The National Society of Film Critics on Sex, Violence and Censorship*, ed. Peter Keough (San Francisco: Mercury House, 1995), 12.
25. See Linda Williams, *Hardcore: Power, Pleasure and the Frenzy of the Visible* (Berkeley/Los Angeles: University of California Press, 1989).

26. Overseen by Attorney General Edwin Meese, the commission sought to halt the liberal impetus that had so embarrassed President Richard Nixon in 1970 following the findings of the Presidential Commission on Pornography and Obscenity. Joseph Slade summarizes Meese's ambitions thus:[it]

> attempted unsuccessfully to link pornography with violence, harassed stores for selling *Playboy*, and published a report so prurient that its critics called it pornographic ... finding new ways to restrict expression was also the mandate ... [its] most lasting consequence was the creation of a special unit of the Justice Department with instructions to circumvent the first amendment by treating all erotic expression as a form of contraband.

Joseph Slade, *Pornography in America* (Santa Barbara, CA: ABC-CLIO, 2000), 193–194.

27. See, e.g., Richard Dyer, *Stars* (London: BFI, 1979); Alan Lovell and Peter Kramer, eds *Screen Acting* (London/New York: Routledge, 1999); and Paul McDonald, *Hollywood Stardom* (Malden MA/Oxford/Chichester: Wiley-Blackwell, 2013).
28. Kate Egan and Sarah Thomas, "Introduction: Star Making, Cult—Making and Forms of Authenticity," in *Cult Film Stardom: Offbeat Attractions and Processes of Cultification*, eds Kate Egan and Sarah Thomas (London/New York: Palgrave Macmillan, 2013), 8.
29. Stuart Muirhead, "The Cock, The Thief, The Wife and Her Lovers," *Neon* (April 1997), 70.
30. Dyer, *The Matter of Images*, 111.
31. Ibid.
32. Ibid., 112.
33. Ibid.
34. Matt Hills, "Cult Movies with and without Cult Stars: Differentiating Discourses of Stardom," in *Cult Film Stardom: Offbeat Attractions and Processes of Cultification*, eds Kate Egan and Sarah Thomas (London/New York: Palgrave Macmillan, 2013), 22.
35. Ibid., 26.
36. David Black, "Charactor; or, The Strange Case of Uma Peel," in *Cult Television*, eds Sara Gwenllian Jones and Roberta E. Pearson (Minneapolis: University of Minnesota Press, 2004), 105.
37. Robin Bougie, *Graphic Thrills, American XXX Movie Posters 1970 to 1985* (Guildford: FAB Press, 2014), 15.
38. Nevertheless, the film features interviews with not only white males but also black male and female members of the public.
39. Eve Kosofsky Sedgwick, *Between Men: English Literature and Male Homosocial Desire* (Colombia University Press: New York, 1985), 1.
40. Susann Paasonen and Laura Saarenmaa, "The Golden Age of Porn: Nostalgia and History in Cinema," in *Pornification: Sex and Sexuality in Media Culture*, eds Susanna Paasonen, Kaarina Nikunen and Laura Saarenmaa (Oxford/New York: Berg, 2007), 32.
41. As my friend and colleague Thomas Joseph Watson pointed out to me, it is quite possible here that the interviewee had in mind Larry Holmes, who was the world heavyweight boxing champion at the time of the film's production, an altogether different model of masculinity.
42. Other female performers had already made contributions to nonpornographic films by 1981, including Marilyn Chambers' lead in *Rabid* (David Cronenberg, 1976) and

Constance Money and Annette Haven's (uncredited) minor speaking roles in *10* (Blake Edwards, 1979). Fellow male lead Jamie Gillis also had a brief speaking part in *Nighthawks* (Bruce Malmuth, 1981), playing a scene opposite Sylvester Stallone and Lindsay Wagner.

43. It has been confirmed by several biographical and documentary sources (including the *Wadd* documentary and the Sugar and Nelson biography) that Holmes never graduated from high school, and certainly never entered into higher education.

9

From Opera House to Grindhouse (and Back Again): Ozploitation in and beyond Australia

Alexandra Heller-Nicholas

Ever since European settlers laid claim to Australia in 1788, white Australia has struggled with the construction of a viable national identity. Although flourishing briefly with films like the iconic *The Story of the Kelly Gang* (Charles Tait, 1906), it was not until the 1970s that an Australian film industry could be identified *per se*. This so-called "new wave" was supported financially by the federal government as a conscious, national identity-building project, in order to create "a national voice" and "a sense of national purpose."[1] The government therefore saw Australian filmmaking at this time as a potent forum for the construction, consolidation, and dissemination of a film-based national brand, as seen in internationally acclaimed films like *Picnic at Hanging Rock* (Peter Weir, 1975). These movies were felt to show the world how sophisticated Australia could be. It was in this context that Australian exploitation film—commonly referred to today as "Ozploitation"—was critically dismissed at home during its peak period of production during the 1970s and 1980s, seen to be tangible evidence of an increasing American dominance over Australian culture. It was simultaneously marked by its vernacular: a distinct, dramatic, and deliberate celebration of a proudly parochial Australian crudity. So while the influence of American cinema may have been strong, as these films sought to appeal to foreign and local audiences through a particular utilization of recognizable exploitation genre tropes, Ozploitation was also a vehicle for Australian-specific meanings to flow outwards into these foreign markets. This chapter explores a fundamental tension in Ozploitation between absence and presence, manifesting in the interplay of white Australia's desire to position itself culturally as a part of the Western world. This manifested through its dedication to particular exploitation subgenres, while simultaneously often emphasizing (consciously or not) their geographical distance from the original sources. Ozploitation films relied

The author wishes to thank Anthony C. Bleach and John F. Lennon for their feedback on an earlier draft of this chapter. Some of the ideas here were previously teased out in my article "Dark Forces: Excess and Absence in Harlequin and Beyond," *Metro Magazine* 162 (September 2009): 98–102.

heavily on a palette of influences similar to those that permeated the US grindhouse circuit, from rape-revenge to slasher, martial arts to sexploitation. This chapter maps the tensions between national identity, ideology, and history in what was commonly dismissed as a purely imported cinematic form.

Welcome to Ozploitation

Ozploitation encompasses approximately sixty[2] horror, action, and sexploitation comedy films produced during its heyday. Considering the cultural flows both into and out of these films, it is perhaps appropriate that the very word "Ozploitation" itself is one that evolved by necessity out of a dialogue between an Australian and a non-Australian filmmaker. Mark Hartley's documentary *Not Quite Hollywood* (2008) spearheaded recent interest in this category of Australian filmmaking, and his desire to validate local "trash" cinema gains authority in part from the inclusion of American cult film darling and grindhouse champion Quentin Tarantino. According to Jake Wilson, Hartley's project was in large part justified by Tarantino's passion for this particular subject, calling these films "Aussiesploitation." Hartley adapted this to Ozploitation, and the name has stuck. Wilson states:

> Hartley himself maintains that he simply needed a buzzword meaning Australian genre filmmaking of the revival era—but words, like films, have a life of their own, and the gesture of superimposing "Aussie" on "exploitation" is unavoidably heavy with significance. Strictly speaking, "exploitation" does not designate a genre at all, but rather the use of genre as a pretext for the showcasing of some marketable attraction: sex, violence, grotesquery, but also novelty of any kind, in form as well as content.[3]

As will be explored further, this notion of "marketable" was crucial in the Australian context: what the federal government deemed appropriate for a national cinema and what audiences wanted to in fact see (both in Australia and internationally, including on the grindhouse circuit), were in most instances very different things.

Ozploitation burst into the popular imagination with "ocker" films, bawdy comedies that flourished during the early and mid 1970s. The word itself pertains to a distinctly Australian kind of uncouthness, and it was in this spirit that the ocker films rejected sophistication and instead were proudly uncultured, embracing beer, boobs, and belching. According to Graeme Turner, "the ocker films represented a masculine, populist and cheerfully vulgar view of Australian society." He continues, "Australian social practices and idiosyncrasies were celebrated for their own sake, rather than for their contribution to world culture, while beer, sex, and bodily functions figured large in the action. The films depended on a very specific definition of Australian-ness."[4] Critical and institutional nervousness around the popularity of these lowbrow movies saw a shift toward a supposedly higher-quality national cinema. Consequently, Ozploitation almost vanished from the cultural memory as more somber, art-house fare became representative of the national cinema. But with the celebratory documentary *Not Quite*

Hollywood released in 2008, the issuing of local DVD releases of key Ozploitation titles, and Australian exploitation retrospectives appearing on the national film festival circuit, Ozploitation has recently had a revival. From a critical perspective, it offers a specific national instance of Paul Watson's claim that exploitation film "provides a parallax view through which the domains of history and theory can be rethought."[5]

Tarantino is positioned in *Not Quite Hollywood* as a kind of exploitation expert, one coming from a notably external, non-Australian perspective. Tarantino's affection for Ozploitation became known in Australia when he praised the kind of filmmaking celebrated in *Not Quite Hollywood* at the Australian premier of *Kill Bill: Volume One* in 2003. Tarantino describes the event in an interview with Hartley as follows:

> When I had the Sydney premiere of Kill Bill, a good section of the Australian film industry were [sic] out in the audience that night. I knew that they're snobs, and I live to stick a weed up the ass of snobs, so I dedicated it to Brian Trenchard-Smith: "If you don't like Brian Trenchard-Smith, you ain't gonna like this movie so get the fuck out right now. I've just warned you!"

The placement of this anecdote within *Not Quite Hollywood* itself and in the promotional material that accompanied its release is a clear manifestation of a specific kind of oppositionality, recalling Jeffrey Sconce's notion that a taste for trash stakes a claim in a specific oppositional system.[6] This sense of opposition to legitimate authority pervades Australia's colonial history and its origins as a British penal settlement, manifesting in the mythic "wild colonial boys" legacy that still permeates Australian popular discourse in the figure of the supposedly lovable "larrikin."[7] That *Not Quite Hollywood* gave voice to this spirit through an American director is significant, and similar cultural flows in Ozploitation will provide the focus of this chapter's attention.

The taste-driven duality between mainstream and exploitation film fractures even further in the case of Australian cinema. The lessons of the "Australian history war"—a catch-all for public discourse surrounding the relationship between the British colonization of Australia and its Indigenous peoples—have demonstrated the political force of writings of Australian history. The binary divide that marks the Australian history wars found its enduring imagery in a speech by the renowned historian Geoffrey Blainey in his infamous 1993 Latham Lecture. According to Anna Clark:

> Blainey's assessment not only gave (the debate) a powerful emblem; it also fuelled the disquiet over Australia's past. He argued that on any measure, the "balance sheet" of Australian history had been largely a success, and his imagery was adopted by a number of conservative historians, politicians and commentators. But it spawned an equally powerful reaction from those who dissented—they proudly donned black armbands and accused Blainey and his supporters of underplaying Australia's colonial legacy, and of wearing "white blindfolds."[8]

While the broader debates that mark the Australian history wars may at first appear on the periphery to discourse surrounding Australian exploitation film, there is arguably no coincidence that discussion of Australian history—be it political history or film history—is marked by claims staked on an oppositional binary. "Cultural phenomena only exist in so far as people 'read' them, ascribe them meaning; they are constituted as cultural in the act of reading," says Andrew Tudor. "Accordingly, the artefacts that form the basis for a cultural history are not fixed. They are constructed and reconstructed by their consumers long before they fall into the historian's hands."[9] In the case of *Not Quite Hollywood*, there are a finite number of films produced within the Ozploitation period, and the restrictions of a two-hour documentary allow only a sampling of those titles. But judgments of taste—based on the desire to legitimize some texts and (by association) ghettoize others—govern the writing of Australian film history, both before and in the aftermath of the documentary's release. Whether consciously or not, *Not Quite Hollywood*—through its championing of Ozploitation and its attempt to rewrite it back into the narrative of Australian culture—presents Australian film history itself as a tension between its own kind of binaries that mimic the Australian history wars.

Marked as it is by an either/or binary understanding of Australia's colonial history, the "history war" in this national context provides the template upon which the relationship between competing film histories—Ozploitation and that of more mainstream, critically celebrated movie fare—are defined in *Not Quite Hollywood*. If this tension can be conceived as a metaphorical battle, then even just by his direct involvement in the coining of the term "Ozploitation" itself, Quentin Tarantino can be fairly identified as the heavy artillery. Tarantino's foreignness is crucial here, as it is a clear instance of the oft-cited Australian cultural phenomenon of the "cultural cringe." Coined in a famous essay by A.A. Phillips in 1950, in the Australian context the term refers to "an assumption that the domestic cultural product will be worse than the imported article."[10] The notion of the cultural cringe to white Australian culture is so central that it is worth quoting at some length:

> The devil of it is that the assumption (that the domestic cultural product will be worse than the imported article) will often be correct. The numbers are against us, and an inevitable quantitative inferiority easily looks like a qualitative weakness, under the most favourable circumstances—and our circumstances are not favourable. We cannot shelter from invidious comparisons behind the barrier of a separate language; we have no long-established or interestingly different cultural tradition to give security and distinction to its interpreters; and the centrifugal pull of the great cultural metropolises works against us ... The Cringe mainly appears in an inability to escape needless comparisons. The Australian reader, more or less consciously, hedges and hesitates, asking himself "Yes, but what would a cultivated Englishman think of this?" No writer can communicate confidently to a reader with the "Yes, but" habit; and this particular demand is curiously crippling to critical judgment.[11]

This notion has direct relation to the role of Quentin Tarantino in the retrospective articulation, definition, and championing of Ozploitaiton cinema. The "ploitation" suffix alone clearly seeks to consciously align it with the kinds of "grindhouse traditions" Tarantino celebrates elsewhere—sexploitation, blaxploitation, nunsploitation, and so on—and the director's blessing solidifies this strategy. Indeed, the role of Tarantino in thinking through the relationship of Ozploitation to grindhouse traditions cannot be underemphasized: according to Jason Bailey, the very word "grindhouse" was in large part introduced into the mainstream with Quentin Tarantino and Robert Rodriguez's 2007 double bill of the same name.[12] This appears to be a cultural variation of what Leon Hunt has identified as Tarantino's status as a "gatekeeper auteur." Discussing the relationship between Tarantino and Asian cinema, Hunt observes:

> The "Asianisation" of Euro-American cinema has been dependent on "gatekeeper" figures—producers attuned to cults surrounding Hong Kong, Japanese and South Korean cinema, auteurs displaying their connoisseurship of Asian cinema or acting as patrons to cult Asian films and directors.[13]

Tarantino's brand seeks to emphasize his knowledge of film cultures as yet widely unknown, the director acting as a kind of cultural translator who brings exotic, foreign forms into the Western mainstream. In the case of Asian cinema, Hunt notes that "Tarantino's public persona embraces his Asiaphile fanboy credentials, which have been evident throughout his career."[14] Likewise, a similar process was at work in Tarantino's relationship to Ozploitation: be it a reference in *Kill Bill* to *Patrick* (Richard Franklin, 1978) or, in his *Grindhouse* entry *Death Proof*, to *Fair Game* (Mario Andreacchio, 1986). While not perhaps as numerous as those to Asian cinema in his oeuvre, examples such as the aforementioned introduction to *Kill Bill* in Sydney in 2003 demonstrate a similar strategy to mark his "fanboy credentials" on the Ozploitation front, also.

Tarantino's relationship to Ozploitation—both "here" (in terms of his knowledge) and "not here" (in terms of his status as a non-Australian)—and his pivotal role in the retrospective delineation of the Ozploitation category *per se* all underscore Australia's liminal cultural status: a part of the West in terms of language and a broader cultural palette, but also distant from it in terms of pure geography. This tension between absence and presence comes to the fore in a consideration of the relationship between the Australian genre films that have been retrospectively considered to fall under the "Ozploitation" banner and their relation to the grindhouse traditions that Tarantino has so consciously linked to his personal brand.

The symbolic involvement of Tarantino in inscribing Australian genre filmmaking into the culture war rhetoric that *Not Quite Hollywood* attempts to mimic explicitly links it to grindhouse traditions. *Not Quite Hollywood*'s reliance on Tarantino's authoritative voice as knowledgeable outsider means that its reassessment of Australian film history extends (rather than subverts) the habitual rewriting of Australian history that marks Australia's "history war" rhetoric, dependent in large part on a combination of Tarantino's own brand as a "gatekeeper auteur" with the broader tendencies of white Australia toward the cultural cringe. Stepping beyond these attempts to retrospectively construct Australian film history, however, the defining formal and thematic articulation of a uniquely Australian excessive absence within Ozploitation has a greater significance than simply a missing piece in the jigsaw puzzle of the nation's film history. It demonstrates just how deeply embedded the notion of "exploitation" is to this rewriting of history in a nation transfixed upon the creation of a cohesive postcolonial identity. Even the very title "Not Quite Hollywood" speaks to a stream of national cinema production that is defined by the tensions governing transnational flows. Before these are unpacked, it is necessary to further explore the relationship between Australian film history and the tenuous construction of a postcolonial national identity.

Australian film history and the search for identity

Not Quite Hollywood's mission to reinsert Ozploitation into the dominant film history narrative provides a useful stepping-stone to articulate historiographical questions directly relevant to the broader national body politic, particularly those linked to its status as simultaneously "Western" yet remote from the West. This can be understood in relation to how alternate histories deviate from the dominant telling of Australian film history that generally contends that, despite a boom in the early twentieth century, Australian cinema suffered a long period of stagnation as local distribution and exhibition practices bowed under the dominance of the Hollywood system. Television was introduced to Australia in 1956, and by the 1960s government at both state and federal levels sought to establish a sustainable local film industry. This sparked the so-called renaissance of the Australian film industry in the 1970s, which was "almost entirely the result of government subsidy and investment."[15]

Liberal[16] prime minister John Gorton is a key figure in this rebirthing of the national cinema. According to Philip Adams, "Gorton was alarmed by foreign ownership of Australian industry and agriculture, so it was a simple matter to direct this anxiety into what we described as 'the American ownership of our imagination.'"[17] In 1972, under Prime Minister William McMahon, the Australian Film Development Corporation (AFDC) was formed. When Labor's Gough Whitlam replaced McMahon as prime minister in December that year, Whitlam's reputation as a patron of the arts made the continuing support of his government a certainty. Whitlam created an Arts Ministry that included the Australian Film and Television School. As both Graham Shirley and Brian Adams, and Andrew Pike and Ross Cooper observe,[18] this period was a time of increased nationalistic spirit, and efforts to create a confident, cohesive national identity via the arts were embraced by the public and government alike. Scott Murray concurs, noting that for those reared in the "cinematically barren" 1950s and 1960s, having its own film industry would show Australia's progress in becoming a "cultured" nation.[19]

The Australian Film Commission (AFC) officially replaced the AFDC in 1975, and the industry's grounding shifted again with the introduction of color television, a rise in inflation, and the controversial dismissal of Gough Whitlam at the end of the year. As Pike and Cooper indicate, from this point "it became increasingly difficult for local producers to rely on the local market to recover costs, and the industry moved towards a reliance on the government not only to provide investment capital but also to carry the burden of the deficit, allowing private investors to recover their capital from a film's first earnings."[20] This shift in focus from a local audience to an international market demographic was reflected in the type of films being produced. This was also influenced by a pattern of tax cuts that indirectly encouraged drive-in friendly Ozploitation movies: first in 1978,[21] and later in 1981 with the notorious 10B(A) amendment to the Income Tax Assessment Act that bestowed generous tax breaks to film production investors. For Scott Murray, this dramatically influenced quality and encouraged a turn toward more commercial product, as "overnight, the control over what films were made shifted from government bodies to the investment brokers, most of whom had no experience of, or real interest in, the cinema."[22] Ozploitation flourished in Australia during what is widely considered this tumultuous yet productive shift from the 1970s into the 1980s.

The earliest films produced in the 1970s were predominantly movies made in generic styles that were popular with cinema-going audiences. The first locally produced film of this era with significant government support was the ocker movie *The Adventures of Barry McKenzie* (Bruce Beresford 1972), which was both a financial and popular success. Capitalizing upon the newly introduced adult "R" rating in 1971, it was a loosely strung together series of sexploitation vignettes that followed a young Australian every-yob in Britain. While *The Adventures of Barry McKenzie* was preceded by two notable sex comedies—the quasi-documentary *The Naked Bunyip* (John B. Murray, 1970) and *Stork* (Tim Burstall, 1971)—it was not until the groundbreaking financial success of *The Adventures of Barry McKenzie* that the Ozploitation movement began in earnest. It triggered a spate of lighthearted sex romps like *The True Story of Eskimo Nell* (Richard Franklin, 1974), *Plugg* (Terry Bourke, 1975), *The Love Epidemic* (Brian Trenchard-Smith, 1975), *Australia after Dark* (John Lamond, 1975), *Felicity* (John Lamond, 1979), and *Fantasm* (Richard Franklin, 1976). *Alvin Purple* (Tim Burstall, 1973) fared so well at the Australian box office that it grossed over half as much as *Star Wars* (George Lucas, 1977) in constant dollars.[23]

So why did the Australian film industry need to look for an overseas audience when it was doing so well at home? The answer is more cultural than fiscal. The ocker movies were a zeitgeist-defining cultural phenomenon, for both their visceral, exploitative content and also in regard to their political significance at a time when the government sought to establish a local on-screen film presence. But by 1974, ocker films were falling out of favor with the very system that had facilitated their success. Their very success led critics and officials to wonder if the investment of government money was even necessary. More so, the white Australian ocker presented in these films celebrates a life of uncouth but essentially joyous bacchanalia.[24] The popularity of these proudly crass films flagged them as a concern for politicians and the cultural elite, and consequently commercial films were rejected in favor of what the AFC felt was more appropriate for the representative national cinema. Between 1974 and 1977, this marked a shift in focus from the ocker films (and other lowbrow genres) to the creation of high-quality cinema.[25]

Consequently, it was only a few years into the development of this revamped Australian film industry that a tension manifested between commercial, popular film and what government bodies like the AFC viewed as "quality," art-house cinema. So politically oriented was this shift that Susan Dermody and Elizabeth Jacka refer to these latter titles collectively as "the AFC genre."[26] Consisting predominantly of period dramas like Peter Weir's 1975 film, *Picnic at Hanging Rock*, Dermody and Jacka note the cultural dominance of this type of film became so strong that any reference to "Australian film" seemed to automatically denote a reference to films of the AFC genre.[27] The success of *Picnic at Hanging Rock* and Gillian Armstrong's *My Brilliant Career* (1979) notwithstanding, they considered these films fundamentally "doomed to failure ... at the box office"[28] because they were seen as elitist in comparison to popular films like the *Barry McKenzie* movies.

These "quality" films marked not only a shift in how Australia was depicted onscreen but also a distinct narrative turn in the dominant story of Australian film history. Now that the New Artiness had been introduced, the commercial was necessarily defined by its oppositional status as un-Australian due to the "Hollywood-ness" (a synonym for mainstream, popular cinema as a whole) of its commercial motive.[29] But for Dermody and Jacka, the genteel nostalgia of the AFC genre was also haunted by "quality" British television drama, particularly that of a nostalgic inclination.[30] That the commercial/popular was effectively coded as American, and the "quality" as British ultimately underscored the active presence of dual cultural colonial pressures implying that (white) Australian identity was marked by its physical and cultural distance from Britain and America. The search for national identity in Australian cinema therefore fluctuated between what was viewed as pandering to "Hollywoodized" commercialism and a more highbrow British or European sensibility.[31] In the dominant telling of Australian cinema history, there has been a fundamental politicization of taste as these "quality" films acted to effectively erase the stain of Ozploitation.

Movements in local film history in Australia were codified through these international influences. It is in this climate that the political agenda that championed the cultural legitimacy of these "quality" Australian films over lowbrow forms did so without any kind of acknowledgment that by doing so, films would have less box-office appeal. This manifests no more clearly than in their starkly different demographic focus: while Ozploitation films sought the mass drive-in market, the so-called AFC films were aimed squarely at the niche international film festival circuit.

In this context, it is worth looking more closely at these earlier popular Australian exploitation films. These lowbrow films were generally disinterested in a vision of Australia as such, and instead were marked by excess, spectacle, and sensation. Films like *Eliza Fraser* (Tim Burstall, 1976) and *Mad Dog Morgan* (Phillipe Mora, 1976) were not interested in profound reflections upon capital-H History, intent instead on titillation and excitement. This commercial and cultural immediacy allowed some autonomy from the notions of "history" and "identity" that dominated the more "quality" films. As *Not Quite Hollywood* tells it, this manifests on-screen as Ozploitation's defining spirit of rambunctious anarchy. Ozploitation does not reject the notion of an Australian identity, but rather allows an expansion of the debates surrounding it.

Paracinema Australian style

Ozploitation's rejection of the highbrow strategies that marked "quality" Australian cinema is demonstrated in the opening scene of *Barry McKenzie Holds His Own*. As the sequel to Ur-Ozploitation film *The Adventures of Barry McKenzie*, it was released a year before *Picnic at Hanging Rock* but consciously acknowledges the shifts that were occurring in official support from lowbrow to more highbrow cinematic forms, and the consequent reputation of ocker films in comparison to their new and more acceptable competition. Sitting in front of a garish painting of a Fosters beer can, a comically pompous government minister (Barry Humphries) announces:

> My name is Senator Douglas Manton, and I am the Australian Minister for Culture. You know, the world has enjoyed some very wonderful cultural renaissances in so far as culture is concerned. The Egyptian Dynasty, the very wonderful Greek Civilization, the grandeur that was Rome, the Italian renaissance, and the artistic glory of France. However, none of these very wonderful moments can compare with the Australian cultural renaissance which is sweeping the world at the present period of time ... I think I can say without fear of successful contradiction that amongst the many fields of artistic endeavor in which we Australians have shown such wonderful leadership, is the art of the motion picture.

Surrounded by flies, the humor stems from the contradiction between the absence of highbrow culture in its mise en scène and the pretentious determination of its bumbling central figure. His declared intention to place the Australian film industry among the great traditions of Western art is hilariously paradoxical: the search for a highbrow, sophisticated national identity is futile because, it implies, Australia is neither highbrow nor sophisticated. But despite its explicit rejection of its classier and "quality" competitors, *Barry McKenzie Holds His Own*—like so many other films of its ilk—still shares many of their thematic concerns.

According to Sconce, paracinema functions most clearly as an oppositional category, defined against the mainstream.[32] He claims that viewing pleasure for paracinematic audiences stems from an engagement with non-diegetic filmic aspects. Because paracinematic tastes are by definition opposed to the mainstream, paracinematic audiences are therefore required to be just as familiar with this mainstream style, if only to define their own aesthetic in opposition to it. It is within this oppositional reading strategy that Sconce notes the centrality of excess to paracinema. While stylistic excess in non-paracinematic forms adds an air of "artistic bravado" to the *development* of a film's diegesis, in paracinema this excess *transcends* the diegesis, demanding the "profilmic and extratextual aspects of the filmic object itself" be employed in a reading of the text in question. The near-fetishistic fascination paracinematic audiences have with these non-diegetic surface elements (unconvincing sets and acting, shoddy scriptwriting, haphazard cinematography and editing) to some degree quarantines these features from the films' diegetic core.[33]

This is a useful position from which to approach the above speech from *Barry McKenzie Holds His Own*, as it demonstrates how Ozploitation transcends its diegetic confines via excessive self-reflexivity. Films like this tantalizingly invite liberation from the burdens of Australian identity that weigh upon "quality" cinema. Australian trash cinema defines itself against the preference for "quality" film, and therefore employs excess as a political weapon. This self-reflexivity can be seen in other Ozploitation films, most notably Brian Trenchard-Smith's postapocalyptic action film *Dead End Drive-In* (1986). Turning its titular drive-in into a suburban battleground, it is the very site where exploitation film is exhibited that becomes a tangible space for chaos and violence to reign supreme. To make sure the extra-diegetic wink to the Ozploitation-literate audience is not missed, Trenchard-Smith screens his *own* films in the drive-in within the movie. At one point, his notorious *Turkey Shoot* (1982) has one of the characters so transfixed that she complains about having to eat. The protagonist Crabs (Ned Manning) even has a conversation with the drive-in manager about the turmoil: "How long has it been like this?" he asks. "Like this?" replies Tommy (Peter Whitford); "It's the state of things, son. Economic conditions." From within its own diegesis, the film claims that the unruliness that dominates the drive-in—precisely the kind of space where the films of Brian Trenchard-Smith are exhibited—is shamelessly economic. This overblown dystopia sarcastically mocks the supposed negative effects Ozploitation film is assumed to have upon its supposedly mindless, trash-loving audience.

This model of excessive, extra-diegetic commentary need not be as literal as *Dead End Drive-In* and *Barry McKenzie Holds His Own*. *Thirst* (Ron Hardy, 1979) demonstrates a similar self-reflexive meditation on Ozploitation when viewed in relation to the foreign commercialization of local bodies. Kate (Chantelle Contouri) is kidnapped by a mysterious group called the Hyma Brotherhood, which run a human blood dairy to farm a clean, healthy food supply for a vampire bourgeoisie. Factions within the Brotherhood debate how to most effectively indoctrinate the oblivious Kate (a direct descendent of legendary sixteenth-century Hungarian serial killer and suspected vampire Elizabeth Báthory) to their cause—either through brainwashing and conditioning (as suggested by the villainous Mrs. Cameron, played by Shirley Cameron) or via the more genteel persuasions of Dr. Fraser (David Hemmings). Stripped to its basic narrative components, the protagonist battles the commercialization of an imported phenomenon, refusing to acknowledge her susceptibility to her primal desires. The film's equating of vampirism to commercial genre film could appear to be an attack on Ozploitation, but this reading is subverted as the simplistic plot is superseded by hyperactive formal and visceral excess. After blood showers, bleeding walls, and even a Dame Edna Everage look-alike vampire feeding off a young victim, it is in the film's final moments that Kate finally submits to the vampiric Dr. Fraser: "I am one of you." Kate and the spectator are released from the elitist confines of acceptable behavior as she surrenders to the knowledge that she cannot fight her base desires. Both can now frolic freely in the gritty perversions of exploitation in all its senses.

Although in this instance "excess" refers to glut, the quantitative aspects of the word may belie its significance to Ozploitation. For Carol Laseur, excess is a defining component of Australian exploitation cinema (and exploitation film in general) as the "density of practices clearly suggests the capacity of the exploitation film to lay bare the conventions and values of a culture."[34] It is what she describes as the "moreness"[35] of exploitation film that consciously positions these films in opposition to an amorphous sense of "the mainstream": "Much of the pleasure of the exploitation film may well be precisely situated in the recognition of its satirical parody of a pompous high cultural (bourgeois) set of aesthetic proclamations."[36] But excess in Ozploitation may function in a far more complex way than this quality of "moreness" that Laseur suggests. Just as Australian film history has been so robustly haunted by the looming cultural forces of Britain and the United States—places whose absence is overwhelming, and in a sense excessive—a similar paradox permeates many Australian trash films of this era internally.

Ozploitation films are marked by a similar kind of excessive absence. This overwhelming sense of "something missing" is intrinsic to how Ozploitation film engages with Australia's wider cultural and political concerns, and marks a broader search for a cohesive national identity that is inherent to "history war" rhetoric. This sense is most explicit in *Night of Fear* (Terry Bourke, 1972) and *Patrick* (Richard Franklin, 1978), where horror is constructed through an excessive absence of spoken dialogue. In *Patrick* this is diegetic, as the title character (played by Robert Thompson) unleashes his telekinetic whirlwind of violence while lying comatose and mute in a hospital bed. In *Night of Fear* (originally a TV pilot that ended up getting cinema release), muteness is less a narrative element as its most striking formal feature. The absence of spoken language in the film is arresting—there is no dialogue, and the only human sounds are screams, pants, and other prelingual utterances. There are other strategies that demonstrate this excess of absence: the protagonist in the supernatural drama *The Survivor* (David Hemmings, 1980) is a pilot who suffers from amnesia, and the story is predicated upon his status as a present body that is bereft of the power to recollect the events that led him to his surviving a plane crash. At the film's conclusion, it is revealed he was never a "survivor" at all: rather, he existed purely in a neither-here-nor-there realm that parallels Australia's own sense of alienation from the rest of the world. That these films hinge so intently upon absence reflects a deeper, broader cultural concern. Through its isolation from the rest of the world, white Australia suffers from a constant, disorienting sense that "something is missing." Indeed, this sense of alienation—what the historian Geoffrey Blainey famously identified as "the tyranny of distance" in his 1968 book of the same name[37]—may be claimed to be one of the most recurrent themes in white Australian art, and indicates a direct parallel between the debates of the history wars and Ozploitation cinema.

The overwhelming and inescapable absences that mark Ozploitation are not specific to horror variants, but it is here that it is most intensely articulated. *Razorback* (Russell Mulcahy, 1984) follows the search for a missing tourist and a killer wild boar that cannot be found. The final girls in *Nightmares* (John Lamond, 1980), *Next of Kin* (Tony Williams, 1982), and *Alison's Birthday* (Ian Coughlan, 1979) are all orphans. *Long Weekend* (Colin Eggleston, 1978) goes as far as to lack a coherent malevolent entity, its plot hinging on a general sense that nature is retaliating against a city couple camping in the bush. There are other generic examples: the action-thriller *The Chain Reaction* (Ian Barry, 1980) includes an amnesiac protagonist (absent of memory) and a mute assassin (absent of voice). In all these examples, the voids are excessive. The diegetic and non-diegetic dominance of absence demonstrates how excess can be ironically emphasized through overt negation, resulting in the privileging of other elements to spectacularly overcompensate. Patrick's visual display of violence far outweighs his inability to speak, while *Night of Fear* effectively replaces dialogue-fuelled plot and character development by strapping an abundance of body horror to its bare-bones narrative framework. Therefore, this excess of absence in fact manifests as a tension created by the paradoxical excess of an absent-presence.

There are of course many non-Ozploitation (and non-Australian) paracinematic (and non-paracinematic) texts that feature a similar emphasis upon a sense of "something missing."[38] But it is in the Australian context that this excessive absence is so intrinsically and powerfully relevant to broader cultural and political issues. Because of the extreme specificity of this formal and thematic motif to national identity and to dominant political discourse, this hyperactive and paradoxical excess of absence marks Ozploitation as a distinctly Australian form, just as much as their surface iconography (kangaroos, hats with corks, the Sydney Opera House, etc.).

Grindhousing Ozploitation/Ozploiting grindhouse

There were a number of strategies employed both to garner commercial success at home and to profit on the lucrative international film distribution market. Perhaps most obviously was the regular practice of casting non-Australian actors, often in the leads. Notoriously, Richard Franklin's *Roadgames* (1981) starred Stacy Keach and Jamie Lee Curtis, the latter in particular cast on the back of her recent "scream queen" status in films like *Halloween* (John Carpenter, 1978), *Terror Train* (Roger Spottiswoode, 1980), and *Prom Night* (Paul Lynch, 1980). *Roadgames*' inclusion of two American leads is predicated on a wobbly coincidence that a young American hitchhiker would just happen to be picked up by an American truck driver in the middle of regional Australia. *Razorback* starred the American actor Gregory Harrison, familiar to Australian and American audiences already from appearances in TV movies like *Wonder Woman* (1975) and the Karen Black vehicle *Trilogy of Terror* (1975), and series like *M.A.S.H*, *Barnaby Jones*, and particularly *Trapper John M.D*, in which he appeared for five years between 1979 and 1984.

It was not only American actors who were considered potential audience-bait for foreign markets. The martial arts superstar Jimmy Wang Yu was a familiar face in films that were popular on US grindhouse circuits, and starred in Trenchard-Smith's *The Man from Hong Kong* (1975). He was cast alongside the Australian actor George Lazenby, who was internationally recognizable for his brief role as James Bond in *On Her Majesty's Secret Service* (Peter R. Hunt, 1969). Trenchard-Smith also directed *Turkey Shoot* (1982), with central roles filled by the American actors Steve Railsback and Olivia Hussey. While Railsback had starred as Charles Manson in the 1976 television movie *Helter Skelter*, Hussey had earned a degree of legitimacy for her award-winning performance in Franco Zeffirelli's *Romeo and Juliet* (1968), but had more recently appeared in film fare with less highbrow appeal, such as the proto-slasher *Black Christmas* (Bob Clarke, 1974) and the dystopian Japanese science fiction film *Virus* (Kinji Fukasaku, 1980) alongside Sonny Chiba. Again recalling Leon Hunt's identification of Quentin Tarantino as a "gatekeeper auteur," Chiba has been anointed particular significance by Tarantino in his grindhouse canon: aside from granting Chiba's *The Street Fighter* (Shigehiro Ozawa, 1974) a place in his "Official Top 20 Grindhouse Movies" list,[39] the Japanese martial arts star is also mentioned in 1993's *True Romance* (directed by Tony Scott but written by Tarantino), and was cast in the role of Hattori Hanzo in *Kill Bill*.

Thirst included a memorable performance by Henry Silva, who, despite becoming a familiar face in a number of important Hollywood films like *The Manchurian Candidate* (John Frankenheimer, 1962), also appeared in a number of spaghetti westerns and *poliziottesco* movies that he made while living in Europe. *Thirst* also notably included the British actor David Hemmings. Although forever linked to art-house cinema for his starring role in Michelangelo Antonioni's iconic *Blowup* (1966), Hemmings, too, appeared in a number of films that played on the grindhouse circuit: *Barbarella* (Roger Vadim, 1968), *Fragment of Fear* (Richard C. Sarafian, 1970), and *Voices* (Kevin Billington, 1973), and his work in Italy led to his starring roles in *The Heroin Busters* (Enzo G. Castellari, 1977) and of course Dario Argento's *Deep Red* in 1975. Hemmings was a key Ozploitation figure, and he even directed a number of Ozploitation films such as *The Survivor* (1981), based on a James Herbert novel and starring fellow British actors Robert Powell and Jenny Agutter, and Joseph Cotten in his last film role. Hemmings also directed the New Zealand film *Race for the Yankee Zephyr* (1981), a film that was originally intended to be Australian, but Hemmings wanted so many non-Australians on the cast—Lesley Ann Warren, George Peppard, Donald Pleasence, and Ken Wahl—that Australian Actors Equity made it impossible for the film to be produced within Australia and it was rewritten to be set in New Zealand.

Hemmings also costarred in the remarkable *Harlequin* (Simon Wincer, 1980), again working with fellow British actor Robert Powell. This a crucial film when looking at the mechanics governing transnational flows both into and out of Ozploitation, and is in many ways typical of Ozploitation film created with a specifically American market in mind. Because of the substantial reduction of previously generous government financial support, from 1975 onwards it was clear that "new Australian films were unable to recoup their costs from domestic screenings alone."[40] Ozploitation producer Antony I. Ginnane has acknowledged the necessity to appeal to an international audience, commenting that "we tried to present *Harlequin* as not being set in Australia ... This was part of a deliberate strategy to help sell the film in foreign markets."[41] This political conspiracy thriller wears this desire to woo foreign markets on its sleeve, with its big-name foreign cast (Hemmings, Powell, and Broderick Crawford), an Americanized political system, and the inclusions of right-hand-drive cars, American flags at political rallies, and even a Dixie band.

But it would be incorrect to dismiss *Harlequin* as lacking local "cultural odor," to borrow a phrase from Koichi Iwabuchi, who uses the term "to focus on the way in which cultural features of a country of origin and images or ideas of its national, in most case stereotyped, way of life are associated positively with a particular product in the consumption process."[42] Diegetically, this is most apparent in the disappearance of Deputy Governor Eli Steele (Jack Ferrari) while diving off a beach that opens the film and sparks its storyline. It would have certainly been impossible for Australian audiences to separate this from the similar disappearance of Prime Minister Harold Holt in 1967, who disappeared while swimming at a beach in Victoria: the conspiracy theories that are even today still attached to the real-life disappearance of Holt would have been extremely potent for local audiences in terms of the central themes of political corruption that structure the film (an aspect that non-Australian audiences quite possibly would not have even recognized). And aside from structuring the enigma of its central character around a clearly imported Rasputin mythology, the way that this figure is articulated and defined through his ability to be both absent and present—its structuring spectacles rely on Powell's character's ability to be both seen and unseen, to make things appear and disappear—is a significant aspect of Ozploitation more generally, latching it meaningfully to its context of production.

Casting was of course not the only avenue through which Ozploitation cinema sought to induce itself into foreign exploitation markets. Most immediately, Ozploitation films were predominantly action, horror, and soft-core sex romps, ascribing to an already-established pattern of genre film production that had demonstrated success abroad. As happened particularly with European films that were repackaged for the American grindhouse market, Australian films were often renamed when sold overseas with new titles designed for more immediate genre-recognition in this new market: *Turkey Shoot* was released in the United States as *Escape 2000* (recalling films like Alberto De Martino's horror film *Holocaust 2000* (1977) and Radley Metzger's 1969 sexploitation film *Camille 2000*); *Harlequin* became *Dark Forces* (likely riffing on the iconography of *Star Wars*); and *The Man from Hong Kong* was known as *The Dragon Flies*, its new title evoking instant connections with successful kung fu films like *Enter the Dragon* (Robert Clouse, 1973) and *The Way of the Dragon* (Bruce Lee, 1972). Perhaps most famously John Lamond's *Snapshot* (1979) was released in the United States as both *The Day after Halloween*, *The Day before Halloween*, and *The Night after Halloween*, making no attempt to disguise its desire to profit from the recent success of John Carpenter's *Halloween* the year before (in spite of the fact that *Snapshot* is not set on Halloween, and makes no reference to it).

Rather than simply a one-way process of cross-cultural translation (from vernacular Australian to American grindhouse), the longevity of some key elements of the original Ozploitation era is even today still manifesting in often-overt ways in American genre film. For instance, *Snapshot*'s central motif of an evil ice cream van recently appeared in Marcel Sarmiento's structuring story in the horror anthology *V/H/S: Viral* (2014), and as noted earlier, Tarantino references Richard Franklin's *Patrick* in *Kill Bill*, and *Fair Game* (Mario Andreacchio, 1986) in *Death Proof* (2007). In the latter, Tarantino works through the intersection of masculinity and car culture that is of central concern to a number of well-known Australian exploitation films, such as *The Cars that Ate Paris* (Peter Weir, 1974) and, of course, the *Mad Max* series (George Miller, 1979, 1981, 1985, 2015). Even more obvious, however, is the fact that two of the most iconic Ozploitation films have been recently remade, both with the notable inclusion of Australian genre film producer Antony I. Ginnane. *Not Quite Hollywood* director Mark Hartley has remade Richard Franklin's *Patrick* (released in America as *Patrick: Evil Awakens*). Hartley's remake also included internationally recognizable names like Charles Dance and Rachel Griffiths. At the time of writing, John Hewitt's 2014 remake of Brian Trenchard-Smith's *Turkey Shoot* has also been doing the festival circuit, and aside from the inclusion of some Australian cast members who may be recognizable to those who know the original, its mélange of accents and international locations mean there is very little to identify the film as specifically Australian.

For better or for worse, the cultural flow between Ozploitation and traditions popularly imagined—particularly through "gatekeeper auteurs" such as Quentin Tarantino—as being linked to grindhouse distribution circuits was a dialogue that these recent films suggest has a continuing legacy. Ozploitation provides a conceptual wormhole to reassess the nation's entire cultural project through its role in Australian film history. While self-reflexively filling the role of oppositional, lowbrow Other, Ozploitation applies its own trash-perspective to the foundations upon which notions of Australian history and white identity are based. As Trenchard-Smith said in 2008, lamenting the disappointing local performance of *Not Quite Hollywood*, "cinema is a fluid and irrational universe."[43] It can tell us things we may not always expect to hear from certain areas of culture, in ways that might surprise us.

Notes

1. Philip Adams, "Two Views," *Cinema Papers* 44–45 (1984), 71.
2. This is how many films appear in the following book that accompanied the release of *Not Quite Hollywood* (Mark Hartley, 2008): Paul Harris, *Not Quite Hollywood: The Official Handbook* (Melbourne: Madman Entertainment, 2008).
3. Jake Wilson, *Mad Dog Morgan* (Strawberry Hills: Currency Press, 2015), 77.
4. Graeme Turner, *Film as Social Practice* (Abingdon: Routledge, [1988/2006]), 192.
5. Harris, *Not Quite Hollywood*, 71.
6. Jeffrey Sconce, "Trashing the Academy: Taste, Excess, and an Emerging Politics of Cinematic Style," *Screen* 36:4 (1995): 371.
7. See Melissa Bellanta, *Larrikins: A History* (St. Lucia: University of Queensland Press, 2012).
8. Anna Clark, "The History Wars," in *Australian History Now*, eds Anna Clark and Paul Ashton (Sydney: NewSouth Press, 2013), 157.
9. Andrew Tudor, *Monsters and Mad Scientists: A Cultural History of the Horror Movie* (Oxford: Basil Blackwell Ltd., 1989), 1.
10. A. A. Phillips, "The Cultural Cringe," *Meanjin* 9:4 (1950): 299.
11. Ibid.
12. Jason Bailey, *Pulp Fiction: The Complete Story of Quentin Tarantino's Masterpiece* (Minneapolis: Voyageur Press, 2013), 13.
13. Leon Hunt, "Asiaphilia, Asianisation and the Gatekeeper Auteur: Quentin Tarantino and Luc Besson," in *East Asian Cinemas: Exploring Transnational Connections on Film*, eds Leon Hunt and Leung Wing-Fai (London: I.B. Tauris, 2008), 220.

14. Ibid.
15. Andrew Pike and Ross Cooper, *Australian Film 1900–1977: A Guide to Feature Film Production* (Melbourne: Oxford University Press, 1980), 305.
16. The two leading parties in Australian politics are the Australian Labor Party and the Liberal Party of Australia. References to the these parties must emphasize the capital "L"—the Liberal Party is the traditionally more conservative party, while the Australian Labor Party's name stems from its roots in the labor/union movement.
17. Philip Adams, "Introduction," in *A Century of Australian Cinema*, ed. James Sanine (Port Melbourne: William Heinemann Australia, 1995), ix.
18. Graham Shirley and Brian Adams, *Australian Cinema: The First Eighty Years* (Sydney: Currency Press, 1989), 249; Pike and Cooper, *Australian Film 1900–1977*, 306.
19. Scott Murray, "Australian Cinema in the 1970s and 1980s," in *Australian Cinema*, ed. Scott Murray (North Sydney: Allen & Unwin, 1994), 71.
20. Pike and Cooper, *Australian Film 1900–1977*, 305–306.
21. Ibid., 306.
22. Murray, "Australian Cinema in the 1970s and 1980s," 96.
23. John Hinde, "*Barry McKenzie* and *Alvin* Ten Years Later," in *An Australian Film Reader*, eds Albert Moran and Tom O'Regan (Sydney: Currency Press, 1985), 186.
24. As discussed in *Not Quite Hollywood*, the success of the *Barry McKenzie* films was somewhat ironic as the creator Barry Humphries intended the films to be parodic. His anti-ockerism backfired by appealing to the very demographic he intended to mock.
25. Tom O'Regan, "Cinema Oz: The Ocker Films," in *The Australian Screen*, eds Albert Moran and Tom O'Regan (New York: Penguin Books, 1989), 95.
26. Susan Dermody and Elizabeth Jacka, *The Screening of Australia: Anatomy of a National Cinema*, Vol. 2 (Sydney: Currency Press, 1988), 31.
27. Ibid.
28. Ibid., 33.
29. O'Regan, "Cinema Oz: The Ocker Films," 95.
30. Dermody and Jacka, *The Screening of Australia*, 34.
31. Stuart Cunningham, "Hollywood Genres, Australian Movies," in *An Australian Film Reader*, eds Albert Moran and Tom O'Regan (Sydney: Currency Press, 1985), 235.
32. Sconce, "Trashing the Academy," 372.
33. Ibid., 387.
34. Carol Laseur, "Australian Exploitation Film: The Politics of Bad Taste," *Continuum* 5:2 (1992): 371.
35. Ibid., 370.
36. Ibid., 371.
37. Geoffrey Blainey, *The Tyranny of Distance: How Distance Shaped Australia's History* (Melbourne: Macmillan, 1968).
38. In terms of horror alone, there are movies from around the world about orphans (*The Omen* (Richard Donner, 1976), *The Orphan* (John Ballard, 1979), *Magdalena, Possessed by the Devil* (Walter Boos, 1976), *School of Death* (Pedro Luis Ramírez, 1975), and *Twins of Evil* (John Hough, 1971), the final part of Hammer's Karnstein Trilogy); about amnesia (a familiar trope spanning at least back to Hitchcock's *Spellbound* (1945); horror variations from this era ranging from *The Night of the Hunted* (Jean Rollin, 1980) and *Footprints* (Luigi Bazzoni, 1975) through to *Trauma* (Robert M. Young, 1972) or Sergio Sollima's 1972 film, *Devil in the Brain*); and with mute main characters (a trope in rape-revenge films in particular, inspired by *The*

Spiral Staircase (Robert Siodmak, 1945), *Johnny Belinda* (Jean Negulesco, 1948), and of course *The Virgin Spring* (Ingmar Bergman, 1960), ranging across subgeneric instances including *Thriller: A Cruel Picture* (Bo Arne Vibenius, 1974), *Savage Streets* (Danny Steinmann, 1984), and Abel Ferrara's *Ms. 45* from 1981).

39. "Quentin Tarantino's Top 20 Grindhouse Classics," *Grindhouse Cinema Database*, available at www.grindhousedatabase.com/index.php/Quentin_Tarantino's_Top_20_Grindhouse_Classics (accessed December 17, 2015).
40. Shirley and Adams, *Australian Cinema*, 286.
41. Harris, *Not Quite Hollywood*, 36.
42. Koichi Iwabuchi, *Recentering Globalization: Popular Culture and Japanese Transnationalism* (Durham and London: Duke University Press, 2002), 27.
43. Jim Schembri, "Not Quite Hollywood—Brian Trenchard-Smith Chimes In," *The Age*, September 13, 2008, available at http://blogs.theage.com.au/schembri/archives/2008/09/not_quite_holly.html (accessed December 17, 2015).

10

Go West, Brother: The Politics of Landscape in the Blaxploitation Western

Austin Fisher

When *The Legend of Nigger Charley* (Martin Goldman, 1972) opened in downtown theaters across the United States in May 1972, its marketing campaign provided a clear indication of who its target audience was. The film's tagline—"Somebody warn the West. Nigger Charley ain't running no more"—locates it within the cultural moment of the "blaxploitation" cycle, appealing to inner-city black markets through an antagonistic opposition to white America's most hallowed foundation myth. Yet this belligerent tone belies the hesitance and uncertainty toward the Wild West, its landscape, and the attendant tropes that are to be found in the film itself. After the eponymous hero and his two fellow escapees kill their brutal white slave-master and flee into the desert from an antebellum plantation, the first encounter they actually have with "the West" is rather less assured than the tagline suggests. Charley (Fred Williamson) belatedly notices an impending ambush by a group of Native Americans and nervously says "let's keep moving," but the trio are rapidly surrounded and brought to a halt. As the outlaws look around anxiously, one young tribesman reaches out, wipes his fingers down Charley's cheek and checks to see if the color has rubbed off, before confirming to his companions that it has not. A visibly relieved Charley responds by returning the gesture, and our heroes are allowed to go on their way.

On a diegetic level, this scene gives a brief but clear indication that the black outlaws and the Native Americans are in sympathy with each other in their mutual opposition to white oppression. The tribesman's suspicion that the hero's skin color would rub off also serves as a humorous comment on the history of ethnic makeup in Hollywood westerns, described by Tom Engelhardt as "a vast minstrel show in which the Other was represented by a limited set of red-, black-, brown-, or yellow-face masks created by, and if important enough, worn by whites."[1] Simultaneously, however, this scene shows the film's black characters to be bewildered outsiders in both the landscape and the historical setting of the Wild West: caught unawares, and finding themselves out of their depth in the wilderness. This chapter explores how such ambivalence toward the codes of the western genre characterized this and related films' more complex mode of address to their target audiences than the confrontational tone of their paratexts might suggest.

The Legend of Nigger Charley was the most successful of a small hybrid cycle of blaxploitation westerns that played US inner-city circuits in the early to mid 1970s, including *Soul Soldier* (John Cardos, 1972), *Charley One-Eye* (Don Chaffey, 1973), *The Soul of Nigger Charley* (Larry G. Spangler, 1973), *Thomasine and Bushrod* (Gordon Parks Jr. 1974), *Boss Nigger* (Jack Arnold, 1974), and *Take a Hard Ride* (Antonio Margheriti, 1975). Though each film shows people of color uniting in resistance to a racist white America, the divisions between ethnic groups are more revealing than what unites them, consistently placing black outlaws as outsiders in the landscape, which is positioned classically as the terrain of the Native American, but also as that of the white man since it doubles as the Hollywood western's hallowed turf. In these films, black heroes are alienated by both nineteenth-century white society and the great open spaces of the American continent. In their attitudes and outlooks, they instead seem "out of time": anachronistic representatives of a 1970s black urban sensibility, facilitating a mode of address located firmly in these films' immediate distribution contexts. Howard Thompson's review of *The Legend of Nigger Charley* in *The New York Times* gave a clear sense of the blaxploitation western's anachronistic feel, lamenting: "what has a blaring, jazzy rock 'n'roll sound-track got to do with the Old West or old anything?"[2] His question is pertinent, and it is my intention to explore its implications for the films' broader signifying practices in the coming pages.

There is of course nothing new in examining how the racial coding of the western began to unravel toward the end of the 1960s and into the 1970s. Richard Slotkin,[3] Tom Engelhardt,[4] and Stanley Corkin,[5] among others, have argued that the genre faced a crisis as the ideological assumptions on which it had previously thrived were dismantled in the Vietnam era. "Revisionist" westerns of the early 1970s in particular are a *cause célèbre* of politicized reappropriation, focusing in a self-conscious manner on the selective construction of history, and on recovering repressed historical narratives, as taglines for two of the most celebrated such films announced quite overtly. *Soldier Blue* (Ralph Nelson, 1970) was marketed as "the most savage film in history!," while one poster for *Little Big Man* (Arthur Penn, 1970) opened with the words "history lied." The word "history" was at the fore in both marketing campaigns, the films' sympathies for the wronged Native American inverting racial paradigms to register their countercultural outrage and to lay accusations of a continuum of genocidal impulses at white America's door. It is considerably less common to study the blaxploitation westerns, which also sought to reinscribe the classical western genre's racial codes for countercultural purposes—this time in the more confrontational tone of black separatism—and that played on urban grind house circuits a couple of years after these more celebrated revisionist examples. They tend to be left out of both scholarly histories of the western, and those of blaxploitation. Before I examine these films' modes of engagement with the landscapes and ideologies of the classical western, and their political and historical address to a 1970s inner-city audience, I will therefore consider why these scholarly omissions have occurred.

Their omission from accounts of the western might partly be due to the awkward "fit" that black-centered narratives had always had within that genre's mythos. Engelhardt argues that the historical presence of African Americans on the frontier was problematic to a binary construction of inexorable white progress set against the myth of the "vanishing American" (the native who mystically and obligingly "moves aside" to make room for white settlement): "Held in a tyrannical embrace within a democratic society, African-Americans could neither be incorporated into the inclusive narrative nor thrust beyond the geographic boundaries of the nation. Feared yet not an enemy, excluded yet close by, demeaned yet needed, they presented whites with an insoluble dilemma."[6] Moreover, of course, the very presence of black people provided an uncomfortable historical reminder that white American notions of "liberty" extended only so far. For this reason, Engelhardt argues, their enslavement was relegated to an "aberrant sideshow," while the facts that 200,000 black soldiers had fought in the Civil War and that a quarter of late-nineteenth-century cowboys were black were mostly erased from the story in dime novels and western films alike.[7]

Engelhardt's argument places emphasis on the liminal position of black identity within the United States' national narrative, and thereby usefully identifies a generic precedent for the "outsider" status of Charley and the blaxploitation westerns' outlaw heroes. It is, however, in danger of oversimplifying the history of the western genre, since there is in fact a long ancestry of black westerns. One of the early so-called "race movies" (independent, black-produced films responding to the public furor caused by the racism of *Birth of a Nation*[8]) was Oscar Micheaux's 1919 drama *The Homesteader*, which—while not strictly speaking a "western"—explored issues around the settlement of the wilderness, and racial tensions with black homesteaders. In the late 1930s, black-audience musical westerns such as *Harlem on the Prairie* (Sam Newfield, 1937), *The Bronze Buckaroo* (Richard C. Kahn, 1938), *Two Gun Man from Harlem*, and *Harlem Rides the Range* (both Richard C. Kahn, 1939) featured the black "singing cowboy" Herb Jeffries. Julia Leyda examines how these films, though ostensibly anodyne when compared to the earlier race movies' overt focus on contemporary racial politics, encouraged contemporary cultural identification among their audiences in all-black cinemas by employing "strategic anachronisms." She continues: "the result is a western that creates a dual present. The fictional characters appear to be in the classic western setting, the nineteenth century, but the anachronistic dialogue, the titles, and the costumes place the film firmly in the 1930s." This strategy of temporal displacement is further enhanced by three of the above films' titles incorporating the incongruous geographical referent "Harlem"—"the symbolic site of twentieth-century urban African American experience"—into a frontier lexicon.[9]

Indeed, Peter Stanfield has set out in great detail how the 1930s more broadly was a decade in which the western genre, though often supposed to be in crisis just prior to the onset of its golden age with the arrival of *Stagecoach* (John Ford, 1939), was in fact flourishing with rapidly produced series westerns. These were commonly set in a post-frontier West, and merged western iconography with Depression-era maladies of urban industrialization and working-class disenfranchisement, directly to address the concerns of lower-class audiences. Gene Autry himself underlined the extent to which the representation of history was very much subordinated to a contemporary mode of address in the 1930s "singing cowboy" format: "I played a kind of New Deal Cowboy who never hesitated to tackle many of the same problems [as Franklin D. Roosevelt]:

the dust bowl, unemployment, or the harnessing of power. This may have contributed to my popularity with the 1930s audiences."[10] Leyda refers to Stanfield's work to argue for an equivalent process on behalf of the black singing cowboy films, which similarly addressed their audiences' immediate economic and geographical dislocations.[11] In the pages that follow, I will argue that the blaxploitation western inherits the legacy of these low-budget "race westerns," whose overt contemporaneity was plain to see, this time by addressing the upheavals within racial politics in the late 1960s and early 1970s. Simultaneously, however, I shall argue that the blaxploitation western inherits and utilizes certain of the classical Hollywood western's ideological and racial associations, and therefore occupies an uncertain position within that genre's rich and varied history.

Of course, if I am adequately to contextualize these films within their cultural moment (and indeed within the remit of this book), they must also be considered alongside the wider blaxploitation trend of the early 1970s. This cycle of films emerged in response to a crisis in cinema audience numbers (brought about by the rise of television and the incursion of foreign films), and simultaneous shifts in postwar inner-city demographics. *Variety* estimated in 1967 that, while only 10–15 percent of the US population at that time were black, they totaled over 30 percent of audiences in first-run, big-city cinemas.[12] By June 1972, *The New York Times* reported that "an informal survey made on a recent weekend revealed that over half of the patrons for *all* kinds of movies in the theaters on 42nd Street and along Broadway ... were black."[13] The resultant need to adapt cinematic business practices was clear to see, and in the same month *The Boston Globe* reported that "black audiences ... have become a major factor in cities throughout the country. With the number of urban blacks increasing and the move of whites to the suburbs, downtown movie theatre owners in many cities feel they must attract the blacks in order to survive."[14] The films under consideration in this chapter were entwined within this socioeconomic context, emerging at the peak of blaxploitation's popularity after the huge successes of *Sweet Sweetback's Baadasssss Song* (Melvin van Peebles, 1971) and *Shaft* (Gordon Parks, 1971) had demonstrated the lucrative returns on offer to those willing to exploit the inner-city black market. Even once the blaxploitation trend had waned after 1973, as Hollywood's fiscal crises eased and objections from civil rights organizations to such films' racial stereotyping became more audible, these westerns continued to target black markets through both their content and their distribution patterns.[15]

It is therefore notable that the most successful blaxploitation westerns are often omitted or sidelined in literature about blaxploitation, even when the overt focus is on the trend's engagement with established industry genre categories.[16] Novotny Lawrence breaks blaxploitation down into detective, horror, gangster, and cop variants, with brief mentions of westerns coming only in lists and filmographies,[17] while Mikel J. Koven devotes a chapter to "Genre Films" but appraises only *Adios Amigo* (Fred Williamson, 1976) and *Take a Hard Ride* under the "westerns" category, and states that "neither ... are Blaxploitation films."[18] The reasons for such consistent omissions can, I think, be gleaned from the broader scholarly consensus that surrounds blaxploitation's sociopolitical contexts. Donald Bogle and Ed Guerrero both highlight the extent to which blaxploitation was a direct rejection of the integrationism that had characterized postwar "problem films," in particular those featuring the mild-mannered, nonthreatening persona of Sidney Poitier—whom Bogle labeled "the model integrationist hero"[19]—such as *No Way Out* (Joseph L. Mankiewicz, 1950), *Edge of the City* (Martin Ritt, 1957), and *Guess Who's Coming to Dinner* (Stanley Kramer, 1967).[20] Blaxploitation's confrontational separatist messages, articulated and enacted by altogether more assertive black heroes, were seen by producers to be more in tune with the shifts in black sociopolitical consciousness in the era of the Civil Rights and Black Power movements. This critical focus on how blaxploitation films were overtly responding to the contemporary social realities of their intended audiences is of course crucial to an understanding of their success, but it runs the risk of demarcating their modes of engagement with those audiences in an over-prescriptive manner. In a rundown of what constitutes "blaxploitation," Lawrence states that its films "are set in predominantly black urban spaces. Prior to the emergence of these films, all-black Hollywood motion pictures were generally set in the South. Blaxploitation films replace the traditional Southern settings with urban locales in cities like Harlem and Oakland."[21]

The assumption that emerges from such policing of the trend's boundaries is that, in order to qualify as "blaxploitation," a film must engage on a literal level with its target audiences' lived experience, by occupying the same urban spaces and addressing the same social and political issues. Yet this overlooks other, less literal, ways by which the films might address said audiences. The first half of *The Legend of Nigger Charley* is indeed set in the antebellum South, but if another of Lawrence's definitions for blaxploitation holds true—"movies made between 1970 and 1975, by both black and white filmmakers alike, to exploit the black film audience"[22]—then all of the key westerns analyzed in this chapter should be considered in this context. Rather than meeting target audiences in their immediate and contemporary locales, these films adopt particular strategies for the exploitation of this inner-city market, based around cinematic genre convention rather than sociopolitical verisimilitude. The blaxploitation western is such an awkward fit within both of its parent genres precisely because it occupies what Leyda (referring to the 1930s black "singing cowboy" films) called a "dual present"[23]: simultaneously residing in a cinematically and historically "western" setting, while embedding itself in its immediate distribution context. These films are neither here nor there. They are fluid, hybrid texts, displaced both generically and temporally. Running contrary to Lawrence's demarcation of blaxploitation's settings, their rural locales are paradoxically central to their strategies of engagement with their urban audiences. Rather than rejecting the legacy of white America's cinematic myth *par excellence* (to misquote André Bazin[24]), their racial inscriptions are executed through ambivalent appropriation of the received landscapes of the classical Hollywood western, and the attendant ideological implications of those landscapes.

This ambivalence toward the conventions of the Hollywood western is at its most apparent when the films' black heroes encounter other ethnic minority groups. One of the most noticeable and repeated features of blaxploitation westerns—present in *The Legend of Nigger Charley*, and forming a decisive factor in the narrative developments of

Charley One-Eye and *Thomasine and Bushrod*—is a consistent depiction of black outlaws discovering an affinity with Native Americans, the obvious point being that people of color should unite against the white oppressor. In this way, these films can be said to possess crossovers with the more celebrated revisionist western, with the classical genre's tables of racial representation being turned on white society to unmask a genocidal counterhistory. What is notable about these depictions, though, are the differences they posit between black and Native American characters. Far from inverting the classical western's racially coded associations with the landscape, they borrow and utilize them, to present their audiences with black heroes who are alienated by both white society and the great open spaces of the North American continent. This is a key component of a broader and defining sense that these films' black outlaws are anachronistic time travelers, dropped in the middle of the cinematic Wild West from 1970s Harlem.

In each film, the black heroes are shown quite conspicuously to be uncomfortable in the wilderness. *The Legend of Nigger Charley*, for example, makes it very clear that its gang of black outlaws on the run is anything but the western's outlaw archetype of "men who know Indians." They are shown to be ignorant of what the word "squaw" means; they have never heard of the Rio Grande; and when they sit around a campfire to be introduced to the ways of the wild by the itinerant freed slave known as "Shadow," they shelter miserably from the rain, pull faces of disgust at the bush tea Shadow has

Figures 10.1–10.4 Equivalent framings of Native Americans in *Stagecoach* (1939) (10.1, 10.2) and *The Legend of Nigger Charley* (1972) (10.3, 10.4).

served them, and cough and splutter on his pipe. They are also shown to lack guile in the wild since, as already outlined, they are easily ambushed by Native Americans, who seem to appear from nowhere, framing the natives as being "at one" with the landscape.

Furthermore, though it is executed with a lower budget and more basic production values, the aforementioned scene provides a clear visual association with one of the most iconic shots in the history of the western genre, and it inherits its racial coding. This can be demonstrated by a simple shot comparison with the mise-en-scène and camera movement as the lone titular vehicle enters the vast wilderness in *Stagecoach* (John Ford, 1939) (see Figures 10.1–10.4). In each shot, a Native American tribe enters the frame as the camera moves upwards and to the left to "discover" them standing on a high bluff, catching both the viewer and the protagonists—who are naively travelling along an exposed road—unawares. Each therefore offers a visual manifestation of Jim Kitses's seminal "shifting antinomies" paradigm, whereby the western genre negotiates US national identity by setting up a series of binary oppositions broadly symbolizing "wilderness" and "civilization."[25] In each shot, the Native Americans are framed as being tied to or part of the arid landscape in juxtaposition to the protagonists, who are travelling through this landscape as endangered outsiders. *The Legend of Nigger Charley* borrows this association to assert the obvious point that, though they are in sympathy with each other, there are significant cultural differences dividing people of color. Yet, by placing the black heroes in the position of the ambushed traveler usually occupied by whites in the western's generic syntax, the film frames the Native in an altogether classical, not a revisionist, manner.

Indeed, it is certainly not the case that, simply because blaxploitation westerns are apt to frame black and Native American characters as being in sympathy with one another, they necessarily do anything to subvert or challenge the genre's dominant racial stereotypes. *Charley One-Eye* pairs two men referred to only as "The Black Man" and "The Indian" in an uneasy partnership between contrasting ethnicities, reminiscent of similar pairings in numerous spaghetti westerns (an association enhanced further by the film's location shooting in Almería). Accordingly, their ethnic identities are emphasized throughout, with stereotypical assumptions being made about The Indian in particular. He is relied upon and coerced by The Black Man to show resourcefulness in the wild, and to hunt and cook their food, while The Black Man refuses him a sip of whiskey, saying "I know what this stuff does to you redskins. You stay away from it." This characterization (along with the casting of Richard Roundtree, fresh from his starring role in *Shaft*) serves to reinforce The Black Man's role as a talkative, streetwise pragmatist with a cynically urban sensibility, in contrast to the taciturn Indian—a relationship typified by The Black Man asking "how about you and me robbing for a living?," to which The Indian responds "don't know how to rob." "There ain't nothing to know," counters The Black Man; "You just leave that to me."

Gordon Parks Jr.'s *Thomasine and Bushrod* is a transparent reworking of the Bonnie and Clyde legend, moving the real Bonnie and Clyde's 1930s exploits into the relatively more "western" timeframe of 1911 and seeking to advance a more progressive message with a black outlaw couple robbing the (white) rich to give to the (black, Hispanic, and Native American) poor. The film borrows heavily from Arthur Penn's *Bonnie and*

Clyde (1967), by focusing on the construction of the heroes' legendary status with sepia photographs intercut with their exploits, and the outlaws reading newspaper reports of their growing celebrity status. It also resembles Penn's film in the way it plays upon the contemporary countercultural pertinence of the Bonnie and Clyde story, framing its heroes as free-spirited youths rebelling against a bigoted white society, this time overlaid with an explicitly racial dimension as the black outlaw couple find succor in the mountains from a mixed race black/Native American couple. Yet, once again, this affinity between people of color is expressed through age-old associations with a Native connection to the wilderness. Bushrod's ability to tame horses and find his way through tribal holy ground is implicitly linked to the revelation that he is half Comanche, while Thomasine tries in vain to cook on a campfire, and ends up kicking over her impromptu spit in frustration.

While Native American roles in these films tend to draw upon well-worn racial stereotypes, this consistent sense that the black heroes would be more at home in an urban milieu provides the blaxploitation western with a revealing indication of its contemporary mode of address. The use of the western setting to symbolize and foreground these heroes' cultural alienation is not only predicated upon their relationship with natives; it is just as often used to frame their interaction with white society. *The Legend of Nigger Charley* starts with the heroes being incarcerated as slaves in the antebellum South, and only enters recognizably "western" terrain when Charley has killed his slave-master and fled as a fugitive. As he and his companions then enter the wilderness, they are pursued by a white posse, and here it is made clear that white people too are considerably more comfortable in the landscape than are the black outlaws. Upon seeing that their pursuers are still very close behind them, despite a montage of landscape shots suggesting that they have been fleeing for some time, Charley sits on a promontory and comments bitterly: "that damn white man won't let up." This lament is (perhaps deliberately) reminiscent of Butch Cassidy's (Paul Newman's) repeated utterance of "who the hell are those guys?" in *Butch Cassidy and the Sundance Kid* (George Roy Hill, 1969), suggesting that *Thomasine and Bushrod* was not the only blaxploitation western to appropriate for the racial politics of the 1970s a symbol of white rebellion that had been recently reimagined by New Hollywood. The association is certainly apt. Butch Cassidy is here expressing incredulity at the tenacity of the faceless system that pursues the free-spirited heroes through the landscape. By overlaying a racial dimension onto an association with this recently filmed icon of white countercultural sentiment, *The Legend of Nigger Charley* further enhances its contemporary credentials, and emphasizes its heroes' position at the margins of bourgeois society.

In a similar vein, *Boss Nigger* consistently frames the western landscape as being the habitat of the white man, which alienates and endangers black people who dare enter it. An early scene shows a black father and daughter being attacked by white outlaws, their wagon having been overturned and their possessions strewn over the desert floor. The symbolic inversion of the western's racial archetypes is clear to see, with the desecration of the pioneer wagon being committed by whites rather than Native Americans. When the hero (played by Fred Williamson) arrives to save the daughter, it also becomes apparent that black people are unwise to set foot in this terrain, as he asks incredulously "what y'all doing out here anyway?" Her reply—that they are looking for work—is revealing. Though they outwardly resemble the western genre's trope of a vulnerable "pioneer" family, they are in fact seeking to reach an already-founded urban society, rather than settling in the wilderness. The film proceeds to underline this sense that black people do not "belong" in the western's landscape. The hero—a tough, uncompromising black bounty hunter—arrives in town and "sticks it to the Man" by proclaiming himself sheriff, outlawing racial slurs and imprisoning racist whites. Once again, however, it is the white man who is shown to be at home in the great outdoors, in stark and noticeable contrast to the hero who, the moment he leaves the town that he has taken charge of and enters the surrounding countryside, is caught in a laughably simple trap by the white posse seeking to catch him.

It is therefore apparent that, in the blaxploitation western, both white people and Native Americans are frequently shown to "belong" to the western genre and to the historical referents that accompany it. Black people, on the other hand, are consistently framed as conspicuous outsiders. The films utilize associations from the genre's history: framing Native Americans in their age-old role as being "of the land"; and framing whites as being "of the genre," since they too are shown easily to traverse the hallowed turf of white America's film genre *par excellence*. The black heroes are only shown to be in their element when they find an urban environment, as with Fred Williamson's sheriff in *Boss Nigger*, who is itinerant until he happens upon a lawless town, and sees the opportunity to enforce his "black man's law."

Before I draw conclusions about these trends of representation, there are a number of contextual factors that require clarification. I am not, for example, claiming that inner-city black audiences were necessarily inspired by these films. Nor am I claiming that blaxploitation westerns were expounding black nationalist doctrine in anything but the most superficial manner. My argument instead revolves around the identification of a particular mode of address and exploitation in this cultural moment, when US film producers were waking up to the lucrative returns on offer from the domestic black market, and tailoring their products accordingly. This hardheaded economic imperative was, of course, the origin and definition of the term "blaxploitation," and an appeal to black audiences was certainly not the same thing as black agency in the filmmaking process or an equal share of profits for black producers. In her study of the "black film" phenomenon between January 1973 and August 1974, Reneé Ward states plainly: "Black films are a box office bonanza at Chicago's Loop theaters, but mainly for white theater owners, producers and distributors." The picture she paints is a stark one in which, of the fifty-two "black-oriented" films released in the sample period, 75 percent were produced by whites, 57 percent were directed by whites, and none at all were distributed by black-owned companies.[26]

The blaxploitation westerns considered in this chapter were a part of this trend: both *The Legend of Nigger Charley* and *The Soul of Nigger Charley* were directed and produced by white filmmaker Larry G. Spangler, and distributed by Paramount; *Charley One-Eye* was directed by Don Chaffey (white), produced by David Frost's company "David Paradine Productions," and also distributed by Paramount; *Thomasine and Bushrod*, though directed and coproduced by black filmmakers (Gordon Parks Jr. and Max Julien respectively), was distributed by Columbia Pictures; while *Boss Nigger* was written and coproduced by Fred Williamson (black), but directed by Jack Arnold (white) and distributed by Dimension Pictures.[27] Indeed, this factor was a bone of contention in the film press at the time of these films' releases. *The Legend of Nigger Charley* in particular drew the ire of critics in *The New York Times*, with its cynical "whiteness" being singled out in a number of articles during its first downtown and neighborhood runs.[28] One critic, for example, described the sudden trend of movies featuring black cowboys and cops as "products of the same Hollywood minds that made millions of dollars while excluding Blacks from the industry. Now they've discovered a latter-day vein of gold to rip off."[29]

The notion that these films might be merely paying superficial lip service to the concerns of black audiences can to some extent be illustrated by their marketing strategies. Returning to the focus on taglines with which I began this chapter, *Charley One-Eye*'s is particularly revealing: "Somebody told the black man he wasn't a slave anymore. Somebody told the red man this land was his. Somebody lied. Somebody is going to pay." This confrontational tone suggests that the narrative alliance between The Black Man and The Indian is to be predicated on a common grievance against whites, but the film itself sells this promise short. *Charley One-Eye* does not in fact address slavery or land rights at all, but instead revolves around a fugitive soldier, and a Native American whose only grievance and cause to kill a white man appears to be that the said white man shot his pet chicken (the titular "Charley One-Eye"). The sensationalist tagline is clearly present to sell this film to inner-city black audiences eager to see their heroes "stick it to the Man," and this extended to its wider marketing strategy. Reviewing *Charley One-Eye* in the *Chicago Tribune*, Gene Siskel criticized its misleading advertising campaign, in particular an advert in his own paper the previous week that

> contains a picture of Richard Roundtree as Shaft—leather coat, black turtleneck, and revolver exploding from his waist—with the note, "The man you know as SHAFT in an exciting new role, defending 'Charley One-Eye.'" There is a crouching Indian beneath those words … a number of people have stormed out of the Roosevelt Theater upon discovering that "Charley One-Eye" wasn't a "Shaft" adventure.[30]

Yet such opprobrium at "misleading" marketing presumes the "black audience" to be a discrete and politically unified entity. Jon Kraszewski has argued that blaxploitation scholarship focuses too much on the negative polemics and reviews about the films that arose from black pressure groups (and from those sympathetic to their causes). Such a focus, he suggests, constructs a monolithic black spectator and homogenizes "black experience" through a singular, reductive prism of "black nationalism," overlooking the ways in which other factors such as marketing materials "structured the historical reception of blaxploitation in the 1970s."[31] Citing Barbara Klinger's model of cinematic "digressions," whereby promotional materials fracture the film and allow the spectator to follow numerous meanings (by focusing variously on the star, the genre or the director for example),[32] Kraszewski sets out how blaxploitation's marketing strategies "articulated shifting forms of nationalism, black class relations, and anxiety; spectators could choose these articulations or rearticulate them. These ads, then, provided one possible framework that spectators would position their reading of the film within or against."[33] Blaxploitation advertising frequently made use of tropes and slogans associated with revolutionary black nationalist groups to promote films whose narrative content actually had very little to do with such causes. Kraszewski also points out, for example, that while the adverts for *Shaft* suggested that the film's eponymous hero might be an ultraviolent black nationalist, the film itself shows him to be a middle-class police officer.[34] It is not made clear whether the audience members whom Gene Siskel observed storming out of the Roosevelt Theater were asked exactly why they disapproved of *Charley One-Eye*, but the assumption that they hankered after a repeat of *Shaft* should not be taken as read. *Shaft*, too, had provided sensationalist marketing that differed from its more sedate narrative content. Perhaps they were irked that the same trick had been pulled again.

The point is that these films had multiple meanings, and adopted various strategies to profit from black audiences. We should therefore consider the possibility that some of these audiences were not being duped by the vested interests of white capital and their misleading ad campaigns, but were instead critically aware of their own ambivalent relationship to the films, and were free to accept the connotations on offer from the adverts or the films, or not. Certainly, blaxploitation westerns contain numerous indications of self-reflexivity, suggesting (and perhaps catering to) an awareness of the cultural and cinematic heritage into which the films were entering. I have already speculated that the Native's suspicion that Charley's skin color would rub off in *The Legend of Nigger Charley* might serve as a comment on the history of ethnic makeup in westerns. This is certainly one available reading, to an audience familiar with the traditions of black representation in Hollywood. In a similar vein of cultural-historical self-awareness, at one point in *Boss Nigger* Fred Williamson's hero responds to a racial slur in a saloon ("hey nigger, come here and shine my boots") by performing the exaggerated stereotype of a smiling, subservient black man: the "coon" or "pickaninny" archetype from early cinema described by Donald Bogle as an "amusement object and black buffoon ... a harmless, little screwball creation whose eyes popped, whose hair stood on end with the least excitement, and whose antics were pleasant and diverting."[35] After abruptly coming out of this character and dealing deadly justice to these overt racists, the hero is accosted by the town's well-meaning Bostonian schoolmarm, who betrays the systemic prejudice of liberal white America by further affirming the "coon" archetype: "My family had black people working for us. They were good people. They used to sing and dance a lot. I used to love to watch them." *Thomasine and Bushrod*, too, passes comment on the pervasiveness of this character type, when a photographer expresses incredulity at the outlaw couple's ethnicity by saying: "Negroes sing and dance and steal chickens. They don't rob banks."

Of course, the most overt (indeed, unmissable) comment many of these films make on the history of racial slurs in the United States comes in their titles. Their inclusion of "the N word" is purposefully sensational, designed to foment identification among 1970s audiences eager to reclaim the word for an assertive black identity. Indeed, Fred Williamson states this purpose openly in the opening credits of the 2008 VCI DVD release of *Boss Nigger*: "I used the 'N' word to create sensationalism at the box office."[36] As Lawrence points out, such incorporation of racial epithets into film titles also has a long cinematic heritage as films like *Pickaninnies Doing a Dance* (1894), *A Nigger in the Woodpile* (1904), and *The Wooing and the Wedding of a Coon* (1905) attest.[37] Again, the blaxploitation western offers such a reading to a viewer attuned to this cinematic (and broader cultural) history.[38]

In conclusion, blaxploitation westerns' uneasy balancing act between revisionist and classical versions of the western genre can be seen to arise directly from their distribution contexts, constructing a scenario in which black outlaws are spatially and temporally disconnected from their rural surroundings so as to appeal to inner-city black audiences. Though they were in many cases distributed by major studios and made by white filmmakers, these films nevertheless adopted a variety of strategies— some obvious, some less so—for targeting these audiences. My focus has been on how these modes of address played out in these films.

To some extent, the films do of course document a moment of political revisionism in the western genre, when its ideological foundations were being brought into doubt. Yet their engagement with this generic heritage is more complex than such a surface reading might suggest, because they simultaneously demonstrate an inheritance from the genre's more "classical" elements (in particular in their framing of Native Americans), even while they seek to reject those elements' ideologies. If revisionism uncovers specific repressed histories, the blaxploitation western does not fit the bill, because these films were for the most part not addressing the history of black people on the frontier, as more prestigious black-oriented westerns of the time like *Buck and the Preacher* (Sidney Poitier, 1972) were.[39] Instead, these films' negotiation with the genre's history and landscape creates a tension through which their heroes perform a sort of time travel. Their urban sensibilities and articulations of black nationalism are transposed into the ideological and topographical terrain of the Wild West, almost as if they had been dropped there in a modified DeLorean, discombobulated and bewildered, from 1970s Harlem.

This, of course, should come as no surprise, given the target audiences for these films, and it perhaps explains why they do not quite "fit" into genre histories. They are neither urban blaxploitation films nor overtly historical narratives addressing specific events that contributed to the mythic Wild West. Their heroes can instead be seen as agents of transcultural appropriation across space and time. Robert A. Rosenstone sees in Alex Cox's use of creative anachronisms throughout the 1987 biopic *Walker* (such as helicopters, Marlboro packets, computer terminals, and Zippo lighters, all appearing in an 1850s setting) an "interpenetration of past and present" that purposefully destroys any surface realism of historical representation, thereby foregrounding the continuities that lie behind the construction of historical narratives: "Beyond destroying the surface realism of the film, they work to demystify the pretensions of professional history, cast into doubt notions of historical distance and objectivity, and insist that the questions we take to the past always arise from our current concerns."⁴⁰ For Rosenstone, *Walker* thus comments simultaneously on both the ideological construction of history and the traditions of representation that surround its subject: the American mercenary William Walker. Though *Walker* deploys anachronisms in a more overt manner than do *The Legend of Nigger Charley* or *Boss Nigger*, in their appeal to 1970s audiences blaxploitation western protagonists offer equivalently jarring readings around how dominant histories are constructed, how modes of ethnic representation operate, and how they persist into the present.

Notes

1. Tom Engelhardt, *The End of Victory Culture: Cold War America and the Disillusioning of a Generation* (New York: BasicBooks, 1995), 41.
2. Howard Thompson, "The Legend of Nigger Charley," *The New York Times* (May 18, 1972), 55.
3. Richard Slotkin, *Gunfighter Nation: The Myth of the Frontier in Twentieth-Century America* (New York: Atheneum, 1992).
4. Engelhardt, *The End of Victory Culture*.
5. Stanley Corkin, *Cowboys as Cold Warriors: The Western and US History* (Philadelphia: Temple University Press, 2004).
6. Engelhardt, *The End of Victory Culture*, 28.
7. Ibid., 22, 30, 34.
8. See Donald Bogle, *Toms, Coons, Mulattoes, Mammies and Bucks: An Interpretive History of Blacks in American Films* (New York: Continuum, 2001), 101–116.
9. Julia Leyda, "Black-Audience Westerns and the Politics of Cultural Identification in the 1930s," *Cinema Journal* 42:1 (2002): 62–64.
10. Peter Stanfield, *Hollywood, Westerns and the 1930s: The Lost Trail* (Exeter: University of Exeter Press, 2001), 90.
11. Leyda, "Black-Audience Westerns," 64.
12. Cited in Ed Guerrero, *Framing Blackness: The African American Image in Film* (Philadelphia: Temple University Press, 1993), 83.
13. James P. Murray, "Now, a Boom in Black Directors," *The New York Times* (June 4, 1972), D11. Emphasis in original.
14. George McKinnon, "Movies: Especially for the Blacks," *The Boston Globe* (June 2, 1972), 18. Also notable here is David Church's argument that, so synonymous was inner-city movie-going with black audiences by this period, the cultural disdain aimed at grind houses carried a decidedly racially charged component: "It is difficult not to detect an echo of racial anxiety in fears the 'wrong' films and 'wrong' audiences would spread to higher-class and less inner-city parts of the New York area beyond 42nd Street" (David Church, *Grindhouse Nostalgia: Memory, Home Video and Exploitation Film Fandom* (Edinburgh: Edinburgh University Press, 2015), 86).
15. Without wishing to labor the point, since these films' targeting of black audiences is perhaps self-evident, a snapshot of their release patterns shows how focused their distribution strategy was, even after the blaxploitation trend was past its peak. A one-page display ad of releases across the Chicago area from the *Chicago Tribune* of May 6, 1975 (B6), shows *Boss Nigger*'s extensive second run playing exclusively

in South Side cinemas: the Maryland on East 63rd Street, the Rhodes on East 79th Street, the Beverly on West 95th Street, the Jeffery on East 71st Street, the Double drive-in on West Columbus Avenue, and the Halsted on South Halsted Street.

16. This is not to say that these films have been entirely overlooked in scholarship. The release of Quentin Tarantino's own "blaxploitation western" *Django Unchained* (2012) has led to a degree of attention being paid to them, albeit as conduits through which to explore Tarantino's networks of citation. See, e.g., Johannes Ferle, "'And I Would Call It "A Southern"': Renewing/Obscuring the Blaxploitation Western," *Safundi: The Journal of South African and American Studies* 16:3 (2015): 294–297.
17. Novotny Lawrence, *Blaxploitation Films of the 1970s: Blackness and Genre* (New York: Routledge, 2008).
18. Mikel J. Koven, *Blaxploitation Films* (Harpenden: Kamera, 2010), 141.
19. Bogle, *Toms, Coons*, 175.
20. Ibid., 175–183; Guerrero, *Framing Blackness*, 70–75.
21. Lawrence, *Blaxploitation Films*, 19.
22. Ibid., 18.
23. Leyda, "Black-Audience Westerns," 63.
24. André Bazin, "The Western, or the American Film *par excellence*," in *What Is Cinema? Volume 2* (London: University of California Press, 2005), 140–148.
25. Jim Kitses, *Horizons West: Anthony Mann, Budd Boetticher, Sam Peckinpah: Studies of Authorship within the Western* (London: Thames and Hudson, 1969), 11.
26. Reneé Ward. "Black Films, White Profits," *The Black Scholar* 7:8 (1976): 13–14.
27. *Boss Nigger*'s association with the independent company Dimension Pictures perhaps sets it apart as a film that was not distributed for the profit of one of the major studios. Dimension was, however, very much geared toward the programmatic exploitation of profitable markets. For more on Dimension's marketing strategies, see Fred Olen Ray, *The New Poverty Row: Independent Filmmakers as Distributors* (London: McFarland, 1991), 149–174.
28. George Gent, "Black Films Are In, So Are Profits," *The New York Times* (July 18, 1972), 22; Clayton Riley, "Shaft Can Do Everything—I Can Do Nothing," *The New York Times* (August 13, 1972), D9; Lonne Elder III, "This May Seem Bitter," *The New York Times* (December 17, 1972), D19.
29. Riley, "Shaft Can Do Everything," D9.
30. Gene Siskel, "Charley One-Eye," *Chicago Tribune* (May 9, 1973), C8.
31. John Kraszewski, "Recontextualizing the Historical Reception of Blaxploitation: Articulations of Class, Black Nationalism, and Anxiety in the Genre's Advertisements," *The Velvet Light Trap* 50 (2002): 48.
32. Barbara Klinger, "Digressions at the Cinema: Reception and Mass Culture," *Cinema Journal* 28:4 (1989): 11–13.
33. Kraszewski, "Recontextualizing the Historical Reception of Blaxploitation," 49.
34. Ibid., 59.
35. Bogle, *Toms, Coons*, 7.
36. It is therefore notable that the packaging of the same DVD titles the film simply as *Boss*, perhaps pointing to an increased squeamishness around this word in the twenty-first century. As Ferle demonstrates, this very issue has come to the fore in the discourse surrounding *Django Unchained* (2012) (Fehrle, "And I Would Call It 'A Southern,'" 291–293).

37. Lawrence, *Blaxploitation Films*, 1.
38. It is worth mentioning *Blazing Saddles* (Mel Brooks, 1974) in this context, since this also addresses American cinema's uneasy relationship with racial slurs, albeit in an altogether more comedic manner. Its depiction of a black sheriff arriving in a racist frontier town perhaps places it as an inspiration for *Boss Nigger*, which was released the following year, but it was not aimed so purposefully at black audiences as were the blaxploitation westerns considered here, and is therefore outside the remit of this chapter.
39. The notable exception to this rule is *Soul Soldier*, which addresses the history of the Buffalo Soldiers.
40. Robert A. Rosenstone, *Visions of the Past: The Challenge of Film to Our Idea of History* (Cambridge, MA: Harvard University Press, 1995), 148–149.

11

Red Power, White Movies: *Billy Jack*, *Johnny Firecloud*, and the Cultural Politics of the "Indiansploitation" Cycle

David Church

As low-budget independents working outside or on the margins of corporate capital, the exploitation filmmakers who served grind houses had long sought short-term economic returns from sensationalized depictions of timely or controversial subject matter—and the tumultuous racial politics of the 1960s–1970s civil rights movement were no exception. Given the common tendency for discussions of race in the United States to be metonymically condensed into considerations of the African American experience, it is no surprise that much critical attention has been paid to the appropriative influences between Black Power rhetoric and the early-1970s rise of blaxploitation films. Yet, while slavery understandably retains its discursive centrality as the "original sin" contradicting the American national project's higher ambitions of freedom and equality, the history of colonization and extermination faced by Native American peoples is far less often invoked. Indirectly inspired by the well-publicized political activism of groups like Indians of All Tribes and the American Indian Movement (AIM), a short-lived cycle of films—sometimes termed "Indiansploitation"—nevertheless emerged during blaxploitation's boom years, addressing this notably different historical legacy of racism and genocide. Although these films may have imitated blaxploitation's highly marketable popularization of an often violent, racially marked (anti)hero, they also resonated with the growing political consciousness of Native Americans and their non-Indigenous allies, and thus stand as an important but oft-neglected development in exploitation cinema's transcultural impetus.

Blaxploitation films emerged during a period of severe economic downturn within the wider US film industry, with the unexpected success of films like *Sweet Sweetback's Baadasssss Song* (Melvin Van Peebles, 1971) and *Shaft* (Gordon Parks, 1971) heralding the industry's sudden "discovery" of black audiences as a potential audience hitherto underserved by the genre films that frequently played urban grind houses. Both independent producers and major studios jumped on the trend, their films influencing one another until the cycle gradually exhausted audience demand in the mid- to late 1970s, by which point the film industry had economically restabilized and a deliberate catering to black audiences gave way to films with more interracial crossover appeal.¹ By contrast, although movie theaters have long been located on or near tribal reservations,² the far smaller (and hence less profitable) potential Native American audience for exploitation films cannot fully account for why Indiansploitation films emerged concurrent with blaxploitation. Nor does the fact that white writers and producers were largely responsible for these films simply equate to a mercenary act of one-way cultural appropriation of racial discontent—a long-held criticism of blaxploitation that has since been complicated by recent scholarship.³ Rather, these films—while politically limited and sometimes stereotypical in their depictions of Native Americans—also index the "Red Power" movement that reached its height between the 1969–1971 Alcatraz occupation and the 1973 siege of Wounded Knee. With the movement gaining currency among not just Indigenous activists but also via transcultural alliances with Black Power and white countercultural activists, these films about the retributive violence exacted by modern-day Native Americans represent a notable extension of the era's growing awareness of Indigenous rights issues.

In this chapter, I do not claim that Indiansploitation films like *Billy Jack* (Tom Laughlin, 1971), *Johnny Firecloud* (William Allen Castleman, 1975), and *Angry Joe Bass* (Thomas G. Reeves, 1976) are "realistic," "positive," or "authentic" representations of Native Americans—if such a thing could be said to truly exist in the realm of the fiction film. In fact, most of these films star non-Indigenous actors in redface and rely on a plethora of stereotypical traits even as they attempt to generate empathy with their protagonists. Although the historical legacies of African American slavery and Native American extermination share important parallels and differences, exploitation cinema's capitalization on anger over racial inequality has still tended to uphold the wider cultural condensation of blackness as the quintessential symbol of American race relations. As such, this chapter attempts to avoid conflating these different histories of genocide, but some slippage is inevitable on my part. This is due to not only Indiansploitation filmmakers' partial imitation of the blaxploitation formula with Native American themes—a cinematic echo of how the Red Power movement gained momentum and inspiration from 1960s African American advances in self-determination—but also my own intellectual debt to the abundance of existing scholarship on blaxploitation.

Much like blaxploitation, then, I argue that the political value of Indiansploitation films resides more in the retributive fantasies they offer—including to audiences beyond Native Americans themselves—than in some essentialized notion of "Indianness" to which they do not necessarily aspire. Indeed, by foregrounding the concept of race as stylized *performance* instead of biological truth, we can better account for the political resonance generated in their specific historical context.⁴ It was, after all, the superficial and even stereotypical connotations of Indianness (e.g. spirituality, environmentalism, communalism) that—for better or worse—made Native American issues so appealing to the era's various countercultural interests.⁵ By exploring the threads of integrationist and separatist politics echoed in different films within the cycle, we can thereby understand how white filmmakers briefly capitalized on intersecting facets of Red Power activism, while still creating films whose ideological strategies might render them appealing to white and Indigenous audiences alike.

Transcultural influences and the rise of Red Power

Responding to America's changing racial politics, the early-1970s marketplace for both major-studio and exploitation films engendered multiple cycles with potential appeal across ethnic lines. Examples include not only the crossover white audience for blaxploitation films but also the lucrative African American viewership of East Asian kung fu films at urban grind houses.[6] Furthermore, black protagonists began appearing in major-studio westerns like *100 Rifles* (Tom Gries, 1969) and *Buck and the Preacher* (Sidney Poitier, 1972), not only complicating the genre's longtime equation between white/Anglo heroes and raced/Indian villains but also bridging between the meager integrationism of 1960s social-problem films and later, more separatist blaxploitation westerns like *The Legend of Nigger Charley* (Martin Goldman, 1972), *Thomasine & Bushrod* (Gordon Parks Jr., 1974), and *Take a Hard Ride* (Antonio Margheriti, 1975).[7]

These same years likewise saw a much-discussed spate of revisionist westerns that explicitly reversed the genre's old racial dichotomies by depicting white cowboys and cavalrymen as villains and Native Americans as sympathetic heroes or avengers. Ranging from prominent offerings like *Little Big Man* (Arthur Penn, 1970), *A Man Called Horse* (Elliot Silverstein, 1970), and *Soldier Blue* (Ralph Nelson, 1970) to more exploitative pictures like *Navajo Joe* (Sergio Corbucci, 1966), *Cry Blood, Apache* (Jack Starrett, 1970), *Chato's Land* (Michael Winner, 1972), and *Apache Blood* (Vern Piehl, 1975), these films have often been read as a generic reaction to the political advances of the civil rights era—including the rise of American Indian activism.[8] Yet, as valuable as these films may be in reformulating generic tropes, they still unfold in a mythic, premodern West, offering allegorical value at the expense of more explicitly evoking the Red Power movement. As Jodi Byrd says, "The possibility of an eruption of unanticipated Indian violence and the expectation of the hostile Indian savage seeking revenge for historical crimes remain a powerful threat within non-Indian imaginings,"[9] and I would argue that the political efficacy of such imagined threats is better served in modern dress. For this reason, I see the aforementioned westerns as an important cinematic thread intersecting with the Indiansploitation films under consideration in this chapter, but I instead focus on *contemporary* narratives of Native American retribution.[10]

The desire for political retribution—violent or otherwise—for a long history of forced removal, broken treaties, and cultural extermination had engendered the rise of Red Power activism by the mid-1960s. Federal efforts to terminate tribal sovereignty and force cultural assimilation had remained strong through the 1950s, but the liberation era led to organized political resistance both in the courts and on the ground. A series of "fish-ins" in the Pacific Northwest saw Native American activists reasserting their treaty rights to maintain tribal self-sufficiency by harvesting seafood on and outside reservation land. The resulting string of legal conflicts was not resolved until Judge George H. Boldt's landmark decision in *United States v. Washington* (1974), which saw the federal government finally siding with tribal treaty rights. Meanwhile, a series of well-publicized demonstrations on federal land focused public attention on Indigenous land rights and substandard living conditions. These included the 1969–

1971 occupation of Alcatraz Island by Indians of All Tribes; the 1970 return of the sacred Blue Lake (New Mexico) area to the Taos Pueblo; the 1970 occupation of Fort Lawton, Seattle, by United Indians of All Tribes; and the 1972 cross-country Trail of Broken Treaties march to Washington, DC, which culminated with AIM members occupying and sacking the federal Bureau of Indian Affairs (BIA) building. Although Red Power protests would persist throughout the 1970s, the movement arguably reached its peak of public visibility and sympathy when AIM's 1973 armed occupation of Wounded Knee on the Pine Ridge Indian Reservation, South Dakota—initially staged as a protest over corruption within the tribal government—resulted in a violent siege by federal troops at the site of the infamous 1890 Wounded Knee massacre.

Native American tribes do not necessarily share a common culture or past, since cultural differences often existed between individual tribes and regional affiliations. Furthermore, unlike other racially marked groups in the United States, Native Americans already had long-standing (if unfulfilled) promises of intranational sovereignty through specific land bases and treaties.[11] Accordingly, Native American activists did not want their causes to be simply perceived as derivative of the civil rights movement spearheaded by African Americans. In his foundational and widely read Red Power manifesto, *Custer Died for Your Sins*, the author and activist Vine Deloria Jr. argues that viewing civil rights as a *racial* issue instead of a cultural or ethnic issue has not only reduced discussion of race to blackness but also denied the significant differences both within and between presumed racial categories. "The most common attitude Indians have faced has been the unthoughtful Johnny-come-lately liberal who equates certain goals with dark skin," he notes. "This type of individual generally defines the goals of all groups by the way he understands what he wants for the blacks."[12]

In her indispensable history *Hippies, Indians, and the Fight for Red Power*, Sherry L. Smith details how white, middle-class New Leftists who had supported the African American civil rights movement had become increasingly alienated from the growing separatism of late-1960s Black Power rhetoric. Still desiring to "authenticate" their political involvement by championing social justice for more "authentic," non-white peoples, the counterculture gradually gravitated toward Native American issues. The predominantly white counterculture may have envisioned the vaunted mysticism, environmentalism, and communalism of Indigenous cultures as spiritual predecessors to the cultural alienation of latter-day hippies, but their sometimes-superficial romanticization of Indigeneity nevertheless succeeded in garnering wider attention for Red Power struggles and even spurred some younger Native Americans to increasingly revalue their own culture. As Smith says, these transcultural investments in Indianness were certainly not unproblematic, but they still "represented the absolute antithesis of the assimilation and acculturation models that had prevailed for centuries."[13]

Several social-problem films about modern-day Indigenous life appeared during these years, capitalizing on spreading public awareness of Native American politics. Based on Clair Huffaker's 1967 novel *Nobody Loves a Drunken Indian*, Carol Reed's *Flap* (1970) raises issues of Indigenous land rights within the lightweight context of a major-studio comedy about a man named Flapping Eagle (Anthony Quinn), who quixotically leads a one-man Native uprising. After Red Power activists raised a controversy over the film's planned use of the novel's original title, Warner Bros. made the retitled film's topical appeal further visible on its posters: "A warning to the mayor: FLAP is here! The Indians have already claimed Alcatraz. City Hall may be next. *You have been warned.*" Several years later, Twentieth Century Fox contributed *When the Legends Die* (Stuart Millar, 1972), an adaptation of Hal Borland's 1963 novel about a young Ute man torn between traditional Indigenous lifeways and cultural assimilation after he becomes a successful rodeo rider. Framed as a generational tension between the precocious Tom Black Bull (Frederic Forrest) and his white rodeo mentor, Red Dillon (Richard Widmark), the film's updating of the novel's setting from the early twentieth century to the present day was calculated to resonate with the youth audience's alienation from parental cultures.

Perhaps the most interesting example, however, is GSF Productions' independent release *Journey through Rosebud* (Tom Gries, 1972), which is about a white hippie named Danny (Kristoffer Tabori) who befriends Frank (Robert Forster), a cynical young Sioux, while traveling through South Dakota's Rosebud Indian Reservation in an attempt to evade the draft. Rather than move to the ghettos of Chicago and risk losing their cultural heritage, the reservation's politically engaged youth decide to organize and reassert the treaty rights that should prevent them from starving on their own land, staging an armed protest to release a local man accused of illegally harvesting food animals. Although many of the Native Americans scorn the appearance of the "goddamn hippies," Danny eventually develops a romance with a local Sioux activist (Victoria Racimo), while Frank becomes more self-destructive after the white organizers of a competitive demolition-derby circuit exclude him from participating in the sort of lucrative traveling competitions that benefited *When the Legends Die*'s protagonist. After Frank dies in a car crash and Danny finds his tenuous tribal relationships severed, he returns to the open road and an uncertain future. Although it plays into the revisionist western's trope of the white man who desires to "go Native," the film's depiction of armed political standoffs was remarkably prescient of the following year's events at the Pine Ridge reservation just adjacent to Rosebud.

While this handful of contemporary social-problem films lacks the more lurid emphasis on violent retribution that the exploitation film market would capitalize upon through blaxploitation-style tropes, these films still demonstrate the timeliness and potential countercultural appeal of Red Power issues. *Variety*, for example, deemed *Rosebud*'s box-office prospects "dubious, although it may do well in big city liberal strongholds," with its serious themes and sparse narrative a "hard sell" in comparison to the more flippant and star-powered *Flap*'s respectable returns.[14]

The *Billy Jack* series

Without sacrificing the transcultural resonance of the era's Red Power issues, exploitation cinema's marshalling of a politically charged Native protagonist to the more populist genre thrills of ass-kicking heroism found its most influential model in white filmmaker Tom Laughlin. Working under various pseudonyms as writer, director, and star, Laughlin made a four-film series about a character that even Vine Deloria (although dismissing the films as "dreadful") grudgingly called an "overwhelming symbol of the fascination that Indians held for other Americans in the sixties," and a series that "struck a responsive chord in majority hearts and minds."[15]

Introduced in American International Pictures' *The Born Losers* (1967), one of the many late-1960s biker films cycling off from the success of *The Wild Angels* (Roger Corman, 1966), Billy Jack (Laughlin) is a "half-breed" former Green Beret turned liberal-minded vigilante. Repeatedly derided as an "Injun," Billy runs afoul of a biker gang terrorizing a California coastal town (Figure 11.1), but his efforts to intervene where the police do not also results in his arrest and a hefty fine. Like *When the Legends Die*'s Tom Black Bull, Billy is a skilled rodeo competitor, but the next competition is not soon enough to win the money to pay his fine, and he is unable to support himself as a wild horse tamer since the animals have been vanishing (in the sequel, we see that white poachers have been killing wild horses on reservation land for dog food). When the gang subsequently steals Billy's meager savings, a series of violent confrontations ensue as he attempts to recover his ticket out of legal jeopardy.

Meanwhile, the biker gang is on trial for raping several local teenagers after the women acceded to visit the gang's hideout, fascinated with their rebelliously nonconformist image. The gang begins threatening them against testifying in an upcoming trial, and the narrative's central conflict soon becomes the question of whether the women should further endanger their personal safety to testify on behalf of the law and order championed by their parental generation. The victims also include Vicky (Elizabeth James), a bikini-clad college student whose independence is marked by her lone driving of a motorcycle; apparently entreating upon the biker gang's masculinist domain, she is raped after she refuses to be sexually initiated as the

Figure 11.1 Billy Jack confronts the biker gang after they repurpose a "No Indians" sign from a local business, in *The Born Losers* (1967).

gang's newest "mama." After befriending Billy, Vicky must decide whether to be like the younger victims and retreat into a sheltered life of white privilege or to risk her life for the common good. When the gang captures Vicky on the eve of the trial, Billy infiltrates their hideout and eventually turns them over in a police raid—though he is shot and wounded by a sheriff after being mistaken for one of the miscreants.

More than willing to use his hapkido martial-arts training against the gang, Billy's vigilantism positions him outside the law, yet he often acquiesces to the legal system's authority—whether in the fine initially leveled against him or the impending trial against the gang. This ambivalence is little coincidence, since the era saw the outlaw biker's "raw, spiritual freedom" celebrated in countercultural quarters as a figure inheriting the "Noble Savage" trope long associated with Native Americans.[16] The film thus finds the conflict between Billy and the villainous gang symbolizing an ideological tension between "good Indians" and "bad Indians" at a time when Native American and countercultural politics were both gaining wider sympathies. The biker gang's very motto, "Born to Lose," even echoes the implication that Billy's racialized identity marks his inherent (counter)cultural difference—a more "authentic" difference from the white bikers' voluntarily adopted social deviance.

In this regard, Billy's Indianness also helps explain his ostracism as a returned Vietnam veteran whose extralegal activities often pit him against local sheriffs—a trope that would be subsequently repeated in *Journey through Rosebud*, *Johnny Firecloud*, and *Angry Joe Bass*. As Sherry Smith observes, the counterculture often drew parallels between past military massacres of the Native Americans and present massacres of the Vietnamese, with both groups posited as similarly resisting European colonialism.[17] As a "half-breed" uneasily positioned between two worlds, then, Billy's status as a veteran now opposed to the war implicates him as both colonizer and colonized; he may somewhat share the bikers' resistance to the dominant culture's laws, but it is also implied that his ethnicity gives him a premodern moral/spiritual high ground that the hedonistic bikers lack. Yet, the fact that Billy is the only Native character in the film suggests that his "important roles for a liberal audience—environmental steward, precolonial subject, and spiritual guardian" (all traits that would be amplified in the sequel)—serve to render him not only highly visible via stereotype but also a paradoxical embodiment of "ghostly" Indigeneity that has been otherwise absented into a premodern past. As a solitary vigilante, he thus serves as what Michelle H. Raheja calls a nostalgic figure for already-vanished Native American lifeways that are ostensibly distanced from the era's collective struggles over political self-determination—and yet, his very status as the film's lone Native American (notably played by a white man) also serves as an uncanny reminder of white guilt over the cultural genocides that Red Power activism was attempting to redress.[18]

Following *The Born Losers*'s modest success as a biker film, Laughlin further styled himself as a countercultural hero through the tumultuous production and distribution history of its 1971 follow-up *Billy Jack*. After Laughlin independently produced the film, Twentieth Century Fox acquired the distribution rights, but Laughlin stole the film's soundtrack when the studio threatened to alter the film. After Laughlin reacquired the film, Warner Bros. next agreed to distribute it, but Laughlin sued the studio for dumping it into drive-ins, grind houses, and other areas of the exploitation film circuit in 1971. Warner Bros. settled with Laughlin, allowing him to reissue the film on his own terms for an even split of the profits. Laughlin "four-walled" the film by renting out theaters at a flat rate (thus allowing him to collect all the proceeds), and then used market research to saturate local television with demographically targeted advertising. "Separate ads foregrounded romance, countercultural/anti-Vietnam War aspects, action, and martial arts—a varied campaign designed to reach a broad spectrum of moviegoers." When the $800,000 film became a tremendous hit upon its May 1973 reissue, earning over $32 million, Laughlin's strong-arm tactics against the majors were vindicated; he not only earned a far larger share of the profits than his original distribution deals would have allowed but the larger industry began experimenting with four-walling and localized saturation advertising.[19] Countering *Variety*'s suggestion the previous year about *Journey through Rosebud*, then, *Billy Jack*'s reissue proved that Native American political themes did well beyond just urban liberal enclaves when marketed to appeal to transcultural and multigeneric interests. The film's rerelease on the very day after the seventy-one-day Wounded Knee occupation ended could not have been better timed.

Billy Jack opens with a confrontation between Billy and white poachers (including a local sheriff) on reservation land in the American Southwest, setting up the film's central conflict over sovereignty. Billy is the unofficial guardian of Freedom School, a liberal alternative school and multiracial/countercultural refuge run by the soft-spoken pacifist Jean (played by Laughlin's wife, Delores Taylor). After one of the poachers savagely beats his hippie daughter Barbara (Julie Webb) for coming home from San Francisco pregnant, Billy hides her at the school, which is located on the reservation and therefore a different legal jurisdiction. Barbara soon falls for Martin (Stan Rice), a young Native student who is targeted by local bigots after he is suspected of being the baby's father. After an escalating series of confrontations between the students and bigots—with Billy often stepping in to deliver some hapkido payback—Jean is raped and Martin killed, but Jean urges Billy to control his rage, lest his vengeance jeopardize the school's existence.[20] When the authorities finally come to take Barbara from the school, she and Billy hole up in a nearby church where a Wounded Knee-style shootout ensues—ending once Jean convinces Billy to surrender and, by standing trial, bring attention to Red Power issues.

As in *The Born Losers*, Billy fits the popular 1970s trope of the male vigilante seeking revenge against rapists (as also seen in *Straw Dogs* (Sam Peckinpah, 1971) and *Death Wish* (Michael Winner, 1974))—but throughout he is depicted as less violent and far more spiritual than in the previous entry. Unlike the previous film, his unspoken love for Jean has led him toward pacifism, as she encourages Billy not to follow a retributive path of further destruction. Like the teenage rape victims in *The Born Losers*, Billy is now positioned as the character who must altruistically reconcile himself with the common good instead of simply following a selfish desire for revenge. Since he is no longer the only Native American character, protecting the Freedom School means protecting not only the Indigenous rights to be enjoyed by young people like Martin but also the countercultural youth drawn to Native spirituality and literal relocation onto Native land. Indeed, Billy explicitly notes that white youth have turned to Native American ways after seeking spiritual answers not provided by drugs or the religion of their parents. "Being an Indian is not a matter of blood; it's a way of life," he concludes, freely opening notions of "Indianness" to countercultural participation.

On the one hand, then, Billy is no longer depicted as a "lone" Native character, suggesting that he is not just a ghostly remnant of a premodern past, but rather one of many Native Americans struggling to survive on the reservation against continual threats to their sovereignty. This political dimension is all the more foregrounded in *Billy Jack* because, unlike *The Born Losers*, the savagely violent and bigoted villains are not an "outsider" group like a biker gang, but prominent white townspeople themselves. On the other hand, the film dilutes the notion of "Indianness" to the point that it becomes accessible to white counterculture members as a trendy mantle that can be discarded at any time to reassert their racial privilege. As valuable as Billy's fostering of transcultural sympathy may be, for example, his statement about Indianness as a way of life also questions the very blood-quantum laws that (for better or worse) provide a legal justification for tribal membership and sovereignty in the first place. Furthermore, he may tell Jean that he'll stop being a vigilante when the law is applied equally to all, but Jean's own moral struggles with adhering to her pacifism are narratively developed in more detail than Billy's stand for Native American rights. When the film ends on a note of solidarity with Red Power—the Freedom School students standing and defiantly raising their fists (Figure 11.2) as the police car carrying Billy drives by—it thus feels like an abrupt shift from the film's primary emphasis on pacifism, an idea that a Vietnam-era audience could perhaps more readily rally behind.

Despite the film's cumulative success at the box office, some Native American critics derided it as "traditional American Western lore dressed in buckskins, authenticated

Figure 11.2 After Billy finally surrenders at the church, the multiracial, countercultural Freedom School students raise their fists in solidarity, in *Billy Jack* (1971).

by an intense Lutheran belief that justification by faith alone is sufficient."[21] Billy also represents common stereotypes of the Indian as violent, mystical, attuned to nature, and unafraid to die in vain.[22] Other critics were more charitable, saying it "does not patronize Indians, and it finds value for life today in Indian ways of living."[23] "Here, for once, is a film that finds part of the solution right in the problem," said another, "a film that harnesses violence in support of peace and brotherhood."[24] Still another suggests that this ideological ambivalence ensured the film's box-office success by appealing to different cultural fantasies: "*Billy Jack* wants to be realistic in its approach to social issues, but finds that for dramatic effectiveness it must use the stock figures of melodrama … Billy Jack is a superhero for an age that needs superheroes, but he is also a man who needs lecturing about nonviolence in an era too 'realistic' to believe in them."[25] Although the film's critical reputation has not greatly improved over the years, more recent critics like Scott Richard Lyons acknowledge "an entire generation of young Indian men … wearing variations of what is now considered to be the standard American Indian Movement (AIM) uniform, but which was originally Billy Jack's iconic outfit," testifying to not only the film's cultural influence upon Indigenous viewers but also its even-handed resonance with Red Power and leftist debates over violent versus nonviolent resistance.[26]

The inevitable sequel, *The Trial of Billy Jack* (1974), actually spends little time drawing attention to Red Power issues through Billy's involuntary manslaughter trial. Billy instead uses his time on the witness stand recalling a My Lai-inspired massacre he saw in Vietnam and denouncing Nixonian foreign policy. Throughout the film, Laughlin pays far more attention to the Freedom School's continuing struggles with corrupt local government and business interests once Billy is released from prison and begins a spiritual purification process. Indeed, the film's prologue betrays its primary interest in white countercultural issues instead of Red Power, listing the number of casualties at real-life student protests like Kent State University before including the fictional Freedom School shootout as the most recent incident. Although there are long sequences dedicated to Native Americans arguing about resistance to white corporate encroachment on tribal lands, the film offers even fewer action scenes than its predecessor. The end result is an overly long, meandering series of scenes featuring Billy, Jean, and their comrades speechifying on leftist views about Vietnam, Nixon, tribal rights, child abuse, government corruption, and civil disobedience. Gripping cinema it is not. Less a coherent narrative than a guidebook to The World According to Tom Laughlin, the film was modestly successful as a follow-up to the previous year's phenomenon, but the series clearly saw diminishing generic and economic returns.

By eschewing the earlier films' vigilante genre thrills in favor of greater political grandstanding, Laughlin gradually lost the multigeneric viewership that *Billy Jack* had fostered through potentially exploitative appeals to martial-arts action and countercultural rebellion. A further film, *Billy Jack Goes to Washington* (1977), appeared several years later, but Laughlin's remake of the Frank Capra classic did not even garner a theatrical run and was instead sold to television syndication. Nevertheless, Lyons reads the trajectory of the series as "a civil rights roadmap, moving as it does from defense of oppressed individuals (*The Born Losers*), to militant confrontation with 'legitimate' power structures (*Billy Jack*), to engagement with the court system (*The Trial of Billy Jack*), and finally to an attempted seizing of power using national electoral politics (*Billy Jack Goes to Washington*)."²⁷ This reading is important, because even if the series represents an integrationist approach to Native American issues, it was only one direction that the Red Power movement was unfolding as its more radical elements subsided in Wounded Knee's wake. Indeed, as Billy Jack gradually became less violent and more macropolitically involved in liberal causes, another exploitation film would emerge to pick up the far bloodier and more radically separatist elements of the era.

Johnny Firecloud

Although derivative of *Billy Jack*'s far greater renown, William Allen Castleman's 1975 film *Johnny Firecloud* is arguably the quintessential example of a Native American-themed exploitation film, albeit one that has garnered virtually no critical attention despite its strong screenplay and performances. Whereas Laughlin blanched at the thought of *Billy Jack* being merely consigned to drive-ins and grind houses, *Johnny Firecloud* revels in its sleazier pedigree—but without wholly sacrificing political resonance. Sexploitation specialists Entertainment Ventures, Inc. (EVI) were veteran producers of some of the highest-budgeted soft-core films of the late 1960s, but when hard-core porn began dominating the sex film market in the early 1970s, the company branched out into R-rated general-release films for economic survival. EVI head David F. Friedman managed to raise $220,000 (his largest budget ever) for *Johnny Firecloud*, and the major studios were so hungry to cash in on *Billy Jack*'s success that Laughlin's original distributor, Twentieth Century Fox, made a deal with the sexploiteers for *Firecloud*'s foreign distribution rights. Their budget already recouped from the Fox deal, EVI profitably retained distribution rights for the United States and Canada (including playing the film at the Lyric theater on New York City's 42nd Street, among other grind houses), and later syndicated it to television.²⁸

As in *Billy Jack*, Johnny Firecloud (Victor Mohica) is another veteran whose Indianness sets him at odds with the local bigots who effectively run a tiny Southwestern town. Local gangleader Herb Colby (Ralph Meeker) is especially out for Johnny's blood after the latter impregnated Colby's daughter, June (Christina Hart), just prior to Johnny's deployment to Vietnam. Kept apart by her father, June lost the baby and has since become an alcoholic. Meanwhile, Johnny has returned to town out of his love for June, which opens him to constant harassment from Sheriff Jesse (David Canary) at Colby's command. Johnny's grandfather, Chief White Eagle (Frank DeKova), is also an alcoholic, but whereas June's racial/class privilege allows her addiction to unfold behind closed doors, White Eagle serves his addiction at the price of debasing himself in public for the amusement of Colby's men—especially at the aptly named Thunderbird Bar, wallpapered with Indian kitsch, where Colby holds court. When Johnny arrives at the bar to beat up the baddies and take his grandfather home, we quickly see the film's indebtedness to blaxploitation in the broadly caricatured conflict between racist white villains and rebelliously heroic men of color, much as the one-time taboos on miscegenation and Native-on-white violence fuel the conflict in ways that earlier generations of Native American and African American representation would not have lauded.[29]

Yet, unlike Billy Jack, Johnny has turned his back on his ethnic heritage, ashamed of what has become of his grandfather and the poverty-stricken reservation where he grew up. Despite his grandfather's appeals for Johnny to return and rediscover his rich heritage, the younger man accuses White Eagle of wanting to join the white man's world without knowing how. Initially, Johnny would rather integrate with white society beyond the reservation, even at the cost of his birthright to become the new chief upon his grandfather's death. He reminds White Eagle how the "fire cloud" that gave him his name—the atomic bomb tested on the day of Johnny's birth—marked "the beginning of a new age," an age divorced from seemingly outdated notions of tribal sovereignty. This generational divide is not one-sided, however, since Johnny's friend Nenya (Sacheen Littlefeather) is a young woman who also left the reservation, but has returned to teach at the reservation school, college-educated and proud of her Indigenous heritage (Figure 11.3).

Yet, Johnny's refusal to be "just another Indian" changes after he reconciles with June, and Colby subsequently arranges his arrest on a phony rape charge.[30] While Johnny is in prison, White Eagle dons a traditional headdress and is lynched by a mob after demanding Colby release his grandson. Johnny soon escapes, but Colby's men rape and beat Nenya to death (a scene betraying EVI's sexploitation background) when they come to the reservation school looking for the fugitive—another instance of sexual violence prompting vengeance in the cycle, but this time a Native woman savaged by white cowboy types.[31] With White Eagle and Nenya both murdered, all those who challenged Johnny to embrace his heritage are gone, so he decides to finally take a stand for tradition and seek vengeance as the tribe's de facto chief. One of the film's taglines—"They taught him today's violence ... He gave them yesterday's revenge!"—suggests the more stereotypically "Indian" methods of Johnny's bloody retribution: death by scalping, by tomahawk, by dynamite, by bag of rattlesnakes pulled over the head, and by burial up to the head to let the vultures do the rest. After Johnny strikes back against Colby, June leaves town, prepared to testify against her father, and Jesse's final confrontation with Johnny in the desert foothills ends in a stalemate.

Instead of *Billy Jack*'s less confrontational appeals to pacifism and long scenes of moral wrestling over vigilantism, *Johnny Firecloud* makes no qualms about the redemptive power of violence when ostensibly rooted in the rediscovery of one's "true" Indigenous heritage. Much as blaxploitation films ideologically marked a shift from an earlier generation's belief in African American integrationism to the younger, more militant separatism of Black Power, we can see ideological differences with the Indiansploitation cycle echoing similar divisions within the struggle for Native American civil rights. Within Native American communities, older generations favored change through the decisions of courts and tribal governments, whereas the younger generation was more prone to direct action and public protest.[32] Littlefeather's role as the proud Nenya is particularly significant in this regard (though she also appeared as a political activist in

Figure 11.3 Sacheen Littlefeather, appearing as *Johnny Firecloud*'s Nenya, after her famous Red Power protest at the 1973 Academy Awards ceremony.

The Trial of Billy Jack), since she was cast after having already become one of the most public faces of Red Power by famously declining Marlon Brando's Oscar on his behalf at the 1973 Academy Awards ceremony to protest the Wounded Knee siege. Thus, if the *Billy Jack* series traces the former civil rights strategy as a path through the legal and legislative systems aided by white countercultural allies, *Johnny Firecloud* echoes AIM's more radical politics of armed and potentially violent resistance against white supremacy—but does so at the risk of problematically essentializing Indianness as an inescapable trait associated with premodern cultures. In other words, much as Black Power and its rhetorical outgrowth in the blaxploitation cycle reversed the cultural devaluation of blackness as a point of racial pride, *Johnny Firecloud* celebrates "Old West" associations of Indianness as a fitting brand of retributive self-defense, even at the risk of also portraying Johnny's political transformation as a "natural" regression into savagery.

Like the masculinism touted by many of the more radically separatist proponents of Black Power, *Johnny Firecloud* pays considerable attention to what it supposedly means to "be a man." After Johnny calls Jesse's masculinity into question for being no more than Colby's puppet, the sheriff confesses that he is also a veteran, but was dishonorably discharged for homosexual conduct—a secret that has allowed Colby to blackmail him into subservience. In this light, Jesse's continual harassment of Johnny appears rooted less in personal racism than a sense of displaced anger and shame that his sexuality has potentially cast him as the only person in town as culturally low as Johnny. In their final confrontation, Johnny defiantly asserts that, as chief, he has more independence than Jesse does under Colby's thumb, then goads Jesse over his inability to publicly acknowledge his sexual identity. "You're always crying about justice … well, where's mine?" Jesse exclaims, saying he just wants to "live like a man." "You've got to know what you are and where you belong to live like that," Johnny answers, implying that, unlike remaining meekly in the closet, coming out as gay will not make Jesse any less of a man. Both Johnny and Jesse have been marginalized because of some seemingly inherent trait that they cannot deny—whether race or sexuality—and this intersection of identity factors is all the more poignant in a film appearing amid both the Red Power and gay liberation movements. Despite the more outlandish touches of the film's revenge plot, then, the combative relationship between Johnny and Jesse is portrayed in a surprisingly sensitive way, with Jesse clearly departing from the era's stereotypically effeminate depictions of gay men. When both men depart in separate directions for unknown final destinations, the film's open-ended denouement may not picture them comfortably returning to their previous environs, but it at least implies the need for further struggle as they each reclaim their independence.

Angry Joe Bass and the cycle's end

As the decade-long boom in Red Power's public visibility slowed, so too did the brief cycle of Indiansploitation films by the late 1970s. As Philip Deloria suggests, if the white counterculture once turned to freely circulating signifiers of Indianness in a paradoxical bid for "authenticity" amid an increasingly postmodern period of collapsing grand narratives, "for many, postmodern Indianness had become so detached from anything real that it was in danger of lapsing into a bland irrelevance."[33] The low-budget 1976 film *Angry Joe Bass*, a small regional production aping *Johnny Firecloud*, demonstrates the cycle's creative exhaustion and waning political resonance. Like *Johnny Firecloud*, the plot centers on a powerful townsperson, George Hanson (Mike Miller), who leans on local sheriff Bill Hemmings (Rudy Hornish) to break up his daughter Karen's (Molly Mershon) romance with Joe Bass (Henry Bal), a marginalized Native American fisherman. Unfolding on the shores of upper Lake Michigan, tribal fishing rights fuel the central antagonisms, since Bass and his fellow Native fisherman are "illegally" depleting the local trout stock, which businessperson Hanson worries will drive away the tourist trade of sport fishermen. Bass and his friends had previously organized to unsuccessfully fight new laws against commercial fishing, since these laws were a cover for depriving the local Native population of their economic livelihood and thereby driving them out to make room for white land developers. The local Department of Natural Resources (DNR) officer Sheriff Hemmings represents both civic and state authority, but his ineffectual police efforts soon encourage Hanson to hire racist goons against Bass.

Aside from the taboo of miscegenation, however, Karen's parents seem to oppose her romance with Bass less out of racism than classism. They point out that she is college educated and comes from a "good family," whereas the fishermen are all working-class laborers. By constructing a binary opposition between white/middle-class sport fishermen and Native/working-class commercial fishermen, the film oversimplifies the issue of tribal fishing rights, since these correlations between race and class were far more complicated in real life. In actuality, white commercial fishermen were often as opposed to Native fishing rights as sport fishermen (and these tensions continue simmering to this day), despite the 1974 Boldt decision's reaffirmation of treaty rights having already rendered the film's central conflict largely moot by 1976 (though lingering court battles over fishing rights persisted in later decades). *Angry Joe Bass* may correctly (if inadvertently) link the roots of racism to class competition over scarce resources, but its depiction of racial conflict as binaristic shorthand for more complex conflicts over fishing rights does not convincingly fuel the narrative.

The film's overall poor writing and editing are also to blame, since Hemmings actually emerges as a far more "angry" character than Bass. The latter may be beaten up and his home attacked by gunfire, but the sheriff's murderous mental breakdown provides the most scenes of violent retribution. Bass may injure some of Hanson's thugs, but Hemmings racks up the actual body count. As in *Johnny Firecloud*, the sheriff is depicted as sexually "aberrant," but unlike that film's sympathetic depiction of homosexuality, Hemmings is depicted as a sexual predator who projects his repressed sexual urges outward in the form of racism. After he accuses the Native Americans of trying to "rape the lake" through their fishing haul, one of the next scenes ironically finds him attempting to rape a young woman—a crime prevented by Bass's timely arrival. Later, Hemmings accidentally kills his wife while confronting her over an affair with Hanson, whom the distraught sheriff then murders in revenge. Clearly losing his mind and blaming his longtime antagonist Bass for sparking the chain of events, Hemmings finally kills Bass as Karen watches.

This narrative synopsis may already sound murky, but the film's nonlinear structure borders on incoherence. *Angry Joe Bass* resembles an unfinished project, clumsily patched together as a series of flashbacks narrated by Karen's psychiatrists as they attempt to reassemble the events leading to her committal to a mental hospital. Yet, by attempting to mend the narrative's poor continuity, this awkward framing device merely foregrounds the fact that Joe Bass's story is not his own, but rather the messy product of white storytellers. In this respect, the film points toward some of the Indiansploitation cycle's limitations as a whole: in exploitation film tradition, the narrative may posit broadly sketched white antagonists against a Native protagonist, but the fact that these stories derive from the imaginations of white filmmakers demonstrates that Native American self-determination did not extend to the 1970s film industry itself. The DNR official may emerge as the crazed killer, but the political implications of this twist are muted by the fact that Bass's flouting of fishing laws is only an indirect impetus for the killings compared to Hemmings's sexual issues. Furthermore, *Angry Joe Bass* ends with Karen recovering her traumatic memories and leaving the mental hospital, ready to begin her life anew, while Bass remains depicted as a martyr for a poorly defined cause. With its narrative conceit about fishing rights already relegated to old news and its Native protagonist not only ineffectual as an avenger but eventually killed off, it is no surprise that *Angry Joe Bass* signaled the cycle's end.[34]

As Sherry Smith suggests, the Red Power movement achieved results through a combination of the younger, more countercultural generation's penchant for direct action, which widely publicized Native American issues, and the older generation's more methodical path through the legal and political system. More traditional methods of court decisions and legislation may have succeeded in achieving the most substantive political gains in the long run—including passage of the 1975 Indian Self-Determination and Indian Education Assistance Act, which weakened BIA control by allowing tribes to contract with government agencies and administer their own welfare—but both schools of thought ultimately worked in tandem to produce lasting civil rights advances.[35] As the cycle's key texts, Indiansploitation films like *Billy Jack* and *Johnny Firecloud* epitomized these different political approaches in their respective sympathies with integrationism and separatism, peaceful reform and violent resistance.[36] As the product of white filmmakers playing upon transcultural sympathies with Native American issues, these films all had their stereotypical and otherwise politically problematic traits, but altogether the cycle echoed Red Power's own ideologically fraught dynamics, helping explain their potential appeal to viewers beyond politically engaged Native Americans.

Coda

Although I have suggested that these films were derivative of blaxploitation in some respects, Jodi Byrd cautions that differentiating between the historical racial experiences giving rise to such cycles can have certain pitfalls. American discourse has remained hypersensitive to twentieth-century genocides happening elsewhere in the world, such as the Holocaust, but conveniently disavows the earlier genocides wrought by Native American extermination and African American slavery in the service of national expansion on our own continent. This has allowed "competing discourses of the true genocidal moment [to] pit all survivors against each another while reifying the oppressors' innocence and control."[37] On the one hand, then, Red Power activists like Vine Deloria (who himself advocated Native American separatism) are correct to differentiate Native American civil rights from dominant cultural connotations of race as blackness. When White Eagle is lynched in *Johnny Firecloud*, for example, "[t]he fact that the hanging of Indians evokes violence against blacks in the United States, but not the other way around, suggests that Indians ... [are] abjected as sovereign peoples and invisiblized within a racial narrative dominated by black/white relations within U.S. histories of slavery, segregation, and civil rights."[38] On the other hand, popular associations between "noble" Indigenous peoples and premodern culture mean that competing discourses about genocide posit Native Americans as "yet again, the 'logical,' if tragic victims of modernization who stand in the way of progress by competing for needed resources."[39] And yet, when surveying the tremendous impact that the fruits of the African American civil rights movement—including the blaxploitation cycle—still have on popular culture today, in comparison with the far more forgotten legacy of Red Power and Indiansploitation films, the destructively unequal erasure of Native Americans from the cultural landscape should continue to give us pause.

Notes

1. Ed Guerrero, *Framing Blackness: The African American Image in Film* (Philadelphia, PA: Temple University Press, 1993), 80–84, 105, 110–111.
2. Michelle H. Raheja, *Reservation Reelism: Redfacing, Visual Sovereignty, and Representations of Native Americans in Film* (Lincoln: University of Nebraska Press, 2010), 40–41.
3. See, e.g., Novotny Lawrence, *Blaxploitation Films of the 1970s: Blackness and Genre* (New York: Routledge, 2008); Christopher Sieving, *Soul Searching: Black-Themed Cinema from the March on Washington to the Rise of Blaxploitation* (Middletown, CT: Wesleyan University Press, 2011); and Eithne Quinn, *A Piece of the Action: Race and Labor in the Post-Civil Rights Film Industry* (New York: Columbia University Press, forthcoming).
4. Jennifer DeVere Brody, "The Returns of Cleopatra Jones," *Signs* 25:1 (1999): 100, 106; and Tommy L. Lott, "A No-Theory Theory of Contemporary Black Cinema," *Black American Literature Forum* 25:2 (1991): 227–229.
5. Sherry L. Smith, *Hippies, Indians, and the Fight for Red Power* (New York: Oxford University Press, 2012), 6–7, 73.
6. See Sundiata Keita Cha-Jua, "Black Audiences, Blaxploitation and Kung Fu Films, and Challenges to White Celluloid Masculinity," in *China Forever: The Shaw Brothers and Diasporic Cinema*, ed. Poshek Fu (Champaign: University of Illinois Press, 2008), 199–223; Amy Abugo Ongiri, "'He Wanted to Be Just Like Bruce Lee': African Americans, Kung Fu Theater, and Cultural Exchange at the Margins," *Journal of Asian American Studies* 5:1 (2002): 31–40; and Sylvia Shin Huey Chong, *The Oriental Obscene: Violence and Racial Fantasies in the Vietnam Era* (Durham, NC: Duke University Press, 2012).
7. Joshua Gleich, "Jim Brown: From Integration to Resegregation in *The Dirty Dozen* and *100 Rifles*," *Cinema Journal* 51:1 (2011): 2, 6, 12–13, 22, 25.
8. See Jacquelyn Kilpatrick, *Celluloid Indians: Native Americans and Film* (Lincoln: University of Nebraska Press, 1999), chp. 4; Angela Aleiss, *Making the White Man's Indian: Native Americans and Hollywood Movies* (Westport, CT: Praeger, 2005), chp. 7; and M. Elise Marubbio, *Killing the Indian Maiden: Images of Native American Women in Film* (Lexington: University Press of Kentucky, 2006), chp. 5.
9. Jodi A. Byrd, "'Living My Native Life Deadly': Red Lake, Ward Churchill, and the Discourses of Competing Genocides," *American Indian Quarterly* 31:2 (2007): 316.
10. Likewise, modern-set exploitation films that figure supernatural spirits as sources of Native American vengeance—including *The Manitou* (William Girdler, 1978), *Scalps* (Fred Olen Ray, 1983), and every movie about a haunted house built atop an Indigenous burial ground—are beyond the scope of this chapter.
11. Smith, *Hippies*, 10; and Raheja, *Reservation Reelism*, 196–197.
12. Vine Deloria Jr., *Custer Died for Your Sins: An Indian Manifesto* (Toronto and London: Macmillan, 1969), 168–174. Quote at 170. His son, Philip J. Deloria, would later take up the question of the predominantly white counterculture's cultural appropriation of Indianness, in his book *Playing Indian* (New Haven, CT: Yale University Press, 1998), chp. 6.
13. Smith, *Hippies*, 7–8, 49, 65, 143. Quote at 143.

14. Vine, "*Journey through Rosebud*," *Variety* (March 1, 1972), 20.
15. Vine Deloria Jr., "Identity and Culture," *Daedalus* 110:2 (1981): 24.
16. Bill Osgerby, "Sleazy Riders: Exploitation, 'Otherness,' and Transgression in the 1960s Biker Movie," *Journal of Popular Film and Television* 31:3 (2003): 102.
17. Smith, *Hippies*, 28, 100, 190. The My Lai massacre of Vietnamese civilians, for example, concurrently shared newspaper space with the Alcatraz occupation (100).
18. Raheja, *Reservation Reelism*, 107, 120, 124–125. Quote at 120.
19. Aleiss, *Making the White Man's Indian*, 136; Frederick Wasser, "Four Walling Exhibition: Regional Resistance to the Hollywood Film Industry," *Cinema Journal* 34:2 (1995): 57; and Justin Wyatt, "From Roadshowing to Saturation Release: Majors, Independents, and Marketing/Distribution Innovations," in *The New American Cinema*, ed. Jon Lewis (Durham, NC: Duke University Press, 1998), 74–75 (quoted).
20. Since the school's pedagogical methods apparently consist primarily of amateur folk singing and improv theater—as seen in several extended scenes that painfully date the film from today's perspective—the cynic in me wonders if a drastic curricular makeover might not actually be a bad idea.
21. Deloria Jr., "Identity and Culture," 24.
22. Drew Hayden Taylor, "What Ever Happened to Billy Jack?" in *Readings in Aboriginal Studies, Vol. 4: Images of the Indian—Portrayals of Native People*, ed. Joe Sawchuk (Brandon, Manitoba: Bearpaw Publishing, 1995), 173–175.
23. John A. Price, "The Stereotyping of North American Indians in Motion Pictures," *Ethnohistory* 20:2 (1973): 163.
24. Julian Smith, "Between Vermont and Violence: Film Portraits of Vietnam Veterans," *Film Quarterly* 26:4 (1973): 13.
25. Sidney Rosenzweig, "The Dark Night of the Screen: Messages and Melodrama in the American Movie," *American Quarterly* 27:1 (1975): 90, 97.
26. Scott Richard Lyons, "*Billy Jack*," in *Seeing Red: Hollywood's Pixeled Skins—American Indians and Film*, eds. LeAnne Howe, Harvey Markowitz, and Denise K. Cummings (East Lansing: Michigan State University Press, 2013), 158, 161, 163. Quote at 158.
27. Ibid., 162. Despite an aborted 1985 attempt at making *The Return of Billy Jack*, Laughlin continued soliciting donations at his personal website to help him fund a new Billy Jack film, until his death in December 2013. See Sharon Waxman, "Billy Jack Is Ready to Fight the Good Fight Again," *New York Times* (June 20, 2005), available at http://www.nytimes.com/2005/06/20/movies/20jack.html?_r=0 (accessed December 21, 2015).
28. David F. Friedman, Frank Henenlotter, and Mike Vraney, DVD commentary track, *Johnny Firecloud/Bummer!* special-edition DVD, Something Weird Video, 2001.
29. See Sheril D. Antonio, "The Urban-Rural Binary in Black American Film and Culture," *Black Camera* 1:1 (2009): 129; and Lott, "A No-Theory Theory," 224–225. As Jacquelyn Kilpatrick notes, Hollywood cinema had gradually shown Indigenous maidens giving themselves to white men, since this preserved dominant racial hierarchies, but the converse had hitherto remained forbidden (*Celluloid Indians*, 64).
30. The Native American man framed for raping a white woman had formed the plot of another Indiansploitation film, *Camper John* (Sean MacGregor, 1973), which was also released by Cinemation Industries under the alternate titles *Gentle Savage, Once Upon a Tribe*, and *Up Yours, Pilgrim!* Occupying a position somewhere between *Billy Jack* and *Johnny Firecloud*, the film is less inclined toward countercultural interests,

but still focuses on a local Native population collectively rallying in support of the unjustly accused protagonist.

31. According to M. Elise Marubbio:

    > The western often uses the death or rape of the white woman as the catalyst for the hero's regression into savagery, his retaliation against Native Americans, and his regeneration into an American hero. The Celluloid Maiden films of the 1970s, however, invert the racial hierarchy in an embracing of Indianness and the use of the Native woman for this role.
    >
    > (*Killing the Indian Maiden*, 170)

32. Smith, *Hippies*, 13.
33. Deloria, *Playing Indian*, 175.
34. The hard-core adult film *Deep Roots* (Joseph Bardo, 1978) is another late entry demonstrating this cyclical exhaustion, but because its narrative does not directly invoke racism, retribution, or civil rights, it is beyond the specific scope of this chapter. The title's allusion to the then-recent TV miniseries *Roots* (1977)—as suggested by the film's tagline "Deeper Than Throat, More Powerful Than Roots!"—nevertheless emphasizes the uneasy boundaries between Native and African American civil rights struggles. Native American actor Jesse Chacan stars as Billy, a young Indigenous man who sells his allotted parcel of tribal land and sets off on his motorcycle for the Hollywood hills to become a painter and experience life beyond the reservation. Once there, he sleeps with Joan (Anita Sands), a white bride-to-be who excitedly notes that she's "never had an Indian before." By the film's end, Billy (dressed as a stereotypical Indian brave) introduces Joan to the members of a costume orgy where she becomes the climactic centerpiece. *Deep Roots*, then, is ultimately as much about Billy's sexual initiation of Joan, and her abandonment of marriage in favor of sexual freedom, as about Billy's transcultural exploration. Indeed, in a tacked-on denouement, Billy abruptly tells the viewer that "you should never leave where you belong," and he finally returns home to his "deep roots" on the reservation—his talismanic role in opening the white woman to the (sexual) counterculture having apparently been fulfilled.
35. Smith, *Hippies*, 13, 111, 217.
36. The latter variety of Indiansploitation tropes were notably resurrected in Richard Bugajski's underrated film *Clearcut* (1993), in which a mysterious Indigenous man (Graham Greene) kidnaps a white lawyer (Ron Lea) who is poorly defending a Canadian tribe against a lumber company encroaching on tribal land. At the film's climax, the Indigenous man forces the lawyer to watch as he "debarks" the leg of the lumber company owner, cutting all the flesh from his bone, as extralegal retribution for centuries of environmental and cultural destruction.
37. Byrd, "Living My Native Life Deadly," 311, 313, 316, 318. Quote at 313.
38. Ibid., 324.
39. Ibid., 329.

12

Sleazy Strip-Joints and Perverse Porn Circuses: The Remediation of Grindhouse in the Porn Productions of Jack the Zipper

Clarissa Smith

The history of the grind house is well trodden, offering a picture of exhibition spaces that even in their heyday were characterized by a pervasive stench of decline: their outer facades testaments to faded glories, while their interiors bore all the signs of mistreatment and neglect. David Church has explored the advent of domestic video technologies as the final nail in the coffin of the grind house as *locale* and the consequent morphing of the term to reference genre rather than exhibition.[1] And in that morphing grindhouse found a new lease of life on the very technology that brought the films into the domestic sphere. There are similar parallels in histories of pornography; itself a "most elastic textual category,"[2] porn arcades and cinemas were often located (at least in the United States) in the same geographical spaces, and were squeezed out by gentrification at least as quickly as the grind houses. Just as low-rent horror and exploitation films found a new lease of life on VHS, pornography was able to find a very comfortable and lucrative home on that format before, in turn, moving through DVD and into the digital online environment.

Porn has been understood as an engine of innovation: exploiting each new technology as it arrives and, according to some histories, guaranteeing the success of one format (VHS) over another (Betamax), but the picture may be more complex than the simple replacement of one delivery platform with another.[3] As we have moved into the twenty-first century, new patterns of consumption and engagement have taken their toll on professional pornographic productions, particularly through sharing outside of paid-for distribution channels with scenes ripped and repurposed online as vignettes, or converted to gifs as forms of "micro-porn." We could talk of this as exciting evidence of consumer agency,[4] but for porn producers, maintaining the profitability of the pornographic text has proved difficult. Production costs do not disappear even if consumers are clear they want their content for free.

Thus I come to another way in which porn as genre has walked in step with grindhouse. Just as the exploitation-cinema favorites have found their way into rerelease in beautiful packaging and remodeling for the DVD/Blu-ray connoisseur, so too "vintage" pornography has a market, both as collectable and as rerelease. Porn classics from the 1970s and 1980s are being resurrected for a discerning audience with, as can be seen in this description of Vinegar Syndrome's retro-releases, direct appeal to grindhouse nostalgia:

> These were the days of story driven porn, so far removed from the sort of slam bang gonzo crap with crudely blunt titles, plasticene stripper types and scummy guys that dominate the industry these days that you'd think they were from a different planet. So taken in that light, why not market them as long lost grindhouse classics for a mature and freethinking audience?[5]

The pleasures of these reanimations of the "golden era" are interesting in their own right but are not the focus of my discussion here. Instead, I explore contemporary productions that have sought to reanimate the feature format. In an era of Tube sites and illegal downloads, the demise of the professionally produced pornographic DVD is widely predicted.[6] Yet despite declining sales, some larger porn production houses, such as Private, have reaffirmed their commitment to physical product through branding techniques that mark DVD content as *different* and productions that emphasize narrative alongside sexual numbers.[7] Parodies have been the biggest successes of the past decade although Michael Ninn's mix of sex with "sword and sandal" epic imagery in *The Four* (2011) and the more domestic dramas in Elegant Angel's *Wasteland* and New Sensations' *Torn* (both 2012) also achieved awards and volume sales. More interesting, at least for me and hopefully for readers of this book, is another area of DVD production that has direct parallels in the "retrosploitation"[8] reanimation of grindhouse aesthetics and sensibilities practiced by Quentin Tarantino and Robert Rodriguez.

The most dangerous director in XXX

Described as the most dangerous director in XXX,[9] Jack the Zipper (hereafter Zipper) mixes elements of outlier groups (bikers, freaks, sexual outlaws), beautiful women, and hard-core sex. Drawing on cinematic stylings from small-town American horror and the dystopian visions of global exploitation, Zipper's films are excessively stylish remasterings of the experiences and memories of the grind house. Zipper is one of the "new breed" of directors working for the large studios (Vivid, Hustler, and Club Jenna). Having produced and directed thirteen films in a decade,[10] Zipper's high production oeuvre is understood as "alt-porn" (as defined by industry award-givers, reviewers, and marketeers). In his films he invokes the materiality of the grind house as a particular mise-en-scène for sexual license and fantasy, thus its "alt" sensibility owes more to the director's utilization of the cultural capital of cult cinema and its cinematicity[11] than to punky stylings.

The variety of designations given to Zipper's work—alt versus mainstream, professional versus amateur, quality versus mediocre, subcultural versus generic, and excess versus ordinary—are deployed as discursive strategies of distinction for consumers.[12] While there may be a range of problems in focusing on an individual director's work as I do here—for example, reifying content over the spaces and places of consumption;[13] elevating an individual director to the status of artist while everyone else is understood as inferior;[14] suggesting that *some* forms of pornography are more narratively and aesthetically important than others[15]—Zipper's films do bear more than the cursory designation as sexually explicit. My reading here could be seen as driven by a kind of nostalgia for the "golden age" when porn came closest to achieving status as a proper art form,[16] and for the spaces in which golden-age porn was once shown.[17] Such nostalgia *is* at work in the films I examine but Zipper's invocations of a "golden age" are complicated, working across intertextual and spatial dimensions and imagining a particular sexual utopia connected to grindhouse—both as a cinematic form and as a material space.

Like dropping acid at the circus

I am then approaching the narrative possibilities of Zipper's films through their creation of sensibilities, modalities, and atmospheres that invite responses and animations of desire through their "echo [of] past decades, familiar poses, styles and looks."[18] Zipper conjures excitement through associations that may be connected to claims of "exceptionalism," "innovation," and "auteurship." That Zipper's work *is* regarded as exceptional, innovative, and auteurial is indicated in the following review of *Blacklight Beauty* (Pulse, 2006):

> Every once in a great while, a porn opus comes along that quintessentially defines its generation in the annals of XXX history—*Deep Throat, Taboo, New Wave Hookers, The Fashionistas*—these are the works that will forever be regarded as the landmark achievements of our industry, ones that will continue to be revisited and revered for as long as man views smut.
>
> *Blacklight Beauty* is one of those works, which we say without any hesitation or aggrandizement whatsoever. JacktheZipper, who crashed onto the scene two years ago with *Stuntgirl* and has utterly commanded his particular vein of pornmaking ever since (he's collected our Best All-Sex Release Award both of those years, first for *Stuntgirl* and then for the considerably more seedy *Squealer*), has struck some sort of a chord with *Blacklight* that should catapult him to a whole other level of prominence both inside and out of porn circles.[19]

Citing influences as variable as Andrew Blake (the purveyor of classy, stylish, and, for some critics, pretentiously perverse porn) and David Lynch, as well as movies such as *Chopper, Sexy Beast*, and *Forbidden Zone*, and porn from the 1960s and 1970s, it is clear that Zipper seeks to appeal to cinephile, as well as pornophile, audiences. His work deals in genre hybridity and blending (Figure 12.1), variously including elements from cult movies such as *Deliverance*, and twenty-first-century grindhouse throwbacks such as *The Devil's Rejects* (Rob Zombie, 2007): the opening shots of *Stuntgirl 2*, for example,

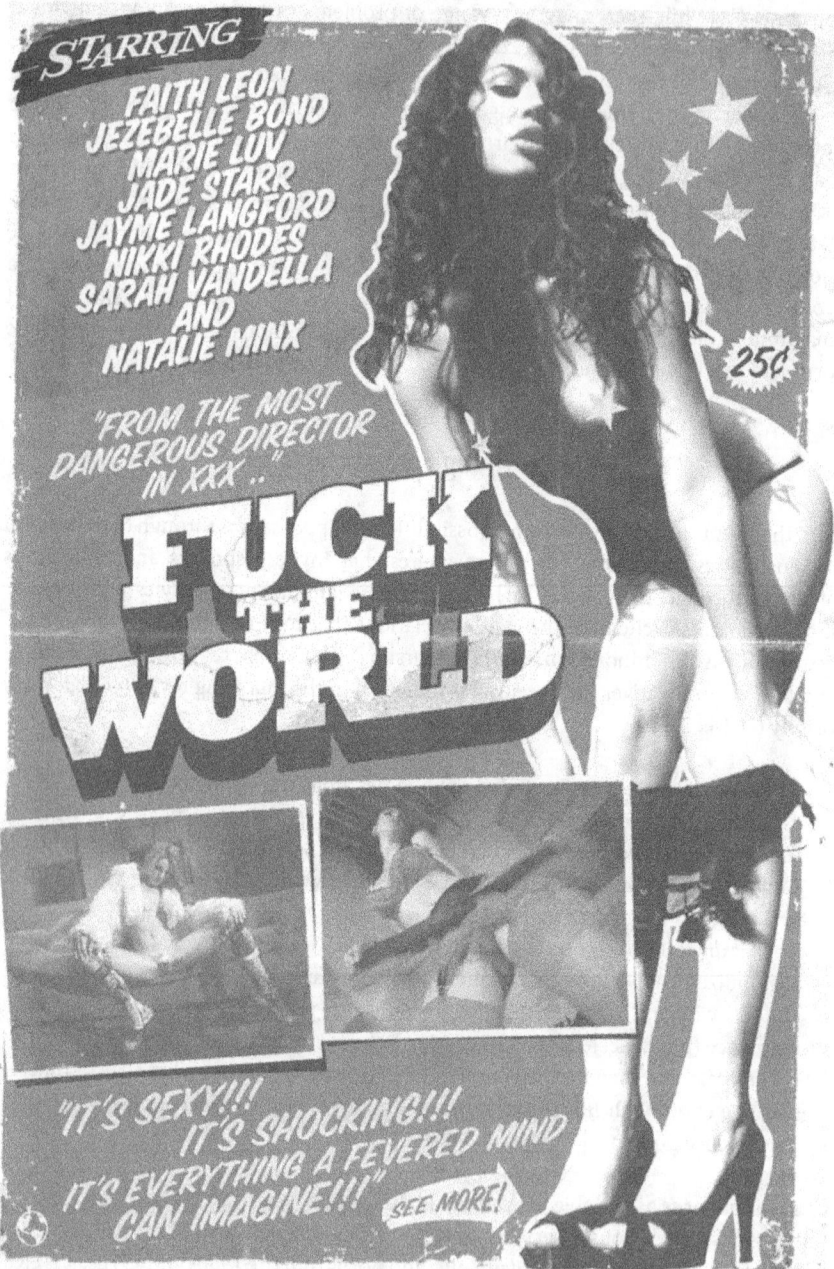

Figure 12.1 Genre hybridity and blending: *Fuck the World*.

directly reference the *Texas Chain Saw Massacre* (Tobe Hooper, 1974), while there is more than a hint of Rinse Dream (Stephen Sayadian) in other titles.

Drawing on the aesthetics and cultural references of exploitation fare—including Manson-influenced cult/biker movies such as *Snuff* (1976), backwoods horror such as *The Hills Have Eyes* (1977), "all girl" road movies such as *The Hitchhikers* (1972), and films of the hard-core "roughie" tradition—Zipper's *King Cobra* (Vivid, 2006) is an initiation narrative. Supposed ingénue Creampuff (Page Morgan) starts the movie with the classic teen voiceover:

> This is the story of how I ran away, lost my virginity, lost my virginity again, ran away again, got kidnapped by bikers and turned into a rowdy biker-bitch. Hope you like it.

We switch to scenes of the motorcycle gang speeding to a motel. As Creampuff slams her room door shut, the bikers force entry. Dressed in a 1950s-style net skirt, she cowers on the bed but is then forced to dance by the Manson-esque gang leader ("He looks like the devil!") and then take part in an orgy. Shot in disconcerting style, the scene features a variety of sexual combinations—Sasha Grey (in rabbit hat/mask) fellates a man, Creampuff is forced to lick girl-gang leader Lanny Barby while the gang leader choreographs the action as another pair fuck—but the camera rarely lingers on any individual coupling, instead constantly cutting away from one grouping to another in ways that mean, as one critic put it, "it doesn't work as a strokeable porn flick."[20] As the camera focuses on the mostly less-than-sexy slapping and pulling of Creampuff's hair, the soundtrack tells us that others in the room are having more fun: a stylistic choice reminiscent of roughie-director Doris Wishman's tendency to cut away to table legs just as the action gets sexual.[21] This style of cutting, along with nontraditional camera angles and split-screen presentation, absolutely refuses "maximum visibility,"[22] causing at least one critic to scratch his head and "wonder if [Zipper's] works are a way to lash out against the industry in some manner."[23]

In an interview Zipper laid out his problems with the marginal status of pornography:

> Porn is a powerful industry but it's a bastard art form. There is no reason why the human race has to make a dirty secret or a joke out of something so basic and intrinsic and vital to our nature. Everything I do as an adult director is an attempt to rise above that—making XXX makes me think about life and death—the life-force and how mysterious and precious it really is, embodied in these beautiful, beautiful women. It's sad that as a society we don't try harder to elevate these ideas in each other. Pornography as it is defined now has a power and significance that's largely untapped, in my opinion.[24]

Thus Zipper differentiates his work from mainstream pornography to rise above "the bastard art form." Central to that differentiation is his claim to "outsider" status.

Elements of Zipper's history are known. Originally a tattoo artist, art school graduate, photographer, and member of a punk band, he hails from New York, placing him outside of the mainstream and within "punk" heritage. In interviews he claims no connections to the porn industry before *Stuntgirl*, his debut film from 2004. This may or may not be true; there are indications that Zipper has worked widely in the industry since 1998, but that only matters in so far as it highlights the mythologizing potential of his pseudonym[25] and, by extension, his brand of authorship.[26] The use of an alias hides the "real" man, his politics and his history, to construct a particular identity for the filmmaker.

There is, of course, obvious connection to the notorious murderer of Victorian London, but also the double entendre of the zipper and the laddishness of the name Jack: "Jack is an idea. Jack is a myth. Lust and obsession—always hungry never satisfied."[27] The alias gives an edge but also establishes its own rules, characteristics, and identity. By working for major companies like Hustler, Vivid, and Club Jenna, Zipper clearly is not out-of-industry; yet he trades on his status as maverick, differentiating his work from others in terms of its visceral qualities. The alias also, as Zipper himself asserts, enables a particular position for his viewers: "The person watching gets to play Jack for a while. The Boogie Man or Santa Claus depending on your orientation, I suppose."

Seamy and squalid

In *Squealer* (Hustler, 2005) the seamy underside of society is represented in all its squalid glory: Gram Ponante's review describes the DVD as "*Grapes of Wrath*-meets-*Deliverance*–meets-*Charlotte's Web*–meets-*The Silence of the Lambs*-meets-Audrey Hollander's mouth."[28] *Squealer*'s opening sequences see four women experiencing car troubles and, having taken shelter in an abandoned farmstead, find themselves at the mercy of a gang of hillbillies who proceed to train the women as sex slaves. Various sexual enactments take place. In that this is a DVD sold *as* pornography, and the scenes feature sexual acts, there might be nothing particularly unusual about any of these scenes. Yet *Squealer* goes beyond the purely formulaic sexual numbers: its narrative offers Audrey Hollander as a kidnap victim, revealed in the boot of a car, tied up, obviously beaten, silk dress torn, her stockings ripped. She is a classy lady brought low by her kidnapper. In subsequent scenes, Hollander and her female companions are taken on a journey into the impure, unclean, and contaminated areas of US life— the ruined shack stuck out in the wilds (shot at Sable Ranch, the archetypal Western setting used by Rob Zombie in *The Devil's Rejects* (2005)). Produced for Hustler, *Squealer* cost $46,000 and took three days to shoot but much longer to edit.[29] As one reviewer commented:

> Ever wish that your favorite horror movie would turn hardcore, and then suddenly shift into snuff? Ever wanted to see Leatherface pop a load in some biz-nitch's face before she died like a dead dog bloating in the road? Do your fantasies consist

of a Rob Zombie retro recombination creating the ultimate amalgamation of carnality and creepy? Well, Jack The Zipper's latest opus, the appropriately named *Squealer* may just be the movie to satisfy your sickening urges. Engaging to look at, deplorable to defend and somewhere between erotic and retarded on the sexual scale, this backwoods S&M sleaze fest takes the concept of dirty girls doing disgusting things to new heights of harrowing horribleness.[30]

Even as that review rejects Zipper's vision of masturbation fodder, it recognizes the ways in which *Squealer* encourages a form of cult reading: rewarding recognition of cinematic stylings in which something particularly pornographic and, at the same time, peculiarly *grindhouse* is revealed. The mix of stylings, frenetic couplings, and problem personalities engaging in sexual scenes are all reminiscent of the classic hard-core roughie, such as *Slaves in Cages* (Carl Borch, 1971) and *The Abduction of Lorelei* (Richard Rank, 1977). So too, the replication of the "roughie template," whereby the victimized woman turns the table on her male aggressors, but with a slight twist in that the men discover women more than equal to match and exceed their sexual appetites.

Focusing on the grotesque aspects of sex, this is not clean, sophisticated, or stylish sex in the consumerist mode: it is firmly anchored in the grindhouse imaginary. Very much aware of its antecedents, Zipper's titles offer elements of meta-textuality with clear references to the ways in which pornography has been constructed as the *sine qua non* of female oppression. Mixing elements that are not supposed to be mixed[31] and using precarious locations and situations, urban wastelands, and incredibly sexy women, horror and sex are offered together in a way that highlights the pleasurable and, indeed, masturbatory possibilities of fear and sexual excitement. There is darkness, cruelty, and perhaps willful bad taste. *Stuntgirl, Squealer,* and *Blacklight Beauty (BLB)* have all won awards, but critics are not uniformly impressed, and some have expressed reservations about whether or not Zipper's films are porn at all.[32]

Antiporn argumentation focuses on pornography's normalizing of the supposedly intrinsically male desires to punish, mold, and manipulate women into sexual objects. The shaming of Audrey Hollander in *Squealer*, her training as a sex slave, could be seen as the ritualistic attempt to bring female sexuality under control (see Figure 12.2). In various scenes, Hollander is subjected to "degrading treatment": she is locked in the cellar and urinated on as she tries to emerge from it. Moreover, repeated gang bangs and scenes of slapping all contribute to a picture of bringing the woman to heel. Yet at the same time, Hollander does not play submissive, but instead, in an illustration of what Zipper calls his "pressure cooker" style of direction, the narrative places Hollander in particularly problematic scenarios, which produce a unique performance from her. Here, the physical containments of female sexuality familiar to audiences of grindhouse cinema are represented: women are tied to chairs, trussed up shibari style, abandoned in a lonely shack, and imprisoned in cellars, and one woman is confined in a basket that enables access to her genitals. But where the roughie leaves the specifically *sexual* violences to the female body off-scene (slapping etc. as a *displacement* of sex), *Squealer* offers its viewers hard-core violations. As Jonathan Lake Crane has argued:

Figure 12.2 Audrey Hollander goes to the dark side in *Squealer*.

ever fascinated with the abuse of the flesh, violence signifies, in all its glorious splendor, an attempt to grasp the feel of the real. Nothing ... screams "this is real" better than skin and bone under assault.[33]

Carl Plantinga suggests "disgusting things may also attract the viewer, creating a push and pull between curiosity and fascination on the one hand and aversion and repulsion on the other."[34] But more than this, *Squealer* and the rest of Zipper's oeuvre attempt to create a mode of viewing that is multilayered. While, as one critic noted, the "camera angles and editing are very arcane and antithetical to good porn production,"[35] I suggest that they enable an engagement with Zipper's films as a sensibility beyond the "simple" fact of masturbatory arousal: from the vision of a star-name doing something different from her familiar performances, and moving beyond the usual formats of all-too-well-known acts, to a form of cinephilia—even *pornophilia*—which, in marketing terms, establishes, and crucially brands, this director as different, edgy, creative.

Squealer ends with *Deliverance*-style music as two women gyrate in a dark doorway. Audrey's face is partially glimpsed over the other woman's shoulder; she looks directly and conspiratorially at the camera as the screen goes black: she has become "one of them," an example of what Zipper calls his performers' "witchery," which marks the porn star as *different* from ordinary women. It is possible to see *Squealer's* pygmalian schooling of women as a kind of retro-sexism: the paracinematic styling of the sexual action, the excessiveness of the presentation of sex, contributes to the "[transformation] from porn starlets to the personification of feminine power and primal animal lust." But at the same time, these performances offer a dynamic riposte to the ubiquity of "amateur" porn and its promise that pornography is best when it offers "pictures of real people with real desires, having real sex in real places."[36]

In *Enter the Peepshow* (Club Jenna, 2010), the sex lives of the weird and wonderful types who populate the sideshow—the clown, fortune-teller, sword-swallower, and the escape artist—are brought into focus. Dressed in circus outfits, alt-porn stars Hollie Stevens, Ariel Adore, Rebeca Linares, and Zoe Minx gyrate and gurn to the camera in a fusion of grotesque burlesque and avant-garde presentation, while Sasha Grey's scenes employ the "strait-jacket" and "glory hole" to significant effect. The mashing together of the circus, the madhouse, and hard-core sex is, by turns, thrilling, intriguing, and disturbing. In one scene, Ariel Adore fellates Murrugun "the Mystic": a renowned fire-eater and sword-swallower currently to be seen on AMC's reality TV show, *Freakshow* (2013–). Sword-swallowing has an obvious sexual symbolism, often used as an "alias" for the blow job, but its connotations are brought full circle when Ariel is filmed deep-throating Murrugun's penis as he slips a sword down his own throat. The obviously risky thrills on offer here double the idea of the porn performance and its requisite *skills*. Zipper's stars produce spectacular *performance*. Performance becomes a thing of wonder: a recognition of the strange, magical possibilities of sex in the arousing yet perilous professional world of carnival and, by their juxtaposition, pornographic entertainments.

The sensationalist setup of the "freaks" in *Enter the Peepshow*, the "enfreakment"[37] of performers through camerawork and sound, draws directly on the pleasures of attraction/repulsion that characterized grindhouse features. The scenes make explicit the ways in which viewers may well indulge in particular hypocrisies: watching women performing sex for their masturbatory interests while viewing them as deviant *because* they perform. The traditional coupling of aggressive women and the sexual dangers they might pose is brought to the fore in Zipper's films and, at the same time, mocks the desire to view that which viewers might also condemn. The crisscrossing of sexual tableaux with images of madness and/or freakishness creates the impression of the mystical, dangerous, and seductive secret world of the sideshow even as it appears to question its audiences. *Enter the Peepshow* may certainly be an immersive experience for viewers, but it does not provide *easy* viewing—the closing credits give the command to "Comfort the disturbed ... Disturb the comfortable," a direct challenge to think about *who* is the most disturbed in the performer/viewer nexus of the porn film.

Stop reading films?

While there are intertextual references (tropes, expressions, styles, images and sounds, and clichés) aplenty in Zipper's filmography—many more than I have managed to recognize—I am not so much interested in being able to demonstrate my subcultural capital here. Rather it seems to me that Zipper's intertextualities and clichés are as much about *sensibility*, *place*, and the mythologizing of *those*, as they are about fidelity to or quotation of some original text(s) once screened on 42nd Street. Zipper's films may have imitative elements but they are not parodies. *Blacklight Beauty*, *Squealer*, and *King Cobra* offer particular complications of the separations between cult, cinema, and pornography. Drawing explicitly on grindhouse imagery, Zipper's films rewrite the rules governing porn's supposed drive to "extreme visibility" and the "money shot" in ways that memorialize, reanimate, and crucially interrogate the mythos of the spaces, ambiences, and weird characters who were said to frequent the grind house.

In his demand that pornography not become *just* another film genre in the film studies curriculum, John Champagne highlights the importance of the transiences and contingencies of the "cultural and social rituals and practices"[38] of the gay porno arcade. For arcade audiences, the film and its contents were unimportant: customers rarely watched the scenes they paid to view, choosing instead to explore the sexual opportunities of the space where sexual excitement, fear, and hedonism could be observed and experienced. Of course, this is very similar to the stories told about the grind house, that the "audience was busy, with massage parlor girls and streetwalkers pecking around for business in the aisles. Black transvestites offering 'honey, you want anything for $5?' were a constant. Leftover disco-era clones in cowboy hats hovered near the well-travelled toilets."[39]

As others argue in this book and elsewhere,[40] the myths of the grindhouse have particular purchase and power for audiences. Elena Gorfinkel suggests that "For cinephiles, Times Square has an especial bio of significance," and that cult fans fixate "with a mixture of longing for a semipublic space and sociosexual scene, a scene inextricable from and facilitated by the adult film theaters."[41] Beneath the surface of such longings lies the reminiscer's imagined social positioning among the misfits "meet[ing] partners by flashing or sitting with a ready-to-go erection in a little, recessed row, accepting or rejecting offers of sex."[42] However, the one who reminisces in this way is *not* one of the sexual actors—he or she simply *watches* those *Others* challenge the socio-sexual order. The misfits' "ready-to-go erections" and willing mouths serve as reassuring confirmation of the cinephile's "normalcy" at the same time as the performers' bodies "symbolize ... a potential for individual freedom denied by cultural pressures towards standardisation."[43] It is precisely the hypocrisies of this mythos that Zipper brings to life in Blacklight Beauty.

Taking nine months to complete, *Blacklight Beauty* was shot in the Burgundy Room in Hollywood, recreating a seedy joint on a backlot in small-town USA. In one scene featuring Allie Sin[44] the mise-en-scène makes clear reference to the infamous toilet at New York's *CBGB's* and the foul ambience of the grind house restroom. The DVD's nine scenes dispense with the "nice" bedrooms or luxurious apartments of aspirational pornographies, instead making a virtue of the spaces for live and/or filmed sexual performances whose frequenters are lowlifes, drunks, and bizarre clowns. The settings in *Blacklight Beauty* breach the public/private divide: sex happens in the toilet; adjacent to, and on, the poledance stage; on a bar and—in the most obvious of its homages to grindhouse—in a shabby screening room. In the following analysis of that scene, Zipper plays to the fantasy of grind houses as places where the party never stopped, and is a visual confirmation of Champagne's insistence that porn films rarely mattered in the porno-theater. But I also want to demonstrate how this scene invites sensing sensuality through viewers' embodied recognitions of the particular carnalities of "private" sex in public space and through that sensoria offers a riposte to the cozy mythologizing of grindhouse's sexual outlaws.

In a small screening room a porno film plays[45] while Faith Leon—illuminated by the beam from a single flashlight—leans, naked except for her jacket, against the wall (see Figure 12.3). As she masturbates, a man approaches and takes over her task. They engage in fellatio, and another man comes along ... Faith takes both on, again revealed in a single flashlight: one man takes her from behind while she fellates the other. The glow from the screen casts minimal light on the action, but as the scene progresses additional flashlights make movement more observable. Faith insists one guy "fuck her throat"; changes of position occur, accompanied by idiosyncratic cuts; and, consequently, when other men appear, it is difficult to be sure of their number. Various permutations follow: Faith fellates one man after another; she rides one man cowgirl while sucking another and masturbating at least two others. Crouched on the floor, she administers handjobs in turn to five men and intermittently licks and sucks their penises. Her hair has lost its blow-dried bounce and her makeup is smeared in an approximation of a clown's huge blacked eyes and grotesque mouth, testifying to her exertions.

A particular Zipper conceit presents men as the archetypal "dick." Their faces are rarely seen, and their bodies rarely displayed. In *BLB*, all the men wear the same black pants and T-shirts and, as a consequence, are not individualized. These are dark and anxious bodies, and, crucially, anonymous. The men approach Faith without removing their clothing, though at different points, some appear in only their socks. There is no

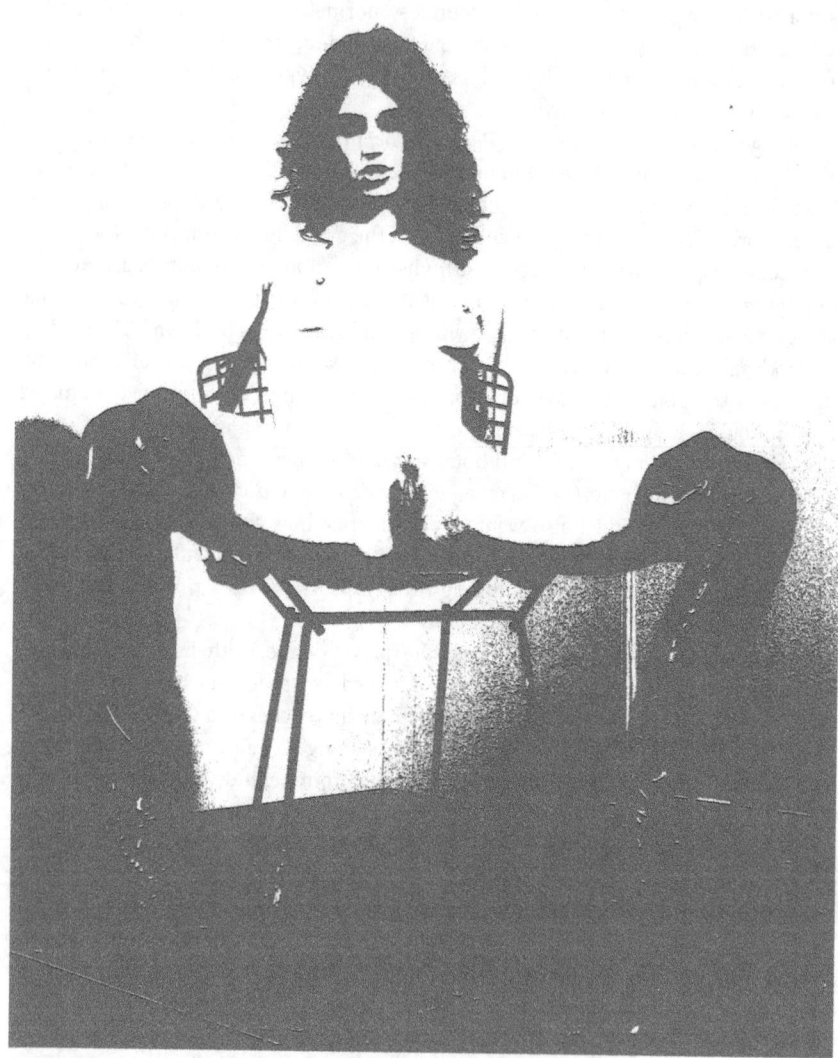

Figure 12.3 Faith Leon in *Blacklight Beauty*.

doubt that Faith *executes* the sexual acts and, apart from the minor frigging that begins this scene, there is no demonstration that any of her "partners" are concerned about giving her a good time. Even so, the idea that she might be merely a vessel for male pleasure is refused by the incredibly aggressive style of her performance. Faith goes at it with energy and raw vigor, her aggressive facial expressions—in the few moments of penetration as she grinds on her penetrator, and vigorously fellates or masturbates the other men around her—refusing a reading of her as simply *there* for male consumption.

Eyes wide, and her teeth bared, Faith stares aggressively at the camera. Assailed by cocks, a longer view of her shows her lasciviously smiling at each of the guys in assertive anticipation of the coming money shots. The freeze frame on the first ejaculation into her mouth captures its shiny abundance, but there are no appreciative smiles from her; she doesn't pander to the "pop" as masculine achievement. The scene ends with repeated shots of her pugnaciously opening her mouth, sticking out her tongue to disclose the semen there. Thus Faith's performance, which, in its belligerent physicality, flirts with but ultimately rejects the idea of the "degradation" and "objectification" of women in porn, challenges the normative impulse to render the female porn star's body as abject.

Sound, Space and Fantasy

Across all the films discussed here, dialogue is fairly minimal and avoids the post-sync "sounds of pleasure" that Linda Williams has suggested is a part of "porno-performativity."[46] Intra-diegetic grunts and groans pepper individual scenes though they are rougher, perhaps more animalistic, than the standard soundtrack. As in Zipper's other films, the soundtrack for *Blacklight Beauty* is dominated by a unique music score—in this instance created by Myiasis B. and DJ Kraddy. Mixing forms of original ambient jazz with rock and punk, the switches of styles punctuate the various vignettes on the DVD, creating different moods and reflecting the various modes of sex on offer. Cherry 2000's "Teenage Freak" accompanies a girl-on-girl scene featuring a large double-ended dildo; Pilar Bauman's "Fuck on a Washing Machine" gives an exciting tempo to the Allie Sin bathroom scene; while the Redneck Casanovas provide the theme for Sin's threesome on the bar.

In Faith's scene, her introduction is accompanied by hi-hat and snare drum with a grunge tempo, which morphs to an ambient jazz feel. As the action "hots" up, the same score takes on an industrial rock tenor reminiscent of Nine Inch Nails and, later, Marilyn Manson. The music changes as she grunts, and becomes more insistent at moments when the action becomes more chaotic; slo-mo/freeze frame camera work also stretches out the tempo, as the drumbeat slows and speeds up again. The switches of tempo, style, and form create an unusual yet particularly evocative sonotope combined with lighting textures, and the tight-packed performers, conveying the physicality of sex in a down-and-dirty environment.[47] As Smith argues:

> If fantasy is best understood as the setting of a scene, and sound is uniquely able to convey the experience of space, then sound design emerges as a central aspect

of the representation of sexual fantasy in adult film. Sound is a powerful—perhaps the most powerful—index of setting, and the choice of sonotope employed in a particular scene profoundly shapes the subsequent experience of fantasy … a well-designed soundscape can do much to shape the experience of cinematic sexual fantasy … one more adept at evoking an immersive experience of fantasy than the visual depiction of the mechanics of sex."[48]

Moving beyond porno-performativity, porn should then be regarded as both aural and visual.[49] Sound, in Zipper's films, contributes to a kind of porno-cinematicity. In this twenty-minute scene with its multiple cuts and partners, realistic presentation of each sexual coupling is refused to significant effect. The musical moves give the impression of time passing—accompanying, though not necessarily always in sync with, the pace of the visuals (or even with the sexual action) – providing shape to the fantasy of the "marathon" Faith has accomplished, and thus emphasizing her endurance.[50]

Vivien Sobchack suggests that images may be about more than simply seeing or following a narrative: they bring with them "the sense and sensibility of materiality," offering sensory experiences of the "real" and "as if real."[51] In so doing, film encourages the "reflexive … turn toward my own carnal, sensual, and sensible being to touch myself touching, smell myself smelling, taste myself tasting, and, in sum, sense my own sensuality."[52] As a body genre, pornography no doubt encourages viewers to consider its effects on their own bodies, but I suggest that Faith's scene in *BLB* may also offer a further and particular dimension to the always already assumed (as an incitement to masturbation) embodiment of its viewers through its staging of a particular sensorium of the grind house. The darkness of the mise-en-scène—broken only by flickering lights from the screen and handheld torches, glimpses of purple velveteen cinema seating, the pressing of anonymous bodies, and frenetic sound—pricks personal memories (hasn't everyone been to a cinema?) but invokes cultural memories of the carnal physicalities and possibilities of New York's Times Square in the 1970s.

For the purely judgmental observer, the scene I have described here could be considered no more than the usual multiple blow job scene ending in bukkake found across innumerable compilation DVDs. But Faith's performance and its staging are not simply about numeric excess or the pop-shots. This scene both literalizes the anonymous and random sexual activities of grindhouse mythos and animates reflection on the "transgressions" those tales of seedy public sex imply. As I have already indicated, descriptions of grindhouse audiences bring bodies and sexual behaviors to life in the service of sensationalist narratives that highlight the "dangers" braved by the cinephile who attempts to watch his cult movie surrounded by pimps, prostitutes, and johns. The cultural "shock" experienced by such voyeurs[53] depends in part on the idea of the exoticism of eroticized "oddities" engaged in sexual congress: a kind of "extra-cinema of attractions" whose characters are refused any psychological motivations or individual personalization except in imputing to them a sleazy, animalistic, monologic desire to fuck. Faith's scene brings to life the "radical laissez-faire" and "unimaginable things [taking] place in darkness" that characterize memories of the grind house and, in so doing, offers a direct challenge to the non-personhood those memories ascribe to "faceless urban misfits [seeking] sexual solace"[54] in those spaces.

In his own words, Zipper's films are like:

> A thrill ride at a carnival. The movies are most definitely adult movies, porn movies, whatever your terminology—they've just been recast to be more timeless. Like a message in a bottle. I don't think they try to be anything they're not, it's always wall-to-wall sex.

In producing his "wall-to-wall sex" films, Zipper deploys imagery drawn from grindhouse themes of horror and exploitation to craft "cult" pornographies that bear repeat viewings and that also animate the experience of the grind house as a site of outlaw sex. By employing a "grindhouse" lens, Zipper is not simply indulging in fond memory. Rather, the tropes outlined above amplify something fundamental about the "wall-to-wall sex" in his films. Zipper's challenge to the bastard art form is his reanimation, in an era where amateur porn has become the big story, of the exceptional status of the performer *qua* porn *star*.

Recognizing the standard critique of pornography as always already about sex, Zipper claims a particular orientation to the familiar accusations of homogeneity: "Porn is like the blues—you only have 3 chords, but you can play them forever. I wanna be the John Lee Hooker of porn." The self-mythologizing and attribution of cult-classic status for his films is clear, but more than this I want to suggest that his work offers a critique of the ubiquity of sex as *ordinary* in the age of amateur porn by its referencing of the down and dirty public sex of the grind house. Zipper's films feature a coterie of star-names including Audrey Hollander, Kimberley Kane, Allie Sin, and Sasha Grey (actresses who have had more or less mainstream successes), but—as discussed above—he intends in employing those recognized faces to bring out their "witchery" and the "radioactive nature of sex," highlighting the porn stars' difference from the "ordinary citizenry." Zipper describes his directorial modus operandi as putting stars into "the pressure cooker" so that these mainstream stars produce performances that are unlike those they offer in more conventional big-studio productions. Zipper and his films are interesting to explore, both as illustrations of the diversity of productions contained within the category of alt-porn and as a means of exploring the cultural legacy and mythology of the grind house theater and the sexual freedoms it supposedly offered.

In the mise-en-scène of the DVDs discussed here, Zipper pays homage to screening places and to forms of cinema that have particular resonances and affective dimensions for audiences. The grind house is seen in traces across these contemporary porn performances, appealing to forms of cinephilia: "the love that never dies."[55] The focus on place, and its revivification and reification in grindhouse nostalgia, is often regarded as a rather retrograde memorializing, as David Church argues:

> The latter-day exploitation fan who imagines him/herself as a grindhouse patron participates in the construction and continued circulation of cultural memories

about a downmarket, largely lawless urban exhibition site where the viewer's lived experiences as a theatre-goer might seem sensuously to mirror the sleazy spectacles seen on-screen.[56]

Of course such claims tend to essentialize audiences and my textual readings here may be just as guilty of "diagnosing desire."[57] I am willing to admit that this chapter is about my own relation to Zipper's films, that perhaps what they animate for me are particular sets of remembrances of my own first forays into the "sexual underground" that was London's Soho in the late 1970s and early 1980s—the pre-AIDS period—and late-night cult film viewing in local fleapits. Still, this speaks to a sensibility that is surely shared: my *experiences* were based in the UK but are filled with the images and references of American exploitation cinema.

For *this* viewer, Zipper's narratives rely on the idea of an era in which pornography belonged on the boundaries, and where sexual *adventures* were the province of oddballs and deviant "Others." Zipper employs cultural memories in order to index an *idea* of the grind house, not an historical reality, offering viewers the pleasures of a bygone era, the reinvigoration of what Benson-Allott suggests is a "cinematic utopia, an idealized theatrical *nonplace that never was*."[58] In his creative uses of the past, the explicit references to exploitation cinema and to the places, and spatial, sexual, possibilities of the grind house theater, Zipper comments on what he has described as the "basically factory system" of contemporary pornographies.[59] The freakshow, the nightclub, and the grind house are memorialized for Zipper's viewers but these memories are surely not their own. The pornophile viewer of *Blacklight Beauty* or *King Cobra* is viewing the signifiers of pastness made possible on DVD in order to experience pornography as "the last cultural frontier … [and its] wild and guilty pleasures."[60]

Notes

1. David Church, "From Exhibition to Genre: The Case of Grindhouse Films," *Cinema Journal* 50:1 (2011): 1–25.
2. Jeffrey Sconce, "'Trashing' the Academy: Taste, Excess, and an Emerging Politics of Cinematic Style," *Screen* 36:4 (1994): 371–393.
3. Kevin Heffernan, "Seen as a Business: Adult Film's Historical Framework and Foundations," in *New Views on Pornography: Sexuality, Politics, and the Law*, eds Lynn Comella and Shira Tarrant (Santa Barbara: Praeger, 2015).
4. Helen Hester, Bethan Jones, and Sarah Taylor-Harman. "Giffing a Fuck: Non-Narrative Pleasures in Participatory Porn Cultures and Female Fandom," *Porn Studies* 2:4 (2015): 356–366.
5. DVD review of Vinegar Syndrome, available at https://thirdeyecinema.wordpress.com/2013/02/23/dvd-review-adults-only-vinegar-syndromes-drive-in-collection-vol-3-anthony-spinellis-expectations-and-confessions/ (accessed November 5, 2013).
6. Bob Johnson, "DVD Makers: DVD Still King," *XBiz.com*, July 29, 2010, available at http://www.xbiz.com/articles/123470/DVD (accessed March 5, 2012).

7. Enrico Biasin and Federico Zecca, "Contemporary Audiovisual Pornography: Branding Strategy and Gonzo Film Style," *Cinéma & Cie* 9:1 (2009): 133–150; Rhett Pardon, "Private Plans on Releasing More Titles Each Month," *XBiz.com* (November 21, 2011), available at http://www.xbiz.com/news/news_piece.php?id=141303&mi=all&q=DVD (accessed March 5, 2012); Clarissa Smith, "'It's Important You Don't Smell a Suit on It': Aesthetics of Alt Porn," in *Porn after Porn: Contemporary Alternative Pornographies*, eds Enrico Biasin, Giovanna Maina, and Federico Zecca (Milano-Udine: University of Udine Press, 2014); Chauntelle Ann Tibbals, "Gonzo, Trannys, and Teens—Current Trends in US Adult Content Production, Distribution, and Consumption," *Porn Studies* 1:1–2 (2014): 127–135.
8. David Church, *Grindhouse Nostalgia: Memory, Home Video and Exploitation Film Fandom* (Edinburgh: Edinburgh University Press, 2015).
9. This epithet is used on numerous review sites such as hotmovies.com as well as on Zipper's own website. It is impossible to know if this is his own description of himself or one bestowed by a reviewer.
10. Leaving aside the "lost to the world" *True Grit XXX* (2012), following the failure of Pleasure Dynasty. Compared with mainstream movie production, one title per year may seem extremely productive but in the world of pornography this is very modest.
11. Caetlin Benson-Allott, *Killer Tapes and Shattered Screens: Video Spectatorship from VHS to File Sharing* (Berkeley and Los Angeles: University of California Press, 2013).
12. Jane Juffer, *At Home with Pornography: Women, Sex, and Everyday Life* (New York: New York University Press, 1998); Biasin and Zecca, "Contemporary Audiovisual Pornography"; Smith, "It's Important You Don't Smell a Suit on It."
13. John Champagne. "'Stop Reading Films!': Film Studies, Close Analysis, and Gay Pornography," *Cinema Journal* 36:4 (1997): 76–97.
14. Susanna Paasonen, *Carnal Resonance: Affect and Online Pornography* (Boston: MIT Press, 2011).
15. In electing to examine the work of this particular director, I am aware of Andrew Sarris's caution that auteur theory can value the personality of the director in ways that reify the "few brave spirits" managing "to overcome the gravitational pull of the mass of movies" (Sarris in John Caughie, *Theories of Authorship* (Boston: Routledge & Kegan Paul, 1981), 65.)
16. Susanna Paasonen and Laura Saarenmaa, "The Golden Age of Porn: Nostalgia and History in Cinema," in *Pornification: Sex and Sexuality in Media Culture*, eds Susanna Paasonen and Laura Saarenmaa (Oxford: Berg, 2007), 23–32.
17. Church, *Grindhouse Nostalgia*; Elena Gorfinkel, "Tales of Times Square: Sexploitation's Secret History of Place," in *Taking Place: Location and the Moving Image*, eds John David Rhodes and Elena Gorfinkel (Minneapolis: University of Minnesota Press, 2011).
18. Susanna Paasonen, "Epilogue: Porn Futures," in *Pornification: Sex and Sexuality in Media Culture*, eds Susanna Paasonen, Kaarina Nikunen, and Laura Saarenmaa (Oxford: Berg, 2007), 166.
19. Peter Warren, "Blacklight Beauty Movie Review," *AVN*, October 1, 2006, available at http://www.avn.com/movies/67834.html (accessed August 7, 2011).
20. Don Houston, "Review: *King Cobra*," *XCritic*, March 3, 2008, available at http://www.xcritic.com/review/32373/lanny-barby-king-cobra/ (accessed August 22, 2015).

21. Moya Luckett, "Sexploitation as Feminine Territory: The Films of Doris Wishman," in *Defining Cult Movies: The Politics of Oppositional Taste*, eds Mark Jancovich, Antonio Lazaro Reboll, Julian Stringer, and Andy Willis (Manchester: Manchester University Press, 2003), 142–156.
22. Linda Williams, *Hard Core: Power, Pleasure and the "Frenzy of the Visible"* (London: Pandora, 1990).
23. Houston, "Review: *King Cobra*."
24. Jack the Zipper, in Joanne Cachapero, "Crazy World of Jack the Zipper," *Xbiz.com*, 2008, available at http://www.xbiz.com/articles/127921 (accessed July 11, 2011).
25. His anonymity is preserved by the absence of photographs of him in any industry publications and in interviews he insists on being addressed, and written about, as Jack.
26. I am drawing on Andrew Sarris's conception of auteurist criticism, that the "distinguishable personality of the director [acts] as a criterion of value" (in "Notes on the Auteur Theory in 1962," *Film Culture*, Winter 62/3 (1962)).
27. Unless attributed elsewhere, all quotations from Zipper are from personal email communications with me during 2011.
28. Gram Ponante, "DVD Review: Squealer," *Fleshbot*, April 7, 2006, available at http://straight.fleshbot.com/165747/dvd-review-squealer (accessed August 21, 2015).
29. Zipper has suggested, in interviews, that the film was his own vision, not something expected by Hustler but partly inspired by the hillbilly persona of Larry Flynt. In a podcast (available at http://www.jackthezipper.com/ podcast), Zipper states that his only interest in satisfying Hustler was to get the six hard-core scenes on camera, thereafter the narrative and visual layers of the production were his alone.
30. Alec Knight, DVD Review: *Squealer*, XCritic, September 27, 2005, available at http://www.xcritic.com/review/17903/alec-knight-squealer/ (accessed March 5, 2012).
31. Thomas Joseph Watson, "There's Something Rotten in the State of Texas: Genre, Adaptation and *The Texas Vibrator Massacre*," *Journal of Adaptation in Film and Performance* 6:3 (2013): 387–400.
32. Houston, "Review: *King Cobra*"; Knight, DVD Review: *Squealer*.
33. Jonathan Lake Crane, *Terror and Everyday Life: Singular Moments in the History of the Horror Film* (California: Sage Publications, 1994), 168.
34. Carl Plantinga, "Disgusted at the Movies," *Film Studies* 8:1 (2006): 87.
35. Knight, DVD Review: *Squealer*.
36. Sergio Messina, "Realcore, the Digital Porno Revolution," 2009, available at http://www.sergiomessina.com/realcore/index.php (accessed August 10, 2011).
37. Niall Richardson, *Transgressive Bodies: Representations in Film and Popular Culture* (Surrey: Ashgate Publishing, 2012).
38. Champagne, "Stop Reading Films!" 81.
39. Michelle Clifford, "Black and Blue: New York's Roughie Grindhouses and the Films that Played at Them," in *Everything You Know about Sex Is Wrong: The Disinformation Guide to the Extremes of Human Sexuality (and Everything in Between)*, ed. Russ Kick (New York: Disinformation, 2006), 153.
40. See Glenn Ward's contribution to this volume and Church, *Grindhouse Nostalgia*.
41. Gorfinkel, "Tales of Times Square," 65.
42. Clifford, "Black and Blue," 158.
43. Richardson, *Transgressive Bodies*, 168.

44. I have written about Sin's performance in this scene in "Reel Intercourse: Doing Sex on Camera," *Hard to Swallow: Reading Pornography Onscreen*, eds Darren Kerr and Claire Hines (London: Wallflower, 2012), 194–214.
45. Various scenes in *BLB* were post-produced to replicate the cheap and imperfect visuals of grindhouse and the film playing in the background to this scene looks like an old, damaged film print.
46. Williams, *Hard Core*, 124; see also Rich Cante and Angelo Restivo, "The Voice of Pornography," in *Keyframes*, eds Matthew Tinkcom and Amy Villarejo (New York: Routledge, 2001), 207–227.
47. Likewise, music as scene-setter plays a central role in *Enter the Peepshow*, though it is perhaps more obvious in its allusions. With a discordant "screamer" soundtrack mixing industrial electronica and discordant circus marches, the fast-cut, low-angle photography, and kaleidoscope visuals and intertitles, the discordances of the carnival are brought to life as affective *experiences*.
48. Jacob Smith, "Sound and Performance in Stephen Sayadian's Night Dreams and Café Flesh," *The Velvet Light Trap* 59 (Spring, 2007): 22.
49. Music and sound in pornography have received more attention in recent years, for example, chapters in *Earogenous Zones: Sound, Sexuality and Cinema*, ed. Bruce Johnson (London: Equinox, 2010).
50. It is also perfectly possible that these tempo changes may provide the rhythm for a viewer's masturbation—I don't think that significantly alters any of the points I make here.
51. Vivian Sobchack, *Carnal Thoughts, Embodiment and Moving Image Culture* (Berkeley and Los Angeles: University of California Press, 2004), 76.
52. Ibid.
53. I use this term absolutely intentionally to reference the "viewer's" separateness from the individuals they describe.
54. Jack Stevenson, "Grindhouse and Beyond," in *From the Arthouse to the Grindhouse: Highbrow and Lowbrow Transgession in Cinema's First Century*, eds John Cline and Robert G. Weiner (Maryland: Scarecrow Press, 2010), 129–152.
55. Thomas Elsaesser. "Cinephilia, or the Uses of Disenchantment," in *Cinephilia: Movies, Love and Memory*, eds Marijke de Valck and Malte Hagener (Amsterdam: Amsterdam University Press, 2005), 41.
56. Church, *Grindhouse Nostalgia*, 74.
57. Champagne, "Stop Reading Films!"
58. Benson-Allot, *Killer Tapes*, 132
59. Quoted in Cachapero, "Crazy World of Jack the Zipper."
60. Zipper quoted in Michael Hayes, "Vivid Hires JacktheZipper," *XBiz.com*, August 23, 2006, available at http://www.xbiz.com/news/16665 (accessed August 22, 2015).

Select Bibliography

42nd Street Pete. "A Lost Saturday Night at the Venus." In *Grindhouse Purgatory* 1.1, edited by Peter Chiarelli, 7–9, 2013.

Abel, Richard. *The Red Rooster Scare: Making American Cinema*. Berkley: University California Press, 1999.

Adams, Philip. "Introduction." In *A Century of Australian Cinema*, edited by James Sanine, vii–xi. Port Melbourne: William Heinemann Australia, 1995.

Aleiss, Angela. *Making the White Man's Indian: Native Americans and Hollywood Movies*. Westport, CT: Praeger, 2005.

Altman, Rick. *Film/Genre*. London: BFI, 1999.

Antonio, Sheril D. "The Urban-Rural Binary in Black American Film and Culture." *Black Camera* 1.1 (2009): 116–135.

Austin, Bruce A. "Portrait of a Cult Film Audience: *The Rocky Horror Picture Show*." *Journal of Communication* 31.2 (1981): 43–54.

Bailey, Jason. *Pulp Fiction: The Complete Story of Quentin Tarantino's Masterpiece*. Minneapolis: Voyageur Press, 2013.

Barefoot, Guy. "Who Watched that Masked Man? Hollywood's Serial Audiences in the 1930s." *Historical Journal of Film, Radio and Television* 31.2 (2011): 167–190.

Bazin, André. "The Western, or the American Film *par excellence*." In *What Is Cinema? Volume 2*. London: University of California Press, 2005.

Bellanta, Melissa. *Larrikins: A History*. St. Lucia: University of Queensland Press, 2012.

Benson-Allott, Caetlin. *Killer Tapes and Shattered Screens: Video Spectatorship from VHS to File Sharing*. Berkeley and Los Angeles: University of California Press, 2013.

Bermel, Albert. *Farce: A History from Aristophanes to Woody Allen*. New York: Simon and Schuster, 1982.

Betz, Mark. "Art, Exploitation, Underground." In *Defining Cult Movies: The Cultural Politics of Oppositional Taste*, edited by Mark Jancovich, Antonio Lazaro-Reboll, Julian Stringer and Andy Willis, 202–222. Manchester: Manchester University Press, 2003.

Betz, Mark. "High and Low and in Between." *Screen* 54.4 (2013): 495–513.

Biasin, Enrico and Federico Zecca. "Contemporary Audiovisual Pornography: Branding Strategy and Gonzo Film Style." *Cinéma & Cie* 9.1 (2009): 133–150.

Björklund, Elisabet. *The Most Delicate Subject: A History of Sex Education Films in Sweden*. Lund, Sweden: Critica Litterarum Lundensis, 2012.

Black, David. "Charactor; or, The Strange Case of Uma Peel." In *Cult Television*, edited by Sara Gwenllian Jones and Roberta E. Pearson. Minneapolis: University of Minnesota Press, 2004.

Blainey, Geoffrey. *The Tyranny of Distance: How Distance Shaped Australia's History*. Melbourne: Macmillan, 1968.

Bodroghkozy, Aniko. "Reel Revolutionaries: An Examination of Hollywood's Cycle of 1960s Youth Rebellion Films." *Cinema Journal* 41.3 (2002): 38–58.

Bogle, Donald. *Toms, Coons, Mulattoes, Mammies and Bucks: An Interpretive History of Blacks in American Films*. New York: Continuum, 2001.

Bordwell, David, Janet Staiger and Kristin Thompson. *The Classical Hollywood Cinema: Film Style & Mode of Production to 1960*. London: Routledge and Kegan Paul, 1985.

Bougie, Robin. *Graphic Thrills, American XXX Movie Posters 1970 to 1985*. Guildford: FAB Press, 2014.

Bowser, Eileen. "Mack Sennett vs Henry Ford." In *Slapstick Comedy*, edited by Tom Paulis and Rob King, 107–113. New York: Routledge, 2010.

Boym, Svetlana. *The Future of Nostalgia*. New York: Basic Books Press, 2001.

Brand, Simon. *Picture Palaces and Fleapits*. Sydney: Dreamweaver, 1983.

Byrd, Jodi A. "'Living My Native Life Deadly': Red Lake, Ward Churchill, and the Discourses of Competing Genocides." *American Indian Quarterly* 31.2 (2007): 310–332.

Canjels, Rudmer. *Distributing Silent Film Serials: Local Practices, Changing Forms, Cultural Transformation*. New York: Routledge, 2011.

Cante, Rich and Angelo Restivo. "The Voice of Pornography." In *Keyframes*, edited by Matthew Tinkcom and Amy Villarejo, 207–227. New York: Routledge, 2001.

Caughie, John. *Theories of Authorship*. Boston: Routledge & Kegan Paul, 1981.

Cha-Jua, Sundiata Keita. "Black Audiences, Blaxploitation and Kung Fu Films, and Challenges to White Celluloid Masculinity." In *China Forever: The Shaw Brothers and Diasporic Cinema*, edited by Poshek Fu, 199–223. Champaign: University of Illinois Press, 2008.

Champagne, John. "'Stop Reading Films!': Film Studies, Close Analysis, and Gay Pornography." *Cinema Journal* 36.4 (1997): 76–97.

Chiarella, Peter, ed. *Grindhouse Purgatory* 1.1, 2013.

Chong, Sylvia Shin Huey. *The Oriental Obscene: Violence and Racial Fantasies in the Vietnam Era*. Durham, NC: Duke University Press, 2012.

Church, David. "From Exhibition to Genre: The Case of Grind-House Films." *Cinema Journal* 50.4 (2011): 1–25.

Church, David. *Grindhouse Nostalgia: Memory, Home Video and Exploitation Film Fandom*. Edinburgh: Edinburgh University Press, 2015a.

Church, David. "One on Top of the Other: Lucio Fulci, Transnational Film Industries, and the Retrospective Construction of the Italian Horror Canon." *Quarterly Review of Film and Video* 32.1 (2015b): 1–20.

Clark, Anna. "The History Wars." In *Australian History Now*, edited by Anna Clark and Paul Ashton. Sydney: New South Press, 2013.

Clifford, Michelle. "Black and Blue: New York's Roughie Grindhouses and the Films That Played at Them." In *Everything You Know about Sex Is Wrong: The Disinformation Guide to the Extremes of Human Sexuality (and Everything in Between)*, edited by Russ Kick, 153–163. New York: Disinformation, 2006.

Cook, David. "Movies and Political Trauma." In *American Cinema of the 1970s*, edited by Lester D. Friedman. New Brunswick, NJ: Rutger's University Press, 2007.

Corkin, Stanley. *Cowboys as Cold Warriors: The Western and US History*. Philadelphia: Temple University Press, 2004.

Crane, Jonathan Lake. *Terror and Everyday Life: Singular Moments in the History of the Horror Film*. California: Sage Publications, 1994.

Crang, Mike. "Rethinking the Observer: Film, Mobility, and the Construction of the Subject." In *Engaging Film: Geographies of Mobility and Identity*, edited by Tim Cresswell and Deborah Dixon, 13–31. New York and Oxford: Rowman and Littlefield, 2002.

Csaba, Fabian Faurholt and Anders Bengtsson. "Rethinking Identity in Brand Management." In *Brand Culture*, edited by Jonathan Schroeder and Miriam Salzer-Mörling, 118–135. Abington: Routledge, 2006.

Cunningham, Stuart. "Hollywood Genres, Australian Movies." In *An Australian Film Reader*, edited by Albert Moran and Tom O'Regan, 53–74. Sydney: Currency Press, 1985.

Deloria Jr., Vine. *Custer Died for Your Sins: An Indian Manifesto*. Toronto and London: Macmillan, 1969.

Deloria, Philip J. *Playing Indian*. New Haven, CT: Yale University Press, 1998.

Dermody, Susan and Elizabeth Jacka. *The Screening of Australia: Anatomy of a National Cinema*, Vol. 2. Sydney: Currency Press, 1988.

Derrida, Jacques. "Archive Fever." In *The Archive*, edited by Charles Merewether, 76–79. London: Whitechapel Gallery/MIT Press, 2006.

DeVere Brody, Jennifer. "The Returns of Cleopatra Jones." *Signs* 25.1 (1999): 91–121.

Doherty, Thomas. "This Is Where We Came In: The Audible Screen and the Voluble Audience of Early Sound Cinema." In *American Movie Audiences: From the Turn of the Century to the Early Sound Era*, edited by Melvyn Stokes and Richard Maltby, 143–163. London: BFI, 1999.

Doherty, Thomas. *Teenagers and Teenpics: The Juvenilization of American Movies in the 1950s*. Philadelphia: Temple University Press, 2002.

Donahue, Suzanne Mary. *American Film Distribution: The Changing Marketplace*. Ann Arbor: UMI Research Press, 1987.

Dworkin, Andrea. *Pornography: Men Possessing Women*. London: The Women's Press, 1981.

Dyer, Richard. *Stars*. London: BFI, 1979.

Dyer, Richard. *The Matter of Images*. London: Routledge, 1993.

Eco, Umberto. *The Limits of Interpretation*. Bloomington: University of Indiana Press, 1994.

Edwards, Phil. *Shocking Cinema: The Breaking of Movie Taboos*. Beaconsfield: Mentmore Press, 1987.

Egan, Kate. *Trash or Treasure? Censorship and the Changing Meanings of the Video Nasties*. Manchester: Manchester University Press, 2007.

Egan, Kate and Sarah Thomas. "Introduction: Star Making, Cult—Making and Forms of Authenticity." In *Cult Film Stardom: Offbeat Attractions and Processes of Cultification*, edited by Kate Egan and Sarah Thomas, 1–17. Basingstoke: Palgrave Macmillan, 2013.

Elsaesser, Thomas. "Cinephilia, or the Uses of Disenchantment." In *Cinephilia: Movies, Love and Memory*, edited by Marijke de Valck and Malte Hagener, 27–44. Amsterdam: Amsterdam University Press, 2005.

Engelhardt, Tom. *The End of Victory Culture: Cold War America and the Disillusioning of a Generation*. New York: BasicBooks, 1995.

Ernst, Wolfgang. *Digital Memory and the Archive*, edited by Jussi Parikka, Minneapolis: University of Minnesota Press, 2013.

Ferle, Johannes. "'And I Would Call It "A Southern"': Renewing/Obscuring the Blaxploitation Western." *Safundi: The Journal of South African and American Studies* 16.3 (2015): 294–297.

Friedberg, Anne. *Window Shopping: Cinema and the Postmodern*. Berkeley: University of California Press, 1993.

Friedman, Andrea. *Prurient Interests: Gender, Democracy, and Obscenity in New York City, 1909–1945*. New York: Columbia University Press, 2000.

Gartman, David. *Auto Opium: A Social History of American Automobile Design*. London and New York: Routledge, 1994.

Gleich, Joshua. "Jim Brown: From Integration to Resegregation in *The Dirty Dozen* and *100 Rifles*." *Cinema Journal* 51.1 (2011): 1–25.

Gomery, Douglas. *The Hollywood Studio System*. London: BFI/MacMillan, 1986.

Gomery, Douglas. "The Economics of the Horror Film." In *Horror Films: Current Research in Audience Preferences and Reactions*, edited by James Weaver and Ron Tamborini, 49–62. New York: Routledge, 1996.

Gore, Chris. "Foreword: Grinding Out a New Form of Entertainment." In *From the Arthouse to the Grindhouse: Highbrow and Lowbrow Transgression in Cinema's First Century*, edited by John Cline and Robert G. Weiner, ix–x. Lanham, MD: Scarecrow, 2010.

Gorfinkel, Elena. "Tales of Times Square: Sexploitation's Secret History of Place." In *Taking Place: Location and the Moving Image*, edited by John David Rhodes and Elena Gorfinkel, 55–76. Minneapolis: University of Minnesota Press, 2011.

Guerrero, Ed. *Framing Blackness: The African American Image in Film*. Philadelphia: Temple University Press, 1993.

Halbwachs, Maurice. *On Collective Memory*, translated by Lewis A. Coser. Chicago: University of Chicago Press, 1992.

Hall, Sheldon. "Tall Revenue Features: The Genealogy of the Modern Blockbuster." In *Genre and Contemporary Hollywood*, edited by Steve Neale, 11–26. London: BFI, 1998.

Hanby, Terry. "Brands—Dead or Alive?" *Journal of the Marketing Research Society* 41.1 (1999): 7–18.

Harris, Paul. *Not Quite Hollywood: The Official Handbook*. Melbourne: Madman Entertainment, 2008.

Hawkins, Joan. *Cutting Edge: Art-Horror and the Horrific Avant-Garde*. Minneapolis: University of Minnesota Press, 2000.

Hawkins, Joan. "Midnight Sex-Horror Movies and the Downtown Avant-garde." In *Defining Cult Movies: The Cultural Politics of Oppositional Taste*, edited by Mark Jancovich, Antonio Lázaro Reboll, Julian Stringer, and Andy Willis, 223–233. Manchester: Manchester University Press, 2003.

Heffernan, Kevin. *Ghouls, Gimmicks, and Gold: Horror Films and the American Movie Business, 1953–1968*. Durham and London: Duke University Press, 2007.

Heffernan, Kevin. "Seen as a Business: Adult Film's Historical Framework and Foundations." In *New Views on Pornography: Sexuality, Politics, and the Law*, edited by Lynn Comella and Shira Tarrant, 37–56. Santa Barbara: Praeger, 2015.

Heidenry, John. *What Wild Ecstasy: The Rise and Fall of the Sexual Revolution*. New York: Simon and Schuster, 1997.

Hester, Helen, Bethan Jones, and Sarah Taylor-Harman. "Giffing a Fuck: Non-Narrative Pleasures in Participatory Porn Cultures and Female Fandom." *Porn Studies* 2.4 (2015): 356–366.

Higgins, Scott. *Matinee Melodrama: Play and the Art of Formula in the Sound Serial*. New Brunswick: Rutgers University Press, 2016.

Hillier, Jim and Aaron Lipstadt. "The Economics of Independence: Roger Corman and New World Pictures, 1970–1980." *Movie* 31/32 (1986): 43–53.

Hills, Matt. "Cult Movies with and without Cult Stars: Differentiating Discourses of Stardom." In *Cult Film Stardom: Offbeat Attractions and Processes of Cultification*, edited by Kate Egan and Sarah Thomas, 21–36. Basingstoke: Palgrave Macmillan, 2013.

Hinde, John. "*Barry McKenzie* and *Alvin* Ten Years Later." In *An Australian Film Reader*, edited by Albert Moran and Tom O'Regan, 184–187. Sydney: Currency Press, 1985.

Hoberman, J. and Jonathan Rosenbaum. *Midnight Movies*. New York: De Capo Press, 1991.
Hollows, Joanne. "The Masculinity of Cult." In *Defining Cult Movies: The Cultural Politics of Oppositional Taste*, edited by Mark Jancovich, Antonio Lazaro-Reboll, Julian Stringer, and Andy Willis, 35–53. Manchester: Manchester University Press, 2003.
Horton, Andrew. "Turning On and Tuning Out at the Drive-In: An American Phenomenon Survives and Thrives." *Journal of Popular Film* 5.3/4 (1976): 233–244.
Hunt, Leon. "Asiaphilia, Asianisation and the Gatekeeper Auteur: Quentin Tarantino and Luc Besson." In *East Asian Cinemas: Exploring Transnational Connections on Film*, edited by Leon Hunt and Leung Wing-Fai, 220–236. London: I. B. Tauris, 2008.
Hutchings, Peter. "Resident Evil? The Limits of European Horror: *Resident Evil* versus *Suspiria*." In *European Nightmares: Horror Cinema in Europe since 1945*, edited by Patricia Allmer, David Huxley, and Emily Brick, 13–24. New York: Wallflower Press, 2012.
Huyssen, Andreas. *Present Pasts: Urban Palimpsests and the Politics of Memory*. Palo Alto, CA: Stanford University Press, 2003a.
Huyssen, Andreas. "Trauma and Memory: A New Imaginary of Temporality." In *World Memory: Personal Trajectories in Global Time*, edited by Jill Bennett and Rosanne Kennedy, 16–29. Basingstoke: Palgrave Macmillan, 2003b.
Huyssen, Andreas. "Nostalgia for Ruins." *Grey Room* 23 (2006): 6–21.
Inglis, Ruth. *Freedom of the Movies*. Chicago: University of Chicago Press, 1947.
Iwabuchi, Koichi. *Recentering Globalization: Popular Culture and Japanese Transnationalism*. Durham and London: Duke University Press, 2002.
Jancovich, Mark. "Cult Fictions: Cult Movies, Subcultural Capital, and the Production of Cultural Distinctions." *Cultural Studies* 16.2 (2002): 306–322.
Jenkins, Henry. *Convergence Culture: Where Old and New Media Collide*. New York and London: New York University Press, 2006.
Jeremy, Ron. *Ron Jeremy: The Hardest (Working) Man in Showbusiness*. New York: Harper Collins, 2007.
Johnson, Bruce, ed. *Earogenous Zones: Sound, Sexuality and Cinema*. London: Equinox, 2010.
Johnson, Eithne and Eric Schaefer. "Soft Core/Hard Gore: *Snuff* as a Crisis in Meaning." *Journal of Film and Video* 45.2/3 (1993): 40–59.
Juffer, Jane. *At Home with Pornography: Women, Sex, and Everyday Life*. New York: New York University Press, 1998.
Juno, Andrea. "Interview: Frank Henenlotter." In *Re/Search: Incredibly Strange Films*, edited by Jim Morton, 8–17. San Francisco: Re/Search Publications, 1986.
Kerekes, David and David Slater. *Killing for Culture: An Illustrated History of Death Film from Mondo to Snuff*. London: Creation, 1994.
Kilpatrick, Jacquelyn. *Celluloid Indians: Native Americans and Film*. Lincoln: University of Nebraska Press, 1999.
King, Rob. *The Fun Factory: The Keystone Film Company and the Emergence of Mass Culture*. Berkeley: University of California Press, 2009.
Kipnis, Laura. "How to Look at Pornography." In *Pornography: Film and Culture*, edited by Peter Lehman, 118–129. New Brunswick: Rutgers University Press, 2006.
Kitses, Jim. *Horizons West: Anthony Mann, Budd Boetticher, Sam Peckinpah: Studies of Authorship within the Western*. London: Thames and Hudson, 1969.
Kleinhans, Chuck. "The Change from Film to Video Pornography." In *Pornography: Film and Culture*, edited by Peter Lehman, 154–167. New Brunswick: Rutgers University Press, 2006.

Klenotic, Jeff. "'Four Hours of Hootin' and Hollerin'": Moviegoing and Everyday Life Outside the Movie Palace." In *Going to the Movies: Hollywood and the Social Experience of Cinema*, edited by Richard Maltby, Melvyn Stokes, and Robert Allen, 130–154. Exeter: University of Exeter Press, 2007.

Klinger, Barbara. "Digressions at the Cinema: Reception and Mass Culture." *Cinema Journal* 28.4 (1989): 11–13.

Klinger, Barbara. *Beyond the Multiplex: Cinema, New Technologies, and the Home*. Berkeley and Los Angeles: University of California Press, 2006.

Kosofsky Sedgwick, Eve. *Between Men: English Literature and Male Homosocial Desire*. New York: Columbia University Press, 1985.

Koszarski, Richard. *An Evening's Entertainment: The Age of the Silent Feature Picture, 1915–1928*. Berkeley: University of California Press, 1990.

Koven, Mikel J. *Blaxploitation Films*. Harpenden: Kamera, 2010.

Kraszewski, John. "Recontextualizing the Historical Reception of Blaxploitation: Articulations of Class, Black Nationalism, and Anxiety in the Genre's Advertisements." *The Velvet Light Trap* 50 (2002): 48–61.

Kronhausen, Phyllis and Erberhard Kronhausen. *The Sex People: A Professional View of Sensuous Celebrities and Erotic Entertainers—Who They Are and Why They Do It!* Chicago, IL: Playboy Press, 1975.

Krutnik, Frank. "'Be Moviedom's Guest in Your Own Easy-Chair': Hollywood Radio and Movie Adaptation." *Historical Journal of Film, Radio and Television* 33.1 (2013): 24–54.

Landis, Bill and Michelle Clifford. *Sleazoid Express*. New York and London: Fireside/Simon and Schuster, 2002.

Laseur, Carol. "Australian Exploitation Film: The Politics of Bad Taste." *Continuum* 5.2 (1992): 366–377.

Lawrence, Novonty. *Blaxploitation Films of the 1970s: Blackness and Genre*. New York: Routledge, 2008.

Le Goff, Jacques. *History and Memory*, translated by Steve Rendall and Elizabeth Claman. New York: Columbia University Press, 1992.

Lewis, Jon. *Hollywood vs. Hardcore: How the Struggle over Censorship Saved Hollywood*. New York: New York University Press, 2002.

Leyda, Julia. "Black-Audience Westerns and the Politics of Cultural Identification in the 1930s." *Cinema Journal* 42.1 (2002): 46–70.

Lithgow, James and Colin Heard. "Underground USA and the Sexploitation Market." *Films and Filming* (August 1969): 19–29.

Lott, Tommy L. "A No-Theory Theory of Contemporary Black Cinema." *Black American Literature Forum* 25.2 (1991): 221–236.

Lovell, Alan and Peter Kramer, eds. *Screen Acting*. London: Routledge, 1999.

Lowry, Ed. "Dimension Pictures: Portrait of a '70s Independent." *The Velvet Light Trap* 22 (1986): 74.

Luckett, Moya. "Sexploitation as Feminine Territory: The Films of Doris Wishman." In *Defining Cult Movies: The Politics of Oppositional Taste*, edited by Mark Jancovich, Antonio Lazaro Reboll, Julian Stringer, and Andy Willis, 142–156. Manchester: Manchester University Press, 2003.

Lyons, Scott Richard. "Billy Jack." In *Seeing Red: Hollywood's Pixeled Skins—American Indians and Film*, edited by LeAnne Howe, Harvey Markowitz, and Denise K. Cummings, 158–166. East Lansing: Michigan State University Press, 2013.

Marubbio, M. Elise. *Killing the Indian Maiden: Images of Native American Women in Film*. Lexington: University Press of Kentucky, 2006.

Mathijs, Ernest and Jamie Sexton. *Cult Cinema*. Oxford: Wiley-Blackwell, 2011.

Mathijs, Ernest and Xavier Mendik. "Cult Case Studies: Introduction." In *The Cult Film Reader*, edited by Ernest Mathijs and Xavier Mendik, 163–172. Maidenhead: Open University Press, 2007.

May, Kirse Granat. *Golden State, Golden Youth: The California Image in Popular Culture, 1955–1966*. Chapel Hill: University of North Carolina Press, 2002.

Mayer, Ruther. *Serial Fu Manchu: The Chinese Supervillain and the Spread of Yellow Peril Ideology*. Philadelphia: Temple University Press, 2014.

McDonald, Paul. *Hollywood Stardom*. Oxford: Wiley-Blackwell, 2013.

McNair, Brian. *Striptease Culture*. London: Routledge, 2002.

McNeil, Legs and Jennifer Osbourne (with Peter Pavia). *The Other Hollywood: The Uncensored Oral History of the Porn Film Industry*. New York: Regan Books/Harper Collins, 2006.

Mendik, Xavier, ed. *Peep Shows: Cult Film and the Cine-Erotic*. London and New York: Wallflower Press, 2012.

Morton, Jim, ed. *Re/Search: Incredibly Strange Films*. San Francisco: Re/Search Publications, 1986.

Muller, Eddie and Daniel Faris. *That's Exploitation! The Forbidden World of "Adults Only" Cinema*. London: Titan Books, 1996, 8–9.

Murray, Scott. "Australian Cinema in the 1970s and 1980s." In *Australian Cinema*, edited by Scott Murray, 71–146. North Sydney: Allen & Unwin, 1994.

Newman, Michael Z. "Indie Culture: In Pursuit of the Authentic Autonomous Alternative." *Cinema Journal* 48.3 (2009): 16–34.

Nora, Pierre. *Realms of Memory: Rethinking the French Past*, edited by Lawrence D. Kritzman, translated by Arthur Goldhammer, 3 vols. New York: Columbia University Press, 1968.

Nowell, Richard. "There's More than One Way to Lose Your Heart: The American Film Industry, Early Teen Slasher Films, and Female Youth." *Cinema Journal* 51.1 (2011a): 115–140.

Nowell, Richard. *Blood Money: A History of the First Teen Slasher Cycle*. New York: Continuum, 2011b.

Nowell, Richard. "Targeting American Women: Movie Marketing, Genre History, and the Hollywood Women-in-Danger Film." *InMedia* 3 (2013), available at http://inmedia.revues.org/600 (accessed May 27, 2016).

Nowell, Richard. "'For Girls': Hollywood, the Date-Movie Market, and Early-1980s Teen Sex Comedies." *Post-Script* 33.2 (2014): 16–32.

O'Regan, Tom. "Cinema Oz: The Ocker Films." In *The Australian Screen*, edited by Albert Moran and Tom O'Regan, 75–98. New York: Penguin Books, 1989.

Oberholtzer, Ellis P. *The Morals of the Movies*. Philadelphia: Penn Publishing, 1922, 56–57.

Olney, Ian. *Euro Horror: Classic European Horror Cinema in Contemporary American Culture*. Bloomington and Indianapolis: Indiana University Press, 2013.

Ongiri, Amy Abugo. "'He Wanted to Be Just Like Bruce Lee': African Americans, Kung Fu Theater, and Cultural Exchange at the Margins." *Journal of Asian American Studies* 5.1 (2002): 31–40.

Osgerby, Bill. "Sleazy Riders: Exploitation, 'Otherness,' and Transgression in the 1960s Biker Movie." *Journal of Popular Film and Television* 31.3 (2003): 98–108.

Paasonen, Susanne. "Epilogue: Porn Futures." In *Pornification: Sex and Sexuality in Media Culture*, edited by Susanna Paasonen, Kaarina Nikunen, and Laura Saarenmaa, 161–170. Oxford: Berg, 2007.

Paasonen, Susanna. *Carnal Resonance: Affect and Online Pornography*. Boston: MIT Press, 2011.

Paasonen, Susanna and Laura Saarenmaa. "The Golden Age of Porn: Nostalgia and History in Cinema." In *Pornification: Sex and Sexuality in Media Culture*, edited by Susanna Paasonen and Laura Saarenmaa, 23–33. Oxford: Berg, 2007.

Perren, Alisa. "A Big Fat Indie Success Story? Press Discourses Surrounding the Making and Marketing of a Hollywood Film." *Journal of Film and Video* 56.2 (2004): 18–31.

Pike, Andrew and Ross Cooper. *Australian Film 1900–1977: A Guide to Feature Film Production*. Melbourne: Oxford University Press, 1980.

Price, John A. "The Stereotyping of North American Indians in Motion Pictures." *Ethnohistory* 20.2 (1973): 153–171.

Puchalski, Steven. *Slimetime: A Guide to Sleazy, Mindless Movies*. Revised and Updated Edition. Manchester: Critical Vision/Headpress, 2002.

Quinn, Eithne. *A Piece of the Action: Race and Labor in the Post-Civil Rights Film Industry*. New York: Columbia University Press, forthcoming.

Radner, Hilary. *Neo-feminist Cinema: Girly Films, Chick Flicks, and Consumer Culture*. New York: Routledge, 2011.

Raheja, Michelle H. *Reservation Reelism: Redfacing, Visual Sovereignty, and Representations of Native Americans in Film*. Lincoln: University of Nebraska Press, 2010.

Ray, Fred Olen. *The New Poverty Row: Independent Filmmakers as Distributors*. London: McFarland, 1991.

Read, Jacinda. "The Masculinity of Cult: From Fan-Boys to Academic Bad-Boys." In *Defining Cult Movies: The Cultural Politics of Oppositional Taste*, edited by Mark Jancovich, Antonio Lázaro Reboll, Julian Stringer, and Andy Willis, 54–70. Manchester: Manchester University Press, 2003.

Richardson, Niall. *Transgressive Bodies: Representations in Film and Popular Culture*. Surrey: Ashgate Publishing, 2012.

Ricoeur, Paul. *Time and Narrative*, Vol 1. Chicago: University of Chicago Press, 1984.

Robinson, Jeffrey. "Good Evening—Here Are the Nudes." *Penthouse* 7.12 (1973): 87–92.

Rodowick, D. N. *The Virtual Life of Film*. Cambridge, MA and London: Harvard University Press, 2007.

Romao, Tico. "Engines of Transformation: An Analytical History of the 1970s Car Chase Cycle." *New Review of Film and Television Studies* 1.1 (2003): 31–54.

Rosenstone, Robert A. *Visions of the Past: The Challenge of Film to Our Idea of History*. Cambridge, MA: Harvard University Press, 1995.

Rosenzweig, Sidney. "The Dark Night of the Screen: Messages and Melodrama in the American Movie." *American Quarterly* 27.1 (1975): 88–98.

Sarris, Andrew. "Notes on the Auteur Theory in 1962." *Film Culture* 62/3 (Winter, 1962): 1–8.

Schaefer, Eric. *Bold! Daring! Shocking! True! A History of Exploitation Films, 1919–1959*. Durham and London: Duke University Press, 1999.

Schaefer, Eric. "'I'll Take Sweden': The Shifting Discourse of the 'Sexy Nation' in Sexploitation Films." In *Sex Scene: Media and the Sexual Revolution*, edited by Eric Schaefer. Durham and London: Duke University Press, 2014.

Schiller, Dawn. *The Road through Wonderland: Surviving John Holmes*. Aurora, IL: Medallion Press, 2010.

Sconce, Jeffrey. "'Trashing' the Academy: Taste, Excess and an Emerging Politics of Cinematic Style." *Screen* 36.4 (1995): 371–393.

Segrave, Kerry. *Drive-In Theaters: A History from Their Inception in 1933*. Jefferson, NC: McFarland, 1992.

Shirley, Graham and Brian Adams. *Australian Cinema: The First Eighty Years*. Sydney: Currency Press, 1989.

Sickels, Robert C. "1970s Disco Daze: Paul Thomas Anderson's *Boogie Nights* and the Last Golden Age of Irresponsibility." *Journal of Popular Culture* 35.4 (2002): 49–60.

Sieving, Christopher. *Soul Searching: Black-Themed Cinema from the March on Washington to the Rise of Blaxploitation*. Middletown, CT: Wesleyan University Press, 2011.

Singer, Ben. "Serials." In *Oxford History of World Cinema*, edited by Geoffrey Nowell-Smith, 105–110. Oxford: Oxford University Press, 1996.

Singer, Ben. *Melodrama and Modernity: Early Sensational Cinema and Its Contexts*. New York: Columbia University Press, 2011.

Slotkin, Richard. *Gunfighter Nation: The Myth of the Frontier in Twentieth-Century America*. New York: Atheneum, 1992.

Smith, Clarissa. "Reel Intercourse: Doing Sex on Camera." In *Hard to Swallow: Reading Pornography Onscreen*, edited by Darren Kerr and Claire Hines, 194–214. London: Wallflower, 2012.

Smith, Clarissa. "'It's Important You Don't Smell a Suit on It': Aesthetics of Alt Porn." In *Porn after Porn: Contemporary Alternative Pornographies*, edited by Enrico Biasin, Giovanna Maina and Federico Zecca, 57–82. Milano-Udine: University of Udine Press, 2014.

Smith, Jacob. "Sound and Performance in Stephen Sayadian's *Night Dreams* and *Café Flesh*." *The Velvet Light Trap* 59 (Spring, 2007): 15–29.

Smith, Julian. "Between Vermont and Violence: Film Portraits of Vietnam Veterans." *Film Quarterly* 26.4 (1973): 10–17.

Smith, Phyll. "'Poisoning Their Daydreams': American Serial Cinema, Moral Panic and the British Children's Cinema Movement." *lwu: Literatur in Wissenschaft und Unterricht* XLVII 1/2 (2014): 39–54.

Smith, Sherry L. *Hippies, Indians, and the Fight for Red Power*. New York: Oxford University Press, 2012.

Snelson, Tim. "'From Grade B Thrillers to Deluxe Chillers': Prestige Horror, Female Audiences, and Allegories of Spectatorship in *The Spiral Staircase* (1946)." *New Review of Film and Television Studies* 7.2 (2009): 173–188.

Snelson, Tim. *Phantom Ladies: Hollywood Horror and the Home Front*. New Brunswick: Rutgers University Press, 2015.

Sobchack, Vivian. *Carnal Thoughts, Embodiment and Moving Image Culture*. Berkeley and Los Angeles: University of California Press, 2004.

Stamp Lindsey, Shelley. "Is Any Girl Safe? Female Spectators at the White Slave Films." *Screen* 37.1 (1996): 1–15.

Stamp, Shelley. *Movie-Struck Girls: Women and Motion Picture Culture after the Nickelodeon*. Princeton: Princeton University Press, 2000.

Stanfield, Peter. *Hollywood, Westerns and the 1930s: The Lost Trail*. Exeter: University of Exeter Press, 2001.

Stanfield, Peter. *Horse Opera: The Strange History of the 1930s Singing Cowboy*. Urbana: University of Illinois Press, 2002.

Stanfield, Peter. "Intent to Speed: Cyclical Production, Topicality, and the 1950s Hot Rod Movie." *New Review of Film and Television Studies* 11.1 (2013): 34–55.

Stanfield, Peter. *The Cool and the Crazy: Pop Fifties Cinema*. New Brunswick: Rutgers University Press, 2015.

Stevens, Brad. *Abel Ferrara: The Moral Vision*. Guildford: FAB Press, 2004.

Stevenson, Jack, ed. *Fleshpot: Cinema's Myth Makers and Taboo Breakers*, 2nd edition. Manchester: Headpress, 2002.

Stevenson, Jack. "Grindhouse and Beyond." In *From the Arthouse to the Grindhouse: Highbrow and Lowbrow Transgession in Cinema's First Century*, edited by John Cline and Robert G. Weiner, 129–152. Maryland: Scarecrow Press, 2010a.

Stevenson, Jack. *Scandinavian Blue: The Erotic Cinema of Sweden and Denmark in the 1960s and 1970s*. Jefferson, North Carolina: McFarland, 2010b.

Sugar, Jennifer and Jill C. Nelson. *John Holmes: A Life Measured in Inches*. Albany, GA: Bear Manor Media, 2008.

Taylor, Drew Hayden. "What Ever Happened to Billy Jack?" In *Readings in Aboriginal Studies, Vol. 4: Images of the Indian—Portrayals of Native People*, edited by Joe Sawchuk, 173–182. Brandon, Manitoba: Bearpaw Publishing, 1995.

Thorsen, Isak. "Family Porn—The Zodiac Film: Popular Comedy with Hard-Core Sex." *Journal of Scandinavian Cinema* 4.3 (2014): 289–304.

Thrower, Stephen. *Nightmare USA: The Untold Story of the Exploitation Independents*. Guilford: FAB Press, 2007.

Tibbals, Chauntelle Ann. "Gonzo, Trannys, and Teens—Current Trends in US Adult Content Production, Distribution, and Consumption." *Porn Studies* 1.1–2 (2014): 127–135.

Tompkins, Joe. "Bids for Distinction: The Critical-Industrial Function of the Horror Auteur." In *Merchants of Menace: The Business of Horror Cinema*, edited by Richard Nowell, 203–214. New York: Bloomsbury Academic, 2014.

Tudor, Andrew. *Monsters and Mad Scientists: A Cultural History of the Horror Movie*. Oxford: Basil Blackwell Ltd., 1989.

Turner, Graeme. *Film as Social Practice*. Abingdon: Routledge, 2006.

Vela, Raphael. *With the Parents' Consent: Film Serials, Consumerism and the Creation of the Youth Audience*. Unpublished PhD thesis. University of Wisconsin-Madison, 2000.

Walker, Johnny. *Contemporary British Horror Cinema: Industry, Genre and Society*. Edinburgh: Edinburgh University Press, 2016.

Waller, Gregory A. "Auto-Erotica: Some Notes on Comic Softcore Films for the Drive-In Circuit." *Journal of Popular Culture* 17.2 (1983): 135–141.

Walters, Trevor. *The Picture Palaces of Melbourne: A History of Melbourne's Picture Theatres*. Melbourne: Trevor Walters, 2003.

Ward, Reneé. "Black Films, White Profits." *The Black Scholar* 7.8 (1976): 13–24.

Wasser, Frederick. "Four Walling Exhibition: Regional Resistance to the Hollywood Film Industry." *Cinema Journal* 34.2 (1995): 51–65.

Watson, Thomas Joseph. "There's Something Rotten in the State of Texas: Genre, Adaptation and *The Texas Vibrator Massacre*." *Journal of Adaptation in Film and Performance* 6.3 (2013): 387–400.

Weldon, Michael. *The Psychotronic Encyclopedia of Film*. London: Plexus, 1983.

Weldon, Michael. *The Psychotronic Video Guide*. London: Titan Books, 1996.

Williams, Linda. *Hard Core: Power, Pleasure and the "Frenzy of the Visible."* London: Pandora, 1990.

Wilson, Jake. *Mad Dog Morgan*. Strawberry Hills: Currency Press, 2015.

Winston-Dixon, Wheeler. *Lost in the Fifties: Recovering Phantom Hollywood*. Carbondale: Southern Illinois University Press, 2005.

Wood, Robin. *From Vietnam to Reagan … and Beyond: Expanded and Revised Edition*. New York: Columbia University Press, 2003.

Wyatt, Justin. "From Roadshowing to Saturation Release: Majors, Independents, and Marketing/Distribution Innovations." In *The New American Cinema*, edited by Jon Lewis, 64–86. Durham and London: Duke University Press, 1998.

Wyatt, Justin. *High Concept: Movies and Marketing in Hollywood*. Austin: University of Texas Press, 1994.

Wyatt, Justin. "Revisiting the 1970s' Independent Distribution and Marketing Strategies." In *Contemporary American Independent Film: From the Margins to the Mainstream*, edited by Christine Holmund and Justin Wyatt, 229–244. London: Routledge, 2005.

Contributors

Dean Brandum is completing his PhD at Deakin University, Australia, developing a methodology of determining the viability of British films at the US box office in the 1960s. He has taught cinema studies at several universities, has written for a number of publications, and maintains the website www.technicolouryawn.com, which details the history of film exhibition in his native Melbourne.

David Church is Lecturer in Comparative Cultural Studies at Northern Arizona University. He specializes in genre studies and histories of film distribution and reception. His books include *Grindhouse Nostalgia: Memory, Home Video, and Exploitation Film Fandom* (2015) and *Disposable Passions: Vintage Pornography and the Material Legacies of Adult Cinema* (Bloomsbury, 2016).

Austin Fisher is Senior Lecturer in Film and Television Studies at Bournemouth University in the UK, author of *Radical Frontiers in the Spaghetti Western* (2011) and editor of *Spaghetti Westerns at the Crossroads* (2015). He serves on the Editorial Boards of the *Transnational Cinemas* and *[in]Transition* journals, and is Co-Chair of the SCMS "Transnational Cinemas" Scholarly Interest Group.

Kevin Heffernan teaches media history in the Division of Film and Media Arts at Southern Methodist University. His writings on exploitation film, European and Asian cinema, and pornography have been published in many journals and anthologies. He is the author of *Ghouls, Gimmicks and Gold: Horror Films and the American Movie Business, 1952–1968* (Duke University Press, 2007) and is currently writing a history of American moving-image pornography from 1994 to the present, which is tentatively titled *Channels of Pleasure* and another book tentatively titled *From Beavis and Butt Head to Tea Party Nation: Dumb White Guy Politics and Culture in America*.

Alexandra Heller-Nicholas is a film critic, writer, and researcher from Melbourne, Australia. She is a coeditor of the journal *Senses of Cinema*, cohost of the Triple R radio film program *Plato's Cave*, and author of books including *Rape-Revenge Films: A Critical Study* (McFarland, 2011), *Found Footage Horror Films: Fear and the Appearance of Reality* (McFarland, 2014), and *Devil's Advocates: Suspiria* (Auteur, 2015). She is also Adjunct Research Fellow at the Institute of Social Research at Swinburne University of Technology.

Neil Jackson is Lecturer in Film Studies at the University of Lincoln, UK. He has published on horror and exploitation cinema in a variety of books and journals and is coeditor of *Snuff: Real Death and Screen Media* (Bloomsbury, 2016). He is currently preparing a study of Hollywood and its representation of the adult film industry.

Richard Nowell teaches at Charles University in Prague. He is the author of *Blood Money: A History of the First Teen Slasher Film Cycle* (Continuum, 2011) and the editor of *Merchants of Menace: The Business of Horror Cinema* (Bloomsbury, 2014), and he has published articles in various journals including *Cinema Journal*, the *Journal of Film & Video*, *Postscript*, and the *New Review of Film & Television Studies*.

Robert J. Read received his PhD from McGill University and is currently an independent film scholar. His research focuses on the emergence of the low-budget independent film industry during the silent era and its parallel development with the Hollywood studio system. He is presently finishing a book entitled *A Squalid-Looking Place: Independent Poverty Row Film Production, 1929–1940*.

Clarissa Smith is Professor of Sexual Cultures in the Centre for Research in Media and Cultural Studies at Sunderland University. She researches sex, sexual identities, and sexual representations in contemporary culture, and is a founding editor of the journal *Porn Studies*.

Phyll Smith is a lecturer/researcher at the University of East Anglia. His research focuses on the cultural politics of fringe and ephemeral media, particularly their seriality and discursive functions. He has written extensively on British sound Serials, and is the author of *The Last English Revolutionary: Tom Wintringham 1898–1949* (Sussex Academic/London School of Economics) and a forthcoming book *Tijuana Bibles and the Pornographic Re-imagining of Hollywood*. His PhD thesis is titled *American Sound Serials: Their Audience and Exhibition* and he coordinates the research network on To Be Continued ... Serials, series and sequential viewing.

Peter Stanfield is Professor of Film at the University of Kent. He has written two monographs on the Western and a substantial body of research on popular music and film. Recent publications include *Maximum Movies-Pulp Fictions: Film Culture and the Worlds of Samuel Fuller, Mickey Spillane, and Jim Thompson* (Rutgers, 2011) and *The Cool and the Crazy: Pop Fifties Cinema* (Rutgers, 2015). He is currently working on a full-scale study of serial production and the 1960/70s biker movie cycle.

Johnny Walker is Senior Lecturer in Media at Northumbria University. He is the author of *Contemporary British Horror Cinema: Industry, Genre and Society* (Edinburgh University Press, 2015), coeditor of *Snuff: Real Death and Screen Media* (Bloomsbury, 2016), and cofounder of Bloomsbury's Global Exploitation Cinemas book series.

Currently, he is working on a history of video rental culture in 1980s Britain for the University of Exeter Press.

Glenn Ward lectures in the history of art and design at the University of Brighton. His main research interests lie in the visual cultures of cinema and in the interrelationships between avant-garde, marginal, and popular screen cultures. His work has appeared in collections such as *The Transnational Fantasies of Guilermo del Toro* (Palgrave, 2015) and *Latsploitation, Exploitation Cinemas, and Latin America* (Routledge, 2009).

Index

Note: locators followed by 'n' refer to notes

Abel, Richard 49 n.45
Academy Pictures Corporation 96
Adams, Brian 168, 178 n.18, 179 n.40
Adams, Philip 168, 177 n.1, 178 n.17
Addio Zio Tom (Jacopetti & Prosperi, 1971) 59
Adios Amigo (Williamson, 1976) 184
adult films 7, 138–9, 142 n.9, 145–7, 150, 152, 155–6, 158 n.4, 226, 230
The Adventures of Barry McKenzie (Beresford, 1972) 169, 171
African Americans 8, 182–3, 197–200, 208, 212, 215 n.34
Agutter, Jenny 175
Alcatraz occupation 198, 200, 214 n.17
Al Dubin song "42nd Street" 20
Aleiss, Angela 213 n.8, 214 n.19
Alilunas, Peter 143 n.24
Alison's Birthday (Coughlan, 1979) 173
All Tribes and the American Indian Movement (AIM) 197, 200, 206, 209
Allen, Robert 49 n.52
Allmer, Patricia 10 n.15
Altman, Rick 33, 47 n.8
alt-porn stars 225
Alvin Purple (Burstall, 1973) 169
America Graffiti (Lucas, 1973) 93
American automobile industry 99, 106 n.21
American Dream 17
American Gigolo (Schrader, 1980) 65
American Grindhouse (Drenner, 2010) 15–18, 20, 23–4, 26–7
American horrors 17
American International Pictures 109, 132, 202
Anderson, Gotha 132–3, 136
Anderson, Paul Thomas 148, 159 n.20
Angels Die Hard (aka *Violent Angels*, 1970) 74

Angels from Hell (Kessler, 1968) 74–5
Angels Hard as They Come (Viola, 1972) 74
Angels' Wild Women (Adamson, 1972) 74–5
Angel Unchained (Madden, 1970) 74–5, 80, 82–4, 89 n.10, 91 nn.51–2, 91 n.54, 91 nn.56–8
Angry Joe Bass (Reeves, 1976) 198, 203, 210–12
Animal House (Landis) 123
anti-porn protests 21, 25
Antonio, Sheril D. 214 n.19
Apache Blood (Piehl, 1975) 199
Artforum magazine 24
Ashton, Paul 177 n.8
Atamian, Armand 148
audiences
 adult 101
 American Grindhouse's 15–16, 24
 Australian context 62–3, 68, 164, 169, 174, 176
 "biker movies" 6, 87
 black 181, 184, 189–93, 197–8
 consumption habits 6–7, 150
 cult movies 219
 drive-in 56, 62, 96, 105, 110, 113, 121
 42nd Street in 1933 1
 girls as 116–17
 lower-class 183
 in Melbourne 57–9, 61
 middle-class 32, 34–6, 38, 40, 42, 45–6
 non-normative viewing 38–41
 Ozploitation films 163
 paracinematic 24, 171
 porn film 225–6, 230–2
 scary movies 119
 theater-going 2, 4, 23, 57–8
 transient 20
 unruly 31–47
 urban 185

working-class 38–9, 73, 87, 183, 210
youth/younger 83, 102
Austin, Bruce A. 127 n.97
The Australian Film Commission (AFC) 168–70
Australian Film Development Corporation (AFDC) 168
auteurism 14, 25
Autopsy (Crispino, 1975) 67
Autry, Gene 183

B.A.D. Cats (television program, 1980) 103
Bad Girls Go to Hell (Wishman, 1965) 138
Bailey, Jason 167, 177 n.12
Baker/Malco theater 43
Barbarella (Vadim, 1968) 175
Barefoot, Guy 49 n.48
Barnaby Jones (series) 174
Barry McKenzie Holds His Own 171–2
Basket Case (Henenlotter, 1982) 22
Bazin, André 185, 194 n.24
Behind the Door (Hellman, 1974) 68
Behind the Green Door (Mitchel and Mitchel, 1972) 138
Bel Ami (Torn, 1977) 141
Bellanta, Melissa 177 n.7
Bengtsson, Anders 123 n.10
Benson-Allott, Caetlin 232, 233 n.11
Bermel, Albert 134, 137, 142 n.10, 142 n.12, 142 n.16
Besson, Luc 11 n.26, 177 n.13
Better Theatres 31, 47 n.1
Betz, Mark 19, 29 n.26, 48 n.23, 124 n.19
Biasin, Enrico 233 n.7, 233 n.11
Bickle, Travis 23
biker movie
  AIP's production plan 74, 76–7, 79–80, 82–5, 89 n.18, 90 n.32
  audience 73–4, 76, 78, 80, 83–5, 87–8
  beach vs. 76, 78
  consumption 73–4
  creative alliances 85–6
  GP rating 83–4
  low-budget 81, 86–7
  post-1967 90 n.27
  press reception 77, 83–4, 87
  production principles 87
  protest films 76–7, 83
  serial production 73–89
  seriality components 74–5, 85
  soundtrack 78, 86, 90–1 n.50
Bikers in Outer Space 76
Billy Jack (Laughlin, 1971) 198, 202–9, 212, 214 n.27, 214–15 n.30
Billy Jack Goes to Washington (Laughlin, 1977) 206–7
Birds Do It, Bees Do It (Noxon & Rosten, 1974) 61
Björklund, Elisabet 142 n.5
Black Angels (Merrick, 1971) 74
Black Christmas (Clark, 1974) 4, 175
Black, David 152, 160 n.36
Black Emanuelle Goes East (D'Amato, 1976) 67
Blacklight Beauty (Pulse, 2006) 219, 223, 226–9, 232, 233 n.19
Black Power movement 8, 185
Black Sunday (Frankenheimer, 1977) 64
Blainey, Geoffrey 165, 173, 178 n.37
blaxploitation westerns
  black audiences 184, 189–92, 193 nn.14–15, 195 n.38, 197–8, 213 n.6
  black characters 181–92
  black identity 183, 185–7, 189
  cult film circles 2, 10 n.9
  cultural moment 8, 181–4, 187–9, 191–21
  early to mid-1970s 8, 182
  genre categories 184, 187, 192
  integrationism 185, 199, 208, 212
  low-budget 184, 187
  racism 182–92, 193 n.14, 195 n.38
  self-reflexivity indications 191
  separatism 182, 185
  target audiences 181, 185, 192
  transcultural influences 199
Blood for Dracula (Morrissey, 1974) 65
Blood Feast (Lewis, 1963) 17
Bloody Mama (AIP) 83
Blowup (Antonioni, 1966) 175
The Blues Brothers (Landis, 1980) 93
Blu-rays 14–15, 25, 54, 69, 217
Bodroghkozy, Aniko 125 n.52
Bogart, Humphrey 158

Bogle, Donald 184–5, 191, 193 n.8, 194 n.19, 194 n.35
Bold! Daring! Shocking! True! A History of Exploitation Films (1919–1959) 15, 28 n.13, 71 n.15, 91 n.62, 124 n.30
Boldt decision 1974 210
Bonnie and Clyde (Penn, 1967) 187–8
Boogie Nights (Anderson, 1997) 29, 146, 148, 153–4, 159 nn.18–19
Bordellet/Bordello (Ege, 1972) 132–7
Bordwell, David 91 n.60
The Born Losers (Laughlin, 1967) 76, 78, 82–3, 202–6
Boss Nigger (Arnold, 1974) 8, 182, 188–92, 193–4 n.15, 194 n.27, 195 n.38
The Boston Globe (newspaper) 114, 184, 193 n.14
Bougie, Robin 152, 160 n.37
Bowser, Eileen 101, 106 n.27
Boxoffice 103, 104
Boym, Svetlana 23, 29 n.46
brand identity 107–9, 111–13, 116, 119–23
Brand, Simon 70 n.6
Brandum, Dean 4, 6, 53–70
Brick, Emily 10 n.15
Bring Me the Head of Alfredo Garcia (Peckinpah, 1974) 61
Bronze Buckaroo (Kahn, 1938) 183
Buck and the Preacher (Poitier, 1972) 192, 199
Bugs Bunny cartoons 101
Bullitt (Yates, 1968) 93
Bury Me an Angel (Peeters, 1972) 57, 74
Butch Cassidy and the Sundance Kid (Hill, 1969) 188
Byrd, Jodi A. 199, 212, 213 n.9, 215 n.37

Cameo-Royal 19
cameramen 34
Canal Street (New Orleans) 20
Canby, Vincent 95–6, 98, 101, 105 nn.8–9, 105 n.15, 106 n.18, 106 n.28, 113, 120, 126 n.63, 127 n.93
Canjels, Rudmer 74, 89 n.6
Cannibal Apocalypse (Margheriti, 1980) 67, 69
Cannibal Ferox (Lenzi, 1981) 53–4, 67, 70 n.4
cannibal films
  American screening 53–4, 70
  audience 62–3, 68
  drive-in 56, 62
  Italian 4, 6, 53–7, 70
  low-budget 53, 62
  mainstream 56–7, 59, 63, 68–70
  in Melbourne (Australia) 54–8, 65–7, 70
Cannibal Holocaust (Deodato, 1980) 53–4, 67–9
Cannonball (Bartel, 1976) 94, 97, 100
The Cannonball Run (Needham, 1981) 103
Cante, Rich 235 n.46
Canuxploitation 93
carsploitation 6, 93
  audience appeal 96, 99–102, 104–5
  chases and crashes 104
  choice of cars 96, 99–104
  comedy in 101–5
  "country" films 8, 96–7
  crashes 93, 100–1, 104
  demolitions 94, 100–3, 105
  destruction of cars 94, 98–105
  drive-in audiences 95–6, 98, 105
  low-budget films 93, 95, 98, 105
  mainstream 93, 103, 107–12, 114, 116–17, 119, 121–2
  mid-1970s 93
  PG rating 101, 104–5
  police cars 100–2, 104
  regional production 94–8, 105
  repetition and imitation 103, 105
  stunts 98, 100–1
  topicality 94
  violence 101, 105
The Cars that Ate Paris (Weir, 1974) 176
The Case of the Smiling Stiffs (Cunningham, 1973) 61–2
Caughie, John 233 n.15
C.C. and Company (Robbie, 1970) 75
Chaffey, Don 182, 189
The Chain Reaction (Barry, 1980) 173
Cha-Jua, Sundiata Keita 213 n.6
Chambers, Marilyn 152, 160–1 n.42
Champagne, John 226–7, 233 n.13, 234 n.38, 235 n.57
Champlin, Charles 75

Charley One-Eye (Chaffey, 1973) 182, 186–7, 189–91, 194 n.30
Chato's Land (Winner, 1972) 199
The Cheaters (Martino, 1975) 67
Chiarella, Peter 29 n.48, 29 n.50
Chicago Tribune 114, 190, 193–4 n.15
Chinn, Bob 147, 152, 159 n.13
CHiPs (television program, 1977-1983) 103
Chong, Sylvia Shin Huey 213 n.6
Chopper 219
The Choppers (Jason, 1961) 93
Christiane F (Edel, 1981) 68
Chrome and Hot Leather (Frost, 1971) 83
Church, David 2, 5, 8, 10 n.8, 10 n.10, 10 n.15, 10 nn.20–1, 11 n.22, 11 n.24, 11 n.27, 14, 25, 28 n.6, 28 n.12, 28 n.16, 31–3, 47 nn.2–3, 49 n.47, 54, 70 n.3, 124 n.12, 193 n.14, 197–212, 217, 231, 232 n.1, 233 n.8, 233 n.17, 234 n.40, 235 n.56
cinematographers 34
cinephilia 225, 231
Citizen Kane (Welles, 1941) 65
Claman, Elizabeth 28 n.10
Clark, Anna 165, 177 n.8
Class C cinemas 35
Class D cinemas 35
classical exploitation films 15–16
Clifford, Michelle 4, 9 n.2, 10 n.18, 10 n.21, 18, 29 n.41, 29 n.45, 29 n.49, 29 n.53, 30 n.62, 30 n.78, 51 n.72, 53–4, 70 n.2, 234 n.39, 234 n.42
Cline, John 3, 10 n.13, 48 n.23, 235 n.54
A Clockwork Orange (Kubrick, 1972) 62
Club Jenna 218, 222, 225
Club Venus 130
Comella, Lynn 232 n.3
Compton 19
Conley, Tom 9, 11 n.28
continuous houses 35
Cook, David 105 n.3
Cooper, Ross 168, 178 n.15, 178 n.18, 178 n.20
Corkin, Stanley 182, 193 n.5
Corvette Summer (Robbins, 1978) 93, 123
Cotten, Joseph 175
Crane, Jonathan Lake 223, 234 n.33

Crang, Mike 29 n.30, 29 n.33
Crash! (Band, 1976) 100
Cresswell, Tim 29 n.30
Crown International Pictures
 brand identity 107–9, 111–13, 116, 119–23
 cars in 113–16
 Crownsmanship label 107, 111–13, 123 n.4
 drive-in audience 108, 110, 113–16, 118–23
 exploitation cinemas 108–11, 113, 116–17, 119, 122–3
 flagship series 107–8, 110–13, 116–17, 119, 121–2, 123 n.4
 girls in 116–19
 historiography 108–11
 in-house production 107, 117
 junk foods sale 119–20
 mainstream movies 108–12, 114, 116–17, 119, 121–2
 marijuana complementing 121–2
 SoCal Drive-in movies 7, 107, 110, 116, 118, 122, 163
 The Pom Pom Girls Exhibitors Manual 123 n.3, 126 nn.68–9, 127 n.91, 128 n.109
 vehicular patronage characteristics 115, 118
Cry Blood, Apache (Starrett, 1970) 199
Cry of the Banshee 82
Csaba, Fabian Faurholt 123 n.10
Cult Cinema 9 n.5, 11 n.25
cult cinema 2, 7, 218, 226
cult film 2, 5, 8, 14, 18, 53, 164, 232
Cult Movies 13
Cummings, Denise K. 214 n.26
Cunningham, Stuart 178 n.31
Custer Died for Your Sins (Deloria Jr.) 200, 213 n.12
Cycle Savages (Brame, 1969) 75, 87–8

Damiano, Gerard 141, 158 n.4
Danish film industry
 Bedside series 129–32, 134–6, 141, 142 n.6
 censorship laws 130–1, 136, 141

contemporary masculinity 132
folk comedy 129–30
mainstream 129–31, 134, 141
pornography 130, 132, 134–5, 138–41
R-rating 138
sex films 129–41
Danish Film Institute 141
Danish Pastries 7, 129–30, 137–41
 (*I Jomfruens Tegn* (Karlsson, 1973)
Dawn of the Dead (Romero, 1978) 109
Dawn of the Mummy (Agrama, 1981) 69, 71 n.20
The Day after Halloween, The Day before Halloween 176
Dead End Drive-In (Trenchard-Smith, 1986) 172
Deadline Auto Theft (Halicki, 1983) 104
Death Proof (Tarantino, 2007) 27, 167, 176
Death Wish (Winner, 1974)) 204
Deep Red (Argento, 1975) 175
Deep Throat (Damiano, 1972) 138, 158 n.4, 219
Deliverance (Boorman, 1972) 219, 222, 225
Deloria, Philip J. 210, 213 n.12, 215 n.33
Deodato, Ruggero 53, 63–4
the Depression 36, 42
Dermody, Susan 170, 178 n.26, 178 n.30
Derrida, Jacques 25, 30 n.64
Det tossede paradis/Crazy Paradise (Axel, 1962) 129
de Valck, Marijke 235 n.55
DeVere Brody, Jennifer 213 n.4
Devil's Angels (Haller, 1967) 74, 76–8, 82, 89 n.18, 90 n.26
Devil's Island Lovers/Night of the Assassins (Franco, 74) 4
The Devil in Miss Jones (Damiano, 1973) 23, 138
The Devil's Rejects (Zombie, 2007) 219, 222
Didion, Joan 73, 86–7, 89 n.1, 91 n.63
Dilly (Soho) 19
Dimension Pictures 111, 125 n.42, 190, 194 n.27
Dirty Harry (Siegel, 1971) 117
Dirty Mary, Crazy Larry (Hough, 1974) 96–8, 101, 105 n.11, 105 nn.15–16, 106 nn.17–18

Disco Exorcist (Griffin, 2011) 27
Distribpix 139, 143 n.24
Dixon, Deborah 29 n.30
Django Unchained (Tarantino, 2012) 10 n.9, 194 n.16, 194 n.36
Doherty, Thomas 39, 47 n.9, 49 n.52, 125 n.50, 126 n.57
Donahue, Suzanne Mary 124 n.17
Don't Go in the House (Ellison, 1979) 111, 125 n.38
double bills 35, 39–40, 45–6
Double Nickels (Vacek, 1979) 97
Douglas, Kirk 155, 158
Dracula: Prisoner of Frankenstein/The Curse of Frankenstein (Franco, 1972/1973) 4
Dragstrip Riot (Bradley, 1958) 93
Dreadful Pleasures 13
drive-in movies
 biker movies 87, 95–6, 98
 carsploitation 105
 in Melbourne 55–6, 58–9, 61–2, 64, 67–70
 Ozploitation 169–70, 172
 past exhibition context 31
 porn 138–9
 SoCal 107–8, 110, 113–16, 118–22
 social functions 107–8
The Wild Angel 79
"The Dukes of Hazzard" (television program, 1979-1985) 103
DVDs 2, 14–15, 25, 69, 141, 165, 192, 217–18, 222, 229–31
Dworkin, Andrea 25, 30 n.61
Dyer, Richard 145, 151, 158 n.2, 160 n.27, 160 n.30

Easy Rider (Hopper, 1969) 17, 75, 83–4, 90–1 n.50, 112, 121
Eaten Alive (Lenzi, 1980) 53, 67, 69
Eaten Alive!: The Rise and Fall of the Italian Cannibal Film (Waddell, 2015) 69
Eat My Dust (Griffith, 1976) 97, 100, 102–3, 106 n.30
Eco, Umberto 75, 89 n.8

Edge of the City (Ritt, 1957) 185
Edwards, Eric 153
Edwards, Phil 70 n.8
Egan, Kate 10 n.19, 150, 160 n.28, 160 n.34
Eliza Fraser (Burstall, 1976) 170
Elsaesser, Thomas 235 n.55
Elvira Madigan (Widerberg, 1967) 65
Emanuelle in America (D'Amato, 1977) 67
Emmanuelle (Jaeckin, 1974) 62, 65, 68, 76, 138
Emmanuelle 3 (Pallardy, 1980) 68
Emmanuelle 5 (Borowczyk, 1987) 76
Engelhardt, Tom 181–3, 193 n.1, 193 n.4, 193 n.6
Enter the Dragon (Clouse, 1973) 176
Enter the Peepshow (Jenna, 2010) 225–6, 235 n.47
Entertainment Ventures, Inc. (EVI) 207
Ernst, Wolfgang 26, 30 n.65
erotic films 16, 18, 21–2, 53, 64, 129, 131–2, 134, 136, 138, 141, 143 n.21, 160 n.26, 223, 230
Escape 2000 176
E.T. (Spielberg, 1982) 65
Euro horror movies 3–4
Euro Horror: Classic European Horror Cinema in Contemporary American Culture (Olney) 3, 10 n.14
Exhausted: John C Holmes the Real Story (Vincent, 1981)
  cult stardom 150–1
  cultural artefacts 146–52, 156–8
  hard-core features 145–8, 151, 154
  Holmes's status 146–58
  male porn stardom 145–6, 151
  self-reflexive surface 146, 151
The Exorcist (Friedkin, 1973) 62
exploitation cinema
  advertising 25
  alternative model 7
  Australian context 172
  classical 15
  communicative dimensions 119
  cult cinema as 2, 7
  cultural mainstream 108
  economic aspects 17
  explicit references 232
  film consumption 9, 14
  gender and sex 116
  global histories 5–6
  grindhouse memories 22
  identification 3–4
  in 1970s 108–10, 113, 122
  in 1980s 69
  pornography 217
  race relations 8, 198
  sexploitation 19
  transcultural resonance 201
Expose Me Lovely (Weston, 1976) 139

Fair Game (Andreacchio, 1986) 176
Fantasm (Franklin, 1976) 169
Farber, Manny 24
Farewell Uncle Tom (Jacopetti & Prosperi, 1971) 59
Faris, Daniel 21, 29 n.35
The Fashionistas (Stagliano, 2002) 219
Fast Company (Cronenberg, 1979) 93
Fatal Visions 56
Ferle, Johannes 10 n.9, 194 n.16, 194 n.36
Film Daily 36, 40
Film and History Conference (Madison, 2015) 143 n.24
Film Threat (cult magazine) 3
films. *See also specific movies*
  biker 73–89
  blaxploitation 181–93
  cannibal 4, 6, 53–70
  carsploitation 93–105
  Danish 129–41
  exploitation (*See* exploitation cinema)
  grindhouse (*See* grindhouse)
  horror 3–4, 21, 53, 56, 63, 67–9, 76, 85, 109–10, 116, 164, 173–4, 176, 184, 217–18, 221–3
  Indiansploitation 197–212
  Ozploitation 8, 163–77
  porn 7, 9, 18–19, 21, 25, 217–32
  sexploitation 17, 19–21, 25, 27
  skin trade 19
Films and Filming 19, 29 n.27
Findlay, Michael 20, 27
Fireball 500 (Asher, 1966) 76, 93
First Avenue (Seattle) 20

first-run cinemas 32–3, 35, 37, 40–6, 56, 59, 69, 86, 130, 139, 184
Fisher, Austin 1–9, 10 n.9, 181–93
The FJ Holden (Thornhill, 1977) 93
Flaming Creatures 19
Flap (Reed 1970) 200–1
Flash Gordon's Trip to Mars (Beebe and Hill, 1938) 40, 50 n.58
Flesh for Frankenstein (Morrissey, 1973) 62
Fonda, Peter 75, 96
Forbidden Zone 219
Fort Lawton occupation 1970 200
The Four (Chan and Chun, 2011) 218
42nd Street
    black audiences 184
    consumption experience 53
    distribution rights 207
    drive-in circuits 80
    grindhouse concept 5, 13, 19–21, 23
    home viewing 21–2, 27
    imitative elements 226
    international audiences 1933 1
    title song 1, 9
Fragment of Fear (Sarafian, 1970) 175
Frazer, Sid 75
Freaks (Browning, 1932) 16
Freakshow (TV series, 2013) 225
Free Enterprise (Burnett, 1998) 151
Freebie and the Bean (Rush, 1974) 93
Freedom to Love (Kronhausens, 1969) 136
Friedberg, Anne 29 n.51
Friedman, Andrea 28 n.18
Friedman, Lester D. 105 n.3
"Friends" *Couples* (Nosseck, 1975) 117
From the Arthouse to the Grindhouse: Highbrow and Lowbrow Transgression in Cinema's First Century 3, 10 n.13, 48 n.23
Fuck the World 220

Gartman, David 99, 103, 106 n.19, 106 n.22, 106 n.33
The Georgia Peaches (Haller, 1980) 97
Gillis, Jamie 153, 160–1 n.42
Ginger (Shain, 1971) 111
Ginnane, Antony I. 175, 177
Girls with Open Lips (Dietrich, 1972) 67

Gleich, Joshua 213 n.7
The Glory Stompers (Lanza, 1967) 75, 78, 90 n.29
The Godfather (Coppola, 1972, 1974) 59, 62
Goldhammer, Arthur 29 n.32
Gomery, Douglas 41, 43–5, 47, 50 n.62, 50 n.69, 51 n.77
Gone in 60 Seconds (Halicki, 1974) 97, 100–1, 104–5, 105 n.12, 106 n.25
Gone with the Wind (Fleming, 1939) 62
Goodbye 42nd Street (Kern, 1986) 22
Gore, Chris 3–4, 10 n.13, 11 n.22
Gorfinkel, Elena 226, 233 n.17, 234 n.41
Grand Theft Auto (Howard, 1977) 97, 100, 102–3, 106 nn.31–2
Grease (Kleiser, 1978) 123
The Great Gatsby (Clayton, 1974) 59
The Great Lester Boggs (Thomason, 1974) 97
The Great Texas Dynamite Chase (Pressman, 1976) 95
Green Inferno (Roth) 69, 71 n.23
grind/grinding
    definition 33–4
    mill comparison with 33–5
    serial exhibition 35–7
grind house. *See also* exploitation films; grindhouse, early history
    afterimages 25–7
    American context 5, 14, 16–21
    audience 223
    contemporary relevance 5
    continuous theaters 35–7
    cultist viewing practices 14–15, 17, 19, 21, 24
    cultural distinctions, audience 33, 38–9, 45–6
    decline narratives 21–3
    exhibition strategies 31–46
    global presence 4–5, 13
    grindhouse films 3, 6, 13, 15, 22
    middle-class audience 32, 34–6, 38, 40, 42, 45–6
    mythology 1–4, 6, 8–9, 16, 44, 73, 99, 156, 176, 231
    1920s to 1950s serial production 46
    "paracinematic" mythology 4
    psychologized prejudices 40

recollection 21–3
revival 21–3
theaters 1, 54–5, 231–2
transnational aspects 4–5
grindhouse, early history
audience behaviors 31–46
B-picture 41–3
class segregation 32–46
continuous programming 31–2, 34–5, 37, 39, 41, 43, 45–6
cultural and economic history 31, 33, 38–9, 45–6
double-features 32, 40, 42–3
economic structure 31–3, 35, 37–8, 41, 44–7
exhibition context 31–46
factory process comparison with cinema 33–5
grind model 35–7
grind policy 31, 36–7, 42, 44
independent exhibitors 32, 36–7, 39–44, 46
non-normative perceptions 32–3, 38–41
Oxford English Dictionary etymology 31–2
screening practice 34–5, 37, 39–40, 42–6
serial practice 31–43, 45–7
sex films 38, 41, 44
terminology, use of 32–7
Grindhouse Follies 13
grindhouse nostalgia, concept 14, 33, 218, 231
Grindhouse Nostalgia:Memory, Home Video and Exploitation Film Fandom, 2, 10 n.8, 10 n.10, 10 nn.20–1, 11 n.22, 11 n.27, 28 n.12, 47 n.7, 47 nn.2–3, 70 n.3, 193 n.14, 233 n.17, 234 n.40, 235 n.56
Grindhouse Purgatory 23, 27
grinding 33–4, 37
Grizzly (Girdler, 1976) 95
the Grosvenor 55–6
Guerrero, Ed 184–5, 193 n.12, 194 n.20, 213 n.1
Guess Who's Coming to Dinner (Kramer, 1967) 185

Hagener, Malte 235 n.55
Halicki, H.B 97, 100–1, 104–5, 106 n.37
Hall, Sheldon 125 n.44
Hall, Terri 152
Hanby, Terry 123 n.10
Hard Core 135
The Harem 20
Harlem on the Prairie (Newfield, 1937) 183
Harlem Rides the Range (Kahn, 1939) 183
Harlequin (Wincer, 1980) 175–6
Harris, Paul 177 n.2, 177 n.5, 179 n.41
Hartley, Mark 164, 177
Haven, Annette 152, 155, 160–1 n.42
Hawkins, Joan 19, 28 n.25
Heard, Colin 19, 29 n.27
Heat (Morrissey, 1972) 57
Heffernan, Kevin 2, 7, 9 n.6, 129–42, 232 n.3
Heidenry, John 142 n.4
Hellcats (TV series, 1977) 111
Heller-Nicholas, Alexandra 2, 163–77
Hell of the Living Dead (Mattei, 1980) 69, 71 n.20
Hell's Angels '69 74, 76, 79–84, 89 n.7, 90 nn.35–6, 90 nn.38–44
Hells Angels on Wheels (Rush, 1967) 74
Hell's Belles 75
Hell's Bloody Devils 75, 88
Hell's Chosen Few 75
Helter Skelter (TV movie, 1976) 174
Hemmings, David 172–3, 175
Henenlotter, Frank 13, 21–2, 28 n.2, 214 n.28
Herbert, James 175
The Heroin Busters (Castellari) 175
Hester, Helen 232 n.4
Hewitt, John 177
The Hills Have Eyes (Craven, 1977) 109, 221
Higgins, Scott 50 n.61
Hillier, Jim 124 n.20
Hills, Matt 151, 160 n.34
Hinde, John 178 n.23
Hines, Claire 235 n.44
Hippies, Indians, and the Fight for Red Power (Smith) 200, 213 n.5
Hi-Riders (Clark, 1978) 100–1
Hoberman, J. 28 n.14

Hollows, Joanne 124 n.12
Hollywood
  large-budget films 16
  modes of production 17
  profits 44, 46–7
  stills photographers 34
Hollywood Boulevard (Arkush and Dante, 1976) 24–5
Hollywood Boulevard (Los Angeles) 20, 73, 158 n.4
Hollywood Citizen News 77, 80–1, 81, 90 n.24, 90 n.34, 90 n.42
Hollywood Reporter 77, 90 n.23, 91 n.66
Holmes, John C
  brand of celebrity 155
  career 152–3
  drug addiction 148
  heterosexual icon 153–4
  iconic status 147
  pornobiography 154
  role in US adult film industry 145–7, 149, 158
  sexual stamina 150–1
  St. Vincent's interview 156–7
Holmlund, Chris 143 n.24
Holmund, Christine 124 n.29
Holocaust 2000 (Martino, 1977) 176
home cinema 14, 21, 29 n.38
The Homesteader (Micheaux's drama, 1919) 183
home viewing 21–2, 26
horror films 3–4, 21, 56
Horton, Andrew 108, 113–14, 123 n.6, 126 n.65, 126 n.75
The Hot Rock (Yates, 1972) 59
Howard, Ron 97, 102–4
Howe, LeAnne 214 n.26
100 Rifles (Gries, 1969) 199, 213 n.7
Hunt, Leon 11 n.26, 167, 177 n.13
Hussey, Olivia 174
Hustler 218, 222, 234 n.29
Hutchings, Peter 10 n.15
Huxley, David 10 n.15
Huyssen, Andreas 14, 28 n.7, 28 n.9, 29 n.29, 30 n.72

Income Tax Assessment Act (Australia) 169
The Incredible Two Headed Transplant (Lanza, 1971) 15
Incredibly Strange Films (Henenlotter) 13, 22, 28 n.2
Independent Film Journal 98, 101
Indiansploitation 8, 197–9, 208, 210–12, 214 n.30, 215 n.36
  blaxploitation, comparison with 197–9, 201, 207–9, 212
  coda 212
  cycle's end 210–12
  emergence 197–9
  integrationism 198–9, 207–8, 212
  low-budget 197, 210
  political values 197–201, 203–12
  racial politics 197–200, 205, 207, 209–12, 214 n.19, 215 n.31, 215 n.34
  Red Power, depictions of 198–201, 203–7, 209–12
  separatism 198–200, 207–10, 212
  transcultural influences 197–202, 204–5, 212, 215 n.34
Inga (Sarno 1968) 137
Inglis, Ruth 70 n.1
International Alliance of Theatrical Stage Employees (IATSE)) 34
The Island (Ritchie, 1980) 64
Iwabuchi, Koichi 175, 179 n.42

Jacka, Elizabeth 170, 178 n.26, 178 n.30
Jackie Brown (Tarantino, 1997) 15
Jackson County Jail (Miller, 1976) 95
Jackson, Neil 7, 145–58
Jack the Zipper 8–9, 217–18, 223, 234 n.24
  All-Sex Release Award 219
  cinematic stylings 223–6
  history 222
  intertextual references 226–9
  as most dangerous director, XXX 218–19
  narrative possibilities 219–21
  soundtrack 229–32
  space and fantasy 229–32
  "wall-to-wall sex" films 231
Jacobs, Newton P. "Red" 109
Jancovich, Mark 28 n.5, 29 n.26, 48 n.23, 50 n.62, 124 n.19, 124 n.22, 124 nn.11–12, 127 n.80, 234 n.21

Jaws (Spielberg, 1975) 17
JCVD (El Mechri, 2008) 151
Jeffries, Herb 183
Jenkins, Henry 29 n.52
Jeremy, Ron 158 n.6
Johnny Firecloud (Castleman, 1975) 198, 203, 207–12, 214–15 n.30
Johnny Wadd series 152, 154–6
Johnson, Eithne 124 n.18, 126 n.78
Jones, Bethan 232 n.4
Jones, Sara Gwenllian 160 n.36
Joseph, Saul 75
Journey through Rosebud (Gries, 1972) 201, 203, 204
Juffer, Jane 233 n.12
The Junkman (Halicki, 1982) 104, 106 nn.35–6
Juno, Andrea 28 n.2, 29 n.36, 29 n.40
Justine and Juliette (Ahlberg, 1975) 137

Katzen, Jeremy 27
Kennis, Dan 75
Kerekes, David 58, 71 n.13
Kerr, Darren 235 n.44
Kick, Russ 234 n.39
Kill Bill: Volume One 165
Kilmer, Val 146
Kilpatrick, Jacquelyn 213 n.8, 214 n.29
King Cobra (Vivid, 2006) 221, 226, 232, 233 n.20, 234 n.23, 234 n.32
King, Rob 101, 106 n.27, 106 n.29
Kipnis, Laura 148, 159 n.14
Kitses, Jim 187, 194 n.25
Kleinhans, Chuck 147, 159 n.11
Klenotic, Jeff 39, 49 n.52
Klinger, Barbara 14, 18–19, 28 n.4, 28 n.8, 28 n.23, 190, 194 n.32
Koszarski, Richard 49 n.48
Koven, Mikel J. 184, 194 n.18
Kraddy, DJ 229
Kramer, Peter 160
Kraszewski, John 125 n.48, 190–1, 194 n.33
Kritzman, Lawrence D., 29 n.32
Kronhausen, Erberhard 130, 136, 142 n.5
Kronhausen, Phyllis 142 n.5
Krutnik, Frank 50 n.61

Laing, C.J. 152
Landis, Bill 1, 4, 9 n.1, 18, 22–4, 27, 29 n.41, 51 n.72, 53, 70 n.2
Landis, John 15–17, 20
Larsson, Mariah 141 n.1, 143 n.24
Laseur, Carol 172–3, 178 n.34
Last Cannibal World (Deodato, 1977) 53, 63–4, 68–9, 71 n.17
The Last Chase (Burke, 1981) 103
The Last Flight of Noah's Ark (Jarrott, 1980) 65
Las Vegas Lady (Nosseck, 1975) 117
late-night screenings 44
Latham Lecture, 1993 165
Lawrence, Novonty 184–5, 192, 194 n.17, 194 n.21, 195 n.37, 213 n.3
The Legend of Nigger Charley (Goldman, 1972) 8, 181–2, 185–91, 193, 193 n.2, 199
Le Goff, Jacques 28 n.10
Lehman, Peter 159 n.11, 159 n.14
Leslie, John 153
Lewis, Herschell Gordon 15, 17, 27
Lewis, Jon 126 n.76
Leyda, Julia 183–5, 193 n.9, 193 n.11, 194 n.23
Life (magazine) 73
The Life and Times of Grisly Adams (Friedenberg, 1974) 109
Lindsey, Shelley. Stamp 126 n.79
Lipstadt, Aaron 124 n.20
Lithgow, James 19, 29 n.27
Little Big Man (Penn, 1970) 182, 199
Lloyd Bacon 1
Lonely Hearts (Cox, 1982) 68
Long Weekend (Eggleston, 1978) 173
The *Los Angeles Herald Examiner* 77, 81
Los Angeles Theatres Association 35
Los Angeles Times 75–7, 81, 84, 89 n.20, 89 nn.7–9, 91 n.57, 110, 119, 123
The Losers ((aka *Nam Angels*) 74, 82
Lott, Tommy L. 213 n.4, 214 n.29
The Love Epidemic (Lamond, 1979) 169
Lovelace, Linda 152, 156
Lovell, Alan 160
Love Play: That's How We Do It (Wickman 1972) 136
Love Train for the S.S. (Payet, 1977) 67

low-budget movies 7, 13, 45, 53, 62, 81, 86–7, 93, 95, 98, 105, 130, 138, 184, 197, 210
Lowry, Ed 111, 125 n.42
Luckett, Moya 234 n.21
Lyons, Scott Richard 206, 214 n.26

Machete (Maniquis and Rodriguez, 2010) 27
Macon County Line (Compton, 1974) 95
Mad Dog Morgan (Mora, 1976) 170, 177 n.2
Mad Max series (Miller, 1979, 1981, 1985, 2015) 176
The Magnificent Seven (Fuqua, 1960) 82
Maina, Giovanna 233 n.7
mainstream exploitation 3, 7, 9, 17
Major Barbara (Pascal, 1941) 61
Make Them Die Slowly (Lenzi, 1981) 67
male sexuality 151, 223
Malibu Beach (Rosenthal, 1978) 107–8, 111–12, 116, 118, 120–1, 123 n.3, 123 n.7, 123 n.9, 125 n.38, 126 n.59, 126 n.68, 127 n.93, 128 n.109, 128 n.111, 128 nn.116–17
Maltby, Richard 32, 36–7, 47 n.4, 48 n.24, 49 n.52
A Man Called Horse (Silverstein, 1970) 199
The Manchurian Candidate (Frankenheimer, 1962) 175
Man from Deep River (Brandum, 1972) 4, 6, 53–4, 57–9, 61–4, 67–9
The Man from Hong Kong (Trenchard-Smith, 1975) 174, 176
Maniac (Lustig, 1981) 23
Margaret Herrick Library 76
Market Street (San Francisco) 20
Markowitz, Harvey 214 n.26
Marks, Laura Helen 143 n.24
Marubbio, M. Elise 213 n.8, 215 n.31
M.A.S.H (series) 174
The Master Touch (*Un uomo da rispettare*, Lupo, 1972) 93
Mathijs, Ernest 2, 5, 9 nn.4–5, 11 n.25
Mature Pictures 130, 138–9
Maturepix 137–42
May, Kirse Granat 112, 126 n.60
Mayer, Ruther 74, 84, 88, 89 n.4, 91 n.59, 91 n.69

McDonald, Paul 29 n.38, 160 n.27
McNair, Brian 149, 159 n.23
McNeil, Legs 159 n.8
Meese Commission 150
Melbourne (Australia)
  cannibal films 54–8, 65–7, 70
  CBD theatres 55–7, 69
  digital release 69
  double feature tradition 53, 55–6, 59, 61–3, 69–70
  exploitation strategies 54–9, 62–5, 67, 69–70
  grindhouse experience 53–4, 56, 64, 69
  R-classification 55–6
Mendik, Xavier 9 n.4, 28 n.20
Merewether, Charles 30 n.64
Mes nuits avec ... Alice, Pénélope, Arnold, Maud et Richard/Kinky Ladies of Bourbon Street (Lanzac, 1976) 139–41
Midnight Cowboy (Schlesinger, 1969) 20, 27
midnight movie cult 16, 24, 61, 119
mill and grind, comparison 33–5
Milligan, Andy 20
Mondo Cane (Jacopetti, Prosperi, Cavara, 1962) 58
Money, Constance 152, 160–1 n.42
Moran, Albert 178 n.23, 178 n.25, 178 n.31
The Morning After (Lumet, 1972) 138
Morton, Jim 13, 22, 28 n.2
Motion Picture Association of America 83, 110
Motion Picture Herald 39, 77, 80, 89 n.22, 90 n.39
Motion Picture Magazine 39, 49 n.49
Mountain of the Cannibal God (Martino, 1979) 64
Moving Violation (Dubin, 1976) 97, 100–2
Muirhead, Stuart 150, 160 n.29
Muller, Eddie 21, 29 n.35
Murray, Scott 168–9, 178 n.19, 178 n.22
My Brilliant Career (Armstrong, 1979) 170
Myiasis B. 229
My Name Is Bruce (Campbell, 2007) 151
My Tutor (Bowers, 1983) 109

Nader, Ralph 99, 106 n.21
Naked Angels, Nam Angels (aka *The Losers*) 74

The Naked Fist (Santiago, 1981) 67
National Association of Theater Owners 111
National Industrial Recovery Act 42
National Maximum Speed Law 1974 99
Native Americans 8, 181–2, 186–90, 192,
    197–201, 203–8, 210–12, 213 n.10,
    214–15 n.30, 215 n.31, 215 n.34
Navajo Joe (Corbucci, 1966) 199
nazisploitation 93
Neale, Steve 125 n.24
Nelson, Jill C. 147, 158 n.4
New Wave Hookers 219
New World Pictures 109, 111, 124 n.20,
    124 n.31
New York Post 23, 80, 90 n.33
The New York Ripper (Fulci, 1982) 23
New York Times 53, 73, 95–6, 102, 113–14,
    149, 182, 184, 190
Newman, Michael Z. 110, 125 n.33
Next of Kin (Williams, 1982) 173
Nice Dreams (Chong, 1981) 121, 128 n.114
A Nigger in the Woodpile (Weed, 1904) 192
The Night after Halloween 176
Night of Fear (Bourke, 1972) 173–4
Nightmares (Lamond, 1980) 173
Nikunen, Kaarina 160 n.40, 233 n.18
No Way Out (Mankiewicz, 1950) 185
Nobody Loves a Drunken Indian
    (Huffaker's novel 1967) 200
Nora, Pierre 25–6.29 n.32, 30 n.71
Not Quite Hollywood (Hartley's
    documentary) 164–8, 170, 177, 178
    n.24, 179 n.41, 179 n.43
Nowell, Richard 2, 7, 9 n.6, 50 n.62,
    107–22, 124 n.21, 124 nn.15–16,
    125 n.51, 125 n.53, 126 n.79, 127
    n.80, 127 n.89, 128 n.118
Nowell-Smith, Geoffrey 49 n.48
nunsploitation 93, 167
Nympho's Divine Obsession (Kaufman,
    1976) 20

Oberholtzer, Ellis P. 49 n.42, 49 n.44
Oceans 11 (Soderbergh, 1960) 81
ocker films 164, 169, 171
Ole Søltof 129–32, 134–5,
    137, 139
Olney, Ian 3–5, 10 n.14, 10 n.16

On Her Majesty's Secret Service (Hunt,
    1969) 174
Ongiri, Amy Abugo 213 n.6
O'Regan, Tom 178 n.23, 178 n.25, 178 n.31
Organization of Petroleum Exporting
    Countries (OPEC) 99
Osbourne, Jennifer 159 n.8
Osgerby, Bill 214 n.16
The Other Hollywood 146, 159 n.8
Ozploitation films 8, 93, 163–7
    American market 175–7
    casting 176–7
    categories 164–8
    cultural phenomena 163–7, 169–71,
        173–7
    drive-in 169–70, 172
    in 1870s-1980s 163
    exploitation films 163–5, 167–70,
        172–3, 176
    grindhouse strategy 174–7
    history and identity 168–70
    history wars 165–7, 173
    mainstream 165–7, 170–1, 173
    paracinema 171–4

Paasonen, Susanna 154, 160 n.40, 233
    n.14, 233 n.16, 233 n.18
Palladium 129–2, 134, 139, 141
paracinema 1–2, 4, 8, 13, 24, 171, 174, 225
Paramount 63, 74, 86, 121, 189
The Passion of the Christ (Gibson,
    2004) 17
Patrick (Franklin, 1978) 173–4, 176–7
Paulis, Tom 106 n.27
The Pawnbroker (Lumet, 1965) 57
Pearson, Roberta E. 160 n.36
Peep Shows: Cult Film and the Cine-Erotic
    18, 28 n.20
Penthouse 21
Peppard, George 175
Perren, Alisa 120, 128 n.112
Phillips, A.A. 166, 177 n.10
photographers 34, 57, 132, 191, 222
Pickaninnies Doing a Dance (Dickson,
    1894) 192
Pick-Up Summer (Mihalka, 1980) 107
Picnic at Hanging Rock (Weir, 1975) 163,
    170–1

Pike, Andrew 168, 178 n.15, 178 n.18, 178 n.20
Pink Angels (Brown, 1972) 74
Pit Stop (Hill, 1969) 93
Plantinga, Carl 225, 234 n.34
Pleasence, Donald 175
Plugg (Bourke, 1975) 169
Point of Terror (Nicol, 1973) 110
Policewomen (Frost, 1974) 117
Polk County Pot Plane (West, 1977) 98, 100, 105 nn.13–14
The Pom Pom Girls (Ruben, 1976) 107, 111–14, 117–18, 120, 122, 123 n.1, 123 n.3, 125 n.38, 126 n.68–9, 127 n.91, 128 n.109, 128 n.116
Pornografi—en musical/Pornography, a Musical (Ege, 1971) 132
pornography 7, 9, 18–19, 21, 25, 130, 135, 141, 146, 148–9, 151, 153–4, 158, 217, 219, 221–3, 225–6, 230–2. See also porn stardom
   classics 1970s and 1980s 218
   DVD production 217–18, 222, 227, 229–32
   female sexuality 223
   mainstream 145–7, 149–52, 157–8, 218, 221–2, 231
   vintage 217–18
Pornography in Denmark (de Renzy, 1970) 130
pornophilia 225
pornotopian 150
porn stardom 145, 150–1, 154, 158, 225, 229, 231
Poverty Row production 16, 42–4
Powell, Robert 175
Price, John A. 214 n.23
Principle Distribution Corporation (Sol Lesser) 42
Producers Distribution Corporation (PDC) 42
Prom Night (Lynch, 1980) 174
Psycho (Hitchcock, 1960) 15, 17
Psychotronic Encyclopedia of Film 13, 22, 24, 27, 28 n.1, 29 n.42
Psych-Out (Rush, 1968) 76
Puchalski, Steven 22, 26–7, 29 n.43, 29 n.47, 30 n.73
Pygmalion (Asquith, 1938) 61

Quinn, Eithne 213 n.3

Race for the Yankee Zephyr (Hemmings, 1981) 175
Radner, Hilary 117, 127 n.87
Raheja, Michelle H. 203, 213 n.2, 213 n.11, 214 n.18
Railsback, Steve 174
Rated X (Estevez, 1999) 154
Rau, Vivi 134–5
Ray, Fred Olen 213 n.10
Razorback (Mulcahy, 1984) 173–4
Read, Jacinda 14, 28 n.5
Read, Robert J. 6–7, 93–105
Reboll, Antonio Lázaro 28 n.5, 48 n.23, 234 n.21
Redneck County 97
Red Power movement 8, 197–201, 198–201, 203–7, 203–12, 209–12
Red Sonja (Fleischer, 1985) 18
Reems, Harry 153
Reese recommendations 150
Rendall, Steve 28 n.10
Republic Pictures (Herbert Yates) 42
Restivo, Angelo 235 n.46
Revenge of the Cheerleaders (Lerner, 1976) 117
Rhodes, John David 233 n.17
Richardson, Niall 234 n.37, 234 n.43
Ricoeur, Paul 15, 28 n.11
Riot on Sunset Strip (Dreifuss, 1967) 76
Risky Business (Brickman, 1983) 109
Roadgames (Franklin 1981) 174
Roadracers (Swerdloff, 1958) 93
The Road Warrior (Miller, 1981) 93
Robinson, Jeffrey 29 n.37
The Rocky Horror Picture Show (Sharman, 1975) 25, 127 n.97
Rodowick, D. N. 18–19, 21, 26, 28 n.22, 28 n.24, 29 n.38, 30 n.66
Rodox Corporation 130
Rodriguez, Robert 2, 13, 27, 69, 71 n.24, 167, 218
Romao, Tico 113, 126 n.65, 126 n.67
Romeo and Juliet (Zeffirelli. 1968) 174–5
Rosenbaum, Jonathan 28 n.64, 127 n.97

Rosenstone, Robert A. 192–3, 195 n.40
Rosenzweig, Sidney 214 n.25
Roxy Burlesk theater 20
Run, Angel, Run!, 74, 90 n.27

Saarenmaa, Laura 154, 160 n.40, 233 n.16, 233 n.18
Salmaggi, Bob 139
Salzer- Mörling, Miriam 123 n.10
Sandberg, Anders 130, 132–4
Sarris, Andrew 233 n.15, 234 n.26
Satan's Bed 138
Satan's Sadists (Adamson, 1969) 75, 79, 88
Saturday Review 77
The Savage Seven (Rush, 1968) 75, 83
Savages from Hell (Mawra, 1968) 75, 88
Sawchuk, Joe 214 n.22
Schaefer, Eric 2, 9 n.6, 15–17, 19, 28 n.13, 29 n.31, 71 n.15, 86–7, 91 n.62, 124 n.18, 124 n.30, 126 n.78, 143 n.21
Schepelem, Peter 141, 142 n.8
Schiller, Dawn 158–9 n.7
Schlock! The Secret History of American Movies (Greene, 2001) 15
Schroeder, Jonathan 123 n.10
Sconce, Jeffrey 2, 9 n.3, 9 n.7, 14, 24, 28 n.3, 125 n.32, 165, 171, 177 n.6, 178 n.32, 232 n.2
Scorpio Rising (Anger, 1963) 80
Scott, Casey 143 n.24
Sebastiane (Jarman 1976) 62, 71 n.16
second-run cinemas 16, 20, 37, 44, 56, 69, 82
Sedgwick, Eve. Kosofsky 160 n.39
Segrave, Kerry 127 n.92
Seka 147, 152, 155, 157
Selby Jr.Hubert 23
Serena 152
serial pictures 31–42–3, 46, 47 n.9, 49 n.46
sex exploitation 111
A Sex Odyssey (Tressler, 1974) 61
sexploitation films 17, 19–21, 25, 27, 61, 65, 117, 138, 164, 167, 169, 176, 207–8
Sex Rituals of the Occult (Caramico, 1970) 138
Sexton, Jamie 2, 5, 9 n.5, 11 n.25
Sexual Customs in Scandinavia (Knight, 1972) 138

Sexy Beast 219
Shaft (Parks, 1971) 184, 191, 197
Shirley, Graham 178 n.18, 179 n.40
Sickels, Robert C. 29 n.39
Sieving, Christopher 213 n.3
Silva, Henry 175
Silvera, Joey 153
Singer, Ben 49 n.41, 49 n.46, 49 n.48, 50 n.61
Sinister Cinema 13
Siskel, Gene 190–1, 194 n.30
The Sister-in-Law (Ruben, 1974) 117
skin trade films 19
Slater, David 58, 71 n.13
Slave of the Cannibal God (Martino, 1979) 64–5
Sleazoid Express:A Mind-Twisting Tour through the Grindhouse Cinema of Times Square 1, 4, 9 n.2, 10 n.18, 10 n.21, 18, 23, 29 n.41, 29 n.45, 29 n.49, 29 n.53, 30 n.62, 30 n.78, 51 n.72, 54, 70 n.2
Slimetime 27, 29 n.43, 29 n.47
Slotkin, Richard 182, 193 n.3
Smith, Clarissa 8, 217–32, 233 n.7
Smith, Jacob 235 n.48
Smith, Julian 214 n.24
Smith, Phyll 6, 31–47, 49 n.46
Smith, Sherry L. 200, 203, 211–12, 213 n.5
Smokey and the Bandit (Needham, 1977) 103, 105 n.8
Smokey and the Hot Wire Gang (Cardoza, 1979) 97
Snapshot (Lamond 1979) 176
Snelson, Tim 40, 50 n.60, 126 n.79
Snuff (Findlay and Findlay, 1976) 20, 221
Sobchack, Vivian 230, 235 n.51
SoCal Drive-in movies 7, 107, 110, 116, 118, 122, 163
Soldier Blue (Nelson, 1970) 182, 199
Something Weird Video 13, 27, 214 n.28
Sorcerer (Friedkin, 1977) 62
The Soul of Nigger Charley (Spangler, 1973) 182, 189
Soul Soldier (Cardos, 1972) 182, 195 n.39
Soya, Erik 129, 131
A Space Odyssey (Stanley, 1968) 62, 71 n.16

Speed Trap (Bellamy, 1977) 100
Speed Zone (Drake, 1989) 103
Spelvin, Georgina 152, 155
splatter films 1
Squealer (Hustler, 2005) 219, 222–6, 234 n.30
Stagecoach (Ford, 1939) 183, 186, 187
stag films 18
Staiger, Janet 85, 91 n.60
Stamp, Shelley 32, 38, 40, 47 n.5, 49 n.41
Stanfield, Peter 2, 6–7, 9 n.6, 47 n.9, 73–89, 93, 105 n.4, 113, 126 n.66, 183–4, 193 n.10
Star Wars (Lucas, 1977) 169
The Stepmother (Avedis, 1972) 117
Stevens, Brad 159 n.9
Stevens, Marc 153
Stevenson, Jack 18, 21, 28 n.19, 28 n.21, 29 n.34, 129, 137, 139, 142 n.2, 142 n.4, 142 n.6, 142 n.15, 143 n.22, 235 n.54
St Nelson, Jill 147, 158 n.4
Stokes, Melvyn 47 n.4, 49 n.52
Stone (Harbutt, 1974) 62
The Story of Joanna (Damiano, 1975) 20
The Story of the Kelly Gang (Tait, 1906) 163
Straw Dogs (Peckinpah, 1971) 204
The Street Fighter (Ozawa, 1974) 175
Stringer, Julian 28 n.5, 48 n.23, 234 n.21
Stuntgirl 219, 222–3
Stuntgirl 2 219
St. Vincent, Julia 148–9, 153–8, 159 n.17
Sugar, Jennifer 147, 158 nn.4–5, 158 n.7, 159 nn.16–17, 159 n.19, 161 n.43
Superchick (Forsyth, 1973) 117
Superstar, John Holmes (Colberg, 1979) 146
Supervan (Card, 1977) 93
Swank (magazine) 139
Sweet Sweetback's Baadasssss Song (van Peebles, 1971) 184, 197
The Survivor (Hemmings, 1980) 173, 175
Sytten/Soya's 17 131

Taboo 219
Take a Hard Ride (Margheriti, 1975) 182, 184, 199
Take Off (Davis and Weston, 1978) 139

Tamborini, Ron 50 n.62
Tandlæge på sengekanten/Bedside Dentist (Hilbard, 1971) 132
Tarantino, Quentin 2, 8–9, 10 n.9, 11 n.26, 13, 15, 27, 69–70, 71 n.24, 164–7, 175–7, 179 n.39, 194 n.16, 218
Tarrant, Shira 232 n.3
Tartan Films 4
Tartan Grindhouse 4
Taxi Driver (Scorsese, 1976) 20
Taylor, Drew Hayden 214 n.22
Taylor-Harman, Sarah 232 n.4
Tenser, Marilyn 107, 111, 117, 125 n.39, 127 n.81, 127 n.91, 127 nn.85–6
Terminal Island (Rothman, 1973) 110
Terror Train (Spottiswoode, 174) 174
That's Sexploitation (Friedman) 27
Theander, Jans 130
Theander, Peter 130
The Texas Chain Saw Massacre (Hooper, 1974) 125 n.32, 221
Thirst (Hardy, 1979) 172, 175
Thomas Crown Affair (Jewison, 1968) 81
Thomas, Kevin 75, 77, 81, 89 n.9, 90 n.26, 90 n.44, 123, 127 n.93, 128 n.120
Thomas, Paul 153
Thomas, Sarah 150, 160 n.28, 160 n.34
Thomasine and Bushrod (Parks Jr. 1974) 182, 186–9, 191
Thompson, Kristin 91
Thorsen, Isak 142 n.3, 142 n.7, 142 n.13
Thrower, Stephen 124 n.18
Thunder in Carolina (Hemlick, 1960) 93
Thunder and Lightning (Allen, 1977) 97, 101
Tibbals, Chauntelle Ann 233 n.7
Times Square (New York City) 1, 3–4, 14, 18–20, 22–7, 40, 226, 230
Tinkcom, Matthew 235 n.46
Tompkins, Joe 124 n.21
Tonight for Sure (Coppola 1962) 138
Torn (New Sensations, 2012) 218
Trapper John M.D 174
Trashola (Morton) 22
Treasure of the Sierra Madre (Huston, 1948) 81
Trenchard-Smith, Brian 165, 169, 172, 174, 177, 179 n.43

The Trial of Billy Jack (Laughlin, 1974) 206–7, 209
Trilogy of Terror (TV movie, 1975) 174
The Trip (Corman, 1967) 76
Truck Turner (Kaplan, 1974) 15, 125 n.48
True Romance (Scott and Tarantino) 175
The True Story of Eskimo Nell (Franklin, 1974) 169
Tudor, Andrew 166, 177 n.9
Turkey Shoot (Trenchard-Smith, 1982) 172, 174, 176–7
Turner, Graeme 164, 177 n.4
Twentieth Century Fox 96, 201, 203, 207
Two Gun Man from Harlem (Khan, 1939) 183
Two-Lane Blacktop (Hellman, 1971) 93
Tyler, Parker 24

Uden en trævl/Without a Stitch 131
Undulations (Tobalina, 1980) 146
United States v. Washington (1974) 199
Up in Smoke (Chong and Adler, 1978) 121, 123
US adult film industry 146
Used Cars (Zemeckis, 1980) 103

Valley of the Dolls (Robson, 1967) 59
Vampire Hookers (Santiago, 1978) 76
The Van (Grossman, 1977) 107–8, 112–16, 120–1, 123 n.3, 123 n.8, 126 n.68, 126 n.70, 127 n.93, 128 n.116
Van Gelder, Lawrence 102, 106 n.30
Vanity Fair 35
Van Nuys Blvd (Sachs, 1979) 93, 107–8, 111, 113–14, 116, 120, 123
Variety 36–7
Vela, Raphael 49 n.45, 50 n.61
Venus in Furs (Franco, 1969) 14
V/H/S: Viral (Sarmiento 2014) 176
Vices and Virtues (Jancsó, 1976) 67
video nasty 4, 10 n.19
Videoscope 13
Video Vault 13
Villarejo, Amy 235 n.46
Vine, Deloria Jr 200, 202, 212, 213 n.12, 214 nn.14–15
Virus (Fukasaku, 1980) 175
Vivid 218, 222
Voices (Billington, 1973) 175

Wadd: The Life and Times of John C. Holmes (Paley, 1999) 146, 158 n.1
Wahl, Ken 175
Walker (biopic 1987) 192–3
Walker, Johnny 1–9, 10 n.19
Walking Tall (Karlson, 1973) 95
Waller, Gregory A. 117, 127 n.90, 127 n.95
Walters, Trevor 70 n.7
Warburg, Anne-Bi 134
Warburg, Bent 134, 137
Ward, Glenn 5, 10 n.12, 13–27, 51 n.72, 234 n.40
Ward, Reneé 189, 194 n.26
Wargames (Badham, 1983) 109
Warner Bros 1, 20, 201, 203–4
Warren, Harry 20
Warren, Lesley Ann 175
Wasser, Frederick 109–10, 124 n.25, 214 n.19
Wasteland (Elegant Angel, 2012) 218
Watson, Paul 165
Watson, Thomas Joseph 160 n.41, 234 n.31
The Way of the Dragon (Lee, 1972) 176
Wayne, John 78, 155–6, 158
Weaver, James 49 n.50, 50 n.62
Weiner, Robert G. 3, 10 n.13, 48 n.23, 235 n.54
Weldon, Michael 13, 22, 27, 28 n.1, 29 n.42, 29 n.44
Wet and Wild (Findlay) 20, 27
Wharton, Theodore 34
What's Up, Doc? (Bogdanovich, 1972) 93
When the Legends Die (Millar, 1972) 201–2
Wickman, Torgny 130, 136, 142 n.5
The Wild Angels (Corman, 1966) 74–80, 83, 90 n.36, 202
Wild in the Streets (Shear, 1968) 76
Wild Rebels (Grefe, 1967) 74
Williams, Linda 135, 142 n.14, 150, 159 n.25, 229, 234 n.22
Willis, Andy 28 n.5, 48 n.23, 234 n.21
Wilson, Jake 164, 177 n.3
Wing-Fai, Leung 11 n.26, 177 n.13
WINS (magazine) 139

Winsten, Archer 80, 90 n.33
Winston-Dixon, Wheeler 47 n.9
Wishman, Doris 20, 30 n.77, 138, 221, 234 n.21
Wizard of Gore (Lewis, 2007) 27
Wollner, Kurt 111, 125 n.39
Woman from Deep River (Lenzi, 1981) 67–9, 71 nn.19–20
Wonder Woman (TV movie, 1975) 174
Wood, Robin 124 n.21, 127 n.96
The Wooing and the Wedding of a Coon (Coyne, 1905) 192
World War II 44
Wounded Knee siege (1973) 198, 200, 204, 207, 209

Wyatt, Justin 124 n.29, 125 n.40, 214 n.19

XXL: The John Holmes Story (Hills, 2000) 146
XXX film. *See also* pornography
  director 218–19. *See also* Jack the Zipper; pornography

The Young Graduates (Anderson, 1971) 121
Young Nurses (Cohen, 1973) 76
A Youth in Babylon: Confessions of a Trash-Film King (Friedman) 27

Zecca, Federico 233 n.7, 233 n.12
Zodiac series 141
Zombie, Rob 9, 219, 222–3

www.ingramcontent.com/pod-product-compliance
Lightning Source LLC
Chambersburg PA
CBHW052219300426
44115CB00011B/1758